A SE
DYN
Maur

Sep
and Functional S

Unive

Southern I
University c
Universi

IN

University c

Harvard Busin
E.
Tel-Aviv

Duality,
Separability,
and Functional Structure:
Theory
and Economic Applications

Charles Blackorby
University of British Columbia

Daniel Primont
University of Massachusetts, Boston
and University of British Columbia

R. Robert Russell
University of California, San Diego

NORTH-HOLLAND·NEW YORK
NEW YORK • OXFORD • SHANNON

Elsevier North-Holland, Inc.
52 Vanderbilt Avenue, New York, New York 10017

Distributors outside the United States and Canada:

THOMOND BOOKS
(A Division of Elsevier/North-Holland Scientific Publishers, Ltd).
P. O. Box 85
Limerick, Ireland

Library of Congress Cataloging in Publication Data
Blackorby, Charles.
    Duality, separability, and functional structure.
    (Dynamic economics: theory and applications)
    Bibliography: p.
    Includes index.
    1. Economics, Mathematical.   2. Economics–
Mathematical models.   I. Primont, Daniel, joint
author.   II. Russell, R. Robert, joint author.
III. Title.   IV. Title: Separability.
V. Title: Functional structure.
HB135.B56   330′.01′51   77-22836
ISBN 0-444-00235-9

Manufactured in the United States of America

To W. M. Gorman

Contents

Editor's Preface

This series of monographs and advanced texts is designed to further research on intertemporal decision making and planning, and related analytical techniques.

The present volume is a synthesis and analysis of the theory and applications of separability and functional structure. During the last decade these concepts have proven to be of increasing importance in both theoretical and empirical economics. Separability conditions provide a theoretical framework for the analysis of aggregation and decentralization problems in the theory of consumer demand, production, price indices, money, welfare theory and intertemporal planning. The reader will find that the authors provide far more than a survey of published results. In preparing this systematic analysis of separability and functional structure they derive original results and many refinements and interpretations of prior work.

This volume will both further research on separability and functional structure and make available to the general economist a powerful set of concepts and theorems.

Maurice Wilkinson

Preface

Separability and functional structure are concepts widely employed by economists. This book is an attempt to provide a systematic analysis of both the theory and the application of these concepts. It is therefore substantially more than a mere survey of previously published results. In most instances, either original results are presented or earlier results are refined. Unfortunately, however, there still remain major unsolved issues. We have tried to draw the reader's attention to these problems whenever they appear.

Our intellectual debt to Terence Gorman is monumental. Without his seminal work, our understanding of these issues would be meager indeed.

We were introduced to this subject by George Lady and benefited greatly from our earlier collaboration with him and with David Nissen.

We are also indebted to Erwin Diewert and Bob Pollak. We have drawn heavily not only on their written work, but also upon discussions we have had with them over the years. In addition we are grateful to the editors and referees of *Econometrica*, *The Review of Economic Studies*, *Journal of Economic Theory*, *International Economic Review*, *Annals of Economic and Social Measurement*, *Journal of Econometrics*, and the *Economic Journal* for criticism, suggestions, and patience.

A preliminary version of the entire manuscript was read by Erwin Diewert; substantial portions were read by Bill Schworm and Paul Thomas. In addition we received comments from E. Berndt, Vince Crawford, Knox Lovell, Les Taylor, Kay Unger, and Terence Wales. We thank them even though we have not always adopted their suggestions. Finally, we would like to thank Walt Heller for his invaluable advice regarding the appendix and Rick Emmerson for many beneficial discussions on Chapter 2.

The Departments of Economics at the University of British Columbia and the University of California at San Diego provided logistical support as well as pleasant working environments.

Table of Theorems, Corollaries, and Lemmas

Chapter 3

Chapter 4

1

Introduction

1.1 BRIEF SURVEY OF THE LITERATURE

1.1.1 Separability

The concept of separability was conceived independently by Leontief (1947a, 1947b) and Sono (1945, 1961).[1] A group of variables was said to be separable from the remaining variables in a utility (or production) function if the marginal rates of substitution between variables in that group are independent of the values of variables outside the group. The Leontief-Sono definition requires that the objective function be differentiable. Definitions which eschew differentiability have subsequently been formulated by Debreu (1959a), Stigum (1967), and Gorman (1968b) and by Bliss (1975). Of these, Bliss's definition is more general than that of Debreu, Stigum, and Gorman (see the discussion in chapter 3).

1.1.2 Functional Structure

Both Leontief and Sono noted that separability is equivalent to functional structure; that is, if a group is separable from its complement, it is possible to write the function image as

$$U(X) = \overline{U}(X^c, U^r(X^r)), \qquad (1.1)$$

where $X = (X^c, X^r)$, X^r is the quantity vector corresponding to the separ-

---

[1] Sono's paper, originally published in Japanese in 1945, was later reprinted in English (1961).

able set of variables, and U^r is a real-valued function.[2] U^r can be interpreted as a sectoral utility function or a composite commodity. On the other hand, if U is a production function, we might think of $U^r(X^r)$ as the intermediate output of sector r, which is then combined with X^c to produce $U(X)$. Thus, Leontief-Sono separability allows us to form commodity or input aggregates.

The Leontief-Sono functional structure theorems are, however, local in nature. Global functional representation theorems using the calculus approach were proved by Goldman and Uzawa (1964). Functional structure theorems using analytic and geometric techniques have been proved with very weak regularity conditions by Debreu (1959a), Gorman (1968b), and Koopmans (1972). Recently, by adding a strict monotonicity condition, Pokropp (1972) has even dispensed with continuity of the objective function.

1.1.3 Consumer Budgeting, Decentralization, and Price Aggregation

A decade after the publication of Leontief's separability paper, interest in functional structure and separability was rejuvenated by Strotz (1957, 1959) and Gorman (1959) in the context of consumer budgeting and price aggregation, and by Solow (1955) in the context of constructing a capital aggregate. Consumer budgeting was defined by Strotz (1957: p. 271) as follows: "A decision is first made as to how income should be allocated among the budget branches (given all prices). Each budget allotment is then spent optimally on the commodities in its branch, with no further references to purchases in other branches." Strotz went on to argue that this type of behavior is rationalized by certain separability conditions (viz., "weak separability") regarding the consumer's utility function. Primont (1970) and Gorman (1971) later showed that these separability conditions are necessary as well as sufficient for this decentralization of the optimization problem.

These restrictions on the consumer's preferences imply empirically refutable restrictions on the system of demand functions. The (differential) restrictions implied by (symmetrically) structured direct utility functions, which were first worked out by Sono (1961) and Strotz (1957), were later extended by Goldman and Uzawa (1964) and Pearce (1964). The demand implications of (symmetrically) structured *indirect* utility functions, first examined by Houthakker (1960b), were extended by Houthakker (1965b), Samuelson (1965), and Lau (1969b). The differential restrictions on de-

---

[2]This result, like others reported in our introductory remarks, of course, requires certain unstated conditions. These ideas are made more precise in the chapters that follow.

mand functions implied by nonsymmetrically structured preferences were worked out by Lady and Nissen (1968) and Primont (1970). These restrictions of course imply restrictions on the elasticities of substitution as well (Berndt and Christensen, 1973a; Russell, 1975; Blackorby and Russell, 1976).

A concept which is intimately related to, but distinguishable from, the two stages of Strotz's budgeting procedure is the notion of price aggregation. That is, can the initial income allocation be carried out knowing only price indices—such as the price of "food"—but not necessarily the individual food-component prices? This is the fundamental issue addressed by Gorman (1959) in his elegant analysis of the Strotz consumer-budgeting problem. There are actually two separate but related price-aggregation issues. The first issue concerns the existence of income-allocation functions in which the price arguments are aggregate price indices for each of the budget categories. The second concerns the existence of price aggregates which, when multiplied by the corresponding composite commodity (e.g., food), yield the optimal expenditure on the corresponding budget category. Gorman (1959) established necessary and sufficient conditions for the first of these concepts[3] and a sufficient condition for the latter. Blackorby, Lady, Nissen, and Russell (1970) provided a necessity proof for the latter concept. Dual to the notion of price aggregation is the concept of quantity aggregation, analyzed by Blackorby, Primont, and Russell (1977a)

1.1.4 Duality Theory and Separability

The theory of duality is very important for the theory and application of separability and functional structure. Duality theory in economics has its intellectual origin in the influential works of Hotelling (1932), Roy (1942, 1947), and Wold and Jureen (1953) and has been honed into a powerful tool for theoretical and applied economics by the research of, among others, Samuelson (1953, 1960), Shephard (1953, 1970), McKenzie (1955), Uzawa (1964), McFadden (1966, 1970), Gorman (1968a, 1970), Hanoch (1970), and Diewert (1971, 1974a). For our purposes, the important implication of duality theory is that consumer preferences or production technologies can (under certain conditions) be represented equivalently by the direct utility or production function, the indirect utility or production function (Hotelling, 1932; Roy, 1942, 1947; Wold and Jureen, 1953; Shephard, 1953, 1970; Houthakker, 1960b, 1965c), the cost function (Samuelson, 1953; Shephard, 1953, 1970; Uzawa, 1964), or the transformation function (Shephard, 1953, 1970; Malmquist, 1953; McFadden, 1970;

---

[3]Gorman's theorem was later extended by Blackorby, Primont, and Russell (1977b).

Gorman, 1970, 1975). This fact is important for functional structure because a structural property of one of these functions does not generally imply that the dual functions have any structural properties. Thus, in general, endowing the primal function with structure has different implications than does endowing the dual function(s) with structure. Hence, duality helps to extend the class of structures that can be imposed on preferences or production technologies. Moreover, the conjunction of primal and dual structure frequently implies additional structure about both.

Interest in functional structure and duality was stimulated by Houthakker (1960b, 1965b) and Samuelson (1965). These papers examined the implications of simultaneous additivity of direct and indirect utility functions. Houthakker and Samuelson's results were extended by Lau (1969a) and Blackorby, Primont, and Russell (1975b). Functional structure theorems which exploit the duality between cost and transformation functions have been proved by Gorman (1970, 1975), McFadden (1970), and Blackorby and Russell (1975).

1.1.5 Nonsymmetric Structures

Most research on functional structure has focused on structures induced by symmetric separability conditions—i.e., group r is separable from group s if and only if group s is separable from group r. The formulation of separability due to Leontief (1947a, 1947b) and Sono (1945, 1961) is, however, inherently nonsymmetric. The theory of nonsymmetrically structured functions was developed by Blackorby and Lady (1967), Lady and Nissen (1968), and Primont (1970). Duality theorems for nonsymmetrically structured preferences and technologies were proved by Blackorby, Nissen, Primont, and Russell (1974).

1.1.6 Applications of Separability

The abundance of applications of separability in theoretical and empirical economics is testimony to its putative usefulness. This usefulness emanates from the fact, emphasized by the early writings of Leontief (1947b), Solow (1955), Strotz (1957), and Gorman (1959), that separability is intimately related to aggregation and decentralization. These latter two concepts play prominent roles in much economic analysis.

We have already noted that certain separability conditions rationalize a two-stage optimization procedure (Strotz, 1957; Green, 1964; Gorman 1971). This in turn provides a theoretical rationalization for the econometric estimation of sectoral demand systems. Thus, the computational problems attendant upon the estimation of systems of demand functions for large numbers of commodities can be circumvented by estimating sectoral demand systems separately and then estimating a single function which allocates total expenditure to the separate branches of the "utility tree" (see, e.g., Heien, 1974; Braithwait, 1975; Deaton, 1975; Anderson, 1976; McMenamin, Pinard, Russell, and Boyce, 1977). Moreover, all demand studies abstract from some aspect of the allocation problem faced by real-world decision makers. They ignore the leisure-work decision as well as the intertemporal wealth-allocation decision. These abstractions can be rationalized by appropriate separability restrictions (see, e.g., Diewert, 1974c; Darrough, 1975).

It is also common in both theoretical and applied economic research to use aggregate commodities and prices. Most consumer-demand studies work with commodity aggregates and hence require (at least implicitly) separability assumptions. In production theory, separability is used to construct an aggregate capital stock from its heterogeneous components (Solow, 1955; Fisher, 1965, 1968a, 1968b) and to rationalize the use of value-added production functions (Arrow, 1974).

Separability restrictions can also be invoked to rationalize aggregation across agents (Klein 1946; Nataf, 1948; Gorman, 1953, 1968a; Green, 1964; Stigum, 1967; Fisher, 1969; Pokropp, 1972).

Finally, separability has been applied to the theory of money (Yasui, 1944; Morishima, 1952; Negishi, 1964), the theory of externalities (Winter, 1969; Bergstrom, 1970), social choice (Archibald and Donaldson, 1976), the theory of time discounting (Koopmans, 1960), the theory of intertemporal-planning consistency and intergenerational conflict (Blackorby, Nissen, Primont, and Russell, 1973), the theory of cost-of-living subindices (Pollak, 1975a, 1975b; Blackorby and Russell, 1977), the notion of effective protection (Woodland, 1976a), and undoubtedly many other problems that have escaped our attention.

1.1.7 Testing for Separability

Separability has been employed as a maintained (untested) hypothesis in the works cited above. Recent developments in the specification of functional forms and in nonlinear-estimation algorithms have made it possible to test separability with a minimum of maintained hypotheses. Flexible functional forms (forms which can provide a second-order approximation to an arbitrary twice differentiable function[4]) have been specified by Lau

---

[4]See Lau (1974a) for a discussion of the meaning of second-order approximations.

and Mitchell (1971) [transcendental logarithmic ("translog") function]; by Diewert (1971, 1973a) [generalized Leontief, mean of order two, and generalized Cobb-Douglas]; and by Kadiyala (1971–2), Hasenkamp (1973), and Denny (1974) [the quadratic mean of order ρ]. The translog specification has been used to test for separability by Christensen, Jorgenson, and Lau (1973, 1975), Jorgenson and Lau (1975), Christensen and Manser (1975, 1977), Berndt and Christensen (1973b, 1974a, 1974b), Berndt and Wood (1975), and Boyce and Primont (1976a, 1976b). The generalized Leontief function has been used by Woodland (1975) to test separability restrictions, but as of the time of this writing, the quadratic mean of order ρ has not been used to test structural hypotheses.

As it turns out, maintained hypotheses that are implicit in these tests are much stronger than one would like (see Blackorby, Primont, and Russell, 1977c); for example, the translog specifications cannot model nonhomothetic separability (unless it is also additive separability). Hence, testing for separability is equivalent to testing for a hybrid of additive separability and homothetic separability.

1.2   OUTLINE OF THE BOOK

The remainder of the book is divided into three parts. The first lays out the duality theory needed for the study of functional structure and separability (chapter 2) and carefully develops—in the simplest possible setting—the theory of separability and functional structure (chapter 3). Our treatment of duality theory differs somewhat from our treatment of separability and functional structure in the succeeding chapters. We do not provide proofs of all duality results used in the later chapters, but where possible cite proofs that are readily accessible in the duality literature. However, as our regularity conditions differ from those adopted in other treatments of duality, most results that we need require proof. The Appendix provides these proofs (as well as explicit references to proofs of results that we do not prove). On the other hand, *all* results about functional structure and separability are proved. Although many of the results in this book (or something close to them) have appeared in the literature cited above, almost all proofs of familiar propositions are altered—many substantially so.[5]

---

[5]A notable exception is the elegant—but lengthy and difficult—proof of the theorem and lemmas of Gorman's important paper (1968b) on the structure of utility functions. We have taken this proof directly from Gorman, merely doubling its length in order to make it more accessible.

Chapter 3 develops the theory of separability and functional structure in the case where there is only one separable group [implying equation (1.1) above]. Almost all of the important aspects of this theory can be learned from this special case. Developing the theory for this simplest case frees the essentially simple idea of separability from the complications generated by complex structures. There is an unfortunate tendency to think of the two (or perhaps three) common types of *structures* [induced by "weak separability", "strong separability", and perhaps "Pearce (1961) separability"] as the different "types" of separability. Focusing on the case where one set is separable from its complement (and *not* necessarily conversely) may elucidate the fact that while there are slightly different *definitions* of separability[6] (attributable in part to different maintained regularity conditions), there is basically one *kind* of separability. Positing a set of separability relationships between certain elements of a partition of the set of variables then *induces* a particular structure. If the concept and properties of separability itself are understood, proofs of propositions regarding most functional structures are fairly straightforward to work out[7]. It is this fact which motivates the structure of the book. Functional-representation theorems and duality theorems for the simple case of one separable group are proved in chapter 3. These results are then used to prove analogous theorems for more complex structures in part II of the book.

We might also note that the structure of the book makes it useful for the reader who is interested in the rudiments of the theory of separability and functional structure, but not so interested in the array of complex structures induced by separability. This reader can simply read chapter 3 and use what he needs out of part II.

Chapter 4 contains representation and duality theorems for symmetrically structured preferences. The separability results—where each group in a partition is separable from its complement—are proved by quite simple applications of the theorems of chapter 3.

Complete separability—where arbitrary unions of groups are separable from their complements—is a completely different matter. The basic functional-representation theorem is not a straightforward extension of the results of chapter 3; indeed, the proofs of theorems 4.7 and 4.3 (which is used in the proof of theorem 4.7), adapted from Gorman (1968b), are the most difficult proofs in the book. Complete separability induces a (group-wise) additive structure, and proof of this fact requires a novel argument in the theory of functional equations.

We have noted above that decentralization and aggregation are so

---

[6]See section 3.2 for a discussion of these alternative definitions.

[7]An important exception to this statement is presented by the complete separability representation theorem of Gorman (1968b). This proof is hard no matter what you know.

intimately related to the theory of separability and functional structure as to be almost parts of it. We therefore include in part II a chapter on decentralization and aggregation as they relate to the symmetrically structured preferences or technologies developed in chapter 4.

We have also noted above that separability is not an inherently symmetric concept (that is, group r separable from group s does not imply group s separable from group r). Although this fact was explicitly recognized by Leontief (1947a) and Sono (1961), much of the profession appeared to lose track of it in the elaborate treatment of symmetric separable structures. Part II concludes with a chapter on nonsymmetric structures, in particular complete recursivity and recursivity—the nonsymmetric analogues of completely separable and separable structures. As it turns out, counterparts to most of the results for symmetric structures proved in chapters 4 and 5 go through for completely recursive structures. On the other hand, almost no duality, decentralization, or aggregation results go through for recursive structures. Basically, this is because recursive structures have a "public good" property which vitiates decentralization (and apparently other properties).

Part III contains some applications of separability and functional structure. Chapter 7 relates separability to certain equality conditions for the Allen elasticities of substitution and to alternative notions of neutral technological progress. In particular, it is shown that equality of the elasticities of substitution between variables i and k and between variables j and k is equivalent to separability of the pair of variables $\{i,j\}$ from the kth variable in the cost (and transformation) functions. This means that it is possible to test for separability of the cost function by testing for appropriate equality conditions on the elasticities of substitution. Moreover, if certain homotheticity conditions are satisfied, the theorems on duality and functional structure, proved in chapters 3, 4, and 6, can be invoked to relate separability of the direct or indirect utility or production function to the equality conditions for the elasticities of substitution.

It is also shown in chapter 7 that three alternative notions of Hicks-neutral technological progress are equivalent, respectively, to separability of the production function, separability of the transformation functions, and multiplicative separability of the production function. These three concepts are shown to be equivalent if and only if the production function is "input-homogeneous".

Chapter 8 surveys the possible uses of separability in the econometric estimation of theoretically plausible demand systems and discusses the potential of testing for separability using flexible functional forms. In particular, we explore the set of structures that can be modeled by these various flexible forms.

Chapter 9 develops a theory of cost-of-living and standard-of-living subindices—i.e., cost-of-living indices and standard-of-living indices for subsets of commodities. Statistical agencies commonly publish cost-of-living indices for categories such as food, clothing, etc. It turns out that this practice can be rationalized by "conjugate implicit separability" (separability of the cost or transformation function).

The book concludes with a discussion of intertemporal planning consistency and intergenerational conflict. The intertemporal consistency problem arises if a planner (a society or an individual) cannot precommit future planners (future generations or the same individual at different points in time) to follow an intertemporal plan. If the planner formulates an optimal plan (from the perspective of today) and executes the first portion of the plan, there is no guarantee that tomorrow's planner will follow the remainder of the plan. In fact, in general the planner won't. We show that only if preferences are completely recursive and intertemporally compatible will the first period's plan be followed. If preferences do not conform to this rigid structure, the plan that is actually followed will make sense from no point of view (except perhaps from the perspective of the last generation). We go on to examine a sophisticated planning strategy (essentially a dynamic-programming algorithm) which might be adopted if naive planning is intertemporally inconsistent. Certain existence problems arise in the context of this planning strategy; we therefore prove an existence theorem. Finally, we show that the demand system of an intertemporal society which adopts the sophisticated planning strategy is "rational"—i.e., could have been generated by utility maximization—if and only if preferences have the (nonsymmetric) structure required for intertemporal consistency of naive planning.

As the concluding paragraphs of section 1.1 above might indicate, the topics discussed in Part II of this book by no means exhaust the list of known applications of the theory of separability and functional structure. Moreover, it is no doubt true that an assiduous reading of the literature would uncover many new applications. Indeed, there are without doubt many potential applications of separability and functional structure that are as yet undiscovered. Because of the nature of economic science (in particular, the paucity of degrees of freedom in empirical investigations), researchers have been and will be repeatedly faced with the need to aggregate across variables and to decentralize (implicitly if not explicitly) optimization problems. If this book has a theme, it is that duality, separability, and functional structure have an important role to play in the effective use of aggregation and decentralization concepts in economic research.

I

DUALITY AND SEPARABILITY

2

The Application of Duality Theory to Consumer Preferences and Production Technologies

This book is not about duality per se. Nevertheless, it is impossible to separate the theory and application of functional structure from the theory of duality. In part, this is because a structural property of a primal function does not generally imply that the dual function has any structural properties (nor, of course, conversely). Thus, in general, endowing the primal function with structure has different implications than does endowing the dual function(s) with structure. Hence, duality helps to extend the class of structures that can be imposed on preferences or production technologies. Moreover, the conjunction of primal and dual structure frequently implies additional structure about both.

The relationships between functional-structure hypotheses and the ability to aggregate also provide a link to duality theory. To put it succinctly, price aggregation and quantity aggregation are dual to one another. Indeed, quantity and price aggregation are equivalent to certain structural restrictions on the primal and dual functions.

Finally, the powerful and elegant theorems of duality theory are instrumental in streamlining many of the proofs in the succeeding chapters of this book.

The exposition of duality theory, as applied to the theory of the consumer and the firm in this chapter and in the Appendix is self-contained, though not exhaustive in topical coverage. Basically, the purpose of this chapter is to provide the minimal background which is required in order to proceed with the theory of functional structure. Hence, we focus on those aspects of duality theory that are germane to this goal. An Appendix at the end of the book contains proofs (or explicit and precise references to proofs in the duality literature) of the many propositions that underlie the exposition of duality theory in this chapter.

The reader who is interested in further pursuit of the subject of duality theory in economics is referred to the rather extensive literature on the subject; the bibliography of Diewert (1974a) is comprehensive. Our own understanding of duality theory and its importance was considerably enhanced by careful readings of Samuelson (1953, 1960, 1965), Shephard (1953, 1970), McKenzie (1955), McFadden (1966, 1970), Gorman (1968a), and Diewert (1971, 1974a).

Section 2.1 contains a general discussion of the class of consumer preferences, or production technologies, that are modeled in the remainder of this book. Section 2.2 examines the duality between direct and indirect utility (or production) functions. Section 2.3 introduces the cost function and the transformation function. The latter function, introduced independently by Malmquist (1953) and Shephard (1953) and more recently discussed by Gorman (1970), McFadden (1970), Hanoch (1970), and Shephard (1970), is a type of distance function which implicitly defines the direct utility (or production) function. It can also be interpreted as an "indirect cost function"—i.e., a "cost function" (or, more evocatively, an "expenditure imputation function") derived from the indirect utility function by a computation that is dual to the derivation of the ordinary (direct) cost function from the direct utility function. It is analogously true that the ordinary cost function can be interpreted as a transformation function which implicitly defines the indirect *utility* function.

The complete dual structure which integrates these four equivalent representations—direct and indirect utility, cost, and transformation functions—of consumer preferences or production technologies is summarized in section 2.4.

2.1 CONSUMER PREFERENCES AND PRODUCTION TECHNOLOGIES

2.1.1 Preferences

The consumption space is represented by the nonnegative Euclidean n-orthant,[1]

$$\Omega^n = \left\{ (x_1, \ldots, x_n) = X \in \mathbf{R}^n \,|\, X \geqslant 0^n \wedge X \neq 0^n \right\},$$

where $\mathbf{R}^n$ is Euclidean n-space, 0^n is the n-dimensional zero vector, and $x_i \in \Omega^{(i)}$ is the ith coordinate of the consumption vector X.

---

[1]The origin of $\mathbf{R}^n$ is deleted from the consumption space for convenience in what follows.

We assume that the consumer's preference ordering, $\succcurlyeq$, on Ω^n is transitive, reflexive, complete, and *continuous*[2] (i.e., $\{X \in \Omega^n | X \succcurlyeq \hat{X}\}$ and $\{X \in \Omega^n | X \preccurlyeq \hat{X}\}$ are closed for all $\hat{X} \in \Omega^n$). Hence, by a theorem of Debreu (1954: theorem II), the consumer's preference ordering is representable by a continuous, real-valued utility function, $U: \Omega^n \rightarrow \mathbf{R}$. In addition, we assume that consumer preferences are *nondecreasing* [for all $(X, \hat{X}) \in \Omega^{2n}$, if $X \geqq \hat{X}$, then $X \succcurlyeq \hat{X}$] and *convex* [for all $(X, \hat{X}) \in \Omega^{2n}$, if $X \succ \hat{X}$, then $\theta X + (1-\theta)\hat{X} \succ \hat{X}$ for all $\theta \in (0,1)$]. Thus the utility function is nondecreasing and *quasi-concave*.

By quasi-concavity we mean that for all $(X, \hat{X}) \in \Omega^{2n}$, if $U(X) > U(\hat{X})$, then $U(\theta X + (1-\theta)\hat{X}) > U(\hat{X})$ for all $\theta \in (0,1)$. Note that this definition of quasi-concavity is stronger than usual. Not only does it guarantee that "no-worse-than-X" sets are convex, but it also precludes "thick" indifference curves (except, possibly, for a region of global satiation).

We also maintain implicitly (though not explicitly in statements of theorems) that U is not the constant function, i.e., that there exists $(X, \hat{X}) \in \Omega^{2n}$ such that $U(X) > U(\hat{X})$.

These regularity conditions are summarized as

(R-1)   continuity, positive monotonicity, and quasi-concavity.

Of course, if the ordering $\succcurlyeq$ is represented by U, it is also represented by the composition $\Psi \circ U: \Omega^n \rightarrow \mathbf{R}$, where Ψ is increasing in its scalar-valued argument, $U(X)$. That is, the utility indicator is unique only up to a strictly monotone transformation.

2.1.2   Technologies

Although most of this book will be couched in the language of consumer theory, it is equally applicable to the theory of a producer with a technology that converts n inputs into a single output. In this case, the function U represents the producer's technology, and the image $U(X)$ is output. Of course, if U is a production function, it must represent more than the ordering of output levels; that is, monotone transforms of U do not

---

[2]In many applications employing specific functional forms, the domain of the utility function is restricted to a proper subset of Ω^n. Many of the propositions of this chapter are not generally valid if the domain of U is restricted in this manner. This is not, however, a matter of great practical importance since the duality results can frequently be validated specifically for well behaved functional forms. Also, some specific functional forms satisfy the separability conditions of chapters 3, 4, and 6 over a proper subset of Ω^n. Again, the duality results for such functions, defined on the domain for which they are separable, can be verified specifically.

represent the same technology. Thus a production function U is in general invariant only up to a linear transformation (i.e., changes in units seldom matter). Apart from the economic interpretation, this is the formal difference between the theory of the consumer and the theory of the producer. Consequently, most of the discussion of parts I and II will be couched in the language of consumer theory unless the sensitivity of the indicator U to monotone transforms is a critical issue.

2.2 MARSHALLIAN DEMAND FUNCTIONS AND INDIRECT UTILITY FUNCTIONS

2.2.1   The Indirect Utility Function

Corresponding to the consumption vector X is a strictly positive price vector $P \in \Omega_+^n$ (the strictly positive n-orthant). Letting $y \in \Omega_+^1$ denote [3] the scalar-valued expenditure level, $P/y \subset \Omega_+^n$ is the normalized price vector.

The consumer's indirect utility function, $V: \Omega_+^n \to \mathbf{R}$, is defined by

$$V(P/y) = \operatorname*{Max}_{X} \left\{ U(X) | X \in \Omega^n \wedge \frac{P}{y} \cdot X \leqslant 1 \right\}, \qquad (2.1)$$

where

$$\frac{P}{y} \cdot X = \sum_{i=1}^{n} \frac{p_i}{y} x_i$$

is an inner product. Thus, $V(P/y)$ is the maximum utility which can be obtained at normalized prices P/y. If the solution to the maximization problem in (2.1) is unique, V is also defined by

$$V(P/y) = U(\phi(P/y)), \qquad (2.1')$$

where $\phi(P/y)$ is the solution vector of the maximization problem in (2.1). If the solution to the maximization problem in (2.1) is not unique, (2.1') is valid for an arbitrary element in the image of P/y by the demand correspondence, $\tilde{\phi}: \Omega_+^n \to \mathcal{P}(\Omega^n)$, where $\mathcal{P}(\Omega^n)$ is the power set of Ω^n. If the solution is unique, the vector-valued function $\phi: \Omega_+^n \to \Omega^n$ is referred to as the ordinary (Marshallian) demand function. Under our assumptions

---

[3] Ω_+^1 is actually the same as Ω^1. We carry the plus sign to remind the reader that y must be positive.

about U, ϕ is continuous (or $\tilde{\phi}$ is upper hemicontinuous) and V is continuous, nonincreasing, and quasi-convex[4] on Ω^n_+. We summarize the regularity conditions for V as

(R-2) continuity, negative monotonicity, and quasi-convexity.

The preceding paragraph focuses on the fact that utility is indirectly a function of normalized prices; that is, corresponding to any continuous direct utility function (and hence to any continuously representable preference ordering) there is an indirect utility function. Moreover, corresponding to any continuous indirect utility function there is a direct utility function which satisfies the appropriate regularity conditions. Hence, V is an alternative and equally legitimate representation of consumer preferences.

The reconstruction of U from V begins by extending V to the nonnegative orthant (assigning images to boundary vectors) in such a way as to preserve lower semicontinuity.[5] Note that this extended function, say $\overset{*}{V}$, is not necessarily finite; as the price of a good for which the consumer is never sated goes to zero, the maximum utility, $V(P/y)$, may go to $+\infty$. Thus, the extended indirect utility function maps into the extended real line $\mathbf{\bar{R}} = \mathbf{R} \cup \{+\infty\}$. In addition, this extension results in closed lower-level sets of the extended function. That is,

$$\left\{ \frac{P}{y} \middle| \frac{P}{y} \in \Omega^n \wedge \overset{*}{V}(P/y) \leqslant u \right\}$$

is closed $\forall u \in \mathcal{R}(\overset{*}{V})$, where $\mathcal{R}(\overset{*}{V})$ is the range of $\overset{*}{V}$. This extension therefore guarantees the existence of solutions to constrained minimization problems.

Let us therefore use $\overset{*}{V}$ to define $\overset{\circ}{U}:\Omega^n_+ \to \mathbf{R}$ by

$$\overset{\circ}{U}(X) = \min_{P/y} \left\{ \overset{*}{V}(P/y) \middle| \frac{P}{y} \in \Omega^n \wedge \frac{P}{y} \cdot X \leqslant 1 \right\}. \tag{2.2}$$

Let $\overset{*}{U}$ be the extension of $\overset{\circ}{U}$ to the entire nonnegative orthant which preserves upper semi-continuity.[6]

---

[4]V is quasi-convex if $-V$ is quasi-concave. Hence "no-better-than-P/y" sets are convex, and there are no "thick" indifference curves (except possibly for a region of global satiation).

[5]This is also referred to as extending V by continuity from below (Diewert, 1974a). Formally, the extension is defined by making the image of P/y equal to the infimum over u of the closure of the epigraph of V (Rockafellar, 1970: p. 51).

[6]Formally $\overset{\circ}{U}$ is extended to Ω^n by continuity from above by defining the image of X as the supremum over u of the closure of the lower graph of $\overset{\circ}{U}$.

The importance of consumer and producer duality theory is in part reflected in the fact that if $\overset{*}{U}$ satisfies (R−1), then $\overset{*}{U}(X)=U(X)$ for all $X \in \Omega^n$. In other words, (2.2) and the closure operation recapture the original (direct) utility function. Moreover, given an extended indirect utility function $\overset{*}{V}$ satisfying (R−2), a function $\overset{\circ}{U}$ derived from $\overset{*}{V}$ by (2.2) satisfies (R−1). Finally, if $\overline{V}$ is in turn derived from U, the extension of U to the boundary by continuity from above, by (2.1) and extended to the boundary by continuity from below, then we have $\overline{V}=\overset{*}{V}$. These results mean that V and U are equivalent ways of representing a given preference ordering. It is as legitimate to describe consumer preferences by the specification of an indirect utility function as by the specification of a direct utility function.

If the solution vector to the minimization problem in (2.2) is unique, the restricted utility function $\overset{\circ}{U}$ can also be defined by

$$\overset{\circ}{U}(X) = \overset{*}{V}(\xi(X)),$$

where $\xi(X)$ is the unique solution vector. $\xi:\Omega^n_+ \to \Omega^n$ is the price-demand function, or shadow price function, and is continuous if $\overset{*}{V}$ satisfies (R−2). If the solution to the problem in (2.2) is not unique, then substituting an arbitrary element of the image of the demand correspondence, $\tilde{\xi}:\Omega^n_+ \to \mathcal{P}(\Omega^n)$, into the indirect-utility-function image yields $\overset{\circ}{U}(X)$. The correspondence $\tilde{\xi}$ is upper hemicontinuous if $\overset{*}{V}$ satisfies (R−2). Finally, note that $\tilde{\xi}(X)$ is the set of normalized price vectors at which X would be chosen. That is, letting $\overset{\circ}{\xi}$ and $\overset{\circ}{\phi}$ be the restrictions of $\tilde{\xi}$ and $\tilde{\phi}$ to the subsets of Ω^n_+ which map into subsets of Ω^n_+, it is clear that $\overset{\circ}{\xi}=\overset{\circ}{\phi}^{-1}$ (the inverse of $\overset{\circ}{\phi}$).

2.2.2 Roy's Theorem and Its Dual

The ability to represent preferences by either a direct or an indirect utility function is made especially important by a theorem of Roy (1942, 1947) and its dual, Wold's (1943) theorem.[7] These theorems are used to generate the ordinary and inverse demand functions by straightforward differentiation of the indirect and direct utility functions.

Roy's Theorem   *If V is differentiable at P/y, then*

$$\phi(P/y) = \frac{\nabla V(P/y)}{\nabla V(P/y) \cdot P/y}, \tag{2.3}$$

[7]These results were apparently first stated by Konyus and Byushgens (1926) and again by Hotelling [1932]. We have retained the usual names.

where ∇V is the gradient of V and

$$\nabla V(P/y) \cdot \frac{P}{y} = \sum_{i=1}^{n} \frac{\partial V(P/y)}{\partial (p_i/y)} \frac{p_i}{y}.$$

Wold's Theorem   *If U is differentiable at X, then*

$$\xi(X) = \frac{\nabla U(X)}{\nabla U(X) \cdot X}. \tag{2.4}$$

Using the appropriate one-of these two identities, it is trivial to derive ordinary demand functions from a differentiable indirect utility function and to derive inverse demand functions from a differentiable direct utility function. This means, of course, that if an investigator is interested in deriving *ordinary* demand functions from an underlying preference ordering, it is most convenient to specify an *indirect* utility function.

At this point some simple examples are appropriate in order to illustrate the above results. First consider the Cobb-Douglas utility function, defined by

$$U(X) = \prod_{i=1}^{n} x_i^{\alpha_i}, \qquad \alpha_i \geqslant 0, \quad i = 1, \dots, n, \tag{2.5}$$

and let $\alpha = \sum_{i=1}^{n} \alpha_i$. The corresponding indirect utility function is

$$V(P/y) = \max_{X} \left\{ \prod_{i=1}^{n} x_i^{\alpha_i} \mid X \in \Omega^n \wedge \frac{P}{y} \cdot X \leqslant 1 \right\}$$

$$= \alpha^{-\alpha} \prod_{i=1}^{n} \left(\frac{\alpha_i y}{p_i} \right)^{\alpha_i}. \tag{2.6}$$

Moreover, the ordinary demand functions are given by

$$x_i = \phi_i(P/y) = \left(\frac{(p_i/y)\alpha}{\alpha_i} \right)^{-1}, \qquad i = 1, \dots, n,$$

which can be derived either from the direct utility maximization problem or from the indirect utility function by Roy's theorem. Of course, minimizing the indirect utility function (2.6) subject to $(P/y) \cdot X \leqslant 1$ yields the direct utility function (2.5). The images of X by the price-demand functions are

$$\frac{p_i}{y} = \xi_i(X) = \left(\frac{x_i \alpha}{\alpha_i}\right)^{-1}, \qquad i = 1, \ldots, n.$$

They are found either from the minimization problem or from (2.5) using Wold's theorem. Obviously $\overset{\circ}{\phi}$ and $\overset{\circ}{\xi}$ are inverses.

For a second example, consider the homogeneous quadratic utility function, $U: \hat{\Omega}^n \to \mathbf{R}$, defined by

$$U(X) = \tfrac{1}{2} X'AX, \tag{2.7}$$

where X is an $n \times 1$ column vector, A is an $n \times n$ negative definite symmetric matrix, X' (the transpose of X) is a $1 \times n$ row vector, and $\hat{\Omega}^n = \{X \in \Omega^n | AX \geqslant 0\}$.[8] The corresponding indirect utility function is given by

$$V(P/y) = \max_X \left\{ \tfrac{1}{2} X'AX \,|\, X \in \hat{\Omega}^n \wedge (P/y) \cdot X \leqslant 1 \right\}$$

$$= \left[2(P/y)'A^{-1}(P/y) \right]^{-1}, \tag{2.8}$$

and

$$\phi(P/y) = \frac{A^{-1}(P/y)}{(P/y)'A^{-1}(P/y)}$$

is the ordinary demand-function image, which can be derived either from the utility maximization problem, or (since V is differentiable) directly from V via Roy's theorem.

Alternatively, one can start with the indirect utility function as specified in (2.8). The reader can verify that minimizing $V(p/y)$ subject to the constraint $(P/y) \cdot X \leqslant 1$ [and $A^{-1}(P/y) \geqslant 0$] yields the direct utility function specified in (2.7). The indirect demand function image,

$$\xi(X) = \frac{AX}{X'AX},$$

can be found either from the minimization problem or from U via Wold's theorem. Clearly, $\xi = \phi^{-1}$ in this example.

---

[8] The homogeneous quadratic utility function satisfies the monotonicity condition only over the set $\hat{\Omega}^n$ (see Diewert, 1974d).

We conclude this section with a final, instructive example: the Leontief "fixed-proportions" utility function, defined by

$$U(X) = \min\left\{ \frac{x_1}{a_1}, \ldots, \frac{x_i}{a_i}, \ldots, \frac{x_n}{a_n} \right\},$$

where $a = (a_1, \ldots, a_n)$ is a strictly positive vector of parameters. The corresponding indirect utility function is generated by

$$V(P/y) = \max_X \left\{ \min\left\{ \frac{x_1}{a_1}, \ldots, \frac{x_n}{a_n} \right\} \middle| X \in \Omega^n \wedge \frac{P}{y} \cdot X \leqslant 1 \right\}$$

$$= \left(\sum_{i=1}^n a_i \frac{p_i}{y} \right)^{-1} = \frac{y}{\sum_{i=1}^n a_i p_i},$$

and the ordinary demand functions are given by

$$\phi(P/y) = a\left(\frac{y}{\sum_{i=1}^n a_i p_i} \right).$$

This derivation is illustrated in figure 2.1. As any positive price vector [e.g., $\bar{p} = (\bar{p}_1, \bar{p}_2)$] generates an optimum on the ray A, it is apparent that

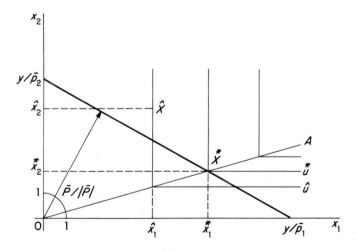

Figure 2.1.

$\phi(P/y)$ is obtained by solving

$$\frac{x_i}{a_i} = \frac{x_n}{a_n}, \qquad i = 1, \ldots, n-1,$$

and

$$\sum_{i=1}^{n} \frac{p_i}{y} x_i = 1$$

for X. V can then be obtained by substitution:

$$V(P/y) = \min\left\{ \frac{a_1 y / \sum_{i=1}^{n} a_i p_i}{a_1}, \ldots, \frac{a_n y / \sum_{i=1}^{n} a_i p_i}{a_n} \right\}$$

$$= \frac{y}{\sum_{i=1}^{n} a_i p_i}.$$

Note that V is differentiable even though U is not. Hence, Roy's theorem can be invoked to derive the demand functions. Note also that indirect indifference surfaces are linear (see figure 2.2). This reflects the intuitive notion that "kinks" are dual to "flat" regions of indifference surfaces.

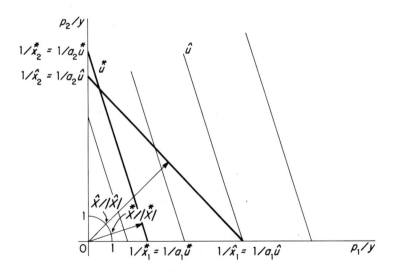

Figure 2.2.

The direct utility function is recovered by solving

$$U(X) = \min_{P/y} \left\{ \left[\sum_{i=1}^{n} a_i \frac{p_i}{y} \right]^{-1} \middle| \frac{P}{y} \in \Omega^n \wedge \frac{P}{y} \cdot X \leqslant 1 \right\}$$

$$= \min \left\{ \frac{x_1}{a_1}, \ldots, \frac{x_n}{a_n} \right\}.$$

The price-demand *correspondence* is given by

$$\tilde{\xi}(X) = \left\{ \frac{P}{y} \in \Omega^n \middle| \frac{p_i}{y} = 0 \; \forall i \text{ satisfying } \frac{x_i}{a_i} > \frac{x_j}{a_j} \right.$$

$$\left. \text{for some } j \wedge \frac{P}{y} \cdot X \leqslant 1 \right\}.$$

This derivation is illustrated in figure 2.2. In this diagram the vector $\hat{X}$ generates a constraint set such that the absolute slope of the constraint boundary, $\hat{x}_1/\hat{x}_2$, is less than the (common) absolute slopes of the indirect indifference lines, a_1/a_2, so that

$$\frac{\hat{x}_1}{a_1} < \frac{\hat{x}_2}{a_2}. \tag{a}$$

Utility is minimized at $p_2/y = 0$ and $p_1/y = 1/\hat{x}_1$. Reversing the slope inequality (a) would yield $p_1/y = 0$ and $p_2/y = 1/\hat{x}_2$. For any X on the ray A (e.g., $\overset{*}{X}$), (a) is converted into an equality, and this in turn results in an uncountably infinite number of optima. U is recovered by

$$U(X) = \begin{cases} \dfrac{1}{a_1(1/x_1)} = \dfrac{x_1}{a_1} & \text{if } \dfrac{x_1}{a_1} \leqslant \dfrac{x_2}{a_2} \\[3ex] \dfrac{1}{a_2(1/x_2)} = \dfrac{x_2}{a_2} & \text{if } \dfrac{x_1}{a_1} \geqslant \dfrac{x_2}{a_2} \end{cases}$$

$$= \min \left\{ \frac{x_1}{a_1}, \frac{x_2}{a_2} \right\}.$$

2.3 HICKSIAN DEMAND FUNCTIONS, COST FUNCTIONS, AND TRANSFORMATION FUNCTIONS

2.3.1 The Cost Function

The set of duality relationships for direct and indirect utility functions is by no means the only such set of relationships. In this section the duality between utility functions and cost functions is described.

If the infimum of the range of U is an element of the range of U, the cost minimization problem, to be defined below, will not have a solution when the level of utility is at its infimum value since the commodity space does not include the origin. Hence, the infimum value of utility is excluded from the cost function's domain. Let $\mathfrak{R}(U)$ be the range of U with its infimum value excluded. The *cost function*, $C:\mathfrak{R}(U)\times\Omega^n_+\to\Omega^1_+$, is defined by[9]

$$C(u,P)= \min_X \{ P \cdot X | X \in \Omega^n \wedge U(X) \geqslant u \} = P \cdot \zeta(u,P), \qquad (2.9)$$

where $\zeta(u,P)$ is the solution vector, if unique, to the minimization problem. Thus, the image of (u,P) by C is the minimum cost of achieving utility level u. Moreover, $\zeta:\mathfrak{R}(U)\times\Omega^n_+\to\Omega^n$ is the constant-utility [or income-compensated, or Hicksian (1946)] vector-valued demand function, and its image value $\zeta(u,P)$ is the (utility- or output-constrained) cost-minimizing consumption or input bundle. If the solution to the minimization problem in (2.9) is not unique, the cost function is given by the inner product of the price vector and an arbitrary element of the image of (u,P) by the constant-utility demand correspondence, $\tilde{\zeta}:\mathfrak{R}(U)\times\Omega^n_+\to\mathfrak{R}(\Omega^n)$. Given the properties of U, C is continuous in (u,P), increasing in u, and nondecreasing, concave, and positively linearly homogeneous (PLH) in P. (Positive linear homogeneity in P is defined as follows: $C(u,\lambda P)=\lambda C(u,P)\forall\lambda>0,\forall(u,P)\in\mathfrak{R}(U)\times\Omega^n_+$.) Whenever C satisfies these properties pertaining to P, we say that C satisfies

(R-3P) continuity, positive monotonicity, positive linear homogeneity, and concavity in P.

If, in addition, C is jointly continuous in (u,P) and increasing in u, we say that C satisfies

---

[9]Alternatively one could define the domain of the cost function to include all values of u in **R**. In this case, if $\mathfrak{R}(U)\neq\mathbf{R}$, then for all $\hat{u}\notin\mathfrak{R}(U)$ such that $\hat{u}\leqslant \inf\{u|u\in\mathfrak{R}(U)\}$, $C(\hat{u},P)=0$, and for all $\bar{u}\notin\mathfrak{R}(U)$ such that $\bar{u}\geqslant \sup\{u|u\in\mathfrak{R}(U)\}$, $C(\bar{u},P)=+\infty$.

(**R-3**) continuity in (u, P), strict positive monotonicity in u, and $(R - 3P)$.

In addition, ζ is continuous ($\tilde{\zeta}$ is upper hemicontinuous) in u and P and homogeneous of degree zero in P. Note that, like the indirect utility function, the cost function is generally defined for positive price vectors only; a minimal cost need not exist for nonpositive price vectors.[10] For example, if the utility function is Cobb-Douglas, with image (2.5), there is no minimum cost of attaining any positive utility if any price vanishes.

Thus, corresponding to any utility function, or preference ordering, is a cost function with the above properties. What is less well known is that corresponding to any cost function with the above properties there is a direct utility function, $\overset{*}{U}: \Omega^n \to \mathbf{R}$, defined as follows:[11]

$$\overset{*}{U}(X) = \max_{u} \left\{ u \in \mathcal{R}(U) \,\middle|\, C(u, P) \leqslant P \cdot X \ \forall P \in \Omega_+^n \right\}. \qquad (2.10)$$

Moreover, $\overset{*}{U}$ is nondecreasing and quasi-concave; continuity of the extension of C to the boundary of price space is required in order to prove continuity of $\overset{*}{U}$. Also, if C is derived from U by (2.9) and $\overset{*}{U}$ is, in turn, derived from C by (2.10), then $\overset{*}{U} = U$. Finally, if U is derived from C by (2.10) and $\overset{*}{C}$ is in turn derived from U by (2.9), then $\overset{*}{C} = C$. Thus, a preference ordering can be represented equivalently by a direct utility function, an indirect utility function, or a cost function.

2.3.2 The Transformation Function

Here we sketch the duality relationship that exists between utility functions and transformation functions. Malmquist (1953), Shephard (1953, 1970), Gorman (1970, 1975), Hanoch (1970), and McFadden (1970) have defined the transformation function $F: \mathcal{R}(U) \times \Omega_+^n \to \Omega_+^1$ as follows:

$$F(u, X) = \max_{\lambda} \left\{ \lambda \in \Omega_+^1 \,\middle|\, U(X/\lambda) \geqslant u \right\}. \qquad (2.11)$$

[10]It is, of course, possible to construct a "cost function" for all nonnegative prices by associating the infimum expenditure with each utility level.

[11]It is not essential that the range of U be known before recovering U from C. Even if the domain of C is defined to include all $u \in \mathbf{R}$ (as in footnote 8) and the maximization (2.10) is carried out letting u range over all the reals, the solution to (2.10) is the same. This is so because if $\hat{u} \notin \mathcal{R}(U)$ and $\hat{u} \geqslant \sup \{u \,|\, u \in \mathcal{R}(U)\}$, then $C(\hat{u}, P) = +\infty$ and the constraint $C(u, P) \leqslant P \cdot X \ \forall P \in \Omega^n$ is violated for all $X \in \Omega^n$. Hence $\hat{u}$ is never attained by the maximization in (2.10). Similarly, if $\hat{u} \notin \mathcal{R}(U)$ and $\hat{u} < \inf\{u \,|\, u \in \mathcal{R}(U)\}$, then $0 = C(\hat{u}, P) < P \cdot X \ \forall P \in \Omega_+^n$ and $\forall X \in \Omega^n$. Thus, $\hat{u}$ never solves the maximization problem in (2.10).

Given $(R-1)$, the properties of the utility function, we have F continuous in (u, X), decreasing in u, and nondecreasing, concave, and PLH in X. Whenever F satisfies these properties pertaining to X, we say that F satisfies

(R-4X) continuity, positive monotonicity, positive linear homogeneity, and concavity in X.

If, in addition, F is jointly continuous in (u, X) and decreasing in u, we say that F satisfies

(R-4) continuity in (u, X), strict negative monotonicity in u, and $(R-4X)$.

As long as X is not a point of global satiation, $U(X) = u$ if and only if $F(u, X) = 1$. Hence, the direct utility function, restricted to Ω_+^n, is implicitly defined by

$$F(u, X) = 1. \tag{2.12}$$

That is, corresponding to F there is a restricted direct utility function, $\overset{\circ}{U} : \Omega_+^n \to \mathbf{R}$, obtained by solving (2.12) for u. (This is always possible, since F is strictly monotonic in u.) If F satisfies $(R-4)$, $\overset{\circ}{U}$ satisfies $(R-1)$. Extending $\overset{\circ}{U}$ to Ω^n by continuity from above yields a mapping $\overset{*}{U} : \Omega^n \to \mathbf{R}$. If F is derived from U—satisfying $(R-1)$—by (2.11), and if $\overset{\circ}{U}$ is in turn derived from F by inversion of (2.12) and extension to the boundary from above, then $\overset{*}{U} = U$. Thus, the extension of $\overset{\circ}{U}$ by continuity from above is in fact continuous. Moreover, if U is derived from F— satisfying $(R-4)$—and $\overset{*}{F}$ is in turn derived from U, then $\overset{*}{F} = F$.

There is an alternative method for deriving U from F: the solution to

$$U(X) = \max_u \left\{ u \in \mathfrak{R}(U) \mid F(u, X) \geq 1 \right\} \tag{2.13}$$

correctly generates the image of U for each positive consumption bundle X.

2.3.3 Duality and Cost and Transformation Functions

The direct utility function, indirect utility function, cost function, and transformation function have been introduced as equivalent representations of the underlying preference ordering. Dual relationships between U and V, between U and C, and between U and F have been sketched. Here we discuss the dual relationships that exist between V and C, between V and F, and between C and F. In doing so, different interpretations of cost and transformation functions become apparent.

Examining the properties of the cost function and the transformation function, $(R-3)$ and $(R-4)$, we note that, except for the direction of monotonicity of the utility variable, these conditions suggest that C could be interpreted as a transformation function and F as a cost function. This is indeed true.

To see this, first consider the relationship between V and C. Define an indirect transformation function by

$$\bar{C}(u,P) = \min_{\lambda}\left\{\lambda\in\Omega^1_+ \mid V(P/\lambda) \geqslant u\right\}. \tag{2.14}$$

We will show that this indirect transformation function is indeed the same as the direct cost function. Rewrite (2.14), using (2.1), as

$$\bar{C}(u,P) = \min_{\lambda}\left\{\lambda\in\Omega^1_+ \mid \max_{X}\left\{U(X)\mid X\in\Omega^n \wedge \frac{P}{\lambda}\cdot X \leqslant 1\right\} \geqslant u\right\}, \tag{2.15}$$

or, recalling that $\tilde{\phi}$ is the vector-valued demand correspondence,

$$\bar{C}(u,P) = \min_{\lambda}\left\{\lambda\in\Omega^1_+ \mid U(\tilde{X}) \geqslant u \wedge \tilde{X}\in\tilde{\phi}(P/\lambda)\right\}. \tag{2.16}$$

However, if $\overset{*}{\lambda}$ solves the optimization problem in (2.16), then $P\cdot\tilde{X}=\overset{*}{\lambda}$, since $P\cdot\tilde{X}>\overset{*}{\lambda}$ implies $\tilde{X}\notin\tilde{\phi}(P/\overset{*}{\lambda})$, and $P\cdot\tilde{X}<\overset{*}{\lambda}$ implies $\tilde{X}$ is feasible at a lower value of λ. Consequently, (2.16) can be rewritten as

$$\bar{C}(u,P) = \min_{\tilde{X}}\left\{P\cdot\tilde{X}\mid U(\tilde{X}) \geqslant u \wedge \tilde{X}\in\tilde{\phi}(P/\lambda)\right\}. \tag{2.17}$$

Next note that the vector which solves

$$\min_{X} P\cdot X \quad \text{s.t.} \quad U(X)\geqslant u \wedge X\in\Omega^n$$

is necessarily a member of $\tilde{\phi}(P/\lambda)$ for some $\lambda\in\Omega^1_+$, namely, the constant value of the equation defining the hyperplane with normal P that supports the u-level set. In other words, the solution to the utility-constrained cost-minimization problem also solves the corresponding expenditure-constrained utility-maximization problem. (The converse does not necessarily hold, because of the possibility of a region of global satiation.) Therefore, (2.17) can be rewritten as

$$\bar{C}(u,P) = \min_{X}\left\{P\cdot X\mid U(X) \geqslant u \wedge X\in\Omega^n\right\} = C(u,P).$$

Therefore $\bar{C}=C$.

Thus, the cost function which is derived from the direct utility function can be thought of as a transformation function of the indirect utility function. Hence, by analogy to (2.12) and (2.13), we can recover the indirect utility function from the cost function either by inverting

$$C(u,P) = 1, \qquad P \in \Omega_+^n, \tag{2.18}$$

in u or by[12]

$$V(P) = \min_u \{ u \in \mathcal{R}(U) | C(u,P) \geq 1 \}. \tag{2.19}$$

Next we show that the transformation function F can be thought of as a cost function derived from the indirect utility function.[13] The easiest way to see this is to write the product of the cost and transformation function as

$$F(u,X) \cdot C(u,P) = \overset{*}{\lambda} P \cdot \overset{*}{X}, \tag{2.20}$$

where $\overset{*}{X}$ is the solution to the minimization problem in (2.9) and $\overset{*}{\lambda}$ is the solution to the maximization problem in (2.11). The latter, given $(R-1)$, implies that $U(X/\overset{*}{\lambda}) = u$ and hence that $X/\overset{*}{\lambda}$ is a member of the feasible set in (2.9). Therefore,

$$\overset{*}{\lambda} P \cdot \overset{*}{X} \leq P \cdot X = \overset{*}{\lambda} P \cdot \frac{X}{\overset{*}{\lambda}} \qquad \forall (P,X) \in \Omega_+^{2n}, \tag{2.21}$$

which together with (2.20) implies that

$$F(u,X) \cdot C(u,P) \leq P \cdot X \qquad \forall (P,X) \in \Omega_+^{2n}. \tag{2.22}$$

The inequalities (2.21) and (2.22) are illustrated in figure 2.3. Note, in particular, that in general $X/F(u,X)$ is not the optimal bundle at prices P. If it were—i.e., if $\overset{*}{X} = X/F(u,X)$—we would refer to the pair (P,X) as *direct conjugates*. Formally, we define the pair $(\bar{P}, \bar{X})$ to be direct conjugates at utility level u if the u-level set is supported at $\bar{X}/F(u,\bar{X})$ by a hyperplane with normal $\bar{P}$ where $\overset{*}{C}(u,\bar{P}) = 1$; hence

$$F(u,\bar{X}) \cdot \overset{*}{C}(u,\bar{P}) = \bar{P} \cdot \bar{X}, \tag{2.23}$$

---

[12]Instead of this evaluation at unit income, we could equivalently interpret P as a vector of normalized prices.

[13]An alternative proof of this result, under different regularity conditions, can be found in Shephard (1970: proposition 44, p. 157). An adaptation of Shephard's proof to accommodate our regularity conditions is contained in the appendix (theorems A.8 and A.11).

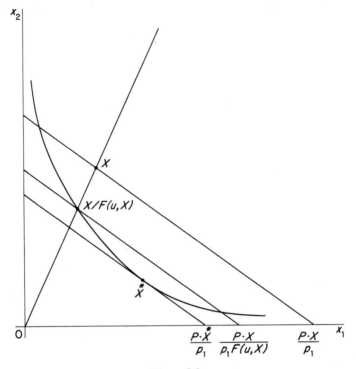

Figure 2.3.

where $\overset{*}{C}$ is the extension of C to $\mathscr{R}(U)\times\Omega^n$ by continuity from above.

We now use this notion of conjugacy to establish that the direct transformation function is a cost function derived from the indirect utility function. Define a function $\Phi:\mathscr{R}(U)\times\Omega^m_+\times\Omega^m\to\mathbf{R}$ by

$$\Phi(u,X,P)=P{\cdot}X-F(u,X)\overset{*}{C}(u,P). \qquad (2.24)$$

For fixed u and X, this is a convex function of P. Letting $X=\overline{X}$, we see from (2.22) and (2.23) that the minimum of $\Phi(u,X,P)$, zero, is achieved at $P=\overline{P}$. Hence,

$$\min_{P}\left\{\Phi(u,\overline{X},P)\big|P\in\Omega^n\right\}=\min_{P}\left\{P{\cdot}\overline{X}-F(u,\overline{X})\big|P\in\Omega^n\wedge\overset{*}{C}(u,P)\geqslant1\right\}$$

$$=\min_{P}\left\{P{\cdot}\overline{X}\big|P\in\Omega^n\wedge\overset{*}{C}(u,P)\geqslant1\right\}-F(u,\overline{X})=0. \qquad (2.25)$$

Therefore,

$$F(u,\overline{X}) = \min_{P} \left\{ P \cdot \overline{X} \,|\, P \in \Omega^n \wedge \overset{*}{C}(u,P) \geqslant 1 \right\}$$

or, using (2.14) and the result that $C = \overline{C}$,

$$F(u,\overline{X}) = \min_{P} \left\{ P \cdot \overline{X} \,|\, P \in \Omega^n \wedge \overset{*}{V}(P) \leqslant u \right\} = \delta(u,\overline{X}) \cdot \overline{X}, \qquad (2.26)$$

where $\delta(u,X)$ is the solution vector for the minimization problem in (2.26). [If the solution is not unique, use an arbitrary element of the set of solution values in the inner product in (2.26).]

Thus, the direct transformation function can be interpreted equivalently as the cost function that is obtained from the indirect utility function. Moreover, $\delta : \mathcal{R}(U) \times \Omega^n_+ \to \Omega^n$ is the constant-utility price-demand, or shadow-price, function. If the solution is not unique, this relationship is given by a shadow-price correspondence, $\tilde{\delta} : \mathcal{R}(U) \times \Omega^n_+ \to \mathcal{P}(\Omega^n)$. Given the regularity conditions, δ is continuous ($\tilde{\delta}$ is upper hemicontinuous) in (u,P) and HDO in X.

In the context of production theory, F represents the evaluation of input vector X at output u and unit expenditure. Only *relative* shadow prices are determined by the gradient of an output level surface, as the evaluation of absolute shadow prices $\delta(u,X)$ implicitly requires normalization on an expenditure level. The constraint in (2.26), $\overset{*}{V}(P) \leqslant u$, implicitly normalizes expenditure to unity. This normalization explains why F is decreasing in u; a higher level of utility u, given unit expenditure, can be obtained only at lower absolute input prices, implying a lower imputation of factor payments. This is illustrated in figure 2.4, where it should be remembered that higher levels of u are represented by indifference curves which are closer to the origin.

The notion of *indirect conjugacy* is defined using the indirect cost and transformation function. Letting $\overset{*}{\lambda}$ be the solution to (2.14) and $\overset{*}{P}$ the solution to (2.26), and following the argument which leads to (2.23), we find that

$$F(u,X)C(u,\overset{*}{P}) = \lambda \overset{*}{P} \cdot X \leqslant P \cdot X \qquad \forall (P,X) \in \Omega^{2n}_+. \qquad (2.27)$$

In figure 2.5, the inequality (2.27) is illustrated. Note that in general the imputed prices $P/C(u,P)$ are not optimal at quantities X. We define the pair $(\overline{P},\overline{X})$ to be indirect conjugates at u if the u-level set is supported at $\overline{P}/C(u,\overline{P})$ by a hyperplance with normal $\overline{X}$ where $\overset{*}{F}(u,\overline{X}) = 1$, in which

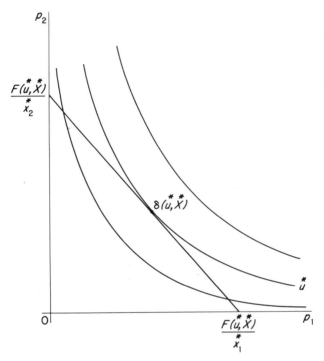

Figure 2.4.

case

$$\overset{*}{F}(u,\overline{X})C(u,\overline{P})=\overline{P}\cdot\overline{X}, \tag{2.28}$$

where $\overset{*}{F}$ is the extension of F to $\mathfrak{R}(U)\times\Omega^n$ by continuity from above.

This in turn allows us to characterize precisely an optimal pair $(\overset{*}{P},\overset{*}{X})$ at $\overset{*}{u}$ as one which is simultaneously directly and indirectly conjugate at $\overset{*}{u}$. That is,

$$\overset{*}{P}\cdot\overset{*}{X}/\overset{*}{F}(\overset{*}{u},\overset{*}{X})=\overset{*}{X}\cdot\overset{*}{P}/\overset{*}{C}(\overset{*}{u},\overset{*}{P}),$$

which implies that

$$\overset{*}{F}(\overset{*}{u},\overset{*}{X})=\overset{*}{C}(\overset{*}{u},\overset{*}{P})=1 \tag{2.29}$$

and

$$U(\overset{*}{X})=\overset{*}{u}=\overset{*}{V}(\overset{*}{P}).$$

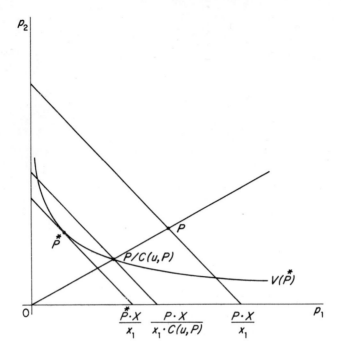

Figure 2.5.

It follows therefore that

$$\overset{*}{X} = \varsigma\left(\overset{*}{u}, \overset{*}{P}\right)$$

and

$$\overset{*}{P} = \delta\left(\overset{*}{u}, \overset{*}{X}\right),$$

which is illustrated in figure 2.6.

Given a transformation function F that has been derived from an indirect utility function $\overset{*}{V}$, by (2.26), V can be recovered from F in a way analogous to the recovery of U from C in (2.10), viz.,

$$V(P) = \min_{u}\left\{u \in \mathcal{R}(U)\,|\,F(u,X) \leqslant P{\cdot}X \ \forall X \in \Omega^{n}_{+}\right\}. \qquad (2.30)$$

Moreover, recalling (2.9) and (2.26), we note that the transformation and cost functions are related by

$$C(u,P) = \min_{X}\left\{P{\cdot}X\,|\,X \in \Omega^{n} \wedge \overset{*}{F}(u,X) \geqslant 1\right\} \qquad (2.31)$$

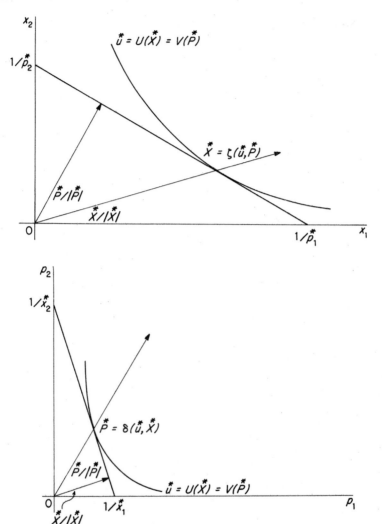

Figure 2.6.

and

$$F(u,X) = \min_{P} \{ P \cdot X \mid P \in \Omega^n \wedge \overset{*}{C}(u,P) \geqslant 1 \}, \tag{2.32}$$

where $\overset{*}{F}$ and $\overset{*}{C}$ are extensions of F and C to $\mathfrak{R}(U) \times \Omega^n$ by continuity from above.

2.3.4 Hotelling's Theorem and Its Dual

It will be recalled from section 2.2 that the duality between direct and indirect utility functions facilitates the expedient derivation of ordinary demand functions by straightforward differentiation using Roy's theorem or its dual (Wold's theorem). The usefulness of the duality between the transformation function and the cost function is similarly enhanced by Hotelling's (1932) theorem and its dual, proved by Shephard (1970):

Hotelling's Theorem *If C is differentiable at (u, P),*

$$\zeta(u, P) = \nabla C(u, P).$$

Shephard's Theorem *If F is differentiable at (u, X),*

$$\delta(u, X) = \nabla F(u, X).$$

Duality implies that a preference ordering (or production technology) can be represented equivalently by a transformation function or a cost function. Hotelling's theorem and its dual, Shephard's theorem, imply that it is most expedient to specify the cost function if one wants to derive Hicksian quantity-demand functions, and to specify the transformation function if one wants to derive Hicksian demand-price functions.

Before concluding, we illustrate these results using the Cobb-Douglas, homogeneous quadratic, and Leontief examples introduced earlier. The cost function which is dual to (2.5) is derived by

$$C(u, P) = \min_{X} \left\{ P \cdot X \mid X \in \Omega^n \wedge \prod_{i=1}^{n} x_i^{\alpha_i} \geqslant u \right\}$$

$$= \alpha \left[\frac{u}{\displaystyle\prod_{i=1}^{n} \left(\frac{\alpha_i}{p_i} \right)^{\alpha_i}} \right]^{1/\alpha}, \tag{2.33}$$

where the Hicksian quantity-demand functions have the images

$$\zeta_j(u, P) = \left(\frac{\alpha_j}{p_j} \right) \left[\frac{u}{\displaystyle\prod_{i=1}^{n} \left(\frac{\alpha_i}{p_i} \right)^{\alpha_i}} \right]^{1/\alpha}, \qquad j = 1, \ldots, n.$$

The direct utility function (2.5) can be recovered from the cost function (2.33) in a large variety of ways. The particular path followed here is simply chosen for pedagogic reasons. In practice, however, this choice can be important, as the paths are not equally difficult. In this example, we recover the indirect utility function by inversion, the transformation function by minimization, and the direct utility function by inversion.

Set the cost-function image (2.33) equal to unity (i.e., normalize income to unity):

$$\alpha \left[\frac{u}{\prod_{i=1}^{n} \left(\dfrac{\alpha_i}{p_i} \right)^{\alpha_i}} \right]^{1/\alpha} = 1,$$

and invert in u to get the indirect utility function,

$$u = \alpha^{-\alpha} \prod_{i=1}^{n} \left(\frac{\alpha_i}{p_i} \right)^{\alpha_i} = V(P). \tag{2.6}$$

Now construct the transformation (indirect cost) function by

$$F(u,X) = \min_{P} \left\{ P \cdot X \mid P \in \Omega_{+}^{n} \wedge \alpha^{-\alpha} \prod_{i=1}^{n} \left(\frac{\alpha_i}{p_i} \right)^{\alpha_i} \leqslant u \right\}$$

$$= \left(u^{-1} \prod_{i=1}^{n} x_i^{\alpha_i} \right)^{1/\alpha}, \tag{2.34}$$

where

$$\delta_j(u,X) = \left(\frac{\alpha_j}{x_j} \right) \left(u^{-1} \prod_{i=1}^{n} x_i^{\alpha_i} \right)^{1/\alpha} \alpha^{-1}, \qquad j = 1,\dots,n,$$

are the compensated price-demand equations.

Setting the transformation function image (2.34) equal to unity and inverting in u yields

$$U(X) = \prod_{i=1}^{n} x_i^{\alpha_i}. \tag{2.5}$$

Continuing the example of the homogeneous quadratic (2.7), we can derive the cost function via (2.9) from the utility function:

$$C(u,P) = \min_X \left\{ P \cdot X \mid X \in \hat{\Omega}^n \wedge \tfrac{1}{2} X'AX \geqslant u \right\}$$

$$= P \cdot \zeta(u,P)$$

$$= (2uP'A^{-1}P)^{1/2}, \tag{2.35}$$

where

$$\zeta(u,P) = A^{-1}P(2u)^{1/2}(P'A^{-1}P)^{-1/2} \tag{2.36}$$

is the image of (u,P) by the vector-valued constant-utility quantity-demand function. Conversely, one can start with the above cost function and retrieve the utility function. A practical way to do this is to use the cost function to derive, say, the transformation function and then invert the transformation function in u. Thus, letting $\hat{\Omega}^n_+ = \{P \in \Omega^n_+ \mid A^{-1}P \geqslant 0\}$,

$$F(u,X) = \min_P \left\{ P \cdot X \mid P \in \hat{\Omega}^n_+ \wedge C(u,P) \geqslant 1 \right\}$$

$$= \min_P \left\{ P \cdot X \mid P \in \hat{\Omega}^n_+ \wedge (2uP'A^{-1}P)^{1/2} \geqslant 1 \right\}$$

$$= \delta(u,X) \cdot X$$

$$= (2u)^{-1/2}(X'AX)^{1/2}, \tag{2.37}$$

where

$$\delta(u,X) = AX(2uX'AX)^{-1/2}, \tag{2.38}$$

the image of (u,X) by the vector-valued constant-utility price-demand function, is the solution to the minimization problem. Next, set $F(u,X)$ equal to one and solve for u. The reader can verify that (2.7) is thus obtained.

Another practical way to retrieve the utility function is to invert the cost function to obtain the indirect utility function; i.e., solve

$$1 = C(u, P/y)$$

for u to get $u = V(P/y)$. From V, U is obtained as in equation (2.2). Next, apply Hotelling's theorem to the cost function to see that it generates the constant-utility quantity-demand function in (2.36). Then, of course, in the dual apply Shephard's theorem to the transformation function to obtain the constant-utility price-demand function in (2.38). Finally, it can be verified that these Hicksian price- and quantity-demand functions are inverses of each other.

Finally, consider the Leontief utility function, with image

$$U(X) = \min\left\{ \frac{x_1}{a_1}, \ldots, \frac{x_n}{a_n} \right\}. \tag{2.39}$$

The dual cost function is derived by

$$C(u, P) = \min_X \left\{ P \cdot X \mid X \in \Omega^n \wedge \min\left\{ \frac{x_1}{a_1}, \ldots, \frac{x_n}{a_n} \right\} \geqslant u \right\}$$

$$= u \sum_{i=1}^{n} a_i p_i, \tag{2.40}$$

and the constant-utility quantity-demand functions are given by

$$\check{\xi}_i(u, P) = a_i u, \qquad i = 1, \ldots, n.$$

Note that, as the cost function is differentiable, these demand functions can be derived using Hotelling's theorem.

The transformation function can be derived from this cost function by

$$F(u, X) = \min_P \left\{ P \cdot X \mid P \in \Omega^n \wedge u \sum_{i=1}^{n} a_i p_i \geqslant 1 \right\}$$

$$= \min\left\{ \frac{x_1}{a_1 u}, \ldots, \frac{x_n}{a_n u} \right\} = \frac{1}{u} \min\left\{ \frac{x_1}{a_1}, \ldots, \frac{x_n}{a_n} \right\},$$

and the constant-utility price-demand correspondences are given by

$$\tilde{\delta}(u, X) = \left\{ P \in \Omega^n \mid p_i = 0 \; \forall i \text{ satisfying } \frac{x_i}{a_i} > \frac{x_j}{a_j} \right.$$

$$\left. \text{for some } j \wedge u \sum_{i=1}^{n} a_i p_i = 1 \right\}.$$

Finally, note that inverting

$$F(u,X) = \frac{1}{u}\min\left\{\frac{x_1}{a_1},\ldots,\frac{x_n}{a_n}\right\} = 1$$

in u yields the direct utility function, and inverting

$$C(u,P) = u\sum_{i=1}^{n} a_i p_i = 1$$

in u yields the indirect utility function.

2.4   CONCLUDING REMARKS

The dual structure outlined in the previous pages is summarized in Figure 2.7. This chart reflects the fact that it is possible to construct any one of the four functions $\{U, V, F, C\}$ from any other function, invoking the appropriate optimization problem signified by the arrow running from the latter function to the former. This, in turn, underscores the important fact that consumer preferences (or production technologies) can be represented equivalently by any one of these four functions. Put differently, the specification of any one of these four functions with the appropriate convexity, monotonicity, and continuity properties is equivalent to specifying a preference ordering (or technology).

This dual structure has been extended by McFadden (1966, 1970), Gorman (1968a), Lau (1969c), and Diewert (1973d, 1974a), who have studied the duality between technology sets and profit functions. We do not exploit this important dual relationship in the study of functional structure that follows.

The existence of these alternative ways of representing a preference ordering is important for the study of functional structure because structure is not necessarily self-dual[14]—i.e., the possession of a particular structural property by one of these functions does not necessarily imply that any of the other three functions (corresponding to the same preferences) possesses this property. This fact enriches the class of structures that can be imposed on the underlying preferences by endowing functional representations with structure.

[14]The notion of self-duality was introduced by Houthakker (1965b).

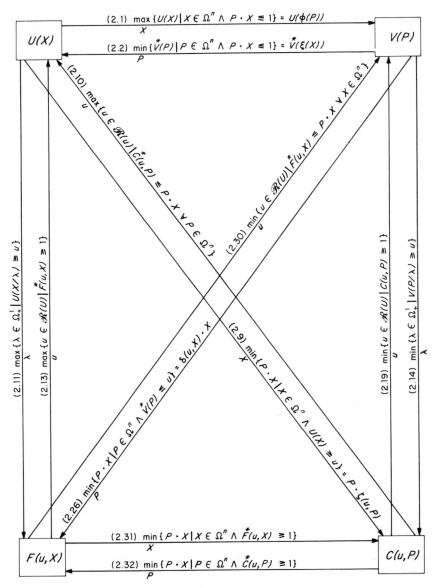

Figure 2.7.

Finally, it is easy to see that the constructive methods of deriving one functional representation of an ordering from another facilitate significantly the constructive proofs of dual relationships between functional structures. Without this elegant dual structure, painstakingly constructed by Diewert, Gorman, Hotelling, McFadden, Samuelson, Shephard, and others, the tasks set forth in this book would be considerably more difficult.

3
Separability

This chapter discusses in some detail the notion of separability. The simplicity of this concept is exploited by carrying out the analysis in the simplest possible setting. The examination of more complicated functional structures is postponed to later chapters.

Separability is defined and illustrated in section 3.1. The following section discusses alternative definitions of separability and relates these definitions to that used in this book. Section 3.3 proves a functional representation theorem which allows us to characterize separability by the structure of the utility function. Representations employing the indirect utility function, the cost function, and the transformation function are introduced in section 3.4. Section 3.5 proves some important results on duality and functional structure. Finally, section 3.6 contains a few concluding remarks.

3.1 THE DEFINITION OF SEPARABILITY

In this section, separability is characterized in terms of the utility (or production) function. This function represents a complete preference ordering (or production technology). The regularity conditions (R-1) (continuity, positive monotonicity, and quasi-concavity) are not needed for many of the results that follow. Appropriate subsets of these conditions (or, frequently, weaker or stronger monotonicity and/or curvature conditions) will be invoked where needed.

3.1.1 Notation

In order to introduce the notion of separability, it is necessary to construct notation which identifies variables and subsets of variables. Let

$$I = \{1, 2, \ldots, n\}$$

be the set of integers which identify the variables over which the preferences are defined. Consider a partition of the set into two subsets:

$$\bar{I} = \{I^c, I^r\}.$$

That is,

$$I^c \cup I^r = I,$$
$$I^c \cap I^r = \varnothing,$$
$$I^c \neq \varnothing,$$

and

$$I^r \neq \varnothing.$$

Corresponding to the binary partition $\bar{I}$, we denote vectors in Ω^n in ways that reflect the partition. First, express Ω^n as a Cartesian product of the appropriate subspaces; i.e.,[1]

$$\Omega^n = \Omega^{(c)} \times \Omega^{(r)}.$$

The dimensions of $\Omega^{(c)}$ and $\Omega^{(r)}$ are given by the cardinalities of I^c and I^r, respectively. A commodity vector, $X \in \Omega^n$, can be written as

$$X = (X^c, X^r).$$

Similarly, a price vector can be written as

$$P = (P^c, P^r).$$

If the ith commodity or price is in the rth category, then x_i is a component of the vector $X^r \in \Omega^{(r)}$ and p_i is a component of the vector $P^r \in \Omega^{(r)}$.

---

[1]Strictly speaking, Ω^n is not the Cartesian product of $\Omega^{(c)}$ and $\Omega^{(r)}$ unless the indices are ordered so that $I^c = \{1, 2, \ldots, n_c\}$ and $I^r = \{n_c + 1, n_c + 2, \ldots, n\}$. In order to avoid complicating the notation, assume that the index set has been ordered to conform to this particular binary partition of I.

3.1.2 Separability Defined

The basic definition of separability which we use [2] exploits the mapping $\beta^r : \Omega^n \to \mathcal{P}(\Omega^{(r)})$, which is defined by

$$\beta^r(X^c, X^r) = \{\hat{X}^r \in \Omega^{(r)} | U(X^c, \hat{X}^r) \geqslant U(X^c, X^r)\}.$$

This mapping defines a set of points in $\Omega^{(r)}$ for each fixed reference vector, (X^c, X^r), such that each point in $\{X^c\} \times \beta^r(X^c, X^r)$ is "no worse than" (X^c, X^r). For example, suppose that $n = 3$, $I^c = \{1\}$, and $I^r = \{2, 3\}$. Then $X^c = x_1$ and $X^r = (x_2, x_3)$. For a particular point $(\bar{X}^c, \bar{X}^r)$ where $\bar{X}^c = \bar{x}_1$ and $\bar{X}^r = (\bar{x}_2, \bar{x}_3)$, the set of points which is equal to $\beta^r(\bar{X}^c, \bar{X}^r)$ is depicted in figure 3.1 by the shaded area.

Geometrically this set may be constructed as follows. Take the set of bundles which are "no worse than" the bundle $(\bar{x}_1, \bar{x}_2, \bar{x}_3)$, and intersect this with the plane

$$\{(x_1, x_2, x_3) | x_1 = \bar{x}_1\}.$$

The projection of this intersection into the two-dimensional nonnegative orthant, $\Omega^{(r)}$, is the shaded area of figure 3.1.

We may generate a collection of subsets of $\Omega^{(r)}$ by fixing X^c at, say, $\bar{X}^c$ and varying the vector X^r throughout the entire domain $\Omega^{(r)}$. For each point X^r, a member of this collection is $\beta^r(\bar{X}^c, X^r)$. This collection of

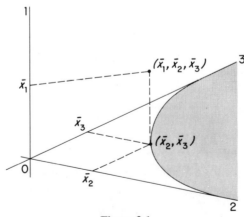

Figure 3.1

---

[2]Alternative definitions and their historical development as well as their relation to our definition are discussed in section 3.2 below.

subsets defines a *conditional ordering*, $\succcurlyeq^r_c$, on the subspace $\Omega^{(r)}$. Specifically, for each pair $(\tilde{X}^r, \overline{X}^r) \in \Omega^{(r)} \times \Omega^{(r)}$ and for some fixed vector $\overline{X}^c$,

$$\tilde{X}^r \succcurlyeq^r_c \overline{X}^r$$

if and only if

$$U(\overline{X}^c, \tilde{X}^r) \geqslant U(\overline{X}^c, \overline{X}^r),$$

which in turn is true if and only if

$$\beta^r(\overline{X}^c, \tilde{X}^r) \subseteq \beta^r(\overline{X}^c, \overline{X}^r).$$

This conditional ordering is clearly complete, reflexive, transitive, and continuous, given continuity of the utility function U. Figure 3.2 illustrates two level sets of this conditional ordering in terms of the example above, where $\tilde{X}^r = (\tilde{x}_2, \bar{x}_3)$ and $\tilde{x}_2 > \bar{x}_2$.

In general this conditional ordering is not independent of the value at which X^c is fixed. However, under the various separability conditions that we shall soon introduce, the conditional ordering will, to a varying extent, be independent of $\overline{X}^c$. One of these separability conditions involves the following property. Consider any collection of subsets of $\Omega^{(r)}$, say

$$B = \{B_1, B_2, \dots\}.$$

This collection is *nested* if, for any two subsets B_1 and B_2 included in the collection, either $B_1 \subseteq B_2$ or $B_2 \subseteq B_1$.

Now consider a particular collection of subsets in $\Omega^{(r)}$ defined by varying both X^r and X^c. A member, $\beta^r(X^c, X^r)$, of this collection is defined for

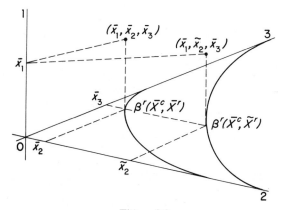

Figure 3.2

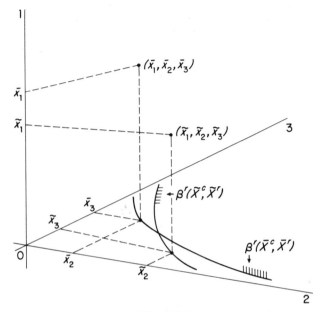

Figure 3.3

each point $(X^c, X^r) \in \Omega^{(c)} \times \Omega^{(r)}$. This collection is not in general a nested collection. This point is illustrated in figure 3.3, where, as before, $I^c = \{1\}$ and $I^r = \{2, 3\}$. In this figure, we consider two points, $(\overline{X}^c, \overline{X}^r)$ and $(\tilde{X}^c, \tilde{X}^r)$, which violate the above nesting property; i.e., we have $\beta^r(\overline{X}^c, \overline{X}^r)$ $\not\subseteq \beta^r(\tilde{X}^c, \tilde{X}^r)$ and $\beta^r(\tilde{X}^c, \tilde{X}^r) \not\subseteq \beta^r(\overline{X}^c, \overline{X}^r)$. Since these sets are not nested, the implied indifference curves that pass through $\overline{X}^r$ and $\tilde{X}^r$ in $\Omega^{(r)}$ intersect each other. We therefore cannot tell anything about consumer preferences between $\overline{X}^r$ and $\tilde{X}^r$ without reference to the consumption of other goods. Thus, if preferences are to be separable, nesting of these sets would seem to be at least a necessary condition.

For a formal definition of separability, partition the set of variable indices into three disjoint subsets, $\{I^p, I^q, I^r\}$. Then $X = (X^p, X^q, X^r) \in \Omega^{(p)}$ $\times \Omega^{(q)} \times \Omega^{(r)} = \Omega^n$. Define a collection of subsets of $\Omega^{(r)}$ as

$$\mathcal{C}^r(\overline{X}^p) = \left\{ \beta^r(\overline{X}^p, X^q, X^r) \,\middle|\, X^q \in \Omega^{(q)} \wedge X^r \in \Omega^{(r)} \right\}$$

for some fixed vector $\overline{X}^p \in \Omega^{(p)}$. The set of variables I^r is said to be *separable in U from the set of variables I^q* if $\mathcal{C}^r(\overline{X}^p)$ is nested for each fixed vector $\overline{X}^p \in \Omega^{(p)}$.[3]

---

[3]This definition of separability is due to Bliss (1975).

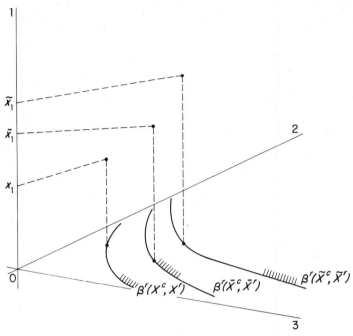

Figure 3.4

One case which is of particular interest is that in which $I^p = \varnothing$ and $I^q = I^c$. This simplifies the definition of separability as follows. Define $\mathcal{C}^r$, a collection of subsets of $\Omega^{(r)}$, as

$$\mathcal{C}^r = \left\{ \beta^r(X^c, X^r) \mid X^c \in \Omega^{(c)} \wedge X^r \in \Omega^{(r)} \right\}.$$

The set of variables I^r is separable in U from the set of variables I^c if $\mathcal{C}^r$ is nested. Continuing our earlier example, figure 3.4 depicts the case in which the set $I^r = \{2, 3\}$ is separable from $I^c = \{1\}$.

3.1.3 Strict Separability Defined

The above notion of separability will be all that is needed in much of what follows. However, at times it will be more convenient or even necessary to employ a slightly narrower concept. The set of variables I^r is said to be *strictly separable in U from the set of variables I^q* if, for each fixed vector $\overline{X}^p$,

$$\beta^r(\overline{X}^p, X^q, X^r) = \beta^r(\overline{X}^p, \tilde{X}^q, X^r)$$

for all $(X^q, X^r) \in \Omega^{(q)} \times \Omega^{(r)}$ and for any $\tilde{X}^q \in \Omega^{(q)}$.

As before, the case in which $I^p = \varnothing$ and $I^q = I^c$ is of particular interest. In this case the set of variables I^r is strictly separable in U from the set of variables I^c if

$$\beta^r(X^c, X^r) = \beta^r(\tilde{X}^c, X^r)$$

for all $(X^c, X^r) \in \Omega^{(c)} \times \Omega^{(r)}$ and for any $\tilde{X}^c \in \Omega^{(c)}$.

3.1.4   Relationships Between Separability and Strict Separability

We now justify our choice of the term "strict separability" by demonstrating that strict separability of I^r from I^c implies separability of I^r from I^c. (A similar argument would apply if I^r were separable from $I^q \subset I^c$.) Consider any two members of $\mathcal{C}$, say $\beta^r(X^c, X^r)$ and $\beta^r(\tilde{X}^c, \tilde{X}^r)$. Completeness of the conditional ordering on $\Omega^{(r)}$, given $\tilde{X}^c$, implies that either

$$\beta^r(\tilde{X}^c, X^r) \subseteq \beta^r(\tilde{X}^c, \tilde{X}^r)$$

or

$$\beta^r(\tilde{X}^c, \tilde{X}^r) \subseteq \beta^r(\tilde{X}^c, X^r).$$

Moreover, strict separability of I^r from I^c implies that $\beta^r(X^c, X^r) = \beta^r(\tilde{X}^c, X^r)$. Substituting this equality into the above we get either

$$\beta^r(X^c, X^r) \subseteq \beta^r(\tilde{X}^c, \tilde{X}^r)$$

or

$$\beta^r(\tilde{X}^c, \tilde{X}^r) \subseteq \beta^r(X^c, X^r).$$

Thus $\mathcal{C}$ is nested and I^r is separable from I^c.

To demonstrate that, in general, separability does not imply strict separability, a simple counterexample will do. Consider the Leontief utility function for the case $n = 3$, i.e.,

$$U(X) = \min\{x_1, x_2, x_3\}.$$

In this case, let $I^c = \{1\}$ and $I^r = \{2, 3\}$. Then

$$\beta^r(X^c, X^r) = \beta'(x_1, x_2, x_3)$$

$$= \{(\hat{x}_2, \hat{x}_3) | \min\{x_1, \hat{x}_2, \hat{x}_3\} \geqslant \min\{x_1, x_2, x_3\}\}.$$

It is easy to verify that the collection of all such sets is nested; thus I^r is separable from I^c.

Next note that

$$\beta^r(2,2,2) = \left\{ (\hat{x}_2, \hat{x}_3) \mid \hat{x}_2 \geqslant 2 \wedge \hat{x}_3 \geqslant 2 \right\}$$

and

$$\beta^r(1,2,2) = \left\{ (\hat{x}_2, \hat{x}_3) \mid \hat{x}_2 \geqslant 1 \wedge \hat{x}_3 \geqslant 1 \right\}.$$

These sets are nested, since

$$\beta^r(2,2,2) \subset \beta^r(1,2,2),$$

but the two sets are not equal. Thus I^r is *not* strictly separable from I^c, since strict separability requires that

$$\beta^r(2,2,2) = \beta^r(1,2,2).$$

The difference between separability and strict separability may be further illuminated by the following result, which we state formally as a lemma.

Lemma 3.1   *If the utility function U is nondecreasing in x_i, then each singleton $\{i\}$ is separable in U from its complement in I. Moreover, if U is increasing in x_i, then each singleton $\{i\}$ is strictly separable in U from its complement in I.*

Proof.   Letting $I^c = I - \{i\}$ and $I^r = \{i\}$, the set

$$\beta^r(X^c, x_i) = \left\{ \hat{x}_i \mid U(X^c, \hat{x}_i) \geqslant U(X^c, x_i) \right\}$$

is simply a half line in $\Omega^1 \cup \{0\}$. Clearly the collection of all such half lines is nested; thus $\{i\}$ is separable in U from I^c.

If U is increasing in x_i,

$$\beta^r(X^c, x_i) = [x_i, +\infty).$$

Since these half lines depend only on the value of x_i,

$$\beta^r(X^c, x_i) = \beta^r(\tilde{X}^c, x_i)$$

for all $(X^c, x_i) \in \Omega^{(c)} \times \Omega^1$; thus $\{i\}$ is strictly separable in U from I^c. $\|$

The main conclusion of the lemma is that when the utility function is nondecreasing, each individual variable is separable from all the other variables. However, when the utility function is not increasing, an individual variable need not be strictly separable. For example, consider the utility function $U:\Omega^2 \to \mathbf{R}$, defined by

$$U(x_1,x_2) = \begin{cases} x_1 \cdot x_2 & \text{if} \quad x_1 \cdot x_2 \leqslant 1, \\ 1 & \text{if} \quad x_1 \cdot x_2 \geqslant 1. \end{cases}$$

U is clearly continuous, nondecreasing, and quasi-concave. Note that $\beta^2(1,1)=[1,+\infty)$ and $\beta^2(2,1)=[\frac{1}{2},+\infty)$. These sets are nested but not equal. Hence $\{2\}$ is separable from $\{1\}$, but it is not strictly separable.

It should be noted, however, that strict monotonicity is *not* necessary for strict separability. To see this, consider the function $U:\Omega^2 \to \mathbf{R}$ defined by

$$U(x_1,x_2) = \begin{cases} x_1 + x_2 & \text{if} \quad x_2 \leqslant 1, \\ x_1 + 1 & \text{if} \quad x_2 \geqslant 1. \end{cases}$$

Clearly, U satisfies (R-1) on Ω^2. Moreover,

$$\beta^2(x_1,x_2)=[x_2,+\infty)$$

if $x_2 \leqslant 1$, and

$$\beta^2(x_1,x_2)=[1,+\infty)$$

if $x_2 \geqslant 1$. Hence, $I^2=\{2\}$ is strictly separable from $I^1=\{1\}$ even though U is not increasing in x_2. The indifference map for this function is illustrated in figure 3.5.

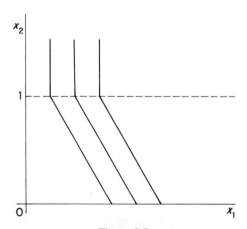

Figure 3.5

Lemma 3.1 suggests that, more generally, strict monotonicity is a sufficient condition for the equivalence of separability and strict separability. In fact, the second half of the lemma is really a consequence of the following result, for which we need a new notion.

We say that U is *locally nonsated* on $\Omega^{(r)}$ if, for every $(X^c, \bar{x}^r) \in \Omega^n$ and $\delta > 0$, there exists an $X^r \in \Omega^{(r)}$ such that $\|X^r - \bar{X}^r\| < \delta$ and $U(X^c, X^r) > U(X^c, \bar{X}^r)$. In what follows, we refer to this property as local nonsatiation on $\Omega^{(r)}$.

A consequence of the assumption of local nonsatiation on $\Omega^{(r)}$ is that the conditional preordering, $\succcurlyeq_c^r$, cannot have "thick indifference curves". More formally, if $\hat{X}^r \in \text{int} \beta^r(X^c, X^r)$ then $\hat{X}^r \succ_c^r X^r$; i.e., if $\hat{X}^r$ is an interior point of $\beta^r(X^c, X^r)$ then $\hat{X}^r$ is strictly preferred to X^r given X^c. This property is used to prove the following theorem:

Theorem 3.1 *Suppose that U is continuous and nondecreasing, and that the set of variables I^r is separable from the set of variables I^c. If U satisfies local nonsatiation on $\Omega^{(c)}$, then I^r is also strictly separable.*

Proof. For any two points (X^c, X^r) and $(\bar{X}^c, X^r)$ (which differ only in the components in I^r), since I^r is separable from I^c, we have, say,

$$\beta^r(X^c, X^r) \subseteq \beta^r(\bar{X}^c, X^r). \tag{a}$$

To show that I^r is also strictly separable given local nonsatiation on $\Omega^{(r)}$ we need to show that these sets are equal. Thus, it suffices to show that

$$\beta^r(\bar{X}^c, X^r) \subseteq \beta^r(X^c, X^r). \tag{b}$$

Suppose not. Then, since the sets are closed, there exists a point $\hat{X}^r$ such that

$$\hat{X}^r \in \text{int}\beta^r(\bar{X}^c, X^r) \tag{c}$$

and

$$\hat{X}^r \notin \beta^r(X^c, X^r). \tag{d}$$

Since U is nondecreasing and satisfies local nonsatiation on $\Omega^{(r)}$, the condition (c) implies that $U(\bar{X}^c, \hat{X}^r) > U(\bar{X}^c, X^r)$. Thus,

$$X^r \notin \beta^r(\bar{X}^c, \hat{X}^r). \tag{e}$$

But, since conditional orderings are reflexive,

$$\hat{X}^r \in \beta^r (\overline{X}^c, \hat{X}^r) \tag{f}$$

and

$$X^r \in \beta^r (X^c, X^r). \tag{g}$$

Then the conditions (d)–(g) together imply that the sets $\beta^r(X^c, X^r)$ and $\beta^r(\overline{X}^c, \hat{X}^r)$ are not nested, contradicting the assumption that I^r is separable. Since the supposition that (b) is false led to a contradiction, (b) must be true. ‖

The logic of the above proof is readily revealed by a graphical example. The condition (a) together with the supposition that (b) is false implies that

$$\beta^r (X^c, X^r) \subset \beta^r (\overline{X}^c, X^r).$$

However, these two sets must have the point X^r in common. Moreover, since U satisfies local nonsatiation on $\Omega^{(r)}$, X^r must be on the boundary of each set. Thus, with well-behaved, convex preferences, we get the diagram in figure 3.6.

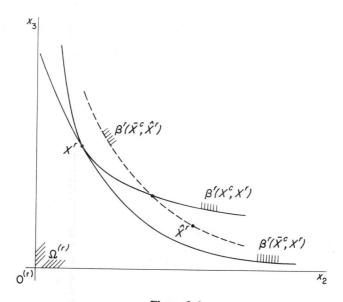

Figure 3.6

Between the boundaries (indifference curves) of the two sets there is a point $\hat{X}^r$ which is strictly preferred to X^r, given $\overline{X}^c$. Note that $\hat{X}^r$ satisfies the conditions (c) and (d). Next, draw through $\hat{X}^r$ an "indifference curve" (the dashed line) which is the boundary of the set $\beta^r(\overline{X}^c, \hat{X}^r)$. This set must lie entirely inside $\beta^r(\overline{X}^c, X^r)$, since $\hat{X}^r$ is strictly preferred to X^r given $\overline{X}^c$. However, this must imply that neither of $\beta^r(X^c, X^r)$ and $\beta^r(\overline{X}^c, \hat{X}^r)$ contains the other, which contradicts the separability assumption of the theorem. This contradiction disappears only if the boundaries of $\beta^r(X^c, X^r)$ and $\beta^r(\overline{X}^c, X^r)$ coincide, making these two sets equal.

There is one final point regarding our separability definitions which should be emphasized. We have defined separability relative to the domain of the utility function, Ω^n. It is quite possible, however, for a function to be separable only over a proper subset of this domain. (For example, the strict separability properties of the Cobb-Douglas utility function hold only in the interior of Ω^n.) It is then easy to modify the separability definitions to restrict the domain over which separability holds.

3.2   ALTERNATIVE DEFINITIONS OF SEPARABILITY

The notion of separability was conceived independently by Leontief (1947a, 1947b) and Sono (1945, 1961) to deal with aggregation problems in producer and consumer theory, respectively. The original paper by Sono was published in Japanese and unfortunately remained relatively unknown outside of Japan until the above-noted English translation appeared in 1961. Leontief and Sono used, however, essentially the same definition of separability. Assume that U is twice differentiable, and let U_i be the partial derivative of U with respect to the ith variable. Further, assume that $U_i(X) > 0 \ \forall X \in \Omega^n, i = 1, \ldots, n.$[4] Then, according to the Leontief-Sono definition, the variables i and j are separable from the kth variable if and only if

$$\frac{\partial}{\partial x_k}\left(\frac{U_i(X)}{U_j(X)}\right) = 0 \qquad \forall X \in \Omega^n. \tag{3.1}$$

That is, the pair $\{i,j\}$ is separable from k if the marginal rate of substitution between i and j is independent of x_k. Referring back to the example illustrated in figure 3.1, where $\{i,j\} = \{2,3\}$ and $\{k\} = \{1\}$, separability requires that every indifference surface, when projected into $\Omega^{(2)}$, have the

---

[4]In this case, our definitions of separability and strict separability coincide.

same slope at $(\bar{x}_2, \bar{x}_3)$. It is easily seen that this rules out possibilities such as those in figure 3.3, as do the definitions which we presented earlier.

The chief disadvantage of the Leontief-Sono definition is that it is a local one and requires differentiability. Thus, if the indifference curve in figure 3.1 had a kink at $(\bar{x}_2, \bar{x}_3)$, the Leontief-Sono definition would not be applicable. On the other hand, there is at least one example where the Leontief-Sono definition makes sense and our definitions do not. It is possible, using this definition, for a set of variables to be separable from a subset of that group. In the two-good case, Leontief-Sono separability of $\{1,2\}$ from $\{2\}$ means that the indifference curves are vertical translates. If $\{1,2\}$ is Leontief-Sono-separable from $\{1,2\}$, the indifference curves are parallel straight lines. However, the equivalence of separability and functional structure is undermined for the case where a set is separable from a subset of itself.[5] It is therefore convenient to exclude this case when dealing with the Leontief-Sono condition. Having done this, (3.1) is equivalent to each of our definitions if the utility function is twice differentiable and increasing. An alternative formulation of the Leontief-Sono separability condition results from carrying out the indicated partial differentiation. That is, the pair, $\{i,j\}$, is separable from k if and only if

$$\frac{U_{ik}(X)}{U_i(X)} = \frac{U_{jk}(X)}{U_j(X)}, \qquad (3.2)$$

where U_{ik} is, of course, the cross partial derivative. Although this identity is no more than an equivalent statement of the Leontief-Sono condition, it is more useful in practice because it is a relationship which is easy to recognize when carrying out differential computations. That is, (3.2) is an explicit differential statement of (3.1)

The definition of separability which we employed in section 3.1 was introduced by Bliss (1975). The definition of strict separability is due to Stigum (1967) and is equivalent to the definiton used by Gorman (1968b). According to the Gorman definition, the set of variables I^r is strictly separable from I^c if the conditional ordering $\succcurlyeq_c^r$, defined earlier, is independent of the components of $\bar{X}^c \in \Omega^{(c)}$.

All three of these definitions of separability are employed in the remainder of this book. To the extent possible, the implications of both separability and strict separability are examined. In some cases, it is necessary to maintain strong regularity assumptions (differentiability and strict monotonicity), in which case the Leontief-Sono concept can be employed. Of course, in these cases the three types of separability are equivalent.

[5]This was pointed out to us by K. Unger.

3.3   SEPARABILITY AND FUNCTIONAL STRUCTURE

3.3.1   Basic Representation and Inheritance
Theorems for the Direct Utility (Production) Function

Perhaps the most fundamental implication of separability is that it allows
one to aggregate the separable group of variables into a single composite
variable in the utility or production function. That is, separability induces
structure on these functions. This fact was salient in the original exposi-
tions of separability by Sono (1945, 1961) and Leontief (1947a, 1947b).
Modern proofs of the functional representation theorems for separable
structures can be found in Debreu (1959a), Stigum (1967), Gorman
(1968b), Koopmans (1972), and Bliss (1975). An alternative proof which
exploits differentiability assumptions can be found in Goldman and
Uzawa (1964). Our proof of the following theorem follows that of Gorman
(1968b).

Theorem 3.2a   *I^r is strictly separable in U from its complement I^c if and
only if there exist functions*

$$U^r : \Omega^{(r)} \to \mathbf{R}$$

and

$$\overline{U} : \Omega^{(c)} \times \mathcal{R}(U^r) \to \mathbf{R}$$

(where $\mathcal{R}(U^r)$ is the range of U^r) such that

$$U(X) = \overline{U}(X^c, U^r(X^r)), \tag{3.3}$$

where $\overline{U}$ is increasing in $U^r(X^r)$.

Proof.   To prove sufficiency [(3.3)⇒strict separability], note that strict
monotonicity[6] of $\overline{U}$ in $U^r(X^r)$ implies that

$$\overline{U}(X^c, U^r(\hat{X}^r)) \geqslant \overline{U}(X^c, U^r(X^r))$$

if and only if

$$U^r(\hat{X}^r) \geqslant U^r(X^r).$$

---

[6]Nonstrict monotonicity would not be sufficient for this equivalence (consider Leontief $\overline{U}$
and U^r functions). Theorem 3.2b considers this problem explicitly.

Hence,

$$\beta^r(X^c, X^r) = \{\hat{X}^r | U(X^c, \hat{X}^r) \geqslant U(X^c, X^r)\}$$

$$= \{\hat{X}^r | U^r(\hat{X}^r) \geqslant U^r(X^r)\}$$

is independent of X^c for all $(X^c, X^r) \in \Omega^{(c)} \times \Omega^{(r)}$.

To prove necessity [strict separability$\Rightarrow$(3.3)], define U^r by

$$U^r(X^r) = U(O^c, X^r) \qquad \forall X^r \in \Omega^{(r)},$$

where O^c is an arbitrary reference vector (which might but need not be the $\Omega^{(c)}$-subspace zero vector). Next define

$$\bar{U} : \Omega^{(c)} \times \mathcal{R}(U^r) \to \mathbf{R}$$

by

$$\bar{U}(X^c, U^r(X^r)) = U(X) \qquad \forall X \in \Omega^n.$$

To prove that $\bar{U}$ is increasing in $U^r(X^r)$, note that

$$U^r(X^r) = U^r(\hat{X}^r)$$

implies that

$$U(\bar{X}^c, X^r) = U(\bar{X}^c, \hat{X}^r)$$

for any reference vector $\bar{X}^c$. Hence,

$$\bar{U}(\bar{X}^c, U^r(X^r)) = \bar{U}(\bar{X}^c, U^r(\hat{X}^r)) \qquad \forall \bar{X}^c \in \Omega^{(c)}.$$

Similarly,

$$U^r(X^r) > U^r(\hat{X}^r)$$

implies that

$$U(\bar{X}^c, X^r) > U(\bar{X}^c, \hat{X}^r) \qquad \forall \bar{X}^c \in \Omega^{(c)},$$

which in turn implies

$$\bar{U}(\bar{X}^c, U^r(X^r)) > \bar{U}(\bar{X}^c, U^r(\hat{X}^r)) \qquad \forall \bar{X}^c \in \Omega^{(c)}. \qquad \|$$

The proof of the existence of the aggregator function U^r is very illuminating because it actually provides a straightforward technique for constructing the function. As this construction is especially useful, it is stated below as a corollary of theorem 3.2a for the purpose of emphasis and easy reference.

Corollary 3.2.0a *The aggregator function U^r in the representation (3.3) can be constructed as follows*:

$$U^r(X^r) = U(O^c, X^r), \tag{3.4}$$

where O^c is an arbitrary reference vector.

Proof. Immediate from the proof of the theorem. ‖

As the reference vector in the construction (3.4) is arbitrary, it will frequently be convenient to choose the cth-subspace zero vector. If, however, a function satisfies the strict separability condition only over a subset of Ω^n, it may be inappropriate to choose the zero vector for reference in the construction of U^r. Consider, for example, a Cobb-Douglas function of three goods with image

$$U(X) = x_1^{\alpha_1} x_2^{\alpha_2} x_3^{\alpha_3}.$$

This function is separable in *any* binary partition over the *restricted* domain Ω_+^3. Consider for example the binary partition in which $I^r = \{2,3\}$ and $I^c = \{1\}$. Letting $x_1 = \bar{x}_1$, where $\bar{x}_1$ is any *nonzero* value, we have the aggregator image

$$U^r(X^r) = U^r(x_2, x_3) = \bar{x}_1^{\alpha_1} x_2^{\alpha_2} x_3^{\alpha_3}.$$

The induced preordering on Ω^r is itself a Cobb-Douglas preference ordering which is invariant with respect to changes in the *positive* "constant" $\bar{x}_1^{\alpha_1}$. Note, however, that choosing $\bar{x}_1 = 0$ in the above construction makes $U^r(X^r) = 0$ everywhere on $\Omega^{(r)}$. The choice is therefore inappropriate. Put differently, $\{2,3\}$ is strictly separable from $\{1\}$ over the domain which excludes the subspace over which $x_1 = 0$. Changing x_1 from $\bar{x}_1 > 0$ to 0 changes the conditional ordering on $\Omega^{(2)}$.

Another important point to notice about this representation theorem is that it is necessary for the macro function $\bar{U}$ to be increasing in the image $U^r(X^r)$. That is, there are many functions which can be written with a functional form as in (3.3) but whose macro function cannot be chosen to be increasing in the aggregator. Such functions do not represent strictly separable preferences. The conditional orderings on $\Omega^{(r)}$ are not in general independent of the values of the components of X^c. In order to illustrate this often misunderstood point, consider again the three-variable Leontief function, with image,

$$U(X) = \min\{x_1, x_2, x_3\}.$$

It will be recalled from the discussion in section 3.1.4 that this function is separable but not strictly separable. Nevertheless, it is possible to rewrite the function image in the form (3.3) without the strict monotonicity assumption.

$$U(X) = \overline{U}(x_1, U^r(X^r)) = \min\{x_1, U^r(X^r)\},$$

where

$$U^r(X^r) = \min\{x_2, x_3\}.$$

Notice, however, that $\overline{U}$ is not increasing in $U^r(X^r)$. For example,

$$\overline{U}(1,1) = \overline{U}(1,2).$$

As the Leontief function is separable but not strictly separable, this example suggests that the weaker separability condition is equivalent to the structure (3.3) without the strict monotonicity condition. This functional-structure characterization is summarized in the following theorem, which follows from that of Bliss (1975).

Theorem 3.2b *Assume that U is continuous and nondecreasing. Then I^r is separable in U from its complement I^c if and only if there exist functions*

$$U^r : \Omega^{(r)} \to \mathbf{R}$$

and

$$\overline{U} : \Omega^{(c)} \times \mathcal{R}(U^r) \to \mathbf{R}$$

such that

$$U(X) = \overline{U}(X^c, U^r(X^r)), \tag{3.5}$$

where $\overline{U}$ is nondecreasing in $U^r(X^r)$.

Proof. To prove sufficiency [(3.5)⇒separability], recall that I^r is separable from I^c if and only if the collection of sets

$$\mathcal{C} = \left\{ \beta^r(X^c, X^r) \mid X^c \in \Omega^{(c)} \wedge X^r \in \Omega^{(r)} \right\}$$

is nested. The argument proceeds by contradiction. Assume that $\mathcal{C}^r$ is *not* nested. Hence there exists a point $(X^c, X^r, \bar{X}^c, \bar{X}^r) \in \Omega^{2n}$ such that

$$\beta^r(X^c, X^r) \not\subseteq \beta^r(\bar{X}^c, \bar{X}^r)$$

and

$$\beta^r(\bar{X}^c, \bar{X}^r) \not\subseteq \beta^r(X^c, X^r).$$

Therefore, there exists a point $\hat{X}^r \in \Omega^{(r)}$ satisfying

$$\hat{X}^r \in \beta^r(\bar{X}^c, \bar{X}^r) \quad \wedge \quad \hat{X}^r \notin \beta^r(X^c, X^r) \tag{a}$$

and another point $\tilde{X}^r \in \Omega^{(r)}$ satisfying

$$\tilde{X}^r \in \beta^r(X^c, X^r) \quad \wedge \quad \tilde{X}^r \notin \beta^r(\bar{X}^c, \bar{X}^r). \tag{b}$$

The definition of β^r and (a) imply that

$$U(\bar{X}^c, \hat{X}^r) \geqslant U(\bar{X}^c, \bar{X}^r) \tag{c}$$

and

$$U(X^c, \hat{X}^r) < U(X^c, X^r). \tag{d}$$

On the other hand, (b) implies that

$$U(X^c, \tilde{X}^r) \geqslant U(X^c, X^r) \tag{e}$$

and

$$U(\bar{X}^c, \tilde{X}^r) < U(\bar{X}^c, \bar{X}^r). \tag{f}$$

Together, (d) and (e) imply that

$$U(X^c, \tilde{X}^r) > U(X^c, \hat{X}^r), \tag{g}$$

while (c) and (f) imply that

$$U(\bar{X}^c, \hat{X}^r) > U(\bar{X}^c, \tilde{X}^r). \tag{h}$$

Using the maintained monotonicity assumption and (3.5), (g) implies that

$$U^r(\tilde{X}^r) > U^r(\hat{X}^r), \tag{i}$$

while (h) implies that

$$U^r(\hat{X}^r) > U^r(\tilde{X}^r), \tag{j}$$

which is a contradiction. Hence $\mathcal{C}^r$ is nested.

To prove necessity, we show that separability implies the existence of a complete, transitive, continuous, and nondecreasing ordering, $\succcurlyeq^r$, on $\Omega^{(r)}$ which may then be represented by a subutility function.

Define the relation $\succcurlyeq^r$ by

$$X^r \succcurlyeq^r \hat{X}^r \quad \Leftrightarrow \quad U(X^c, X^r) \geqslant U(X^c, \hat{X}^r) \quad \forall X^c \in \Omega^{(c)}.$$

Transitivity and monotonicity of $\succcurlyeq^r$ are immediate. We establish completeness and continuity by contradiction. Assume $\succcurlyeq^r$ is *not* complete. Then there exists a point

$$(X^r, \hat{X}^r) \in \Omega^{(r)} \times \Omega^{(r)}$$

such that

$$X^r \not\succcurlyeq^r \hat{X}^r \quad \text{and} \quad \hat{X}^r \not\succcurlyeq^r X^r.$$

This implies the existence of a point $(\overline{X}^c, \tilde{X}^c) \in \Omega^{(c)} \times \Omega^{(c)}$ such that

$$U(\overline{X}^c, X^r) < U(\overline{X}^c, \hat{X}^r)$$

and

$$U(\tilde{X}^c, \hat{X}^r) < U(\tilde{X}^c, X^r).$$

This implies in turn that

$$\hat{X}^r \in \beta^r(\overline{X}^c, \hat{X}^r) \quad \wedge \quad X^r \notin \beta^r(\overline{X}^c, \hat{X}^r)$$

and

$$X^r \in \beta^r(\tilde{X}^c, X^r) \quad \wedge \quad \hat{X}^r \notin \beta^r(\tilde{X}^c, X^r).$$

Hence, $\beta^r(\overline{X}^c, \hat{X}^r) \not\subseteq \beta^r(\tilde{X}^c, X^r)$ and $\beta^r(\tilde{X}^c, X^r) \not\subseteq \beta^r(\overline{X}^c, \hat{X}^r)$, which contradicts the separability assumption.

Assume that $\succcurlyeq^r$ is not continuous. Then there exists an $\hat{X}^r \in \Omega^{(r)}$ such that either

$$\succcurlyeq^r(\hat{X}^r) = \{X^r \in \Omega^r | X^r \succcurlyeq^r \hat{X}^r\}$$

or

$$\leqslant^r(\hat{X}^r)=\{X^r\in\Omega^r|\hat{X}^r\succcurlyeq^r X^r\}$$

is not closed. Suppose the former; then there exist a point $\hat{X}^r\in\Omega^{(r)}$ and a sequence

$$\{(X^r)^\nu\}\subseteq\succcurlyeq^r(\hat{X})$$

with limit point $\overline{X}^r\notin\succcurlyeq^r(\hat{X}^r)$. That is,

$$(X^r)^\nu\to\overline{X}^r,\tag{i}$$

$$U\big(X^c,(X^r)^\nu\big)\geqslant U(X^c,\hat{X}^r)\qquad\forall\nu,\quad\forall X^c\in\Omega^{(c)},\tag{ii}$$

and

$$U(\overline{X}^c,\overline{X}^r)<U(\overline{X}^c,\hat{X}^r)\tag{iii}$$

for some $\overline{X}^c\in\Omega^{(c)}$. Consider the sequence $\{X^\nu\}=\{(X^c)^\nu,(X^r)^\nu\}\subseteq\Omega^\nu$ defined by $(X^c)^\nu=\overline{X}^c\forall\nu$. From (i), (ii), and (iii),

$$X^\nu\to(\overline{X}^c,\overline{X}^r),$$

$$U(X^\nu)\geqslant U(\overline{X}^c,\hat{X}^r)\qquad\forall\nu,$$

and

$$U(\overline{X})<U(\overline{X}^c,\hat{X}^r),$$

violating the continuity of U. A similar argument establishes that non-closedness of $\leqslant^r(\hat{X}^r)$ contradicts the continuity of U.

Thus, $\succcurlyeq^r$ is continuous, transitive, complete, and nondecreasing. By a theorem of Debreu (1954) there exists a continuous, nondecreasing function, $U^r:\Omega^{(r)}\to\mathbf{R}$ such that

$$U^r(X^r)\geqslant U^r(\hat{X}^r)\quad\Leftrightarrow\quad X^r\succcurlyeq^r\hat{X}^r\qquad\forall(X^r,\hat{X}^r)\in\Omega^{(r)}\times\Omega^{(r)}.$$

To complete the proof, simply define $\overline{U}$ so as to satisfy (3.5). Monotonicity of $\overline{U}$ follows immediately from that of U and U^r. $\|$

Note that the sufficiency argument does not use the continuity hypothesis. Thus, the structure (3.5) implies separability if U is nondecreasing.

Throughout the book functions are frequently assumed to satisfy certain regularity properties; e.g., (R-1) is the continuity, quasi-concavity, and positive monotonicity of U. The point of the next theorem is that the macro function and the aggregator function can be picked so that they satisfy the same regularity conditions as the master function. After this theorem, we state and prove similar results regarding other representations of the preference ordering, viz., the indirect utility, cost, and transformation functions.

Theorem 3.3a *Suppose that U is continuous and satisfies the strict separability condition of theorem 3.2a. Then there exist $\bar{U}$ and U^r in the representation (3.3) which are continuous; if in addition U satisfies (R-1), then so do $\bar{U}$ and U^r.*

Proof. The continuity of U^r follows from the continuity of U by the construction in Corollary 3.2.0a.

To prove the continuity of $\bar{U}$, consider a sequence

$$\left\{(X^c)^t, (u_r)^t\right\} \subseteq \Omega^{(c)} \times \mathcal{R}(U^r)$$

converging to $(\overset{*}{X}{}^c, \overset{*}{u}_r) \in \Omega^{(c)} \times \mathcal{R}(U^r)$. If $\overset{*}{u}_r$ is contained in the interior of $\mathcal{R}(U^r)$ (relative to **R**), choose $(X^r, \hat{X}^r) \in \Omega^{(r)} \times \Omega^{(r)}$ such that

$$U^r(X^r) < \overset{*}{u}_r < U^r(\hat{X}^r).$$

If $\overset{*}{u}_r = \max \mathcal{R}(U^r)$, let $\hat{X}^r$ satisfy $U^r(\hat{X}^r) = \overset{*}{u}_r$, and if $\overset{*}{u}_r = \min \mathcal{R}(U^r)$, let X^r satisfy $U^r(X^r) = \overset{*}{u}_r$. If $\mathcal{R}(U^r)$ is degenerate (no commodity in I^r is essential relative to the reference vector O^c),[7] choose $(X^r, \hat{X}^r)$ such that

$$U^r(X^r) = U^r(\hat{X}^r) = \overset{*}{u}_r.$$

As $\Omega^{(r)}$ is arc-connected (in the usual Euclidean topology),[8] there exists an arc $\Theta \subseteq \Omega^{(r)}$ connecting X^r to $\hat{X}^r$. Also, there exists an integer τ such that, for all $t \geqslant \tau$,

$$U^r(X^r) < (u_r)^t < U^r(\hat{X}^r).$$

[If $\overset{*}{u}_r \notin \operatorname{int} \mathcal{R}(U^r)$, one or both of these strict inequalities must be converted to a weak inequality, undermining nothing in what follows.] Continuity of U^r implies that for all $t \geqslant \tau$, there exists an $(X^r)^t \in \Theta$ which

---

[7]See Gorman (1968b: p. 367).

[8]If the separability condition holds only over a proper subset of Ω^n, it must be assumed that $\Omega^{(r)}$ is arc-connected.

satisfies $U^r\big((X^r)'\big)=(u_r)'$. As Θ is homeomorphic to $(0,1)$, it is compact; hence the sequence $\{X^t\}=\{(X^c)',(X^r)'\}$ has a convergent subsequence, say $\{X^{t_\nu}\}=\{(X^c)^{t_\nu},(X^r)^{t_\nu}\}$. Let $\overset{*}{X}=(\overset{*}{X}^c,\overset{*}{X}^r)$ be the limit of this subsequence. [Of course, the $(X^c)^{t_\nu}$ component of this subsequence converges to $\overset{*}{X}^c$ by assumption (on the full sequence).] Continuity of U implies that

$$\lim_{t_\nu\to\infty} U(X^{t_\nu})=U(\overset{*}{X}).$$

By construction, therefore,

$$\lim_{t_\nu\to\infty}\overline{U}\big((X^c)^{t_\nu},(u_r)^{t_\nu}\big)=\overline{U}\big(\overset{*}{X}^c,U^r(\overset{*}{X}^r)\big)$$

$$=\overline{U}\big(\overset{*}{X}^c,\overset{*}{u}_r\big).$$

The proof is completed by showing, by way of contradiction, that this image converges for the full sequence. Suppose that

$$\lim_{t\to\infty}\overline{U}\big((X^c)',(u_r)'\big)\neq\overline{U}\big(\overset{*}{X}^c,\overset{*}{u}_r\big).$$

Then there exist a subsequence $\{(X^c)^{t_\mu},(u_r)^{t_\mu}\}$ and an $\varepsilon>0$ such that

$$\left|\overline{U}\big((X^c)^{t_\mu},(u_r)^{t_\mu}\big)-\overline{U}\big(\overset{*}{X}^c,\overset{*}{u}_r\big)\right|>\varepsilon \tag{a}$$

for all t_μ in the subsequential index set. However, the corresponding subsequence $\{(X^c)^{t_\mu},(X^r)^{t_\mu}\}$, constructed in the same manner as $\{(X^c)^{t_\nu},(X^r)^{t_\nu}\}$ above, itself has a convergent subsequence, say $\{(X^c)^{t_\nu^\mu},(X^r)^{t_\nu^\mu}\}$, converging to $\overset{**}{X}$. Then

$$\lim_{t_\nu^\mu\to\infty}\overline{U}\big((X^c)^{t_\nu^\mu},U^r\big((X^r)^{t_\nu^\mu}\big)\big)=U(\overset{**}{X})=U(\overset{*}{X}),$$

by the continuity of U, contradicting (a). Hence $\overline{U}$ is continuous.

Monotonicity and quasi-concavity are proved as follows. Corollary 3.2.0a is invoked to prove that U^r inherits these properties from U. Exploiting the insensitivity of these properties to strictly monotonic transformations, U^r and $\overline{U}$ are then normalized to establish the monotonicity and quasi-concavity of $\overline{U}$.

Write the mirrored aggregator function image from Corollary 3.2.0a as

$$\overset{\circ}{U}{}^r(X^r)=U(O^c,X^r)\qquad\forall X^r\in\Omega^{(r)}, \tag{b}$$

where O^c is the arbitrary reference vector in $\Omega^{(c)}$. The monotonicity of $\mathring{U}^r$ follows immediately from that of U. To prove quasi-concavity, consider any point $(\hat{X}^r, X^r) \in \Omega^{(r)} \times \Omega^{(r)}$ such that

$$\mathring{U}^r(\hat{X}^r) > \mathring{U}^r(X^r).$$

Using (b), this implies that

$$U(O^c, \hat{X}^r) > U(O^c, X^r).$$

Since U is quasi-concave,

$$U(\theta O^c + (1-\theta)O^c, \theta \hat{X}^r + (1-\theta)X^r)$$
$$= U(O^c, \theta \hat{X}^r + (1-\theta)X^r) > U(O^c, X^r) \qquad \forall \theta \in (0,1)$$

Hence, again by (b),

$$\mathring{U}^r(\theta \hat{X}^r + (1-\theta)X^r) > \mathring{U}^r(X^r) \qquad \forall \theta \in (0,1),$$

proving the quasi-concavity of $\mathring{U}^r$.

Next, $\mathring{U}^r$ is renormalized in a way that preserves its (R-1) properties and, at the same time, gives a representation $\bar{U}$ that also satisfies (R-1). The following construction of U^r was first used by Wold (1943, 1944). Let $\bar{X}^r$ be any vector in the interior of the rth subspace of unit length; i.e.,

$$\bar{X}^r = \frac{X^r}{\|X^r\|} \qquad \text{for some} \quad X^r \in \Omega_+^{(r)}.$$

Hence,

$$\Lambda = \left\{ X^r \in \Omega^{(r)} | X^r = \lambda \bar{X}^r \ \forall \lambda \geqslant 0 \right\}$$

is a ray in $\Omega_+^{(r)}$ with the origin adjoined to it. Define $U^r : \Omega^{(r)} \to \Omega^1$ by

$$U^r(\lambda \bar{X}^r) = \lambda \qquad \forall \lambda \geqslant 0$$

and

$$U^r(X^r) = \lambda \quad \forall X^r \in \Omega^{(r)} \text{ such that } \mathring{U}^r(X^r) = \mathring{U}^r(\lambda \bar{X}^r) \qquad \forall \lambda \geqslant 0.$$

Clearly, U^r is a continuous, strictly monotonic transformation of $\mathring{U}^r$, thereby preserving the properties (R-1).

Now define $\bar{U}: \Omega^{(c)} \times \Omega^1 \to \mathbf{R}$ by

$$\bar{U}(X^c, U^r(X^r)) = U(X) \qquad \forall X \in \Omega^n. \tag{c}$$

The monotonicity of $\bar{U}$ follows immediately from that of U^r and U. To prove quasi-concavity, consider any pair of points, $(X^c, \lambda) \in \Omega^{(c)} \times \mathcal{R}(U^r)$ and $(\hat{X}^c, \hat{\lambda}) \in \Omega^{(c)} \times \mathcal{R}(U^r)$, such that

$$\bar{U}(\hat{X}^c, \hat{\lambda}) > \bar{U}(X^c, \lambda).$$

By construction, $U^r(\hat{\lambda}\bar{X}^r) = \hat{\lambda}$ and $U^r(\lambda\bar{X}^r) = \lambda$. Thus,

$$\bar{U}\left(\hat{X}^c, U^r(\hat{\lambda}\bar{X}^r)\right) > \bar{U}\left(X^c, U^r(\lambda\bar{X}^r)\right),$$

which, together with (c), implies that

$$U(\hat{X}^c, \hat{\lambda}\bar{X}^r) > U(X^c, \lambda\bar{X}^r).$$

The quasi-concavity of U implies that

$$U\left(\theta\hat{X}^c + (1-\theta)X^c, \theta\hat{\lambda}\bar{X}^r + (1-\theta)\lambda\bar{X}^r\right) > U(X^c, \lambda\bar{X}^r) \qquad \forall\theta \in (0,1),$$

which, together with (c), implies that

$$\bar{U}\left(\theta\hat{X}^c + (1-\theta)X^c, U^r\left(\theta\hat{\lambda}\bar{X}^r + (1-\theta)\lambda\bar{X}^r\right)\right) > \bar{U}\left(X^c, U^r(\lambda\bar{X}^r)\right),$$

$$\forall\theta \in (0,1).$$

Since, by construction, $U^r\left([\theta\hat{\lambda} + (1-\theta)\lambda]\bar{X}^r\right) = \theta\hat{\lambda} + (1-\theta)\lambda$ and $U^r(\lambda\bar{X}^r) = \lambda$, this implies that

$$\bar{U}\left(\theta\hat{X}^c + (1-\theta)X^c, \theta\hat{\lambda} + (1-\theta)\lambda\right) > \bar{U}(X^c, \lambda) \qquad \forall\theta \in (0,1),$$

proving the quasi-concavity of $\bar{U}$. $\|$

A simple example provides a geometric interpretation of the construction of $\bar{U}$. Let $m = 2$, $I^c = \{1\}$, and $I^r = \{2, 3\}$. In figure 3.7, $\bar{X}^r = (1/\sqrt{2}, 1/\sqrt{2}) \in \Omega^{(r)}$ is the vector of unit length that generates the ray Λ. This, in turn, gives the hyperplane $\Omega^{(c)} \times \Lambda$, of dimensionality 2, as suggested by the dashed lines. The curved line aa' depicts the intersection of the hyperplane with a level set of U. Letting the scalar $u_r = U^r(X^r)$ vary

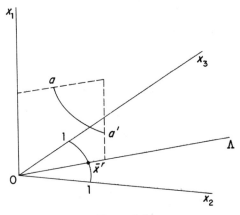

Figure 3.7

over $\mathcal{R}(U^r)=\Omega^1$ and interpreting Λ as the u_r axis (since there is a linear mapping from Λ to Ω^1), aa' can be interpreted as a level set of $\bar{U}$. Of course, other level sets of $\bar{U}$ can be constructed similarly. Hence, a geometric interpretation of a separable set of variables is that preference-ordering information from the separable set can be aggregated up to a scalar value, u_r, measured along the ray Λ. In our example, indifference curves between x_1 and u_r and between x_2 and x_3 convey all of the preference-ordering information represented by U.

Under slightly stronger maintained hypotheses the proof of theorem 3.3a goes through for the weaker separability concept.

Theorem 3.3b *Suppose that U is continuous and nondecreasing and satisfies the separability condition of theorem 3.2b. Then there exist $\bar{U}$ and U^r in the representation (3.5) which are continuous and nondecreasing; if, in addition, U satisfies (R-1), then so do $\bar{U}$ and U^r.*

Proof. The continuity of U^r was proved in the proof of theorem 3.2b. The monotonicity of U^r follows immediately from the monotonicity of U.

To prove the quasi-concavity of U^r, consider any point $(\hat{X}^r, X^r) \in \Omega^{(r)} \times \Omega^{(r)}$ such that

$$U^r(\hat{X}^r) > U^r(X^r).$$

Hence there exists a point $\tilde{X}^c \in \Omega^{(c)}$ such that

$$U(\tilde{X}^c, \hat{X}^r) > U(\tilde{X}^c, X^r).$$

The quasi-concavity of U implies that

$$U(\theta\tilde{X}^c + (1-\theta)\tilde{X}^c, \theta\hat{X}^r + (1-\theta)X^r)$$

$$= U(\tilde{X}^c, \theta\hat{X}^r + (1-\theta)X^r) > U(\tilde{X}^c, X^r) \qquad \forall \theta \in (0,1).$$

This implies that $U^r(X^r) \not\geq U^r(\theta\hat{X}^r + (1-\theta)X^r)$, or

$$U^r(\theta\hat{X}^r + (1-\theta)X^r) > U^r(X^r) \qquad \forall \theta \in (0,1),$$

proving the quasi-concavity of U^r.

All of the properties of $\bar{U}$ may be proved by adapting the corresponding arguments in the proof of theorem 3.3a. ‖

It is worth noting that continuity and monotonicity diminish the significance of the distinction between strict and nonstrict separability with respect to the implications for functional structure and the inheritance of regularity properties. Theorems 3.2b and 3.3b indicate that continuity and monotonicity must be maintained in order to prove the basic equivalence between nonstrict separability and functional structure. On the other hand, the equivalence of structure and strict separability (theorem 3.2a) requires no regularity conditions, and the inheritance results (theorem 3.3a) require continuity only. Parsimonious maintenance of regularity assumptions throughout the remainder of parts I and II would result in an impractical proliferation in the number of theorems and corollaries. Rather than burden the reader with a fastidious distinction between the regularity conditions required in the two cases, we instead maintain continuity and monotonicity in the following theorems and corollaries. Consequently, slightly stronger theorems are frequently available for the case of strict separability than are in fact stated. The interested reader may state and prove such results by analogy to theorems 3.2a and 3.3a.

3.3.2 Separability in the Indirect Utility Function

We proceed now to the definition and representation of separability in the indirect utility function, as well as the inheritance of the maintained regularity conditions (R-2), viz., continuity, quasi-convexity, and negative monotonicity.

To define separability of the indirect utility function, define a new mapping, $\alpha^r : \Omega^n_+ \to \mathscr{P}(\Omega^{(r)}_+)$, whose image is

$$\alpha^r\left(\frac{P^c}{y}, \frac{P^r}{y}\right) = \left\{\frac{\hat{P}^r}{y} \in \Omega^{(r)}_+ \middle| V\left(\frac{P^c}{y}, \frac{\hat{P}^r}{y}\right) \leq V\left(\frac{P^c}{y}, \frac{P^r}{y}\right)\right\}.$$

The set of variables I^r is separable from the set of variables I^c if and only if the collection of sets

$$\left\{ \alpha^r\left(\frac{P^c}{y}, \frac{P^r}{y} \right) \middle| \frac{P^c}{y} \in \Omega_+^{(c)} \wedge \frac{P^r}{y} \in \Omega_+^{(r)} \right\}$$

is nested. In addition, the set of variables I^r is strictly separable from the set of variables I^c if and only if

$$\alpha^r\left(\frac{P^c}{y}, \frac{P^r}{y} \right) = \alpha^r\left(\frac{\bar{P}^c}{y}, \frac{P^r}{y} \right)$$

for all $(P^c/y, P^r/y) \in \Omega_+^n$ and for any $\bar{P}^c/y \in \Omega_+^{(c)}$.

If V is twice differentiable with negative first partial derivatives $V_i(P/y), i = 1, \ldots, n$, then, using Roy's theorem, the Leontief-Sono separability condition can be written

$$\frac{\partial}{\partial (p_k/y)}\left(\frac{V_i(P/y)}{V_j(P/y)} \right) = \frac{\partial}{\partial (p_k/y)}\left(\frac{\phi_i(P/y)}{\phi_j(P/y)} \right) = 0$$

$$\forall P/y \in \Omega_+^n, \quad \forall(i,j) \in I^r \times I^r, \quad \forall k \in I^c.$$

That is, at any set of normalized prices, the ratio of the optimal quantities of the ith and jth commodities in I^r is independent of normalized prices which are not in the rth sector. It is interesting, in this context, to recall that direct separability of I^r from I^c means that ratios of shadow prices in I^r are independent of quantities of commodities in I^c.

The separability condition for the indirect utility function is equivalent to a functional representation:

Corollary 3.2.1 *Assume V to be continuous and nonincreasing. I^r is separable in V from I^c if and only if there exist continuous functions*

$$V^r : \Omega_+^{(r)} \to \mathbf{R}$$

and

$$\bar{V} : \Omega_+^{(c)} \times \mathcal{R}(V^{(r)}) \to \mathbf{R}$$

such that

$$V(P/y) = \bar{V}\left(\frac{P^c}{y}, V^r\left(\frac{P^r}{y} \right) \right) \quad \forall \frac{P}{y} \in \Omega_+^n, \tag{3.6}$$

and $\bar{V}$ is nonincreasing in $V^r(P^r/y)$. If V satisfies (R-2), so does $\bar{V}$, while V^r satisfies (R-1). If in addition I^r is strictly separable from I^c, then $\bar{V}$ is decreasing in $V^r(P^r/y)$.

Proof. Taking note of the reversed monotonicity condition, the sufficiency of the structure (3.6) for separability is proved exactly as in Theorem 3.2b. Proof of necessity and of the inheritance conditions exploits the complete, transitive, reflexive, continuous ordering defined by

$$\frac{P^r}{y} \succcurlyeq_r \frac{\hat{P}^r}{y} \;\;\Leftrightarrow\;\; V\left(\frac{P^c}{y}, \frac{P^r}{y}\right) \leqslant V\left(\frac{P^c}{y}, \frac{\hat{P}^r}{y}\right) \;\; \forall \frac{P^c}{y} \in \Omega_+^{(c)},$$

exactly as the subspace ordering is used in the proofs of Theorems 3.2b and 3.3b, In particular, the aggregator V^r is defined by

$$V^r(P^r/y) \geqslant V^r(\hat{P}^r/y) \;\;\Leftrightarrow\;\; \frac{P^r}{y} \succcurlyeq_r \frac{\hat{P}^r}{y} \;\; \forall\left(\frac{P^r}{y}, \frac{\hat{P}^r}{y}\right) \in \Omega_+^{(r)} \times \Omega_+^{(r)}.$$

$$(3.7a)$$

Proof of the strict (negative) monotonicity property of $\bar{V}$ if I^r is strictly separable from I^c proceeds exactly as in the proof of Theorm 3.2a after defining the aggregator function by

$$V^r(P^r/y) = \left[V(O^c, P^r/y) \right]^{-1}. \quad \| \qquad (3.7b)$$

Notice that V^r is constructed to mirror the properties of the reciprocal of V [equations (3.7)]. This contrasts with the representation (3.3) of a direct utility function in which the aggregator U^r is constructed to mirror the properties of U [equation (3.4)]. The reason for this asymmetry is that V is a nonincreasing function of its arguments and the composition of a decreasing and a nonincreasing function is not necessarily nonincreasing. Hence, were V^r to be defined with the image $V(O^c, P^r/y)$, then $\bar{V}$ would be nonincreasing in normalized prices but *increasing* in $V^r(P^r/y)$. In this case, we could not interpret $\bar{V}$ as an indirect utility function, since it would not be nonincreasing and quasi-convex in its arguments, $(P^c/y, V^r(P^r/y))$. As defined, however, it makes sense to think of $\bar{V}$ as an indirect utility function, although the same cannot be said for the aggregator V^r. The natural interpretation of V^r is that it is the normalized price of one unit of the rth surrogate commodity—i.e., it is a price index. This interpretation may become more persuasive in the course of this chapter.

In general, separability of U does not imply, nor is it implied by, separability of V. Hence, a separable direct utility function represents a different class of consumer preference orderings (technologies) than does a separable indirect utility function. These comments also apply when either U or V is strictly separable. We frequently refer to separability of U as *direct separability* and separability of V as *indirect separability*.

An alternative way to write the indirect utility function is $W : \Omega^1_+ \times \Omega^n_+ \to$ **R**, defined by

$$W(y,P) = V(P/y) \qquad \forall (y,P) \in \Omega^1_+ \times \Omega^n_+. \qquad (3.8)$$

Clearly, W is homogeneous of degree zero in (y,P). Note that separability of I^r from I^c in V is clearly equivalent to separability of I^r from I^c in W. Thus, indirect separability of I^r from I^c implies the existence of continuous functions

$$W^r : \Omega^1_+ \times \Omega^{(r)}_+ \to \mathbf{R}$$

and

$$\overline{W} : \Omega^1_+ \times \Omega^{(c)}_+ \times \mathcal{R}\{W^r\} \to \mathbf{R}$$

such that

$$W(y,P) = \overline{W}(y, P^c, W^r(y,P^r)) \qquad \forall (y,P) \in \Omega^1_+ \times \Omega^n_+, \qquad (3.9)$$

where $\overline{W}$ is nonincreasing in $W^r(y,P^r)$. Clearly, $\overline{W}$ and W^r can be picked so that

$$W^r(y,P^r) = W^r(1, P^r/y) = V^r(P^r/y)$$

and

$$\overline{W}(y, P^c, W^r(y,P^r)) = \overline{W}(1, P^c/y, W^r(1, P^r/y))$$

$$= \overline{V}(P^c/y, V^r(P^r/y)).$$

In addition, if I^r is strictly separable from I^c, the above results apply and $\overline{W}$ is decreasing in $W^r(y,P^r)$.

3.3.3 Separability in the Cost Function

We turn now to examine the implications of separability for the cost function. Let $\gamma^r: \mathcal{R}(U) \times \Omega_+^n \to \mathcal{P}(\Omega_+^{(r)})$ be a mapping whose image is

$$\gamma^r(u, P^c, P^r) = \{\hat{P}^r \in \Omega_+^{(r)} | C(u, P^c, \hat{P}^r) \geqslant C(u, P^c, P^r)\}.$$

The set of variables I^r is separable in C from the set of variables I^c if and only if, for each $u \in \mathcal{R}(U)$, the collection of sets $\{\gamma^r(u, P^c, P^r) | P^c \in \Omega_+^{(c)} \wedge P^r \in \Omega_+^{(r)}\}$ is nested. In addition we say that the set of variables I^r is strictly separable in C from I^c if and only if, for each $u \in \mathcal{R}(U)$,

$$\gamma^r(u, P^c, P^r) = \gamma^r(u, \bar{P}^c, P^r)$$

for all $(P^c, P^r) \in \Omega_+^n$ and for any $\bar{P}^c \in \Omega_+^{(c)}$.

If the cost function C is twice differentiable, with positive first partial derivatives $C_i(u, P)$, $i = 1, \ldots, n$, then we can apply the Leontief-Sono definition of separability: I^r is separable from I^c if and only if

$$\frac{\partial}{\partial p_k}\left(\frac{C_i(u, P)}{C_j(u, P)}\right) = \frac{\partial}{\partial p_k}\left(\frac{\zeta_i(u, P)}{\zeta_j(u, P)}\right) = 0 \qquad \forall(i, j) \in I^r \times I^r, \quad \forall k \in I^c.$$

Thus, separability in the cost function implies that the ratios of income-compensated (Hicksian) demand functions for commodities in group r are independent of prices of commodities not in I^r. Note, however, that this ratio depends upon u, the level of "real income". That is, I^r is not separable from the output or utility variable.

The following theorems characterize the representation of separability in the cost function as well as the inheritance of the maintained regularity conditions.

Theorem 3.4 *Suppose that C is continuous and nondecreasing in P. Then I^r is separable in C from I^c if and only if there exist functions*

$$C^r: \mathcal{R}(U) \times \Omega_+^{(r)} \to \Omega_+^1$$

and

$$\bar{C}: \mathcal{R}(U) \times \Omega_+^{(c)} \times \mathcal{R}(C^r) \to \Omega_+^1$$

such that

$$C(u, P) = \bar{C}(u, P^c, C^r(u, P^r)) \qquad \forall(u, P) \in \mathcal{R}(U) \times \Omega_+^n, \quad (3.10)$$

where $\overline{C}$ is nondecreasing in $C^r(u, P^r)$. If C satisfies (R-3), then $\overline{C}$ and C^r satisfy (R-3P).[8] If, in addition, I^r is strictly separable from I^c, then $\overline{C}$ is continuous, increasing in $C^r(u, P^r)$, and C^r satisfies (R-3).

Before proceeding to a formal proof of Theorem 3.4, some preliminary discussion of the homogeneity condition is instructive. Positive linear homogeneity of the aggregator in prices is needed and has no analogue in the properties of the representation theorems and corollaries for the direct and indirect utility functions. Let $\overset{*}{C}$ be the extension of C to $\mathcal{R}(U) \times \Omega^n$ by continuity from above. If I^r was strictly separable in $\overset{*}{C}$ from I^c for all $(u, P) \in \mathcal{R}(U) \times \Omega^n$, it would be possible to construct $\overset{*}{C}{}^r$ by choosing the cth-subspace zero vector for reference; then the proof would be easy. To see this, let 0^c be the origin of $\Omega^{(c)}$. Consider two cases:

$$\overset{*}{C}(u, 0^c, P^r) > 0 \qquad \text{for some} \quad P^r \in \Omega^{(r)}, \tag{a}$$

and

$$\overset{*}{C}(u, 0^c, P^r) = 0 \qquad \text{for all} \quad P^r \in \Omega^{(r)}. \tag{b}$$

Let the aggregator function be defined by

$$\overset{*}{C}{}^r(u, P^r) = \overset{*}{C}(u, 0^c, P^r).$$

In case (a), since $\overset{*}{C}$ is PLH in P, we have for $t > 0$

$$\overset{*}{C}(u, t0^c, tP^r) = \overset{*}{C}(u, 0^c, tP^r) = t\overset{*}{C}(u, 0^c, P^r);$$

hence $\overset{*}{C}{}^r$ is PLH in P^r. In case (b),

$$\overset{*}{C}{}^r(u, P^r) = 0 \qquad \text{for all} \quad P^r \in \Omega^{(r)},$$

and hence $\overset{*}{C}{}^r$ is trivially PLH in P^r. Such a case is uninteresting, and is easily ruled out. Since I^r is separable, (b) implies that for every fixed reference vector $O^c \in \Omega^c$,

$$\overset{*}{C}(u, O^c, P^r) = \text{constant} \qquad \text{for all} \quad P^r \in I^r;$$

i.e., total cost is independent of prices in the rth sector. If we rule out *inessential* sectors (see section 4.2), case (b) will not be bothersome.

[8](R-3P): Continuity, positive monotonicity, concavity, and positive linear homogeneity in prices (and aggregators) for all u.

If strict separability of a cost function is only defined on a proper subset (say the interior) of Ω^n,[9] the above proof is inoperative. To cover this case and the case in which I^r is separable but not strictly separable, there is an alternative strategy which is used in the proof of theorem 3.4.

Proof of theorem 3.4   Sufficiency of the structure (3.10) for separability is proved exactly as in the sufficiency proof of theorem 3.2b. To prove necessity and inheritance, define the ordering $\succcurlyeq_u^r$ (conditional on the value of u) by

$$P^r \succcurlyeq_u^r \hat{P}^r \quad \Leftrightarrow \quad C(u, P^c, P^r) \geqslant C(u, P^c, \hat{P}^r) \quad \forall P^c \in \Omega_+^{(c)}.$$

As in the proof of Theorem 3.2b, it is easily shown that $\succcurlyeq_u^r$ is complete, transitive, reflexive, and continuous.

Define $\mathring{C}^r$ such that

$$\mathring{C}^r(u, P^r) \geqslant \mathring{C}^r(u, \hat{P}^r) \quad \Leftrightarrow \quad P^r \succcurlyeq_u^r \hat{P}^r \quad \forall (P^r, \hat{P}^r) \in \Omega_+^{(r)} \times \Omega_+^{(r)}.$$

The representation (3.10) is now constructed as in the proof of Theorem 3.2b.

Concavity, and hence quasi-concavity, of $C(u, \cdot)$ implies quasi-concavity of $\mathring{C}^r(u, \cdot)$ by an argument analogous to that in the proof of theorem 3.3b. Monotonicity of $\mathring{C}^r(u, \cdot)$ is likewise immediate.

$\mathring{C}^r(u, \cdot)$ is homothetic if and only if the ordering $\succcurlyeq_u^r$, defined above, has the following property (Katzner, 1970: p. 24):

$$(P^r \succcurlyeq_u^r \hat{P}^r) \quad \Leftrightarrow \quad (tP^r \succcurlyeq_u^r t\hat{P}^r \quad \forall t > 0) \quad \forall (P^r, \hat{P}^r) \in \Omega_+^{(r)} \times \Omega_+^{(r)}.$$

A proof by contradiction establishes this condition. Suppose it is false. Then there exists a point $(P^r, \hat{P}^r) \in \Omega_+^{(r)} \times \Omega_+^{(r)}$ such that $P^r \succcurlyeq_u^r \hat{P}^r$ and $t\hat{P}^r \succ_u^r tP^r$. The latter condition implies that there exists a point $\tilde{P}^c \in \Omega_+^{(c)}$ such that

$$C(u, \tilde{P}^c, tP^r) < C(u, \tilde{P}^c, t\hat{P}^r).$$

Using the homogeneity of C, this implies

$$C\left(u, \frac{1}{t}\tilde{P}^c, P^r\right) < C\left(u, \frac{1}{t}\tilde{P}^c, \hat{P}^r\right),$$

which contradicts the presumption that $P^r \succcurlyeq_u^r \hat{P}^r$. Hence, $\mathring{C}^r$ is homothetic.

[9]As is required, in general, in the theory of duality (see chapter 2).

We now show that $\mathring{C}^r$ can be normalized to be PLH. We have shown that the cost-function image has the representation

$$C(u,P) = \overline{C}\left(u,P^c,\mathring{C}^r(u,P^r)\right), \qquad \text{(a)}$$

where $\mathring{C}^r$ is homothetic; we now show that there exist functions

$$\tilde{C}^r : \mathcal{R}(U) \times \Omega_+^{(r)} \to \Omega_+^1$$

and

$$\tilde{\overline{C}} : \mathcal{R}(U) \times \Omega_+^{(c)} \times \mathcal{R}(\tilde{C}^r) \to \Omega_+^1$$

such that

$$C(u,P) = \tilde{\overline{C}}\left(u,P^c,\tilde{C}^r(u,P^r)\right),$$

$\tilde{C}^r$ is PLH in P^r, and $\tilde{\overline{C}}$ is PLH in $\left(P^c,\tilde{C}^r(u,P^r)\right)$.

By the definition of homotheticity, there exist an increasing function $\psi : \Omega_+^1 \to \Omega_+^1$ and a PLH function $\tilde{C}^r : \Omega_+^{(r)} \to \Omega_+^1$ such that

$$\mathring{C}^r(u,P^r) = \psi(\tilde{C}^r(u,P^r)). \qquad \text{(b)}$$

Define a new function $\tilde{\overline{C}} : \mathcal{R}(U) \times \Omega_+^{(c)} \times \mathcal{R}(\tilde{C}^r) \to \Omega_+^1$ by substituting (b) into (a); i.e.,

$$C(u,P) = \tilde{\overline{C}}\left(u,P^c,\tilde{C}^r(u,P^r)\right) = \overline{C}\left(u,P^c,\psi(\tilde{C}^r(u,P^r))\right).$$

The positive linear homogeneity of $\tilde{\overline{C}}$ follows from that of $\tilde{C}^r$,

$$\tilde{\overline{C}}\left(u,\lambda P^c,\tilde{C}^r(u,\lambda P^r)\right) = \tilde{\overline{C}}\left(u,\lambda P^c,\lambda\tilde{C}^r(u,P^r)\right) \qquad \forall \lambda > 0,$$

and that of C,

$$\tilde{\overline{C}}\left(u,\lambda P^c,\tilde{C}^r(u,\lambda P^r)\right) = \lambda\tilde{\overline{C}}\left(u,P^c,\tilde{C}^r(u,P^r)\right) \qquad \forall \lambda > 0,$$

which imply

$$\tilde{\overline{C}}\left(u,\lambda P^c,\lambda\tilde{C}^r(u,P^r)\right) = \lambda\tilde{\overline{C}}\left(u,P^c,\tilde{C}^r(u,P)\right) \qquad \forall \lambda > 0.$$

This normalization preserves quasi-concavity. Finally, by a theorem of Newman (1969), since the resulting aggregator function, $\tilde{C}^r$, is both PLH and quasi-concave in prices, it is also concave in prices.

Monotonicity of $\overline{C}(u, \cdot)$ follows immediately from that of C and $\overset{\circ}{C}{}^r(u, \cdot)$. Using an argument equivalent to that in the proof of quasi-concavity of $\overline{U}$ in the proof of Theorem 3.3a, one can establish that $\overline{C}(u, \cdot)$ is quasi-concave. Since the above argument showed that $\overline{C}$ can be picked to be PLH in $(P^c, C^r(u, P^r))$, $\overline{C}(u, \cdot)$ is also concave.

If I^r is strictly separable, $\overline{C}$ in (3.10) is increasing, in $C^r(u, p^r)$ by the argument in the proof of Theorem 3.2a. The strict monotonicity of $C^r(\cdot, P^r)$ can be deduced from the representation of C^r:

$$C^r(u, P^r) = C(u, O^c, P^r), \tag{3.11}$$

where O^c is an arbitrary reference vector. Hence, C^r satisfies (R-3).

It remains to show that $\overline{C}$ is continuous. Pick $\{u^t, (P^c)^t, (c^r)^t\} \subseteq \mathfrak{R}(U) \times \Omega_+^{(c)} \times \mathfrak{R}(C^r)$ converging to $(\overset{*}{u}, \overset{*}{P}{}^c, \overset{*}{c}{}^r) \in \mathfrak{R}(U) \times \Omega_+^{(c)} \times \mathfrak{R}(C^r)$. Because $\mathfrak{R}(C^r)$ is open we can pick $(P^r, \hat{P}^r) \in \Omega_+^{(r)} \times \Omega_+^{(r)}$ such that

$$C^r(\overset{*}{u}, P^r) < \overset{*}{c}{}^r < C^r(\overset{*}{u}, \hat{P}^r).$$

The continuity of C^r in $(u, \hat{P}^r)$ implies that there exists a τ such that, for all $t \geqslant \tau$,

$$C^r(u^t, P^r) < \overset{*}{c}{}^r < C^r(u^t, \hat{P}^r).$$

Let $\Theta \subset \Omega_+^{(r)}$ be an arc connecting P^r and $\hat{P}^r$. Continuity and linear homogeneity imply that for all $t \geqslant \tau$ there exists $(P^r)^t \in \Theta$ such that $C^r(u^t, (P^r)^t) = (c^r)^t$. The proof is completed by a subsequential argument as in Theorem 3.3a.

An important and interesting technical difference between separability in the cost function and separability in the direct and indirect utility functions arises because the cost function is defined on a space of dimensionality $n + 1$, whereas the cardinality of I is only n. This means that, although we can aggregate the prices in sector r, in general that aggregate depends upon the level of utility or output, u. As we will see in section 3.4, a rather strong homogeneity assumption needs to be made in order to free the aggregator from the level of utility or output.

The dependence of the aggregator and macro functions on the value of u

also underscores an important contrast between the methods of proof in the representation theorems for strict and nonstrict separability. In particular, the aggregator in the nonstrict-separability representation is constructed by defining a representable subspace ordering, conditional on u, whereas the aggregator in the strict-separability representation can be chosen by the reference-vector technique (3.11).

Of course, if I^r is strictly separable, the representation of $\succcurlyeq^r_u$, defined as in the proof of theorem 3.4, can always be alternatively constructed by the reference-vector technique. If, however, I^r is separable and *not* strictly separable, it is not generally possible to employ the reference-vector construction. Indeed, given a very reasonable assumption (which we invoke several times in the pages that follow), it can be shown that the reference-vector construction is impossible in the absence of strict separability.

The concept that we need is that of (strict) essentiality. The sector I^r is said to be *essential* if, for each $\hat{X}^r \in \Omega^{(r)}$, the set $\{X^r \in \Omega^{(r)} | U(X^c, X^r) = U(X^c, \hat{X}^r)\}$ is a proper subset of $\Omega^{(r)}$ for some $X^c \in \Omega^{(c)}$. That is, for at least one reference vector $X^c \in \Omega^{(c)}$, the conditional preference ordering on $\Omega^{(r)}$ does *not* put all elements into the same indifference class. A sector is said to be *strictly essential* if it is essential for *all* points $X^c \in \Omega^{(c)}$.

We now show that, if I^r is strictly essential and separable and if U^r can be chosen by the reference-vector construction, I^r is *strictly* separable. Suppose that

(a) $U(X) = \bar{U}(X^c, U^r(X^r))$, where $\bar{U}$ is nondecreasing in $U^r(X^r)$.

Presume that

(b) $U^r(X^r) = U(O^c, X^r)$ for some $O^c \in \Omega^{(c)}$, and
(c) $\bar{U}$ is *not* increasing in $U^r(X^r)$ for some interval in $\mathcal{R}(U^r)$.

By strict essentiality and (c), there exists a point $(\bar{X}^r, \hat{X}^r) \in \Omega^{(r)} \times \Omega^{(r)}$ such that

(d) $U^r(\bar{X}^r) > U^r(\hat{X}^r)$, but
(e) $\bar{U}(O^c, U^r(\bar{X}^r)) = \bar{U}(O^c, U^r(\hat{X}^r))$.

However, (b) and (d) imply that

$$U(O^c, \bar{X}^r) > U(O^c, \hat{X}^r),$$

which contradicts (a) and (e). Thus there does not exist a point $O^c \in \Omega^{(c)}$ such that (b) holds.

Consequently, in proving propositions regarding the inheritance of regularity properties, the reference-vector construction can be used in the case of strict—but not nonstrict—separability. In the representation theorems for separable direct and indirect utility functions, this is not an important distinction. It is, however, important in the representation theorem for the separable cost function, because of the dependence of the conditional ordering on the scalar u. Regularity properties of C in P are easily shown to be inherited by the representation of $\succcurlyeq_u^r$, but this is not true of properties in u (see, e.g., Corollary 3.5.2 below) and joint properties in (u, P). On the other hand, the reference-vector technique facilitates proofs of inheritance of properties in u and (u, P). It is for this reason that the regularity properties (R-3) are proved to be inherited by the aggregator in a strictly separable representation, but only (R-3P) are proved to be inherited by the aggregator in a nonstrictly separable representation.

On the other hand, inheritance of (R-3) by $\overline{C}$ is not claimed in either the strict or the nonstrict separability case. In fact, it can be shown that $\overline{C}$ *cannot* satisfy the strict monotonicity property in u (at least if I^c is strictly separable). To see this, consider a pair, (u, P^r) and $(\hat{u}, \hat{P}^r)$, each in $\mathcal{R}(U) \times \Omega_+^{(r)}$, satisfying $\hat{u} > u$ and $C^r(u, P^r) = C^r(\hat{u}, \hat{P}^r)$. (Such a pair can always be found, as can be seen by examining the particular normalization where C^r is PLH.) The reference-vector construction yields

$$C(u, O^c, P^r) = C(\hat{u}, O^c, \hat{P}^r),$$

which, by the definition of $\overline{C}$, implies

$$\overline{C}(u, O^c, C^r(u, P^r)) = \overline{C}(\hat{u}, O^c, C^r(\hat{u}, \hat{P}^r)),$$

which violates the strict monotonicity of $\overline{C}$ in u.

The natural interpretation of C^r is that it is a sector-specific cost function;[10] $C^r(u, P^r)$ is the minimum cost of achieving utility or output level u consuming commodities in sector r at prices P^r. But, in general, the aggregator function yielded immediately by the construction in the above proof [or by (3.11)] is only an ordinal representation of the cost structure with respect to the rth sector of prices. The above theorem simply asserts that there is a normalization of C^r that is PLH. Similarly, $\overline{C}$ might be interpreted as a macro cost function. Unfortunately, as noted above, it does not satisfy all of the regularity conditions (R-3). Moreover, the argument $C^r(u, P^r)$ cannot be reasonably interpreted as a composite price, since it depends upon u as well as P^r.

---

[10]Of course, in the nonstrict separability representation, C^r might not satisfy all of the regularity properties (R-3).

3.3.4 Separability in the Transformation Function

Moving to the transformation function, we find that the technical details are almost the same as for the cost function, although the interpretations are quite different. To begin, define the mapping $\eta^r : \mathcal{R}(U) \times \Omega_+^n \to \mathcal{P}(\Omega_+^{(r)})$, whose image is

$$\eta^r(u, X^c, X^r) = \{\hat{X}^r \in \Omega_+^{(r)} | F(u, X^c, \hat{X}^r) \geqslant F(u, X^c, X^r)\}.$$

The set of variables I^r is separable in F from the set of variables I^c if and only if, for each $u \in \mathcal{R}(U)$, the collection of sets $\{\eta^r(u, X^c, X^r) | X^c \in \Omega_+^{(c)} \wedge X^r \in \Omega_+^{(r)}\}$ is nested. The set of variables I^r is strictly separable from I^c if and only if, for each $u \in \mathcal{R}(U)$, $\eta^r(u, X^c, X^r) = \eta^r(u, \bar{X}^c, X^r)$ for all $(X^c, X^r) \in \Omega_+^n$ and for any $\bar{X}^c \in \Omega_+^{(c)}$.

If F is twice differentiable with positive first partial derivatives $F_i(u, X)$, $i = 1, \ldots, n$, then the Leontief-Sono definition is as follows: I^r is separable from I^c if and only if

$$\frac{\partial}{\partial x_k}\left(\frac{F_i(u, X)}{F_j(u, X)}\right) = \frac{\partial}{\partial x_k}\left(\frac{\delta_i(u, X)}{\delta_j(u, X)}\right) = 0 \qquad \forall(i, j) \in I^r \times I^r, \quad \forall k \in I^c,$$
$$\forall(u, X) \in \mathcal{R}(U) \times \Omega_+^n.$$

This says that, for given u, the ratios of shadow prices associated with goods in sector r are independent of the quantities of commodities in I^c. This ratio does depend in general on the level of utility or output.

It is easy to see that the technical details of separability in the transformation function are the same as in the cost function. That is, the above separability statement allows us to aggregate the commodities in group r, but the aggregator must depend in general upon the level of "real income", u.

Corollary 3.4.1 *Assume that F is continuous and nondecreasing. I^r is separable in F from I^c if and only if there exist functions*

$$F^r : \mathcal{R}(U) \times \Omega_+^{(r)} \to \Omega_+^1$$

and

$$\bar{F} : \mathcal{R}(U) \times \Omega_+^{(c)} \times \mathcal{R}(F^r) \to \Omega_+^1$$

such that

$$F(u, X) = \bar{F}(u, X^c, F^r(u, X^r)) \qquad \forall(u, X) \in \mathcal{R}(U) \times \Omega_+^n, \quad (3.12)$$

where $\overline{F}$ is nondecreasing in $F^r(u, X^r)$. If F satisfies (R-4), *then $\overline{F}$ and F^r satisfy* (R-4X).[11] *If, in addition, I^r is strictly separable from I^c, then $\overline{F}$ is continuous, increasing in $F^r(u, X^r)$, and F^r satisfies* (R-4).

Proof.   As in theorem 3.4.   ‖

F^r can be interpreted as a sector-specific transformation function. [Of course, if I^r is nonstrictly separable from I^c, we cannot be sure that F^r satisfies (R-4).] Alternatively, $F^r(u, X^r)$ can be viewed as the imputed value of X^r computed as the inner product of shadow prices and quantities, where the shadow prices depend on the utility level u and on the direction, $X^r / \|X^r\|$, of X^r.

3.3.5   Inherited Properties of the Macro and Aggregator Functions

In many examples it is desirable to maintain stronger regularity conditions than those represented by (R-1) through (R-4). Most of these stronger maintained conditions on the master function, U, V, C, or F, are inherited by the macro and the aggregator functions. The following theorem and its corollaries state these conditions formally. Proofs are provided only for those propositions which require substantially different modes of proof than already presented.

Theorem 3.5   *Suppose U is continuous and nondecreasing and satisfies the separability assumption of theorem 3.2b. Then $\overline{U}$ and U^r in the representation* (3.5) *can be so chosen that if U has any of the following properties, $\overline{U}$ and U^r possess the same property: (i) strict quasi-concavity, (ii) strict positive monotonicity, (iii) positive homotheticity, and (iv) positive linear homogeneity. If I^r is strictly separable from I^c, then (directional) differentiability of U implies* (v) *(partial) differentiability of $\overline{U}$ and U^r, and, if U is (strictly) concave, U^r can be chosen to be (strictly) concave.*

Proof.   Proofs of the properties (i) and (ii) as well as (strict) concavity are sufficiently similar to the arguments in theorems 3.3a and 3.3b to leave to the reader. (Recall from theorem 3.1 that strict monotonicity of U obviates the distinction between strict and nonstrict separability.) The properties (iii) and (iv) follow from an argument that is formally equivalent to that in theorem 3.4. This leaves (v), differentiability.

The partial differentiability (indeed, the directional differentiability) of U^r follows from the differentiability of U and the construction of U^r in the proof of Theorem 3.2a. The differentiability of $\overline{U}$ with respect of X^c is

---

[11]Continuity, positive monotonicity, concavity, and positive linear homogeneity in input quantities (and aggregators) for all u.

similarly immediate. To prove the differentiability of $\overline{U}$ with respect to $U^r(X^r)$, first note that the directional differentiability of U implies that

$$\lim_{\lambda \to 0_+} \frac{\overline{U}\left(\overline{X}^c, U^r(\overline{X}^r + \lambda X^r)\right) - \overline{U}\left(\overline{X}^c, U^r(\overline{X}^r)\right)}{\lambda} = \lim_{\lambda \to 0_+} \psi(\lambda, \overline{X}^c, \overline{X}^r, X^r)$$

(a)

is unique and finite $\forall (\overline{X}^r, X^r) \in \Omega_+^{(r)} \times \Omega_+^{(r)}$. Noting that, by construction, a positive $U^r(X^r)$ can be guaranteed for all $X^r \in \Omega_+^{(r)}$ (this requires, of course, that U be normalized to map into Ω^1), we define for $X^r > \overline{X}^r$

$$\kappa(\lambda, \overline{X}^r, X^r) = \frac{U^r(\overline{X}^r + \lambda X^r) - U^r(\overline{X}^r)}{U^r(X^r)}.$$

(b)

Note that $\kappa(\lambda, \overline{X}^r, X^r) \to 0$ if and only if $\lambda \to 0$. Consider the limit

$$\lim_{\kappa(\lambda, \overline{X}^r, X^r) \to 0} \frac{\overline{U}\left(\overline{X}^c, \overline{u}_r + \kappa(\lambda, \overline{X}^r, X^r) \cdot u_r\right) - \overline{U}\left(\overline{X}^c, \overline{u}_r\right)}{\kappa(\lambda, \overline{X}^r, X^r)} = \theta(\lambda, X^c, \overline{X}^r, X^r).$$

(c)

If this limit is unique and bounded for all $(\overline{X}^r, X^r) \in \Omega_+^{(r)} \times \Omega_+^{(r)}$, then $\overline{U}$ is differentiable with respect to u_r. To show uniqueness and boundedness, note that substituting the solution of (b) for $U^r(\overline{X}^r + \lambda X^r)$ into $\psi(\lambda, \overline{X}^c, \overline{X}^r, X^r)$ reveals that the numerator of $\psi(\lambda, \overline{X}^c, \overline{X}^r, X^r)$ is equal to the numerator of $\theta(\lambda, \overline{X}^c, \overline{X}^r, X^r)$. Hence, the ratio $\psi(\lambda, \overline{X}^c, \overline{X}^r, X^r)/\theta(\lambda, \overline{X}^c, \overline{X}^r, X^r)$ is equal to

$$\frac{\kappa(\lambda, \overline{X}^r, X^r)}{\lambda} = \frac{U^r(\overline{X}^r + \lambda X^r) - U^r(\overline{X}^r)}{\lambda} \frac{1}{U^r(X^r)}.$$

(d)

The limit of (d) as $\lambda \to 0$ is equal to the directional derivative of U^r times the inverse of $U^r(X^r)$. The differentiability of U^r therefore implies that the ratio of the two limits (a) and (c) is unique and bounded. The differentiability of U then implies boundedness and uniqueness of the limit (c). Hence $\overline{U}$ is partially differentiable. $\parallel$

The next three corollaries are stated without proof, as the arguments follow quite easily by analogy with earlier arguments.

Corollary 3.5.1 *Suppose that V is continuous and nonincreasing and satisfies the separability condition of corollary 3.2.1. If V has any of the following properties, then $\overline{V}$ in the representation (3.6) possesses the same property, while V^r has the corresponding property in theorem 3.5: (i) strict quasi-convexity, (ii) strict negative monotonicity, (iii) negative homotheticity, and (iv) negative homogeneity. If I^r is strictly separable from I^c, then directional differentiability of V implies (v) partial differentiability of $\overline{V}$ and V^r, and if V is (strictly) convex, V^r can be chosen to be (strictly) concave.*

Corollary 3.5.2 *Suppose that C is continuous and nondecreasing and satisfies the separability conditions of theorem 3.4. Then if $C(u, \cdot)$ satisfies any of the properties (i)–(iv) listed in theorem 3.5, $\overline{C}(u, \cdot)$ and $C^r(u, \cdot)$ can be chosen to possess the same property. In addition, if I^r is strictly separable from I^c, each of the following statements holds: (a) if $C(\cdot, P)$ has any of the properties (i)–(iv), then $C^r(\cdot, P^r)$ can be chosen to possess the same properties; (b) if C is (strictly) convex in u, then C^r can be chosen to be so as well; (c) $\overline{C}(u, \cdot)$ and $C^r(u, \cdot)$ inherit (v) from C.*

In the statement of this corollary and of many corollaries and theorems that follow, we speak loosely of the inheritance of differentiability by the macro function. Of course, the formal proposition that has been proved is that if the parent function is directionally differentiable, the macro function can be chosen to be partially differentiable.

Corollary 3.5.3 *Suppose F is continuous and nondecreasing and satisfies the separability condition of corollary 3.4.1. Then if $F(u, \cdot)$ satisfies any of the properties (i)–(iv) listed in theorem 3.5, $\overline{F}(u, \cdot)$ and $F^r(u, \cdot)$ can be chosen to have the same properties. In addition, if I^r is strictly separable from I^c, each of the following statements holds: (a) if $F(\cdot, X)$ has any of the properties (i)–(iv) listed in corollary 3.5.1, then $F^r(\cdot, X^r)$ can be chosen to have the same properties; (b) if F is (strictly) convex in u, then F^r can be chosen to be so as well; (c) $\overline{F}(u, \cdot)$ and $F^r(u, \cdot)$ inherit (v) from F.*

Before proceeding it is worth noting that, in spite of the fact that U^r inherits strict positive monotonicity, it is not true that U^r inherits global nonsatiation on $\Omega^{(r)}$. It is for this reason that we have not maintained the assumption of global nonsatiation (although an examination of the appendix demonstrates that the price paid for this generality, in terms of the difficulty of duality proofs, is nontrivial).

We could have proceeded in the following alternative manner. Suppose that U is continuous, nondecreasing, and globally nonsated but that U^r in (3.5) has a region of global satiation in $\Omega^{(r)}$. Letting $\bar{u}_r = \sup \mathcal{R}(U^r)$ and

$L^r(u_r) = \{X^r \in \Omega^{(r)} | U^r(X) \geqslant u_r\}$, define a new aggregator function:

$$\tilde{U}^r(X^r) = \begin{cases} U^r(X^r) & \forall X^r \notin \text{int } L^r(\bar{u}_r) \\ \hat{U}(X^r) & \forall X^r \in L^r(\bar{u}_r), \end{cases}$$

where $\hat{U}^r$ is any increasing function, satisfying $(\text{R}-1)$, such that $\hat{U}^r(X^r) = U^r(X^r) \forall X^r \in (L^r(\bar{u}_r) - \text{int } L^r(\bar{u}_r))$ (i.e., for all $\bar{X}$ in the boundary of $L^r(\bar{u}_r)$). Define a new macro function, $\tilde{U}$, by

$$U(X) = \tilde{U}(X^c, \tilde{U}^r(X^r)) \quad \forall X \in \Omega^n.$$

Clearly, $\tilde{U}$ and $\tilde{U}^r$ inherit global nonsatiation (as well as the other properties identified in theorem 3.5) and provide a different interpretation of sectoral satiation. The interpretation motivated by our treatment of sectoral satiation is that the quantity of the intermediate good, $U^r(X^r)$, cannot exceed $\bar{u}_r$. The alternative treatment just suggested has the interpretation that, if more than $\bar{u}_r$ of the composite good is produced, the macro function is constant in that direction (i.e., the intermediate good has a zero marginal product for quantities in excess of $\bar{u}_r$). Both interpretations are tenable; we have chosen the former because aggregators constructed as in either Theorems 3.2a or 3.2b are reflections of the overall technology. On the other hand, $\tilde{U}^r$ is obtained from either of these aggregators by a *nonmonotonic* transformation and therefore does not reflect the underlying preference ordering (or technology). Thus, the conversion of U^r to $\tilde{U}^r$ as above deprives the aggregator of one of its more attractive attributes; consequently, we prefer the approach embodied in theorem 3.5 (and its corollaries).

3.4 FUNCTIONAL-STRUCTURE EQUIVALENCES

3.4.1 Equivalence of Separability of the Cost and Transformation Functions

Separability of I^r from I^c in U, V, and F (or in U, V, and C) generally represents different preference or technology structures. However, separability in F and in C are equivalent. This result was established independently by Gorman (1970) and McFadden (1970). In the proof of the following theorem, we follow Gorman's argument. Before proceeding to establish this equivalence, we must cover one small problem.

The problem pertains to the boundary problems confronted in the theory of duality in chapter 2. In particular, C is derived not directly from F, with domain Ω^n_+, but from the extension of F (by continuity from above) to $\mathcal{R}(U) \times \Omega^n$, denoted $\overset{*}{F}$. Similarly, F is derived from $\overset{*}{C}$, the extension of C to $\mathcal{R}(U) \times \Omega^n$ by continuity from above. In order to establish the duality between separability of C and of F, we must therefore show that separability of a function defined on Ω^n_+ implies separability of the appropriate extension of this function to Ω^n.

The following lemma is stated in terms of U but is easily adapted to other representations of the preference ordering or production technology.

Lemma 3.2 *Suppose that $\overset{\circ}{U}$, the restriction of U to Ω^n_+, is continuous and that there exist continuous functions*

$$\overset{\circ}{U}{}^r : \Omega^r_+ \to \mathbf{R} \quad and \quad \overset{\circ}{\overline{U}} : \Omega^{(c)}_+ \times \mathcal{R}(\overset{\circ}{U}) \to \mathbf{R}$$

satisfying

$$\overset{\circ}{\overline{U}}\left(X^c, \overset{\circ}{U}{}^r(X^r)\right) = \overset{\circ}{U}(X) \qquad \forall X \in \Omega^n_+,$$

where $\overset{\circ}{\overline{U}}$ is monotonic. Letting U, U^r, and $\overline{U}$ be extensions of $\overset{\circ}{U}$, $\overset{\circ}{U}{}^r$, and $\overset{\circ}{\overline{U}}$, respectively, to Ω^n, $\Omega^{(r)}$, and $\Omega^{(c)} \times \mathcal{R}(U^r)$ by continuity from above,

$$\overline{U}\left(X^c, U^r(X^r)\right) = U(X) \qquad \forall X \in \Omega^n. \tag{3.5}$$

Moreover, if $\overset{\circ}{U}{}^r$ is homothetic, so is U^r.

Proof. Suppose that, under the hypotheses of the lemma, (3.5) is false for $\overset{*}{X} \in \Omega^n$. Consider a sequence $\{X^\upsilon\}$ in $\{X \in \Omega^n_+ \,|\, U(X) \geqslant U(\overset{*}{X})\}$ converging to $\overset{*}{X}$. The continuity of $\overline{U}$ and U^r from above and the negation of (3.5) at $\overset{*}{X}$ imply that

$$\lim_{\upsilon \to \infty} U(X^\upsilon) = \lim_{\upsilon \to \infty} \overline{U}\left((X^c)^\upsilon, U^r((X^r)^\upsilon)\right)$$

$$= \overline{U}\left(\lim_{\upsilon \to \infty}(X^c)^\upsilon, \lim_{\upsilon \to \infty} U^r((X^r)^\upsilon)\right)$$

$$= \overline{U}\left(\overset{*}{X}{}^c, U^r(\overset{*}{X}{}^r)\right)$$

$$\neq U(\overset{*}{X}),$$

contradicting the continuity of U from above.

Proof of the homotheticity of U^r requires an argument similar to the proof of the structure (3.5) at the boundary. Homotheticity and continuity of $\mathring{U}^r$ imply the existence of a continuous PLH function $\mathring{\overline{U}}^r : \mathring{\Omega}^r_+ \to \mathbf{R}$ and a continuous, increasing function $\mathring{\Psi} : \mathcal{R}(\mathring{\overline{U}}^r) \to \mathbf{R}$, such that

$$\mathring{U}^r(X^r) = \mathring{\Psi}\left(\mathring{\overline{U}}^r(X^r)\right) \qquad \forall X^r \in \Omega^{(r)}_+.$$

Let $\overline{U}^r$ and Ψ be the extensions of $\mathring{\overline{U}}^r$ and $\mathring{\Psi}$ by continuity from above to $\Omega^{(r)}$ and $\mathcal{R}(\overline{U}^r)$, respectively, and suppose that

$$U^r(\overset{*}{X}{}^r) \neq \Psi\left(\overline{U}^r(\overset{*}{X}{}^r)\right) \qquad \text{for some} \quad \overset{*}{X}{}^r \in \Omega^{(r)}. \tag{a}$$

Consider a sequence $\{(X^r)^v\}$ in

$$\{X^r \in \Omega^{(r)} | U^r(X^r) \geqslant U^r(\overset{*}{X}{}^r)\}$$

converging to $\overset{*}{X}{}^r$. Continuity from above of $\overline{U}^r$ and Ψ and (a) imply that

$$\lim_{v \to \infty} U^r((X^r)^v) = \lim_{v \to \infty} \Psi\left(\overline{U}^r((X^r)^v)\right)$$

$$= \Psi\left(\overline{U}^r(\overset{*}{X}{}^r)\right)$$

$$\neq U^r(\overset{*}{X}{}^r),$$

violating the continuity of U^r from above.

Finally, assuming that

$$\overline{U}^r(\lambda\overset{*}{X}{}^r) \neq \lambda\overline{U}^r(\overset{*}{X}{}^r) \qquad \text{for some} \quad \overset{*}{X}{}^r \in \Omega^{(r)}$$

and applying a sequential argument similar to the above establishes the positive homogeneity of $\overline{U}^r$. Hence U^r is homothetic. ‖

Returning to the main point of this subsection, the next theorem establishes the equivalence of separability in C and F. We say that F satisfies local nonsatiation on $\Omega^{(r)}$ if $F(u, X^c, \cdot)$ satisfies local nonsatiation for all $(u, X^c) \in \mathcal{R}(U) \times \Omega^{(c)}$ (actually, nonsatiation for all X^c in the boundary of $\Omega^{(c)}$ would suffice for this and other duality theorems). Local nonsatiation of $\overset{*}{C}$ on $\Omega^{(r)}$ is defined analogously.

Theorem 3.6 *Suppose that U satisfies* (R-1).[12] *Then I^r is separable from I^c in the cost function C if and only if I^r is separable from I^c in the transformation function F. In addition, if $\overset{*}{F}$ and $\overset{*}{C}$, the extensions of F and C*

[12]This implies that C satisfies (R-3) and that F satisfies (R-4).

to the boundary,[13] *satisfy local nonsatiation on* $\Omega^{(r)}$, *then strict separability of* I^r *from* I^c *in* F *is equivalent to strict separability of* I^r *from* I^c *in* C.

Proof.   Lemma 3.2 and the separability of F imply that we can write

$$\overset{*}{F}(u,X) = \bar{F}\left(u, X^c, F^r(u, X^r)\right) \qquad \forall (u, X) \in \mathcal{R}(U) \times \Omega^n, \quad (3.13)$$

where $\bar{F}$ is nondecreasing in $F^r(u, X^r)$. Therefore,

$$C(u, P) = \min_{X} \left\{ P \cdot X \mid X \in \Omega^n \wedge \overset{*}{F}(u, X) \geqslant 1 \right\}$$

becomes

$$C(u, P) = \min_{X} \left\{ P \cdot X \mid X \in \Omega^n \wedge \bar{F}\left(u, X^c, F^r(u, X^r)\right) \geqslant 1 \right\}.$$

The monotonicity of $\bar{F}$ allows us to rewrite this equation as

$$C(u, P) = \min_{X^c, \lambda} \left\{ P^c \cdot X^c + \min_{X^r} \left\{ P^r \cdot X^r \mid X^r \in \Omega^{(r)} \wedge F^r(u, X^r) \geqslant \lambda \right\} \right.$$

$$\left. \left| X^c \in \Omega^{(c)} \wedge \lambda \in \mathcal{R}(F^r) \wedge \bar{F}(u, X^c, \lambda) \geqslant 1 \right\} \right.$$

$$= \min_{X^c, \lambda} \left\{ P^c \cdot X^c + \lambda \min_{X^r/\lambda} \left\{ P^r \cdot X^r / \lambda \mid X^r / \lambda \in \Omega^{(r)} \wedge F^r(u, X^r/\lambda) \geqslant 1 \right\} \right.$$

$$\left. \left| X^C \in \Omega^{(c)} \wedge \lambda \in \mathcal{R}(F^r) \wedge \bar{F}(u, X^c, \lambda) \geqslant 1 \right\} \right.$$

(recall that F^r can be constructed to be a positive function), where the second equality follows from the fact that F^r is PLH in X^r. Let

$$C^r(u, P^r) = \min_{X^r/\lambda} \left\{ P^r \cdot \frac{X^r}{\lambda} \,\middle|\, \frac{X^r}{\lambda} \in \Omega^{(r)} \wedge F^r(u, X^r/\lambda) \geqslant 1 \right\}.$$

Then

$$C(u, P) = \min_{X^c, \lambda} \left\{ P^c \cdot X^c + \lambda C^r(u, P^r) \mid X^c \in \Omega^{(C)} \right.$$

$$\wedge \lambda \in \mathcal{R}(F^r) \wedge \bar{F}(u, X^c, \lambda) \geqslant 1 \right\}$$

$$= \bar{C}\left(u, P^c, C^r(u, P^r)\right). \tag{a}$$

[13]That is, $\overset{*}{F}$ and $\overset{*}{C}$ are the extensions of F and C by continuity from above to $\mathcal{R}(U) \times \Omega^n$.

Moreover, the positive monotonicity of F in λ implies that $\overline{C}$ is nondecreasing in $C^r(u,P')$; hence I^r is separable from I^c in the cost function.

If I^r is separable from I^c in F, and F satisfies local nonsatiation on $\Omega^{(r)}$, theorems 3.1 and 3.2a imply that $\overline{F}$ is increasing in $F^r(u,X')$ in equation (3.13). Repeating the above calculations employing this structure leads to the structure (a), where $\overline{C}$ is increasing in $C^r(u,P')$, implying that I^r is strictly separable from I^c in C.

That (strict) separability of I^r from I^c in C implies (strict) separability of I^r from I^c in F is easily proved by recalling that

$$F(u,X) = \min_P \left\{ P \cdot X \,|\, P \in \Omega^n \wedge \overset{*}{C}(u,P) \geqslant 1 \right\}$$

and interchanging the roles of C and F in the above argument.   ‖

It will be noted that the self-duality of strict separability with respect to F and C requires slightly stronger maintained conditions than does the self-duality of nonstrict separability. In particular, it is necessary to eliminate the possible "thick" indifference surfaces in the subspace $\Omega^{(r)}$ in order for strict separability of F to be equivalent to strict separability of C. The Leontief technology illustrates this point. It will be recalled from chapter 2 that the cost function that is dual to a Leontief technology has the image

$$C(u,P) = u \sum_{i=1}^{n} a_i p_i.$$

Any proper subset I^r is strictly separable in C from its complement, but no subset I^r is strictly separable in the dual transformation function, with image

$$F(u,X) = \frac{1}{u} \min \left\{ \frac{x_1}{a_1}, \ldots, \frac{x_n}{a_n} \right\}.$$

Of course, any subset I^r is nonstrictly separable from its complement in this Leontief structure, (as must be the case since strict separability of I^r from I^c in C implies separability of I^r from I^c in C and hence in F).

It is instructive to inquire why it is that separability of the cost function and of the transformation function are equivalent and that this is the only general equivalence that holds among the six pairs of functional structures that have been introduced. An attempt to apply the strategy of proof of theorem 3.6 to the separability of U and V, say, would reveal that the proof breaks down because the aggregator functions are not homogeneous.

Thus, the duality between the structure of F and of C is apparently attributable to the fact that these functions constitute homogeneous—albeit implicit—representations of the preference ordering or production technology. This suggests that additional separability equivalences could be generated if the conditional orderings on $\Omega^{(r)}$ and/or $\Omega_+^{(r)}$ were assumed to be homogeneous, in which case the aggregator functions could be chosen to be homogeneous (see lemmas 3.3a and 3.3b below). As this is indeed the case, the next subsection turns to a consideration of structures that have the required homotheticity properties.

Before proceeding to a discussion of homothetic separability, we consider an alternative characterization of the dual structure of F and C. In the language of chapter 2, given u, the "price" vector $(P^c, C^r(u, P^r))$ and the "quantity" vector $(X^c, F^r(u, X^r))$ may be either directly or indirectly conjugate. In either case, $F^r(u, X^r) C^r(u, P^r) = P^r \cdot X^r$, a decomposition not generally available with the direct and indirect utility functions. Because of this conjugacy and because F and C implicitly define the utility functions, we sometimes refer to separability of F and C as *conjugate implicit separability* and to separability of U and V as *(explicit) direct* and *indirect separability*, respectively.

3.4.2 Homothetic Separability

We say that a preference ordering on $\Omega^{(r)}$ is homogeneous if indifference between $\bar{X}^r$ and $\hat{X}^r$ implies indifference between $\lambda \bar{X}^r$ and $\lambda \hat{X}^r$ for all $\lambda > 0$. If I^r is separable from I^c in U and if the (Bliss) preference ordering on $\Omega^{(r)}$ is homogeneous, the representation U^r is positively homothetic. We refer to this structure as (direct) *homothetic separability*. Note that this condition does *not* imply homotheticity of U.

Lemma 3.3a   *If I^r is homothetically separable from I^c in U, the aggregator function U^r in the representation* (3.3) *can be chosen to be PLH.*

Proof.   The proof is identical to the proof of the homogeneity part of theorem 3.4, apart from a change in notation and suppression of the variable u.   ‖

Henceforth, when there is little possibility of confusion, we simply consider U^r to have been picked to be PLH without going through the above construction. (In chapter 4 we find, however, that in additive representations this is a nontrival issue.) It is important to notice that homothetic separability does not imply that U is homothetic in its arguments $(X^c, U^r(X^r))$.

I^r is said to be (indirectly) *homothetically separable* from I^c if I^r is separable from I^c in the indirect utility function and the preference ordering on $\Omega_+^{(r)}$ is homogeneous.

Lemma 3.3b *If I^r is homothetically separable from I^c in V, the aggregator function V^r can be chosen to be PLH.*

Proof. The proof is identical to the homogeneity part of the proof of theorem 3.4 with a change in notation. ‖

The cost and transformation functions are necessarily PLH in quantities and prices, respectively. Consequently, as noted in theorem 3.4 and corollary 3.4.1, the aggregators of separable sets in these functions can be chosen to be PLH in X and P, respectively. As it turns out, (direct and indirect) homothetic separability can be characterized in terms of transformation and cost functions. In order to develop this characterization, it is necessary to introduce some additional notation.

Denote the "extended" index set by

$$_0I = I^0 \cup I = \{0, 1, \ldots, n\},$$

where $I^0 = \{0\}$ and 0 represents either the income variable y or the utility (or output) variable u, depending upon the context. Consider the binary partition of $_0I$,

$$_0\bar{I} = \{_0I^c, I^r\} = \{I^0 \cup I^c, I^r\};$$

thus, the first element of the partition contains the utility (or income) variable as well as variable indices for quantities and prices in I^c.

Theorem 3.7 *Assume that the cost function C satisfies the regularity conditions $(R-3)$. Then I^r is separable in C from $_0I^c$ if and only if there exist functions*

$$\bar{C}^r : \Omega_+^{(r)} \to \Omega_+^1$$

and

$$\bar{C} : \mathfrak{R}(U) \times \Omega_+^{(c)} \times \mathfrak{R}(\bar{C}^r) \to \Omega_+^1$$

with images

$$C(u, P) = \bar{C}\left(u, P^c, \bar{C}^r(P^r)\right), \tag{3.14}$$

where $\bar{C}$ and $\bar{C}^r$ satisfy $(R-3)$ and $(R-3P)$, respectively.

Proof. The proof is identical to the proof of theorem 3.4 apart from the change in the index set and its partition and the additional inherited properties of $\bar{C}$. The strict monotonicity of $\bar{C}$ in u follows immediately from the identity (3.14). ‖

As $\bar{C}^r$ is a function of prices only, it does not make sense to interpret it as a total sectoral cost function. In fact, particularly because it is PLH in P^r, it is natural to think of $\bar{C}^r$ as a price index. $\bar{C}^r(P^r)$ is the price of one unit of an aggregate index of commodities in group r; i.e., $\bar{C}^r$ is the sector-specific unit cost function. Therefore, $\bar{C}$ is just an ordinary cost function, defined however on P^c and $\bar{C}^r(P^r)$.

A similar representation result holds for the transformation function F.

Corollary 3.7.1 *Assume that the transformation function F satisfies the regularity conditions* (R $-$ 4). *Then I^r is separable in F from $_0I^c$ if and only if there exist functions*

$$\bar{F}^r : \Omega_+^{(r)} \to \Omega_+^1$$

and

$$\bar{F} : \mathcal{R}(U) \times \Omega_+^{(c)} \times \mathcal{R}(\bar{F}^r) \to \Omega_+^1$$

with images

$$F(u,X) = \bar{F}\left(u, X^c, \bar{F}^r(X^r)\right), \tag{3.15}$$

where $\bar{F}$ and $\bar{F}^r$ satisfy (R $-$ 4) *and* (R $-$ 4X) *respectively.*

Proof. Same as the proof of theorem 3.7, apart from the change in notation. ‖

As $\bar{F}^r$ is a PLH function of quantities only, we can interpret it as a quantity index; hence $\bar{F}$ is a transformation function defined on $\left(u, X^c, \bar{F}^r(X^r)\right)$. Furthermore, it will be shown later that $\bar{C}^r(P^r)$ is the "price" of the "quantity" $\bar{F}^r(X^r)$.

In terms of the new partition, $_0I$, different structural results are obtained by examining the indirect utility function in nonnormalized rather than normalized prices.

Corollary 3.7.2 *Assume that the indirect utility function in nonnormalized prices W satisfies conditions* (R $-$ 2) *in prices and is increasing and continuous in y. Then I^r is separable from $_0I^c$ in W if and only if there exist functions*

$$\bar{W}^r : \Omega_+^{(r)} \to \mathbf{R}$$

and

$$\overline{W} : \Omega_+^1 \times \Omega_+^{(c)} \times \Re(\overline{W}^r) \to \mathbf{R}$$

whose images are defined by

$$W(y, P) = \overline{W}\left(y, P^c, \overline{W}^r(P^r)\right), \tag{3.16}$$

where $\overline{W}^r$ satisfies the conditions (R−1) and is PLH in P^r, and where $\overline{W}$ is continuous and HDO in its arguments, increasing in y, nonincreasing in $\overline{W}^r(P^r)$, nonincreasing in P^c, and quasiconvex in $\left(P^c, \overline{W}^r(P^r)\right)$.

Proof. The representation (3.16) is obtained as in theorem 3.7. However, as W is not generally PLH in P, it remains to show that $\overline{W}^r$ can be chosen to be PLH. As $\overline{W}$ is increasing in y, (3.16) can be inverted in y to obtain

$$y = \overline{W}^{-1}\left(u, P^c, \overline{W}^r(P^r)\right). \tag{a}$$

Thus, I^r is separable from $_0I^c$ in the cost function. By theorem 3.7, there exists a representation in which the aggregator function of (a) is PLH. For the sake of notational simplicity let (a) be such a representation. Then invert the cost function to get the indirect utility function (3.16) in which the aggregator function $\overline{W}^r$ is PLH. ‖

Given the properties of $\overline{W}^r$ and $\overline{W}$, the former can be interpreted as a price index for group r, and $\overline{W}$ can be interpreted as an indirect utility function in y and nonnormalized prices $\left(P^c, \overline{W}^r(P^r)\right)$.

3.4.3 The Homothetic-Separability Equivalence Theorem

This subsection proves a theorem which underscores the profound implications for functional structure and duality of the hypothesis of a homogeneous sectoral ordering. The theorem is also fundamental to the theory of aggregation to be discussed in chapter 5. Before stating the theorem, we prove a well-known result that is instrumental in the proof of the theorem. The statement of the lemma requires some additional notation and separability conditions.

Define the binary partition of the extended index set

$$_0\tilde{I} = \{I^0, I\} = \{\{0\}, I\}.$$

We are interested in the separability of the set I—that is, *all* prices or quantities—from the singleton $\{0\}$, which represents either utility or expenditure. The representations of these structures can be readily inferred from theorem 3.7 and corollaries 3.7.1 and 3.7.2. In order to avoid needless repetition, we eschew formal statements of these representation results.

Lemma 3.4 *Assume that the utility function U satisfies the regularity conditions* $(R-1)$. *Then the following five statements are equivalent*:

(i)   *U is positively homothetic*;
(ii)   *there exist continuous functions $\tilde{C}$ and $\hat{C}$ such that C may be written as*

$$C(u,P)=\tilde{C}(u,\hat{C}(P));$$

(iii) *there exist continuous functions $\tilde{W}$ and $\hat{W}$ such that W may be written as*

$$W(y,P)=\tilde{W}(y,\hat{W}(P)),$$

 where $\tilde{W}$ is increasing in y;
(iv)   *V is negatively homothetic; and*
(v)   *there exist continuous functions $\tilde{F}$ and $\hat{F}$ such that F may be written as*

$$F(u,X)=\tilde{F}(u,\hat{F}(X)).$$

Moreover, (ii), (iii), and (v) imply that C, F, and W can be written in multiplicative form, so that

$$C(u,P)=\psi_c(u)\cdot\hat{C}(P), \qquad (3.17)$$

$$F(u,X)=\frac{\hat{F}(X)}{\psi_f(u)}, \qquad (3.18)$$

and

$$W(y,P)=\psi_w(y/\hat{W}(P)) \qquad (3.19)$$

where $\psi_c\colon \mathcal{R}(U)\to\Omega^1_+$, $\psi_f\colon \mathcal{R}(U)\to\Omega^1_+$, and $\psi_w\colon \Omega^1_+\to\Omega^1_+$ are increasing functions. Finally, if (and only if) U is PLH (equivalently, V is homogeneous *of degree minus one*),

$$C(u,P)=u\hat{C}(P),\qquad(3.20)$$

$$F(u,X)=\frac{1}{u}\hat{F}(X),\qquad(3.21)$$

and

$$W(y,P)=y/\hat{W}(P).\qquad(3.22)$$

Proof.

(i)$\Rightarrow$(ii).[14] Since U is homothetic, there exist functions $\tilde{U}$: $\Omega^n{\rightarrow}\mathbf{R}$ and h: $\mathcal{R}(\tilde{U}){\rightarrow}\mathbf{R}$ such that

$$U(X)=h(\tilde{U}(X))\qquad\forall X\in\Omega^n,$$

where $\tilde{U}$ is PLH and h is continuous and increasing. Let h^{-1} be the inverse mapping of h. Hence $\tilde{U}=h^{-1}\circ U$. Define a new utility variable by

$$v=h^{-1}(u)\qquad\forall u\in\mathcal{R}(U).$$

Then

$$C(u,P)=\min_{X}\{P{\cdot}X\,|\,U(X)\geqslant u\wedge X\in\Omega^n\}$$

$$=\min_{X}\{P{\cdot}X\,|\,\tilde{U}(X)\geqslant v\wedge X\in\Omega^n\}$$

$$=v\min_{X/v}\left\{P{\cdot}\frac{X}{v}\,\Big|\,\tilde{U}(X/v)\geqslant1\wedge\frac{X}{v}\in\Omega^n\right\}$$

$$=v\min_{X}\{P{\cdot}X\,|\,\tilde{U}(X)\geqslant1\wedge X\in\Omega^n\}$$

$$=h^{-1}(u)\tilde{C}(1,P),\qquad(a)$$

where

$$\tilde{C}(1,P)=\min_{X}\{P{\cdot}X\,|\,\tilde{U}(X)\geqslant1\wedge X\in\Omega^n\}$$

---

[14]This argument is essentially the same as Shephard's (1970: p. 93). Note also that for the sake of this argument we have normalized U so that $\mathcal{R}(U){\subseteq}\Omega^1_+$.

is the unit cost function for $\tilde{U}$. Let $\psi_c = h^{-1}$ and $\hat{C}(P) = \tilde{C}(1, P) \; \forall P \in \Omega_+^n$, so that

$$C(u, P) = \psi_c(u) \cdot \hat{C}(P), \tag{3.17}$$

which also satisfies (ii). Finally, when (and only when) U is PLH, $\psi_c(u) = h^{-1}(u) = u$ and thus (3.20) holds.

(ii)$\Rightarrow$(iii). We start with the representation of the cost function

$$y = C(u, P) = \tilde{C}(u, \hat{C}(P)), \tag{b}$$

where $\tilde{C}$ and $\hat{C}$ are continuous. Thus, employing theorem 3.7, I is separable from I^0, and $\tilde{C}$ and $\hat{C}$ can be normalized to be PLH. Assuming, for notational simplicity, that $\tilde{C}$ and $\hat{C}$ are already PLH, we have

$$y = \tilde{C}(u, 1)\hat{C}(P)$$
$$= \psi_c(u)\hat{C}(P), \qquad \text{say,}$$

where ψ_c is an increasing function of u. Solving for u,

$$u = W(y, P) = \psi_c^{-1}(y/\hat{C}(P)) = \psi_w(y/\hat{W}(P)) = \overline{W}(y, \hat{W}(P)),$$

where

$$\hat{W}(P) = \hat{C}(P),$$

$\hat{W}$ is PLH in P, and $\psi_w = \psi_c^{-1}$ is increasing in y. Of course, if (and only if) U is PLH, then $\psi_c(u) = u$ and ψ_w is the identity function, yielding (3.22).

(iii)$\Rightarrow$(iv). We are given the representation

$$u = W(y, P) = \tilde{W}(y, \hat{W}(P)),$$

where $\tilde{W}$ is increasing in y. Solving for y gives a cost function of the form (b). Repeating the argument of (ii)$\Rightarrow$(iii) from this point, retrieval of the indirect utility function gives (3.19). Next define $\hat{V} : \Omega_+^n \to \mathbf{R}$ by

$$\hat{V}(P/y) = \frac{y}{\hat{W}(P)} = \frac{1}{\hat{W}(P/y)}.$$

The indirect utility function V can be written as

$$V(P/y) = W(1, P/y)$$
$$= \psi_w(\hat{V}(P/y)),$$

where $\hat{V}$ is negatively homogeneous, since $\hat{W}$ is PLH. Hence, V is negatively homothetic.

(iv)$\Rightarrow$(v). The derivation of F from V,

$$F(u,X) = \min_{P} \left\{ P \cdot X \,|\, \overset{*}{V}(P) \leqslant u \wedge P \in \Omega^n \right\}$$

is mathmetically equivalent to the problem (a). Hence, noting that lemma 3.2 implies that $\overset{*}{V}$ has the appropriate structure, the result is proved by an argument that is analogous to the one for (i)$\Rightarrow$(ii).

(v)$\Rightarrow$(i). Lemma 3.2 gives us the representation

$$\overset{*}{F}(u,X) = \tilde{F}\left(u, \hat{F}(X)\right),$$

where $\tilde{F}$ and $\hat{F}$ are continuous. Reapplying the argument used for the cost function in (b), we can write

$$F(u,X) = \tilde{F}(u,1)\hat{F}(X).$$

Let $\psi_f(u) = 1/\tilde{F}(u,1)$, thus implying (3.18). Note that ψ_f is increasing in u since F is decreasing. Next solve

$$\frac{\hat{F}(X)}{\psi_f(u)} = 1$$

for u to obtain

$$u = U(X) = \psi_f^{-1}(\hat{F}(X)).$$

Since $\hat{F}$ is PLH and ψ_f^{-1} is increasing, the utility function U is positively homothetic. Finally, if (and only if) U is PLH, $\psi_f = \psi_f^{-1}$ is the identity function and (3.18) reduces to (3.21). $\|$

It is worth noting that the representations (3.17)–(3.19), together with the facts that $C(u,P)$ and $F(u,X)$ are positive and ψ_w is increasing, imply that $\bar{C}$, $\bar{F}$, and $\bar{W}$ are increasing in $\hat{C}(P)$, $\hat{F}(X)$, and $\hat{W}(P)$, respectively. Thus, because of the monotonicity properties of these functions, separability of I from I^0 implies strict separability of I from I^0. Hence the lemma could have been stated in terms of the appropriate separability conditions.

The "(i)$\Leftrightarrow$(ii)" part of this lemma and the associated multiplicative form is due to Shephard (1953, 1970). The "(i)$\Leftrightarrow$(iv)" part has been proved for differentiable functions by Samuelson (1965) and Lau (1969a). These and the other duality results were derived in the context of utility or production functions that are homothetic.

The equivalences of lemma 3.4 could be of interest to a researcher doing an econometric study of a production model, since either testing or maintaining a hypothesis of homotheticity (of U or V) is equivalent to testing or maintaining a hypothesis of separability (in C, F, or W). However, in other contexts, such as models of consumer behavior, homotheticity may not be a desirable maintained hypothesis. A generalization of lemma 3.4 which characterizes the homotheticity of sector-specific utility functions is now given.

Theorem 3.8 *Assume that the utility function satisfies the regularity conditions* (R-1). *Then the following statements are equivalent:*

(i)   *I^r is homothetically separable from I^c in U;*
(ii)   *I^r is separable from $_0I^c$ in C;*
(iii)   *I^r is separable from $_0I^c$ in F;*
(iv)   *I^r is separable from $_0I^c$ in W; and*
(v)   *I^r is homothetically separable from I^c in V.*

In addition, if $\overset{*}{V}$, $\overset{*}{C}$, and $\overset{*}{F}$ (the extensions of V, C, and F to the boundary of Ω^n) and U satisfy local nonsatiation on $\Omega^{(r)}$, "separable" can be replaced by "strictly separable" in (i)–(v).

Proof.

(i)⇒(ii). Since U^r is homothetic, it can be renormalized to be PLH as in lemma 3.3a. Specifically, if $U^r = \psi \circ \overline{U}^r$, where ψ is increasing and $\overline{U}^r$ is PLH, rewrite U as

$$U(X) = \hat{U}\left(X^c, \psi\left(\overline{U}^r(X^r)\right)\right) = \overline{U}\left(X^c, \overline{U}^r(X^r)\right).$$

Define the rth sector-specific cost function, $C^r : \mathcal{R}(\overline{U}^r) \times \Omega_+^{(r)} \to \Omega^1$, by

$$C^r(u_r, P^r) = \min_{X^r}\left\{ P^r \cdot X^r \mid X^r \in \Omega^{(r)} \wedge \overline{U}^r(X^r) \geq u_r \right\}.$$

Lemma 3.4 and the homogeneity property of $\overline{U}^r$ imply that

$$C^r(u_r, P^r) = u_r C^r(1, P^r)$$

$$= u_r \overline{C}^r(P^r), \qquad \text{say.}$$

This means that the cost function can be rewritten as

$$C(u,P) = \min_{X^c,u_r} \left\{ P^c \cdot X^c + \min_{X^r} \left\{ P^r \cdot X^r \mid X^r \in \Omega^{(r)} \wedge \overline{U}^r(X^r) \geqslant u_r \right\} \right.$$

$$\left. \mid (X^c, u^r) \in \Omega^{(c)} \times \mathcal{R}(\overline{U}^r) \wedge \overline{U}(X^c, u_r) \geqslant u \right\}$$

$$= \min_{X^c,u_r} \left\{ P^c \cdot X^c + u_r \overline{C}^r(P^r) \mid (X^c, u_r) \in \Omega^{(c)} \times \mathcal{R}(U^r) \wedge \overline{U}(X^c, u_r) \geqslant u \right\}.$$

Hence,

$$C(u,P) = \overline{C}\left(u, P^c, \overline{C}^r(P^r)\right), \tag{a}$$

where $\overline{C}$ is nondecreasing in $\overline{C}^r(P^r)$ because $\overline{U}$ is nondecreasing in u_r. Thus, I^r is separable from $_0 I^c$ in C. By theorem 3.1, if $\overset{*}{C}$ satisfies local nonsatiation on $\Omega^{(r)}$, then I^r is strictly separable from $_0 I^c$ in C.

(ii)$\Leftrightarrow$(iii). This is easily proved by a simple modification of the proof of theorem 3.6.

(ii)$\Rightarrow$(iv). By theorem 3.7, there exists a representation of C in which $\overline{C}^r$ is PLH. Let (a) be such a representation. Then invert the equation

$$\overline{C}\left(u, P^c, \overline{C}^r(P^r)\right) = y$$

in u to derive an indirect utility function with the required structure,

$$W(y,P) = \overline{W}\left(y, P^c, \overline{C}^r(P^r)\right) = \overline{W}\left(y, P^c, \overline{W}^r(P^r)\right),$$

where $\overline{W}^r$ is PLH. As W and $\overline{W}^r$ are nondecreasing in P^r, $\overline{W}$ is nonincreasing in $\overline{W}^r(P^r)$, implying that I^r is separable from I^c in W. If $\overset{*}{V}$, and hence $\overset{*}{W}$, satisfies local nonsatiation on $\Omega^{(r)}$, then I^r is strictly separable from I^c in W.

(iv)$\Rightarrow$(v). We start with the representation

$$W(y,P) = \overline{W}\left(y, P^c, \overline{W}^r(P^r)\right), \tag{b}$$

where W is nonincreasing (or decreasing) in $\overline{W}^r(P^r)$. If the preference ordering is characterized by a region of global satiation, W is a constant function over a subset of Ω_+^{n+1}. Letting $\overset{\circ}{W}$ be the restriction of W to the subset of Ω_+^{n+1} over which W is increasing in y, we have

$$\mathring{W}(y,P) = \overset{\circ}{\overline{W}}\left(y,P^c,\overline{W}^r(P^r)\right),$$

where $\overset{\circ}{\overline{W}}$ is the corresponding restriction of $\overline{W}$ to a subset of $\Omega_+^1 \times \Omega_+^{(c)} \times \mathcal{R}(\overline{W}^r)$, say S. Invert

$$u = \overset{\circ}{\overline{W}}\left(y,P^c,\overline{W}^r(P^r)\right)$$

in y to obtain the structure (a). By theorem 3.7, $\overline{C}^r(P^r)$ can be normalized to be PLH. Do so. Then upon retrieval of W [i.e., by inverting (a) to get (b) back] we have acquired a PLH aggregator function. For notational ease, let (b) now be that representation. $\overline{W}$ is then extended to the entire space $\Omega_+^1 \times \Omega_+^{(c)} \times \mathcal{R}(\overline{W}^r)$ by the identity

$$\overline{W}\left(\hat{y},\hat{P}^c,\overline{W}^r(\hat{P}^r)\right) = \sup\left\{\overset{\circ}{\overline{W}}\left(y,P^c,\overline{W}^r(P^r)\right)\middle|\left(y,P^c,\overline{W}^r(P^r)\right)\in S\right\}$$

$$\forall\left(\hat{y},\hat{P}^c,\overline{W}^r(\hat{P}^r)\right)\notin S.$$

Since $\overline{W}^r$ is PLH and W is HDO in (y,P), $\overline{W}$ is HDO in $\left(y,P^c,\overline{W}^r(P^r)\right)$; hence we can write

$$W(y,P) = \overline{W}\left(1,\frac{P^c}{y},\overline{W}^r\left(\frac{P^r}{y}\right)\right).$$

From the construction of W this implies that

$$V\left(\frac{P}{y}\right) = \overline{V}\left(\frac{P^c}{y},\overline{V}^r\left(\frac{P^r}{y}\right)\right) = \overline{W}\left(1,\frac{P^c}{y},\overline{W}^r\left(\frac{P^r}{y}\right)\right), \qquad \text{(c)}$$

where $\overline{V}^r(P^r/y) = \overline{W}^r(P^r/y)$, and $\overline{V}$ is nonincreasing (or decreasing) in $\overline{V}^r(P^r/y)$.

(v)$\Rightarrow$(i). By Lemma 3.2, the structure (c) can be extended to Ω^n by continuity from below. From the duality relationships stated in chapter 2 it is clear that the problem

$$\max_{P/y}\left\{-\overset{*}{V}\left(\frac{P}{y}\right)\right\} = \max_{P/y}\left\{-\overset{*}{\overline{V}}\left(\frac{P^c}{y},\overset{*}{\overline{V}}^r\left(\frac{P^r}{y}\right)\right)\right\}$$

subject to $\quad \dfrac{P}{y}\cdot X \leqslant 1, \quad \dfrac{P}{y}\in\Omega^n,$

is mathematically equivalent to the problem

$$\max_X \left\{ U(X) \right\} = \max_X \left\{ \overline{U}\left(X^c, \overline{U}^r(X^r)\right) \right\}$$

$$\text{subject to} \quad \frac{P}{y} \cdot X \leqslant 1, \quad X \in \Omega^n,$$

so that repeating the arguments that establish (i)⇒(v) completes the proof.
||

There is yet another way to characterize homothetic separability. As we have pointed out before, whenever there is a subset of variables separable in U, the corresponding subset is not, in general, separable in F. It is natural then to ask when it is that separability occurs in both U and F simultaneously. The result given below characterizes simultaneous strict separability of U and F in terms of homothetic separability. Thus we are able to extend the characterization of homothetic separability given in theorem 3.8. However, at this time, necessary and sufficient conditions for simultaneous nonstrict separability of U and F are not known.

In the proof of the theorem on simultaneous strict separability of F and U, the following lemma is used:

Lemma 3.5   *Assume that U satisfies (R-1) and that the sector I^c is strictly essential. Then strict separability of I^r from I^c in U implies that U satisfies local nonsatiation for all $X \in \Omega^n$.*

Proof.   Suppose that I^r is strictly separable from I^c and that U violates local nonsatiation. By the quasi-concavity of U, there exists a region of global satiation $L(\sup \mathcal{R}(U))$ with a nonempty interior. Let $\hat{X} \in \operatorname{int} L(\sup \mathcal{R}(U)) = \operatorname{int} L(U(\hat{X}))$. Then

$$\hat{X}^r \in \operatorname{int} \beta^r(\hat{X}^c, \hat{X}^r). \tag{i}$$

By the strict essentiality of I^c, there exists an $\overline{X}^c \in \Omega^{(c)}$ such that $U(\overline{X}^c, \hat{X}^r) < U(\hat{X}^c, \hat{X}^r)$. By the quasi-concavity of U, $(\overline{X}^c, \hat{X}^r)$ is not a point of local satiation, and is therefore in the boundary of $L(U(\overline{X}^c, \hat{X}^r))$. Hence, $\hat{X}^r \notin \operatorname{int} \beta^r(\overline{X}^r, \hat{X}^r)$; together with ($i$), this implies that

$$\beta^r(\hat{X}^c, \hat{X}^r) \neq \beta^r(\overline{X}^r, \hat{X}^r),$$

violating the strict separability of I^r. ||

Theorem 3.9   *Assume that U satisfies the regularity conditions (R-1) and that I^c is strictly essential. Then I^r is strictly separable from I^c in both U and F if and only if I^r is homothetically strictly separable from I^c in U.*

Proof.   *Necessity:* Since I^r is strictly separable from I^c in U and therefore in $\mathring{U}$ (the restriction of U to Ω^n_+),

$$\mathring{\beta}^r(X^c,X^r) = \left\{ \hat{X}^r \in \Omega^{(r)}_+ \,|\, U(X^c,\hat{X}^r) \geqslant U(X^c,X^r) \right\}$$

is invariant with respect to changes in X^c for all values of $X^r \in \Omega^{(r)}_+$. Using the relationship between the transformation function and level sets of U (see chapter 2),

$$\left\{ X \in \Omega^n_+ \,|\, U(X) \geqslant u \right\} = \left\{ X \in \Omega^n_+ \,|\, F(u,X) \geqslant 1 \right\},$$

it is possible to characterize separability of I^r in $\mathring{U}$ in terms of F. To see this, first note that $\mathring{\beta}^r(X^c,X^r)$ is the *intersection* of

$$\left\{ (X^c,\hat{X}^r) \in \Omega^{(c)}_+ \times \Omega^{(r)}_+ \,|\, F\big(U(X^c,X^r),X^c,\hat{X}^r\big) \geqslant 1 \right\}$$

with $\{X^c\} \times \Omega^{(r)}_+$ projected onto $\Omega^{(r)}_+$. Hence, separability of I^r from I^c in $\mathring{U}$ is equivalent to the invariance of

$$\left\{ \hat{X}^r \in \Omega^{(r)}_+ \,|\, F\big(U(X^c,X^r),X^c,\hat{X}^r\big) \geqslant 1 \right\}$$

with respect to changes in X^c $\forall X^r \in \Omega^{(r)}_+$. This, in turn, is equivalent to

$$\left\{ \hat{X}^r \in \Omega^{(r)}_+ \,|\, F\big(U(X^c,X^r),X^c,\hat{X}^r\big) \geqslant 1 \right\}$$

$$= \left\{ \hat{X}^r \in \Omega^{(r)}_+ \,|\, F\big(U(\tilde{X}^c,X^r),\tilde{X}^c,\hat{X}^r\big) \geqslant 1 \right\}$$

$$\forall (X^c,\tilde{X}^c,X^r) \in \Omega^{(c)}_+ \times \Omega^{(c)}_+ \times \Omega^{(r)}_+. \tag{a}$$

Since I^r is also strictly separable from I^c in F,

$$\gamma^r(u,X^c,X^r) = \left\{ \hat{X}^r \in \Omega^{(r)}_+ \,|\, F(u,X^c,\hat{X}^r) \geqslant F(u,X^c,X^r) \right\} \tag{b}$$

is invariant with respect to changes in X^c $\forall u \in \mathcal{R}(\mathring{U})$, $\forall X^r \in \Omega^{(r)}_+$. Thus, strict separability in F implies that

$$\left\{ \hat{X}^r \in \Omega^{(r)} \,|\, F(u,X^c,\hat{X}^r) \geqslant F(u,X^c,X^r) \right\}$$

$$= \left\{ \hat{X}^r \in \Omega^{(r)} \,|\, F(u,\tilde{X}^c,\hat{X}^r) \geqslant F(u,\tilde{X}^c,X^r) \right\}$$

$$\forall (X^c,\tilde{X}^c,X^r,u) \in \Omega^{(c)}_+ \times \Omega^{(c)}_+ \times \Omega^{(r)}_+ \times \mathcal{R}(\mathring{U}). \tag{c}$$

Noting that this invariance holds for all $u \in \mathcal{R}(\mathring{U})$ and letting $u =$

$U(X^c, X^r)$, (b) is equal to

$$\{\hat{X}^r \in \Omega_+^{(r)} | F(U(X^c, X^r), X^c, \hat{X}^r) \geqslant F(U(X^c, X^r), X^c, X^r)\}.$$

Thus, strict separability of I^r from I^c in F implies that

$$\{\hat{X}^r \in \Omega_+^{(r)} | F(U(X^c, X^r), X^c, \hat{X}^r) \geqslant F(U(X^c, X^r), X^c, X^r)\}$$

$$= \{\hat{X}^r \in \Omega_+^{(r)} | F(U(X^c, X^r), \tilde{X}^c, \hat{X}^r) \geqslant F(U(X^c, X^r), \tilde{X}^c, X^r)\}$$

$$\forall (X^c, \tilde{X}^c, X^r) \in \Omega_+^{(c)} \times \Omega_+^{(c)} \times \Omega_+^{(r)}. \tag{d}$$

However, strict essentiality of I^c and strict separability of I^r, together with Lemma 3.5 and Lemma A.1 (in the Appendix) imply that

$$F(U(X^c, X^r), X^c, X^r) = 1. \tag{e}$$

Consequently, the left hand side of (a) is identical to the left hand side of (d). Hence, combining (a) (which is equivalent to the separability of I^r from I^c in $\dot{U}$) and (d) (which is implied by the separability of I^r from I^c in F), we get that (d) is equivalent to

$$\{\hat{X}^r \in \Omega_+^{(r)} | F(U(\tilde{X}^c, X^r), \tilde{X}^c, \hat{X}^r) \geqslant F(U(\tilde{X}^c, X^r), \tilde{X}^c, X^r) = 1\}$$

$$= \{\hat{X}^r \in \Omega_+^{(r)} | F(U(X^c, X^r), \tilde{X}^c, X^r) \geqslant F(U(X^c, X^r), \tilde{X}^c, X^r)\}$$

$$\forall (\tilde{X}^c, X^c, X^r) \in \Omega_+^{(c)} \times \Omega_+^{(c)} \times \Omega_+^r, \tag{f}$$

where we have again invoked (e). This implies that $\gamma^r(u, X^c, X^r)$ is invariant with respect to u as well as X^c. Thus, F is strictly separable in the partition $_0\bar{I}$ and therefore, by corollary 3.7.1, can be written as in equation (3.15).

Because of (e), the direct utility function can be found by inverting

$$\bar{F}\left(u, X^c, \bar{F}(X^r)\right) = 1 \tag{g}$$

in u; this yields

$$U(X) = \overset{*}{U}\left(X^c, \bar{F}^r(X^r)\right) \tag{h}$$

or, more generally,

$$U(X) = \bar{U}\left(X^c, U^r(X^r)\right), \tag{i}$$

where

$$U^r(X^r) = \phi^r\left(\bar{F}^r(X^r)\right)$$

is homothetic (and, of course, ϕ^r is an increasing function).

Sufficiency is an immediate implication of Theorem 3.8.   ‖

A somewhat different way to characterize homothetic strict separability arises from imposing separability simultaneously on the indirect utility function and the cost function.

Corollary 3.9.1 *Assume U satisfies* (R-1) *and that I^c is strictly essential. Then I^r is strictly separable from I^c in both V and C if and only if I^r is homothetically strictly separable from I^c in V.*

Proof.   Follows from theorem 3.9 by duality.   ‖

3.5   CONCLUDING REMARKS

The representation theorems of sections 3.3 and 3.4 evince the intimate relationship between separability and aggregation. The separability of a group of variables from its complement is equivalent to the possibility of forming an aggregate function for that group which can be aggregated consistently into a macro function of the image of the aggregator function and the complementary variables. As the aggregator functions inherit the properties of the parent function,[15] the aggregators U^r, C^r, V^r, and F^r can respectively be interpreted as sectoral utility (or production), cost, reciprocal indirect utility (or production),[16] and transformation functions. Moreover, the macro functions, $\bar{U}$ and $\bar{V}$, also have the properties of direct and indirect utility or production functions in which one of the arguments, $U^r(X^r)$ or $V^r(P/y)$, is a composite commodity or composite normalized price. Although $\bar{F}$ and $\bar{C}$ have some of the properties of transformation and cost functions, the arguments $F^r(u, X^r)$ and $C^r(u, P^r)$ cannot be interpreted as composite commodities or prices.

If the rth sector is implicitly separable from its complement I^c, both F and C have the appropriate separability property. Moreover, the sectoral

---

[15]If I^r is only nonstrictly separable from I^c in the cost or transformation function, we cannot say that the aggregators inherit strict monotonicity in u (see theorem 3.4 and corollary 3.4.1).

[16]Refer back to section 3.4 for a discussion of the reason for making V^r a reciprocal indirect utility function.

transformation and cost functions are related by

$$C^r(u, P^r) = \min_{X^r} \left\{ P^r \cdot X^r \,|\, X^r \in \Omega^{(r)} \wedge \overset{*}{F}{}^r(u, X^r) \geqslant 1 \right\}$$

and

$$F^r(u, X^r) = \min_{P^r} \left\{ P^r \cdot X^r \,|\, P^r \in \Omega^n \wedge \overset{*}{C}{}^r(u, P^r) \geqslant 1 \right\}.$$

It is also possible to define sectoral direct and indirect utility functions by

$$\tilde{U}^r(X^r) = \max_u \left\{ u \in \mathcal{R}(U^r) \,|\, F^r(u, X^r) \geqslant 1 \right\}$$

and

$$\tilde{V}^r(P^r) = \min_u \left\{ u \in \mathcal{R}(V^r) \,|\, C^r(u, P^r) \geqslant 1 \right\}.$$

However, as conjugate implicit separability does not imply explicit separability, these sectoral utility functions cannot generally be aggregated into macro utility functions. Hence their usefulness is limited (see, however, the discussion of conditional utility functions in section 5.2). Similarly, if the direct utility function satisfies the separability condition, we can derive sectoral transformation, cost, and indirect utility functions from U^r by employing the appropriate operations described in chapter 2 (see especially figure 2.4). However, as direct explicit separability does not imply indirect explicit separability or conjugate implicit separability, these derived sectoral functions cannot generally be aggregated consistently into macro functions. A similar statement holds for the derivation of sectoral direct utility, cost, and transformation functions from the aggregator function of a separable indirect utility function.

   If the conditional ordering on $\Omega^{(r)}$ is homogeneous, the above structures fall into place as an integrated system which has a very useful and interesting interpretation. In the first place, it becomes possible to aggregate over commodities and prices alone in the transformation and cost functions. The images of the aggregator functions, $\bar{F}^r$ and $\bar{C}^r$, can be interpreted as a composite commodity and a composite price. Consequently, $\bar{F}$ and $\bar{C}$ can be interpreted as macro transformation and cost functions. Moreover, $\bar{F}^r$ and $\bar{C}^r$ are also the aggregator functions of the utility function and the indirect utility function in nonnormalized prices.

Hence, there are only two aggregators: a quantity index and a price index. Moreover, as will be shown in chapter 5, the product of the two index images, $\bar{C}^r(P^r)\cdot\bar{F}^r(X^r)$, is the optimal expenditure on commodities in sector r if X^r is optimal at prices P^r. This fact is very important for the consistency of two-stage algorithms which employ price and quantity indices (see chapter 5). This algorithm also entails the optimal allocation of sectoral expenditure on commodities in the sector without reference to prices of commodities not in the sector. As shown in chapter 5, this concept—called decentralizability—is also intimately related to separability.

FUNCTIONAL STRUCTURE, DECENTRALIZATION, AND AGGREGATION

4

Representation and Duality
Theorems for Symmetrically
Structured Preferences and Technologies

This chapter extends the results of chapter 3 by allowing for more than one separable group. The implied functional structures are therefore somewhat more complicated than those examined in chapter 3. The structures are simplified, however, by the *assumption* that the separability relation is symmetric; that is, I^r is separable from I^c (the complement of I^r in I) if and only if I^c is separable from I^r. These symmetric structures are classified into two types: (1) (strict)[1] separability of each group of variables from its complement, and (2) (strict) separability of arbitrary unions of groups of variables from their complements. We refer to the first of these notions quite simply as *(strict) separability* of the function (or of the underlying preference ordering or technology) and to the second as *complete (strict) separability* of the function. These two symmetric structures have received considerable attention in the literature. Following Strotz (1959), most researchers have referred to these two structures as "weak separability" and "strong separability", respectively. We prefer the alternative terminology, which is reasonably consistent with the seminal work of Gorman (1968b).

After some preliminary notation is laid out, the chapter begins in section 4.1 with a straightforward generalization of the representation theorems of sections 3.3 and 3.4 to the case of multiple separable sectors. Section 4.2 contains a theorem of Gorman (1968b) on the identification of separable sets. This theorem is very useful in many of the proofs that follow. Section 4.3 examines separable structures in the partition of the extended index set (see subsection 3.4.2), and extends the duality theorems of subsection 3.4.3

---

[1]The distinction between separability and strict separability is discussed in section 3.1.

to these structures. Sections 4.4 and 4.5 are the complete separability analogues of sections 4.1 and 4.3. Section 4.6, however, stands apart from the earlier sections. In this section we analyze the problems associated with the existence of an additive representation when there are only two groups, by extending a theorem of Sono (1945, 1961) which invokes the concept of independence; this latter concept neither implies nor is implied by separability. Section 4.7 invokes the notion of strict independence (a strengthening of Sono's independence condition) to derive multiplicative structures. Finally, the concluding section 4.8 summarizes the relationships between (strict) separability and (strict) independence.

4.1   SEPARABLE STRUCTURES

4.1.1   Notation

Separable structures are defined with respect to a particular partition of the set of variables under consideration. In this chapter, then, commodities are partitioned into m subsets which correspond to a partition of the n prices of these commodities into m subsets. A distinction is made between (1) a partition of n normalized (by total expenditure) prices and (2) a partition consisting of the m subsets of prices or commodities and an $(m+1)$th subset which is a singleton corresponding to total expenditure or utility.

As in chapter 3, let

$$I = \{1, 2, \ldots, n\}$$

be the set of the n variable indices. These indices may be those of the n commodities or the n normalized prices. Let $I^o = \{0\}$, and let

$$_oI = \{0, 1, \ldots, n\} = I^o \cup I$$

be a set of $n+1$ variable indices. They correspond to the indices of the n prices or commodities in I plus an additional index, the number zero. This represents either expenditure or real income, depending upon the context. For example, when discussing cost functions, the number zero refers to the utility indicator u, and in the nonnormalized indirect utility function it represents total expenditure.

We define a partition of I into m subsets as

$$\hat{I} = \{I^1, \ldots, I^r, \ldots, I^m\}.$$

Whenever the ith commodity belongs to the rth category (or sector) of commodities, we write $i \in I^r$. The same convention applies whenever the ith normalized price belongs to the rth sector of normalized prices. A partition of $_oI$ into $m+1$ subsets is

$$_o\hat{I} = \{ I^o, I^1, \ldots, I^r, \ldots, I^m \}.$$

Corresponding to the partition $\hat{I}$, we denote vectors in Ω^n in ways that reflect the partition.

First, express Ω^n as a Cartesian product of appropriate subspaces; i.e.,

$$\Omega^n = \Omega^{(1)} \times \cdots \times \Omega^{(r)} \times \cdots \times \Omega^{(m)}.$$

Strictly speaking, Ω^n is not equal to this Cartesian product unless the indices are ordered so that

$$I^1 = \{ 1, 2, \ldots, n_1 \},$$

$$\vdots$$

$$I^r = \left\{ \sum_{s=1}^{r-1} n_s + 1, \ \sum_{s=1}^{r-1} n_s + 2, \ldots, \ \sum_{s=1}^{r} n_s \right\},$$

$$\vdots$$

$$I^m = \left\{ \sum_{s=1}^{m-1} n_s + 1, \ldots, \ \sum_{s=1}^{m} n_s \right\}.$$

In order to avoid complicating the notation, we assume that the index set has been ordered so as to conform to this partition of I. Note also that the definition of Ω^n implies that the origin is deleted from one of the subspace orthants.

The dimension of $\Omega^{(r)}$ is given by the cardinality of I^r, say n_r. A commodity vector $X \in \Omega^n$ can be written as

$$X = (X^1, \ldots, X^r, \ldots, X^m).$$

Similarly, a price vector can be written as

$$P = (P^1, \ldots, P^r, \ldots, P^m).$$

When the ith commodity or price is in the rth category, x_i is a component of the vector $X^r \in \Omega^{(r)}$ and p_i is a component of the vector $P^r \in \Omega_+^{(r)}$.

Analogous notation applies to the partition $_o\hat{I}$; namely,

$$(u,P)=(u,P^1,\ldots,P^r,\ldots,P^m)\in\Re(U)\times\Omega_+^n,$$

$$(y,P)=(y,P^1,\ldots,P^r,\ldots,P^m)\in\Omega_+^{n+1},$$

and

$$(u,X)=(u,X^1,\ldots,X^r,\ldots,X^m)\in\Re(u)\times\Omega^n.$$

4.1.2 Representation Theorems

Generally speaking, consumer preferences are said to be (*strictly*) *separable* in the partition $\hat{I}$ if each sector I^r is (strictly) separable from its complement in I. We should repeat the statement that although we define (strict) separability below in terms of the utility, cost, and transformation functions, it is the preference orderings induced on the domains of these functions that have structure, and these preference structures are represented by structured (utility, cost, or transformation) functions. With this caveat in mind, we say that a *direct* utility function U is (strictly) separable in the partition $\hat{I}$ if each commodity sector $I^r\in\hat{I}$ is separable from its complement in I.

The representation theorem for a single (strictly) separable set (theorem 3.2) is easily extended to the case of (strict) separability in an m-group partition.

Theorem 4.1 *Suppose the utility function U satisfies the regularity conditions $(R\text{-}1)$.[2] Then U is separable in $\hat{I}$ if and only if there exist $m+1$ functions,*

$$U^r:\Omega^{(r)}\to\mathbf{R},\qquad r=1,\ldots,m,$$

and

$$\hat{U}:\underset{r=1}{\overset{m}{\times}}\Re(U^r)\to\mathbf{R},$$

which satisfy $(R\text{-}1)$ and

$$U(X)=\hat{U}\big(U^1(X^1),\ldots,U^r(X^r),\ldots,U^m(X^m)\big). \tag{4.1}$$

Moreover, if U is strictly separable, $\hat{U}$ is increasing.

---

[2](R-1): continuity, positive monotonicity, and quasi-concavity (see section 2.1).

Proof.   The sufficiency of (4.1) for (strict) separability is established by a repeated application of the sufficiency proof of theorems 3.2a and b. To prove necessity, we hypothesize that I^r is separable from its complement in I, I^c. By theorems 3.2b and 3.3b, this is equivalent to the existence of an aggregator for I^r, $U^r : \Omega^{(r)} \to \mathbf{R}$, and a macro function, $\bar{U} : \Omega^{(c)} \times \mathcal{R}(U^r) \to \mathbf{R}$, both satisfying (R-1), such that

$$U(X) = \bar{U}(X^c, U^r(X^r)).$$

Consider any sector I^s where $s \neq r$, and define $I^t = I^c - I^s$. Since

$$\left\{ \hat{X}^s \in \Omega^{(s)} | U(X^t, \hat{X}^s, X^r) \geqslant U(X^t, X^s, X^r) \right\}$$

$$= \left\{ \hat{X}^s \in \Omega^{(s)} | \bar{U}(X^t, \hat{X}^s, U^r(X^r)) \geqslant \bar{U}(X^t, X^s, U^r(X^r)) \right\},$$

separability of I^s in U from its complement in I is equivalent to separability of I^s in $\bar{U}$ from its complement in $(I - I^r) \cup \{r\}$, where r is the index of the variable $U^r(X^r)$. By theorems 3.2b and 3.3b, this is equivalent to the existence of functions $U^s : \Omega^{(s)} \to \mathbf{R}$ and $\bar{\bar{U}} : \Omega^{(t)} \times \mathcal{R}(U^s) \times \mathcal{R}(U^r) \to \mathbf{R}$, both satisfying (R-1), such that

$$U(X) = \bar{\bar{U}}(X^t, U^s(X^s), U^r(X^r)).$$

Repeated application of this argument proves the result for nonstrict separability. For strict separability, repeat the above argument using theorems 3.2a and 3.3a.   ‖

It might be noted that the equivalence of separability and the structure (4.1) (with a monotonic $\hat{U}$) requires only continuity and monotonicity of U (the other regularity property—quasi-concavity—is unnecessary). Moreover, the equivalence of strict separability and (4.1) with a strictly monotonic $\hat{U}$ requires no regularity conditions on U. We maintain our usual regularity conditions throughout this chapter in order to simplify the exposition.

The inheritance of the regularity properties (R-1) by $\hat{U}$ and U^r is an important feature of the representation theorem 4.1 because it rationalizes the interpretation of the m aggregators U^r, $r = 1, \ldots, m$, as sectoral utility or production functions and of $\hat{U}$ as a macro utility or production function defined over quantities of composite commodities or inputs, $U^1(X^1), \ldots, U^m(X^m)$. In fact, endowing the parent function U with additional properties often bestows these same properties on the macro and aggregator functions. These facts are summarized in the following corollary.

Corollary 4.1.1 *Suppose that U satisfies* (R-1). *If U has any of the following properties, Û and each U^r can be chosen to possess the same property:* (i) *strict positive monotonicity,*[3] (ii) *strict quasi-concavity,* (iii) *homotheticity,*[4] *and* (iv) *positive linear homogeneity. Finally, if U is strictly separable, Û and each U^r inherit differentiability and each U^r inherits (strict) concavity.*

The reader may note that because the conjunction of quasi-concavity and (iv) imply concavity, it follows that if U is concave and PLH, then Û and each U^r can be chosen to be PLH and concave.

As noted in corollary 4.1.1, differentiability and concavity are inherited by U^r if U is strictly separable, but it is not known whether these properties are inherited by aggregators induced by nonstrict separability. This distinction underscores the contrast, noted in chapter 3, between methods of proof of aggregator inheritance properties under strict and under nonstrict separability assumptions. If a function is strictly separable, we can exploit the reference-vector construction of the aggregator function. This constructive technique is so important for the theory of (symmetric or nonsymmetric) functional structure induced by strict separability that we formalize it in the following corollary.

Corollary 4.1.2 *Suppose that U is strictly separable. Then for each aggregator function U^r in* (4.1), *there is an appropriate normalization of the utility function such that*

$$U^r(X^r) = U(O^1,\ldots,O^{r-1},X^r,O^{r+1},\ldots,O^m), \qquad (4.2)$$

where $O^t \in \Omega^{(t)}$, $t = 1,\ldots,r-1,r+1,\ldots,m$, are reference vectors.

Proof. As the order in which the aggregator functions are constructed in the proof of theorem 4.1 is arbitrary, the corollary follows immediately from corollary 3.2.0a. ‖

Recall that quasi-concavity of Û might require a renormalization of the constructed function. (See the proof of theorem 3.3a.)

As in the construction of corollary 3.2.0a, the reference vectors can be—but need not be—the zero vector if the domain of U includes the boundary of the nonnegative orthant.

The representation and inheritance results for (strictly) separable indirect utility, cost, and transformation functions are analogous to theorem 4.1 and its corollaries.

---

[3] Of course, if U is strictly separable, Û necessarily satisfies strict monotonicity.
[4] Of course, Û and each U^r *must* be homothetic if U is.

The indirect utility or production function V is (strictly) separable in the partition $\hat{I}$ if each normalized price sector $I^r \in \hat{I}$ is (strictly) separable from its complement in I.

Corollary 4.1.3 *Suppose the indirect utility function V satisfies the regularity conditions* (R-2).[5] *Then V is separable in $\hat{I}$ if and only if there exist $m+1$ functions,*

$$V^r : \Omega_+^{(r)} \to \mathbf{R}, \qquad r = 1, \ldots, m,$$

and

$$\hat{V} : \underset{r=1}{\overset{m}{\times}} \mathcal{R}(V^r) \to \mathbf{R},$$

such that

$$V(P/y) = \hat{V}\left(V^1(P^1/y), \ldots, V^m(P^m/y)\right), \tag{4.3}$$

where $\hat{V}$ satisfies (R-2) *and each V^r satisfies* (R-1). *In addition, if V has any of the following properties, then $\hat{V}$ can be chosen to possess the same property, and each V^r, $r = 1, \ldots, m$, can be chosen to have the corresponding property listed in corollary 4.1.1: (i) strict negative monotonicity, (ii) strict quasi-convexity, (iii) negative homotheticity, and (iv) negative homogeneity. Finally, if V is strictly separable, then $\hat{V}$ is strictly monotonic, $\hat{V}$ and each V^r inherit differentiability, and each V^r can be chosen (strictly) concave if V is (strictly) convex.*

Proof. By repeated application of corollaries 3.2.1 and 3.5.1. ‖

As in chapter 3, we normalize the aggregator functions V^r, $r = 1, \ldots, m$, to satisfy the regularity conditions (R-1) (continuity, positive monotonicity, and quasi-concavity) and we normalize the macro function $\hat{V}$ to satisfy the regularity conditions (R-2) (continuity, negative monotonicity, and quasi-convexity). Consequently $\hat{V}$ is interpreted as a macro indirect utility or production function, and each V^r, $r = 1, \ldots, m$, is interpreted as a reciprocal indirect utility or production function.

In general, (strict) separability of U in $\hat{I}$ does not imply, nor is it implied by, (strict) separability of V in $\hat{I}$. Hence, a (strictly) separable direct utility function represents a different class of consumer preference orderings (production technologies) than does a (strictly) separable indirect utility function. In addition, it should be noted that the above does not necessarily exhaust the structure in these functions. That is, each aggregator may itself have some structure.

---

[5](R-2): Continuity, negative monotonicity, and quasi-convexity (see section 2.2).

The next two corollaries state the representation results for the cost and transformation functions when (strict) separability with respect to $\hat{I}$ is imposed. The chief difference between these and the preceding results centers on the fact that (strict) separability with respect to $\hat{I}$ does *not* imply (strict) separability with respect to $_0\hat{I}$. That is, the fact that I^r is (strictly) separable from its complement in I does *not* imply that it is (strictly) separable from I^0.

The cost function is (strictly) separable in the partition $\hat{I}$ if each price sector $I^r \in \hat{I}$ is (strictly) separable from its complement in I, i.e., from all prices in the remaining price sectors. Note again that I^r is *not* separable from the utility or output variable, whose index is the single element of I^0.

Corollary 4.1.4 *Suppose the cost function C satisfies the regularity conditions* (R-3).[6] *Then C is separable in $\hat{I}$ if and only if there exist $m+1$ functions,*

$$C^r : \mathcal{R}(U) \times \Omega_+^{(r)} \to \Omega_+^1, \qquad r = 1, \ldots, m,$$

and

$$\hat{C} : \mathcal{R}(U) \times \overset{m}{\underset{r=1}{\times}} \mathcal{R}(C^r) \to \Omega_+^1,$$

all satisfying (R-3P),[7] *such that*

$$C(u, P) = \hat{C}\left(u, C^1(u, P^1), \ldots, C^m(u, P^m)\right). \tag{4.4}$$

Finally, if C is strictly separable in $\hat{I}$, $\hat{C}$ is continuous and the following results hold: (a) *$\hat{C}(u, \cdot)$ is increasing;* (b) *$\hat{C}(u, \cdot)$ and each $C^r(u, \cdot)$ inherit differentiability in P;* (c) *each C^r satisfies* (R-3); *and* (d) *each $C^r(\cdot, P^r)$ inherits* (*strict*) *convexity and positive linear homogeneity in u.*

Proof. Follows from repeated application of theorem 3.4 and corollary 3.5.2. ‖

This corollary underscores an important advantage of working with strict separability of the cost function; in this case, the aggregator functions C^r, $r = 1, \ldots, m$ inherit the regularity properties (R-3) and can there-

---

[6](R-3): Continuity in (u, P), strict positive monotonicity in u, and positive monotonicity, positive linear homogeneity, and concavity in prices (see section 2.3). We emphasize again that the equivalences of the representation (4.4) and separability of C can be proved maintaining only continuity and monotonicity, and if C is strictly separable no regularity conditions are required for this equivalence.

[7](R-3P): Continuity, positive monotonicity, positive linear homogeneity, and concavity in prices. $\hat{C}$ satisfies (R-3P) if it has these properties in $(C^1(u, P^1), \ldots, C^m(u, P^m))$.

fore be interpreted as sectoral cost functions. Under the condition of nonstrict separability, however, it is only known that C^r satisfies (R-3P); strict monotonicity of C^r in u has been neither proved nor disproved. Unfortunately, in neither case does the macro function satisfy (R-3), since $\hat{C}$ is definitely *not* increasing in u. (See the discussion of these points in subsection 3.3.3.) Moreover, the arguments of $\hat{C}$ (other than u) are not really composite prices, since they depend upon the utility or output level as well as upon sectoral prices.

The transformation function is (strictly) separable in the partition $\hat{I}$ if each commodity sector $I^r \in \hat{I}$ is (strictly) separable from its complement in I, i.e., from all commodities in the remaining commodity sectors. Again note that, as with the cost function, I^r is *not* separable from I^0, the singleton set containing the utility or output variable index.

Corollary 4.1.5 *Suppose that the transformation function F satisfies the regularity properties* (R-4).[8] *Then F is separable in $\hat{I}$ if and only if there exist* $m + 1$ *functions*

$$F^r : \mathfrak{R}(U) \times \Omega_+^{(r)} \to \Omega_+^1, \qquad r = 1, \ldots, m,$$

and

$$\hat{F} : \mathfrak{R}(U) \times \underset{r=1}{\overset{m}{\times}} \mathfrak{R}(F^r) \to \Omega_+^1,$$

all satisfying $(R\text{-}4X)$,[9] *such that*

$$F(u, X) = \hat{F}\left(u, F^1(u, X^1), \ldots, F^m(u, X^m)\right). \tag{4.5}$$

Finally, if F is strictly separable in $\hat{I}$, $\hat{F}$ is continuous and the following results hold: (a) $\hat{F}(u, \cdot)$ *is increasing;* (b) $\hat{F}(u, \cdot)$ *and each $F^r(u, \cdot)$ inherit differentiability in X;* (c) *each F^r satisfies* (R-4); *and* (d) *each $F^r(\cdot, X^r)$ inherits* (strict) *convexity and negative homogeneity in u.*

Proof. Follows from the repeated application of corollaries 3.4.1 and 3.5.3. ‖

To avoid tedium in the statements of corollaries 4.1.3–4.1.5, we have not formalized, for the case of strict separability, the reference-vector construction of the aggregator functions. Nevertheless, it is true that, given strict

---

[8](R-4): Continuity in (u, X), strict negative monotonicity in u, and positive monotonicity, positive linear homogeneity, and concavity in X (see section 2.3.2).

[9](R-4X): Continuity, positive monotonicity, concavity, and positive linear homogeneity in X^r or in $\left(F^1(u, X^1), \ldots, F^m(u, X^m)\right)$.

separability, the aggregator functions in corollaries 4.1.3–4.1.5 can be chosen as in corollary 4.1.1. For example, the cost aggregator function C^r can be chosen so that

$$C^r(u, P^r) = C(u, O^1, \ldots, O^{r-1}, P^r, O^{r+1}, \ldots, O^m),$$

where $O^t \in \Omega^{(t)}$, $t = 1, \ldots, m$ $(t \neq r)$, is an appropriate reference vector. Note that in this case the reference vectors cannot be zero vectors, since the domain of C does not include the boundaries of the nonnegative orthant.

4.1.3 Conjugate Implicit (Strict) Separability

(Strict) separability of the utility functions does not imply, nor is it implied by, (strict) separability of the cost or transformation functions. It is the case, however, that the cost function is (strictly) separable if and only if the transformation function is (strictly) separable.

The following theorem is due to Gorman (1970) and McFadden (1970).

Theorem 4.2 *Suppose that C satisfies the regularity conditions $(R\text{-}3)$ and that F satisfies $(R\text{-}4)$. Then C is separable in the partition $\hat{I}$ if and only if F is separable in $\hat{I}$. Moreover, if the extensions of F and C to the boundary are locally nonsated on each $\Omega^{(r)}$, $r = 1, \ldots, m$, then "separable" may be replaced by "strictly separable" in the above statement.*

Proof. Follows from repeated application of theorem 3.6. ‖

Following the nomenclature introduced in chapter 3, we refer to (strict) separability of the cost and transformation functions as *conjugate implicit (strict) separability*. (Strict) separability of the direct and indirect utility functions will sometimes be called explicit direct and indirect (strict) separability, respectively.

4.2 IDENTIFICATION OF SEPARABLE SECTORS

In the preceding section the index set I was partitioned into m disjoint subsets; i.e., no two separable sectors contained common elements. This type of structure was assumed directly; hence there was no problem in identifying the separable sectors. Frequently, however, the structure is implied by other assumptions which have been made. In this case it may be difficult to identify the appropriate partition of the variables. The identification of strictly separable sectors is facilitated by a remarkable theorem due to Gorman (1968b: theorem 1). Suppose that two sets of variable indices, which have a nonempty intersection, and neither of which contains the other, are each strictly separable from their respective complements. The theorem states that the union, the intersection, the differences, and the symmetric difference are each strictly separable from their respective complements. This theorem is very important for our purposes. We present that part of the theorem here that is important for strictly separable structures. The remaining results are reserved for the section on completely strictly separable structures.

Recall from subsection 3.3.3 that a sector I^r is essential if, for each $\hat{X}^r \in \Omega^{(r)}$, the set

$$\{X^r \in \Omega^{(r)} | U(X^c, X^r) = U(X^c, \hat{X}^r)\}$$

is a proper subset of $\Omega^{(r)}$ for at least one point $X^c \in \Omega^{(c)}$. We assume that all sectors are essential. A sector is said to be *strictly* essential if it is essential for *all* points $X^c \in \Omega^{(c)}$.

Let I^r and I^s be two sets of variable indices, i.e., two elements of the power set of I. One of their set differences is

$$I^r - I^s = \{i \in I | i \in I^r \land i \notin I^s \};$$

the other is $I^s - I^r$, defined in a similar manner.

Theorem 4.3 *Assume that U is continuous. If I^r and I^s are each strictly separable from their complements in I, $I^r \cap I^s \neq \emptyset$, $I^r - I^s \neq \emptyset$, $I^s - I^r \neq \emptyset$, and $I^s - I^r$ is strictly essential, then each of the following sets is also strictly separable from its complement in I: (i) $I^r - I^s$, (ii) $I^r \cap I^s$, and (iii) $I^s - I^r$.*

Proof. For convenience, let $I^r = I^1 \cup I^2$ and $I^s = I^2 \cup I^3$. Of course,

$$X = (X^1, X^2, X^3, X^c) \in \Omega^n,$$

$$X^r = (X^1, X^2) \in \Omega^{(r)} = \Omega^{(1)} \times \Omega^{(2)},$$

and

$$X^s = (X^2, X^3) \in \Omega^{(s)} = \Omega^{(2)} \times \Omega^{(3)}.$$

We first prove the strict separability of $I^r \cap I^s = I^2$. By assumption,

$$\{(X^1, X^2) \in \Omega^{(r)} | U(X^1, X^2, \hat{X}^3, \hat{X}^c) \geqslant U(\hat{X}^1, \hat{X}^2, \hat{X}^3, \hat{X}^c)\} \qquad \text{(a)}$$

is independent of $(\hat{X}^3, \hat{X}^c)$, and

$$\{(X^2, X^3) \in \Omega^{(s)} | U(\hat{X}^1, X^2, X^3, \hat{X}^c) \geqslant U(\hat{X}^1, \hat{X}^2, \hat{X}^3, \hat{X}^c)\} \qquad \text{(b)}$$

is independent of $(\hat{X}^1, \hat{X}^c)$.

In particular, (a) implies that the conditional preference ordering on $\Omega^{(2)}$ —a projection of the conditional ordering on $\Omega^{(1)} \times \Omega^{(2)}$—is independent of (X^3, X^c), while (b) implies that the conditional preference ordering on $\Omega^{(2)}$ —a projection of the conditional ordering on $\Omega^{(2)} \times \Omega^{(3)}$—is independent of (X^1, X^c). Together they imply that I^2 is strictly separable from $I^1 \cup I^3 \cup I^c$.[10]

We next prove the strict separability of $I^1 = I^r - I^s$. Then the strict separability of $I^3 = I^s - I^r$ follows by a similar argument, and the proof will be complete.

By Theorem 3.2a, the strict separability of I^r, I^2, and I^s implies the existence of continuous functions $U^2 : \Omega^{(2)} \rightarrow \mathbf{R}$, $g : \Omega^{(1)} \times \mathcal{R}(U^2) \rightarrow \mathbf{R}$, $h : \mathcal{R}(U^2) \times \Omega^{(3)} \rightarrow \mathbf{R}$, $\hat{U} : \mathcal{R}(g) \times \Omega^{(3)} \times \Omega^{(c)} \rightarrow \mathbf{R}$, and $\tilde{U} : \Omega^{(1)} \times \mathcal{R}(h) \times \Omega^{(c)} \rightarrow \mathbf{R}$ such that

$$U(X^1, X^2, X^3, X^c) = \hat{U}\left(g(X^1, U^2(X^2)), X^3, X^c\right)$$
$$= \tilde{U}\left(X^1, h(U^2(X^2), X^3), X^c\right), \qquad \text{(c)}$$

where both g and h are increasing in $U^2(X^2)$, $\hat{U}$ is increasing in $g(X^1, U^2(X^2))$, and $\tilde{U}$ is increasing in $h(U^2(X^2), X^3)$.

Define two more functions,

$$U^1 : \Omega^{(1)} \rightarrow \mathbf{R} \quad \text{and} \quad U^3 : \Omega^{(3)} \rightarrow \mathbf{R},$$

such that

$$U^1(X^1) = U(X^1, O^2, O^3, O^c) = g(X^1, U^2(O^2))$$

and

$$U^3(X^3) = U(O^1, O^2, X^3, O^c) = h(U^2(O^2), X^3).$$

These are representations of the conditional preference orderings on $\Omega^{(1)}$ and $\Omega^{(3)}$ for given reference vectors. What needs to be shown is that these conditional preference orderings are independent of the reference vector choice.

Note that (c) implies

$$U(X^1, X^2, X^3, X^c) \geqslant U(\hat{X}^1, X^2, X^3, X^c) \qquad \text{(d)}$$

---

[10]If a set of variables is strictly separable from a variable k and from a variable k', it is easy to show that it is separable from $\{k\} \cup \{k'\}$. This may not be the case for nonstrict separability.

if and only if

$$g(X^1, U^2(X^2)) \geqslant g(\hat{X}^1, U^2(X^2)).$$ (e)

This follows because (d) is equivalent to

$$\hat{U}\left(g(X^1, U^2(X^2)), X^3, X^c\right) \geqslant \hat{U}\left(g(\hat{X}^1, U^2(X^2)), X^3, X^c\right),$$ (d')

and (d') is equivalent to (e), since $\hat{U}$ is increasing in $g(X^1, U^2(X^2))$. In addition, it follows from the representations in (c) that (d) is equivalent to

$$\tilde{U}\left(X^1, h(U^2(X^2), X^3), X^c\right) \geqslant \tilde{U}\left(\hat{X}^1, h(U^2(X^2), X^3), X^c\right).$$ (f)

Hence it follows that (e) holds if and only if (f) holds. We need to show that (d) holds if and only if

$$U^1(X^1) \geqslant U^1(\hat{X}^1),$$ (d*)

because this is equivalent to the conditional ordering on $\Omega^{(1)}$ being independent of the reference vector. Because of the above list of equivalences, it is sufficient to show that (d*) is equivalent to (e) for all $X^2 \in \Omega^{(2)}$.

Since U^2 is a continuous function and its domain $\Omega^{(2)}$ is connected, the range of U^2 is an interval, say J, on the real line $\mathbf{R}$. By assumption, I^2 is essential (not all of $\Omega^{(2)}$ belongs to the same indifference class); hence J is nondegenerate; i.e., J contains more than one point.

Using Gorman's terminology, we say that $u_2 \in J$ is *joined* to $\hat{u}_2 \in J$ if there are points $X^3 \in \Omega^{(3)}$ and $\hat{X}^3 \in \Omega^{(3)}$ such that

$$h(u_2, X^3) = h(\hat{u}_2, \hat{X}^3).$$ (g)

In this case,

$$\tilde{U}\left(X^1, h(u_2, X^3), X^c\right) \geqslant \tilde{U}\left(\hat{X}^1, h(u_2, X^3), X^c\right)$$ (g-a)

if and only if

$$\tilde{U}\left(X^1, h(\hat{u}_2, \hat{X}^3), X^c\right) \geqslant \tilde{U}\left(\hat{X}^1, h(\hat{u}_2, \hat{X}^3), X^c\right).$$ (g-b)

This is equivalent to the statement

$$g(X^1, u_2) \geqslant g(\hat{X}^1, u_2)$$ (h-a)

if and only if

$$g(X^1, \hat{u}_2) \geqslant g(\hat{X}^1, \hat{u}_2). \tag{h-b}$$

The equivalence of (h-a) and (h-b) is established as follows. Because (e) is equivalent to (f), (g-a) is equivalent to (h-a). Similarly, (g-b) holds if and only if (h-b) holds. Therefore the equivalence of (g-a) and (g-b) establishes the equivalence of (h-a) and (h-b).

If u_2 is joined to $\tilde{u}_2$ and $\tilde{u}_2$ is joined to $\hat{u}_2$, then there exist points X^3, $\overline{X}^3, \overset{*}{X}{}^3$, and $\hat{X}^3$ such that

$$h(u_2, X^3) = h(\tilde{u}_2, \overline{X}^3)$$

and

$$h(\tilde{u}_2, \overset{*}{X}{}^3) = h(\hat{u}_2, \hat{X}^3).$$

In this case we say that u_2 is *connected* to $\hat{u}_2$. Note that u_2 is not necessarily joined to $\hat{u}_2$. Also note that u_2 need *only* be connected to $\hat{u}_2$ for the equivalence of (h-a) and (h-b) to hold; i.e., this equivalence holds for all connected pairs. For, suppose u_2 is connected to $\hat{u}_2$ by the *chain* $\langle u_2, \tilde{u}_2, \hat{u}_2 \rangle$; i.e., u_2 is joined to $\tilde{u}_2$ and $\tilde{u}_2$ is joined to $\hat{u}_2$. Then, since u_2 is joined to $\tilde{u}_2$,

$$g(X^1, u_2) \geqslant g(\hat{X}^1, u_2) \quad \Leftrightarrow \quad g(X^1, \tilde{u}_2) \geqslant g(\hat{X}^1, \tilde{u}_2)$$

and, since $\tilde{u}_2$ is joined to $\hat{u}_2$,

$$g(X^1, \tilde{u}_2) \geqslant g(\hat{X}^1, \tilde{u}_2) \quad \Leftrightarrow \quad g(X^1, \hat{u}_2) \geqslant g(\hat{X}^1, \hat{u}_2).$$

Taken together, these statements imply

$$g(X^1, u_2) \geqslant g(\hat{X}^1, u_2) \quad \Leftrightarrow \quad g(X^1, \hat{u}_2) \geqslant g(\hat{X}^1, \hat{u}_2).$$

This argument easily generalizes to chains of any length.

In general, if u_2 is joined to u_2^1, u_2^1 is joined to $u_2^2, \ldots,$ and u_2^i is joined to $\hat{u}_2$, then we say that u_2 is connected to $\hat{u}_2$ by the chain $\langle u_2, u_2^1, u_2^2, \ldots, u_2^i, \hat{u}_2 \rangle$. The relation "is connected to" is an equivalence relation and therefore partitions J into one or more equivalence classes.

If (h-a) were equivalent to (h-b) for all pairs $(u_2, \hat{u}_2) \in J \times J$, then I^1 would be strictly separable from I^2; hence (d*) would be equivalent to (e) and the proof would be complete. Since this equivalence holds for all connected pairs, it remains to show that, in fact, all pairs are connected. To do this, we first show that each of the above equivalence classes is an interval and then show that there is only one such equivalence class, namely J.

Suppose u_2 and $\hat{u}_2$ are elements of the same equivalence class K and that (without loss of generality) $u_2 > \hat{u}_2$. (If K contains only one element it is still an interval, albeit degenerate.) Pick a real number $\bar{u}_2$ such that $u_2 > \bar{u}_2 > \hat{u}_2$. There will be a pair, u_2^i and u_2^{i+1}, in the chain connecting u_2 and $\hat{u}_2$ such that u_2^i is joined to u_2^{i+1} and, without loss of generality,[11] such that

$$u_2^i \geqslant \bar{u}_2 \geqslant u_2^{i+1}.$$

Then there exist points ${}^iX^3$ and ${}^{i+1}X^3$ such that

$$h\left(u_2^i, {}^iX^3\right) = h\left(u_2^{i+1}, {}^{i+1}X^3\right)$$

$$\leqslant h\left(\bar{u}_2, {}^{i+1}X^3\right)$$

$$\leqslant h\left(u_2^i, {}^{i+1}X^3\right),$$

since h is increasing in u_2. Hence $h(\bar{u}_2, {}^{i+1}X^3)$ is bounded between $h(u_2^i, {}^iX^3)$ and $h(u_2^i, {}^{i+1}X^3)$. The continuity of h on $\Omega^{(3)}$ implies that there exists a point $X^3 \in \Omega^{(3)}$ such that $h(u_2^i, X^3) = h(\bar{u}_2, {}^{i+1}X^3)$. This shows that $\bar{u}_2$ is joined to u_2^i, and hence $\bar{u}_2 \in K$. Therefore, K is an interval.

The final step is to show that there is only one equivalence class. For a proof by contradiction, let J_1 and J_2 be two equivalence classes with a common boundary point $\overset{*}{u}_2$. J, which is an interval, consists of intervals $J_1, J_2, \ldots$ which are the equivalence classes. So J_1 and J_2 are "adjacent", and whether they are open or closed (or neither), they share a common boundary point. Hence $\overset{*}{u}_2$ exists. Additionally, either $\overset{*}{u}_2 \in J_1$, $\overset{*}{u}_2 \in J_2$, or $\overset{*}{u}_2$ is the single element of an equivalence class. Specifically, $\overset{*}{u}_2 \in J$.

By assumption, $I^s - I^r = I^3$ is strictly essential. Hence for all $u_2 \in J$, and in particular for $\overset{*}{u}_2$, there exist points X^3 and $\hat{X}^3$ such that

$$h\left(\overset{*}{u}_2, X^3\right) > h\left(\overset{*}{u}_2, \hat{X}^3\right). \tag{i}$$

Because of the continuity and strict monotonicity in u_2 of h, for some real number $\delta > 0$ define the interval

$$I_+ = J \cap \left[\overset{*}{u}_2, \overset{*}{u}_2 + \delta\right].$$

---

[11] It may seem possible that K contains only two elements. If so, take $u_2^i = u_2$ and $u_2^{i+1} = \hat{u}_2$. But in fact this possibility is ruled out in the proof.

There exists a $\delta > 0$ such that for all $u_2 \in I_+$,

$$h\left(\overset{*}{u}_2, X^3\right) \geqslant h\left(u_2, \hat{X}^3\right) \geqslant h\left(\overset{*}{u}_2, \hat{X}^3\right).$$

Moreover, since h is continuous on $\Omega^{(3)}$, there exists a point $\overset{*}{X}^3 \in \Omega^{(3)}$ such that

$$h\left(\overset{*}{u}_2, \overset{*}{X}^3\right) = h\left(u_2, \hat{X}^3\right)$$

Therefore, $\overset{*}{u}_2$ is connected to each $u_2 \in I_+$. Hence $\overset{*}{u}_2$ belongs to either J_1 or J_2, say J_1.

But by an analogous argument there exists a real number $\epsilon > 0$ such that $\overset{*}{u}_2$ is connected to each

$$u^2 \in I_- = J \cap \left[\overset{*}{u}_2 - \epsilon, \overset{*}{u}_2\right].$$

Hence $\overset{*}{u}_2$ belongs to both J_1 and J_2, which is a contradiction.

Therefore, there is only one equivalence class, and every pair $(u_2, \hat{u}_2) \in J \times J$ is connected. This means that (h-a) is equivalent to (h-b) for all $u_2 \in J$; hence I^1 is strictly separable from I^2. As a subset of I^r, it is also strictly separable from $I^3 \cup I^c$. This establishes the strict separability of $I^r - I^s$. Since I^1 is essential by assumption and is strictly separable, it must be strictly essential. Hence an analogous argument will show that $I^3 = I^s - I^r$ is also strictly separable from its complement in I. $\|$

In what follows we will always assume that the partition of I is disjoint and exhaustive. Theorem 4.3 assures us that as far as strict separability is concerned, disjointness is an innocuous assumption. Nonstrict separability, however, may be another matter. It is not known whether any of the results in theorem 4.3 are true for nonstrictly separable sets.

4.3   HOMOTHETIC SEPARABILITY

In this section we characterize the cases in which the separable structure of a utility, cost, or transformation function is simultaneously present in both the primal and the dual function. These cases involve certain homotheticity assumptions which in turn are equivalent to additional functional structure restrictions.

The direct or indirect objective function U or V is *homothetically (strictly) separable* if it is (strictly) separable in the partition $\hat{I}$ and each aggregator function is homothetic. Note that theis does *not* imply that U or

V is a homothetic function. A careful discussion of homothetic (strict) separability and its implications is postponed until after the discussion of (strict) separability with respect to the extended partition $_0\hat{I}$ of the cost, transformation, and nonnormalized indirect utility function.

4.3.1 Separability in the Extended Partition

The indirect utility or production function in nonnormalized prices is (strictly) separable with respect to the partition $_0\hat{I}$ if and only if each price sector $I^r \in {_0\hat{I}}$ is separable from its complement in $_0I$, i.e., from all prices in the remaining sectors and from the expenditure variable if $r \neq 0$.

Corollary 4.1.6 *Suppose that the indirect utility function V satisfies the regularity conditions* (R-2). *Then the nonnormalized indirect utility function W is separable in the partition $_0\hat{I}$ if and only if there exist $m+1$ functions*

$$\overline{W}^r : \Omega_+^{(r)} \to \mathbf{R}, \qquad r = 1, \ldots, m,$$

and

$$\hat{W} : \Omega_+^1 \times \mathop{\times}_{r=1}^{m} \mathcal{R}(\overline{W}^r) \to \mathbf{R}$$

such that

$$W(y, P) = \hat{W}\left(y, \overline{W}^1(P^1), \ldots, \overline{W}^m(P^m)\right), \qquad (4.6)$$

where $\hat{W}$ is increasing in y, continuous, and HDO; *$\hat{W}(y, \cdot)$ satisfies* (R-2); *and each $\overline{W}^r$ satisfies* (R-3P).

Of course, other properties may be inherited as in corollary 4.1.3.

Proof. Follows from repeated application of corollary 3.7.2.   ‖

The cost function is (strictly) separable in the partition $_0\hat{I}$ if each sector $I^r \in {_0\hat{I}}$ is (strictly) separable from its complement in $_0I$, i.e., from all prices in the remaining sectors and from real income if $r \neq 0$.

Corollary 4.1.7 *Suppose that the cost function C satisfies the regularity conditions* (R-3). *Then C is separable in the partition $_0\hat{I}$ if and only if there exist functions*

$$\overline{C}^r : \Omega_+^{(r)} \to \Omega_+^1, \qquad r = 1, \ldots, m,$$

and

$$\hat{C} : \mathcal{R}(U) \times \underset{r=1}{\overset{m}{\times}} \mathcal{R}(\bar{C}^r) \to \Omega^1_+$$

such that

$$C(u,P) = \hat{C}\left(u, \bar{C}^1(P^1), \dots, \bar{C}^m(P^m)\right), \tag{4.7}$$

where $\hat{C}$ satisfies (R-3) *and each $\bar{C}^r$ satisfies* (R-3P).

Of course, the inheritance properties from corollary 4.1.4 still hold.

Proof.   Follows from repeated application of theorem 3.7.   ‖

Similar results hold for the transformation function. It is (strictly) separable in the partition $_0\hat{I}$ if each sector $I^r \in {_0\hat{I}}$ is (strictly) separable from its complement in $_0I$.

Corollary 4.1.8   *Suppose that the transformation function F satisfies the regularity conditions* (R-4). *Then F is separable in the partition $_0\hat{I}$ if and only if there exist $m+1$ functions,*

$$\bar{F}^r : \Omega^{(r)}_+ \to \Omega^1_+, \qquad r = 1, \dots, m,$$

and

$$\hat{F} : \mathcal{R}(U) \times \underset{r=1}{\overset{m}{\times}} \mathcal{R}(\bar{F}^r) \to \Omega^1_+,$$

such that

$$F(u,X) = \hat{F}\left(u, \bar{F}^1(X^1), \dots, \bar{F}^m(X^m)\right), \tag{4.8}$$

where $\hat{F}$ satisfies (R-4) *and each $\bar{F}^r$ satisfies* (R-4X).

As in Corollary 4.1.5, other properties may be inherited too.

Proof.   Follows from repeated application of corollary 3.7.1.   ‖

It is worth noting that separability of C and F in the extended partition $_0\hat{I}$ generates a much more evocative structure than does separability in the partition $\hat{I}$. In the former case, all of the regularity conditions are inherited by both the macro and the aggregator functions, so that they can be interpreted as cost or transformation functions. This interpretation is made more appealing by the fact that the last m arguments of the macro function induced by separability in $_0\hat{I}$ depend only on prices or quantities and can therefore be interpreted as prices and quantities of composite commodities. It is also worth noting that strengthening separability to strict separability in the extended partition does not significantly extend the inheritance properties of the macro and aggregator functions—only differentiability inheritance is added. Thus, the distinction between non-strict and strict separability of C and F in the extended partition $_0\hat{I}$ is not as important as the similar distinction with respect to the partition $\hat{I}$. This impression is reinforced by the theorems on homothetic separability which appear in the next subsection.

4.3.2   Homothetic Separability and Duality

This section states the equivalences between various separability assumptions. The first theorem, an extension of the results in Blackorby, Primont, and Russell (1975b), relates homothetic (strict) separability of the utility functions to (strict) separability of the cost and transformation functions in the extended partition $_0\hat{I}$. The second result provides another characterization of homothetic (strict) separability. The section concludes with a discussion of overall homotheticity and symmetric separability.

Theorem 4.4   *Assume that U satisfies the regularity conditions* (R-1).[12] *Then the following five structures are equivalent:*

(i) U *is homothetically separable; i.e.,*

$$U(X) = \hat{U}\left(U^1(X^1), \ldots, U^m(X^m)\right),$$

where $\hat{U}$ is monotonic and each U^r is homothetic;
(ii) V *is homothetically separable; i.e.,*

$$V(P/y) = \hat{V}\left(V^1(P^1/y), \ldots, V^m(P^m/y)\right),$$

where $\hat{V}$ is monotonic and each V^r is homothetic;
(iii) W *is separable in $_0\hat{I}$, i.e.,*

$$W(y, P) = \hat{W}\left(y, \overline{W}^1(P^1), \ldots, \overline{W}^m(P^m)\right),$$

where $\hat{W}$ is monotonic;

[12]Of course, if U satisfies (R-1), then V, C, and F satisfy (R-2), (R-3), and (R-4), respectively.

(iv) C is separable in $_0\hat{I}$, i.e.,

$$C(u,P)=\hat{C}\left(u,\bar{C}^1(P^1),\ldots,\bar{C}^m(P^m)\right),$$

where $\hat{C}$ is monotonic;

(v) F is separable in $_0\hat{I}$, i.e.,

$$F(u,X)=\hat{F}\left(u,\bar{F}^1(X^1),\ldots,\bar{F}^m(X^m)\right),$$

where $\hat{F}$ is monotonic.

Moreover, if the extensions of V, C, and F to the boundary are locally nonsated on each $\Omega^{(r)}$, $r=1,\ldots,m$, then "separable" and "monotonic" may be replaced by "strictly separable" and "strictly monotonic", respectively, in the above statement.

Proof. Follows immediately from theorem 3.8. ‖

In view of this theorem, we refer to any of the above five structures as homothetic (strict) separability. If the separability condition of theorem 4.4 is strengthened to strict separability, a rather different characterization of homothetic separability is possible.

Theorem 4.5 *Assume that U satisfies the regularity conditions (R-1). Then the following statements are equivalent to homothetic strict separability:*

(i)   *Both U and F are strictly separable in $\hat{I}$.*
(ii)   *Both V and C are strictly separable in $\hat{I}$.*
(iii) *Both U and C are strictly separable in $\hat{I}$.*
(iv)   *Both V and F are strictly separable in $\hat{I}$.*

Proof. Follows from theorem 3.9 and corollary 3.9.1. ‖

It has been claimed[13] that still another characterization of homothetic strict separability is simultaneous strict separability of the direct and indirect utility functions. A counterexample to this claim is the direct function with image

$$U(X)=U^1(X^1)+\sum_{i\notin I^1}\alpha_i\log x_i,$$

[13]See Lau (1969a: theorem IX).

whose indirect function is given by

$$V(P/y) = V^1(P^1/y) - \sum_{i \notin I^1} \alpha_i \log(P/y),$$

where U^1 (and hence V^1) is *not* homothetic.[14]

4.3.3 Overall Homotheticity and Duality

The importance of sectoral homotheticity in characterizing dual functional structures cannot be overemphasized. In applications where dual results of this nature are required, homothetic separability must be a maintained hypothesis, and as such is quite strong though not nearly as strong as overall homotheticity. However, overall homotheticity does not generate many new relationships as far as separable functional structures are concerned. In order to discuss overall homotheticity, we use the binary partition

$$_0\tilde{I} = \{I^0, I\}.$$

The following theorem characterizes overall homotheticity and (strict) separability.

Theorem 4.6 *If U satisfies* (R-1), *the following structures are equivalent*:

(i) U *is homothetic and separable in* $\hat{I}$; *i.e.*,

$$U(X) = \hat{U}\big(U^1(X^1), \ldots, U^m(X^m)\big), \tag{4.9}$$

where $\hat{U}$ is monotonic.

(ii) V *is homothetic and separable in* $\hat{I}$; *i.e.*,

$$V(P/y) = \hat{V}\big(V^1(P^1/y), \ldots, V^m(P^m/y)\big), \tag{4.10}$$

where $\hat{V}$ is monotonic.

(iii) C *is separable in* $_0\tilde{I}$ *and in* $\hat{I}$; *moreover*,

$$C(u, P) = \Gamma(u)\hat{C}\big(\overline{C}^1(P^1), \ldots, \overline{C}^m(P^m)\big), \tag{4.11}$$

where $\hat{C}$ is monotonic.

---

[14]This particular example is from Samuelson (1969). The statement of theorem VIII in Lau (1969a) provides a more general counterexample.

(iv) F is separable in ${}_0\tilde{I}$ and in $\hat{I}$; moreover,

$$F(u,X) = \Phi(u)\hat{F}\left(\bar{F}^1(X^1),\ldots,\bar{F}^m(X^m)\right), \qquad (4.12)$$

where $\hat{F}$ is monotonic.

(v) W is separable in ${}_0\tilde{I}$ and in $\hat{I}$; moreover,

$$W(y,P) = \Upsilon\left[\frac{\hat{W}\left(\bar{W}^1(P^1),\ldots,\bar{W}^m(P^m)\right)}{y}\right], \qquad (4.13)$$

where $\hat{W}$ is monotonic.

Moreover, if the extensions of V, C, and F to the boundary are locally nonsated on each $\Omega^{(r)}$, $r=1,\ldots,m$, then "separable" and "monotonic" may be replaced by "strictly separable" and "strictly monotonic," respectively, in the above statement.

Proof.   Follows from lemma 3.4 and theorem 4.4.   ‖

We conclude this section by recalling (lemma 3.3) that homothetic aggregator functions can be normalized to be PLH. It therefore makes sense to think of the aggregators of homothetically separable direct and indirect utility functions as quantity indices and price indices, respectively. This is why homothetic separability plays an important role in the theory of price and quantity aggregation developed in chapter 5.

4.4   COMPLETE SEPARABILITY

A function is *completely* (*strictly*) *separable* in the partition $\hat{I}$ if every proper subset of $\hat{I}$ is (strictly) separable from its complement in $\hat{I}$. That is, every union of sectors is (strictly) separable from all variables in the remaining sectors. Hence, it is easily seen that complete (strict) separability is a special case of (strict) separability.

If there are only two sectors (i.e., $m=2$), there is no distinction between separability and complete separability. Thus, we shall assume that there are three or more sectors in the discussions of completely separable functions in this and the following section. (Two-group additivity is treated in section 4.6.)

4.4.1 The Fundamental Theorem of Gorman

Functional-structure representation theorems for completely strictly separable structures have been proved by Debreu (1959a), Gorman (1968b), and Koopmans (1972). We follow the approach of Gorman.

Using the notation in the proof of theorem 4.3, we partition I into four subsets

$$\{I^1, I^2, I^3, I^c\}$$

and examine $I^r = I^1 \cup I^2$ and $I^s = I^2 \cup I^3$. If I^r and I^s are both strictly separable from their complements in I, then so are I^1, I^2, and I^3 by theorem 4.3. In addition, Gorman also showed that $I^1 \cup I^3$ and $I^1 \cup I^2 \cup I^3$ are strictly separable and in doing so provided a representation of the utility function. For the sake of completeness, we bring all of these results together in the following theorem.

Theorem 4.7 (*Gorman, 1968b*) *Suppose the utility function is continuous and all sectors are essential. If* (ā) *I^r and I^s are nonempty and strictly separable from their respective complements in I, if $I^r \cap I^s$, $I^r - I^s$, and $I^s - I^r$ are nonempty, and if $I^s - I^r$ is strictly essential, then* (b̄) *each of the following sets is strictly separable from its respective complement in I:*

(i) $I^r \cap I^s$
(ii) $I^r - I^s$,
(iii) $I^s - I^r$,
(iv) $I^r \cup I^s$,
(v) $(I^r - I^s) \cup (I^s - I^r)$.

In this case, (c̄) *there exist continuous functions $\bar{U}$, U^1, U^2, and U^3 such that*

$$U(X) = \bar{U}\left(U^1(X^1) + U^2(X^2) + U^3(X^3), X^c\right)$$

where $\bar{U}$ is increasing in its first argument. Hence (ā)$\Rightarrow$(b̄) *and* (ā)$\Rightarrow$(c̄). *Moreover,* (c̄)$\Rightarrow$(ā) *and* (c̄)$\Rightarrow$(b̄).

Gorman also states (p. 370) that (b̄) implies (ā). But

$$U(X) = \hat{U}\left(U^2(X^2) + U^1(X^1) \cdot U^3(X^3), X^c\right),$$

where $\hat{U}$ is increasing in its first argument, seems to be a counterexample to this implication. This is not a matter of any importance, however.

Proof.   The proof that (c̄) implies (ā) and (b̄) is a straightforward application of theorem 4.1.

In proving that (ā) implies (b̄) we first note that strict separability of (i), (ii), and (iii) in (b̄) was proved in theorem 4.3. In the proof that follows, the strategy is to show that (ā), (i), (ii), and (iii) imply (c̄), which in turn implies (iv) and (v).

By theorem 4.3, the sets $I^1 = I^r - I^s$, $I^2 = I^r \cap I^s$, and $I^3 = I^s - I^r$ are all strictly separable from their respective complements in I. Thus, by theorem 3.2a, there exist functions

$$U^r : \Omega^{(r)} \to \mathbf{R}, \qquad r = 1, 2, 3,$$

$$g : \mathcal{R}(U^1) \times \mathcal{R}(U^2) \to \mathbf{R},$$

$$h : \mathcal{R}(U^2) \times \mathcal{R}(U^3) \to \mathbf{R},$$

$$\hat{U} : \mathcal{R}(g) \times \mathcal{R}(U^3) \times \Omega^{(c)} \to \mathbf{R},$$

and

$$\tilde{U} : \mathcal{R}(U^1) \times \mathcal{R}(h) \times \Omega^{(c)} \to \mathbf{R}$$

such that

$$U(X^1, X^2, X^3, X^c) = \hat{U}\left(g(u_1, u_2), u_3, X^c\right)$$

$$= \tilde{U}\left(u_1, h(u_2, u_3), X^c\right), \tag{a}$$

where $u_r = U^r(X^r)$, $r = 1, 2, 3$, are the images of the sector-specific utility functions. We want to prove that we can write

$$U(X^1, X^2, X^3, X^c) = \overset{*}{U}\left(a^1(U^1(X^1)) + a^2(U^2(X^2)) + a^3(U^3(X^3)), X^c\right), \tag{b}$$

where the functions a^1, a^2, and a^3 are all continuous, increasing functions of one variable, and $\overset{*}{U}$ is continuous and is increasing in its first argument. This is accomplished by invoking a result proved by Aczel (1966: corollary 1, p. 312). It goes as follows.

The general solution of the functional equation

$$U(x, y, z) = G\left(g(x, y), z\right) = H\left(x, h(y, z)\right),$$

where x, y, and z vary over the same real interval (α, β) and G, g, H and h

are increasing, continuous functions with the same range (α,β), is

$$G(u,z) = F(\phi(u) + c(z)),$$

$$g(x,y) = \phi^{-1}(a(x) + b(y)),$$

$$H(x,v) = F(a(x) + \psi(v)),$$

$$h(y,z) = \psi^{-1}(b(y) + c(z)),$$

where a, b, c, ϕ and ψ are arbitrary increasing and continuous functions, $u = g(x,y)$, and $v = h(y,z)$. Substitution yields

$$U(x,y,z) = F(a(x) + b(y) + c(z)).$$

In order to apply Aczel's result to (a), two issues must be addressed. First, the functions $\hat{U}$, $\tilde{U}$, g, h, U^1, U^2, and U^3 must all have a common range. Second, in the statement of Aczel's theorem, the complement I^c is empty.

The first problem is solved by a simple renormalization procedure. The second is somewhat more complex, so we outline it before proceeding. Note that for every $X^c \in \Omega^{(c)}$ we can think of U as a function defined only over $\Omega^{(1)} \times \Omega^{(2)} \times \Omega^{(3)}$. Hence, for fixed values of X^c we can apply Aczel's theorem. It is then shown that each X^c affects the representation of the preference orderings in $\Omega^{(1)}$, $\Omega^{(2)}$, and $\Omega^{(3)}$ in precisely the same way, namely as a multiplicative constant which can be taken into the macro function in the usual way. This will complete the argument.

The device employed by Gorman in standardizing the ranges is first to restrict all functions to the interiors of their domains and then to renormalize each one so that the range of each is the open interval $(0,1)$. We will show explicitly how this may be done.

First restrict each U^r to $\Omega_+^{(r)}$ for $r = 1,2,3$. The range of each continuous U^r is an open interval on the real line. Transform each U^r so that the range of the resulting composition is $(0,1)$ for each. Denote these transforms by θ^1, θ^2, and θ^3, such that each $\theta^r : \mathfrak{R}(U^r) \rightarrow (0,1)$ is continuous, increasing, and bijective. Define continuous, increasing, bijective functions

$$\overset{*}{g} : (0,1) \times (0,1) \rightarrow \mathfrak{R}(g)$$

and

$$\overset{*}{h} : (0,1) \times (0,1) \rightarrow \mathfrak{R}(h)$$

by the images

$$\overset{*}{g}(\theta^1(u_1),\theta^2(u_2))=g(u_1,u_2)$$

and

$$\overset{*}{h}(\theta^2(u_2),\theta^3(u_3))=h(u_2,u_3).$$

As $\overset{*}{g}$ and $\overset{*}{h}$ are each continuous on the open unit square, their ranges are open intervals. Transform $\overset{*}{g}$ and $\overset{*}{h}$ to make the range of each composition equal to $(0,1)$. Denote these continuous, increasing, bijective transforms by θ^g and θ^h.

Next define increasing, continuous functions,

$$\overset{*}{\hat{U}}:(0,1)\times(0,1)\times\Omega_+^{(c)}\to\mathbf{R}$$

and

$$\overset{*}{\tilde{U}}:(0,1)\times(0,1)\times\Omega_+^{(c)}\to\mathbf{R},$$

by the images

$$\overset{*}{\hat{U}}\left(\theta^g\left(\overset{*}{g}(\theta^1(u_1),\theta^2(u_2))\right),\theta^3(u_3),X^c\right)=\hat{U}\left(g(u_1,u_2),u_3,X^c\right)$$

and

$$\overset{*}{\tilde{U}}\left(\theta^1(u_1),\theta^h\left(\overset{*}{h}(\theta^2(u_2),\theta^3(u_3))\right),X^c\right)=\tilde{U}\left(u_1,h(u_2,u_3),X^c\right).$$

Because of (a), U, $\overset{*}{\hat{U}}$, and $\overset{*}{\tilde{U}}$ all have the same range, which, by continuity, is an open interval.

Having now shown how these transformations may be performed, let us revert to the form in (a), for the sake of notational simplicity, assuming that these normalizations have been employed. U, $\hat{U}$, and $\tilde{U}$ may each be subjected to a common transformation, say L_c, which converts their ranges to the open unit interval $(0,1)$. That is,

$$L_c\big(U(X^1,X^2,X^3,X^c)\big)=\hat{U}_c\big(g(u_1,u_2),u_3\big)$$

$$=\tilde{U}_c\big(u_1,h(u_2,u_3)\big), \qquad (c)$$

where

$$\hat{U}_c\big(g(u_1,u_2),u_3\big)=L_c\big(\hat{U}\big(g(u_1,u_2),u_3,X^c\big)\big)$$

and

$$\tilde{U}_c(u_1, h(u_2, u_3)) = L_c(\tilde{U}(u_1, h(u_2, u_3), X^c)).$$

The subscript c on these functions reminds us that they depend on X^c.

Aczel's result is now applicable to the functional equation in (c). Thus, we can write

$$g(u_1, u_2) = \phi_c(a_c^1(u_1) + a_c^2(u_2))$$

and

$$h(u_2, u_3) = \psi_c(a_c^2(u_2) + a_c^3(u_3)).$$

Again the subscript c reminds us that each of these functions depends on X^c. The rest of the argument consists of showing that X^c affects each a_c^i in the same fashion—through a multiplicative constant.

Given any $X^c \in \Omega^{(c)}$, each a_c^r, $r = 1, 2, 3$, can be normalized so that, when $u_1 = u_2 = u_3 = \bar{u} \in (0, 1)$,

$$a_c^1(\bar{u}) = a_c^2(\bar{u}) = a_c^3(\bar{u}) = 0.$$

Of course, ϕ_c and ψ_c must also be normalized. Again, at the risk of seriously complicating the notation, we indicate how this may be done. For example, let

$$\hat{a}_c^r(u_r) = a_c^r(u_r) - a_c^r(\bar{u}), \qquad r = 1, 2, 3,$$

and

$$\hat{\phi}_c(\hat{a}_c^1(u_1) + \hat{a}_c^2(u_2)) = \phi_c(\hat{a}_c^1(u_1) + a_c^1(\bar{u}) + \hat{a}_c^2(u_2) + a_c^2(\bar{u}))$$

$$= \phi_c(a_c^1(u_1) + a_c^2(u_2))$$

$$= g(u_1, u_2),$$

and similarly for ψ_c. We retain the same notation and assume that the above normalization has already taken place.

Note that $\bar{u} \in (0, 1)$. Write

$$\phi_c(a_c^1(u_1) + a_c^2(u_2)) = \phi(a^1(u_1) + a^2(u_2)) \qquad \text{(d)}$$

whenever $X^c = 0^c$, an arbitrary reference vector. That is, for one particular value of X^c suppress the subscript and then investigate the nature of the change which this entails.

Let $u_2 = \bar{u}$, and (d) becomes

$$\phi_c\big(a_c^1(u_1)\big) = \phi\big(a^1(u_1)\big).$$

Solving for $a_c^1(u_1)$, we have

$$a_c^1(u_1) = \phi_c^{-1}\big(\phi\big(a^1(u_1)\big)\big).$$

Letting

$$\overset{*}{\phi}_c = \phi_c^{-1} \circ \phi, \tag{e}$$

the above solution for $a_c^1(u_1)$ becomes

$$a_c^1(u_1) = \overset{*}{\phi}_c\big(a^1(u_1)\big). \tag{f}$$

Similarly, letting $u_1 = \bar{u}$ gives

$$a_c^2(u_2) = \overset{*}{\phi}_c\big(a^2(u_2)\big). \tag{g}$$

Next, invert (d) to get

$$a_c^1(u_1) + a_c^2(u_2) = \phi_c^{-1}\big(\phi\big(a^1(u_1) + a^2(u_2)\big)\big).$$

Substituting from (e), (f), and (g), we have

$$\overset{*}{\phi}_c\big(a^1(u_1)\big) + \overset{*}{\phi}_c\big(a^2(u_2)\big) = \overset{*}{\phi}_c\big(a^1(u_1) + a^2(u_2)\big),$$

or, changing notation in an obvious way,

$$\overset{*}{\phi}_c(a_1 + a_2) = \overset{*}{\phi}_c(a_1) + \overset{*}{\phi}_c(a_2). \tag{h}$$

This is the well-known Cauchy equation. The function $\overset{*}{\phi}_c$ is continuous and increasing. The arguments a_1 and a_2 each vary over open intervals which contain the origin, since a^1 and a^2 are continuous functions on the domain $(0, 1)$ and were normalized so that $a^1(\bar{u}) = a^2(\bar{u}) = 0$ for some $\bar{u} \in (0, 1)$. Hence the domain of $\overset{*}{\phi}_c$ is (α, β), say, with $0 \in (\alpha, \beta)$.

In order to solve (h) we appeal to a result in Aczel (1966: p. 46, theorem 1), which however requires the domain of definition to be closed. By continuity extend $\overset{*}{\phi}_c$ to the domain $[\alpha, \beta]$. Call the extension $\overset{\hat{*}}{\phi}_c : [\alpha, \beta] \to$

[0, 1]. The solution to the functional equation

$$\overset{*}{\phi}_c(a_1 + a_2) = \overset{*}{\phi}_c(a_1) + \overset{*}{\phi}_c(a_2)$$

is

$$\overset{*}{\phi}_c(\lambda) = k_c \lambda \qquad \forall \lambda \in [\alpha, \beta],$$

where k_c is a positive constant, since $\overset{*}{\phi}_c$ is increasing. However, $\overset{*}{\phi}_c$ and $\overset{*}{\phi}_c$ agree on (α, β). Hence

$$\overset{*}{\phi}_c(\lambda) = k_c \lambda \qquad \forall \lambda \in (\alpha, \beta).$$

Hence

$$\overset{*}{\phi}_c(a^1(u_1)) = k_c a^1(u_1), \qquad k_c > 0,$$

or, because of (f),

$$a_c^1(u_1) = k_c a^1(u_1).$$

Similarly, because of (g),

$$a_c^2(u_2) = k_c a^2(u_2).$$

Putting together these relations yields

$$k_c = \frac{a_c^1(u_1)}{a^1(u_1)} = \frac{a_c^2(u_2)}{a^2(u_2)} \qquad \text{for} \quad u_1 \neq \bar{u} \neq u_2. \tag{i}$$

Applying the same argument to

$$h(u_2, u_3) = \psi_c\big(a_c^2(u_2) + a_c^3(u_3)\big),$$

we get

$$k_c' = \frac{a_c^2(u_2)}{a^2(u_2)} = \frac{a_c^3(u_3)}{a^3(u_3)} \qquad \text{for} \quad u_2 \neq \bar{u} \neq u_3. \tag{j}$$

But (i) and (j) together imply $k_c = k_c'$. Hence

$$a_c^r(u_r) = k_c a^r(u_r), \qquad r = 1, 2, 3. \tag{k}$$

Finally, applying Aczel's result to (c) we get

$$L_c\big(U(X^1,X^2,X^3,X^c)\big)=\overline{U}_c\big(a_c^1(u_1)+a_c^2(u_2)+a_c^3(u_3)\big)$$

$$=\overline{U}_c\big(k_c\big(a^1(u_1)+a^2(u_2)+a^3(u_3)\big)\big)\qquad\forall X^c\in\Omega^{(c)}$$

by substituting from (k). Hence

$$L_c\big(U(X^1,X^2,X^3,X^c)\big)=\widetilde{\overline{U}}\big(a^1(u_1)+a^2(u_2)+a^3(u_3),X^c\big),$$

where $\widetilde{\overline{U}}$ is increasing in its first argument. Finally,

$$U(X^1,X^2,X^3,X^c)=L_c^{-1}\Big(\widetilde{\overline{U}}\big(a^1(u_1)+a^2(u_2)+a^3(u_3),X^c\big)\Big)$$

$$=\overline{U}\big(a^1(u_1)+a^2(u_2)+a^3(u_3),X^c\big),$$

and (b) is satisfied. This result holds when each U^r is restricted to the interior $\Omega_+^{(r)}$ of its domain $\Omega^{(r)}$. Extend each one to the boundary by continuity. Then, working from the inside out, do so for all the other appropriate functions until the result holds for the entire domain of U. ‖

In theorem 4.7, Gorman has provided us with a remarkable result. The existence of two overlapping strictly separable sets in fact implies a much richer class of separable sets. In particular, the intersection $(I^r\cap I^s)$, the two differences (I^r-I^s and I^s-I^r), the symmetric difference $((I^r-I^s)\cup(I^s-I^r))$, and the union $(I^r\cup I^s)$ are separable from their respective complements. Moreover, the capability of aggregating over these separable sets implies much more about the structure of U: it can be represented in additive form. It is this important implication that allows us to prove the equivalence between complete strict separability and a representation of U as (a strictly monotonic transformation of) a sum of m aggregator functions (theorem 4.8). It should be noted that the proof of theorem 4.7 does not go through for nonstrictly separable structures.

We shall want a representation of U in which the aggregator functions and their sums act as sector-specific production or utility functions. That is, we want to pick representations which inherit the regularity properties of the master function. This is ensured by the following normalization:

$$\overline{U}(t,O^c)=t\qquad\forall t\in\Re(U^1+U^2+U^3)$$

and

$$U^r(O^r)=0,\qquad r=1,2,3,$$

in the representation

$$U(X) = \bar{U}\left(U^1(X^1) + U^2(X^2) + U^3(X^3), X^c\right).$$

Then it is easier to show how each U^r inherits properties from U.

The following argument shows how this normalization is acquired. Start with a representation provided by theorem 4.7,

$$U(X) = \overset{*}{U}\left(\overset{*}{U^1}(X^1) + \overset{*}{U^2}(X^2) + \overset{*}{U^3}(X^3), X^c\right), \qquad \text{say.}$$

Define new functions U^r by

$$U^r(X^r) = \overset{*}{U^r}(X^r) - \overset{*}{U^r}(O^r), \qquad r = 1, 2, 3,$$

and a new macro function $\overset{*}{\bar{U}}$ by

$$\overset{*}{\bar{U}}(t, X^c) = \overset{*}{U}(t - d, X^c),$$

where

$$d = \sum_{r=1}^{3} \overset{*}{U^r}(O^r).$$

Hence

$$\overset{*}{\bar{U}}\left(U^1(X^1) + U^2(X^2) + U^3(X^3), X^c\right)$$

$$= \overset{*}{U}\left(\overset{*}{U^1}(X^1) + \overset{*}{U^2}(X^2) + \overset{*}{U^3}(X^3), X^c\right).$$

Next normalize $\overset{*}{\bar{U}}$ to get another macro function which satisfies

$$\bar{U}(t, O^c) = t \qquad \forall t \in \mathcal{R}(U^1 + U^2 + U^3)$$

for the reference vector O^c. Thus

$$U^r(X^r) = \bar{U}\left(U^r(X^r), O^c\right).$$

This may not work for production functions, because some of the transforms just performed may not have been linear.

4.4.2 Representation Theorems

The remainder of this section analyzes complete strict separability with respect to $\hat{I}$ of the utility functions and the cost and transformation functions, employing theorem 4.7 to prove the equivalence of this condition to the familiar additive structure. [15]

Theorem 4.8 *Suppose the utility function U is continuous. Then U is completely strictly separable in $\hat{I}$ ($m>2$) if and only if there exist functions*

$$U^r : \Omega^{(r)} \rightarrow \mathbf{R}, \qquad r=1,\ldots,m,$$

and an increasing function

$$\overset{*}{U} : \sum_{r=1}^{m} \mathcal{R}(U^r) \rightarrow \mathbf{R}$$

such that

$$U(X) = \overset{*}{U}\left(\sum_{r=1}^{m} U^r(X^r) \right). \tag{4.14}$$

Proof. Let $\{R^c, R^r\}$ be an arbitrary partition of the set of sector indices, $R=\{1,\ldots,m\}$, and let $I^c = \cup_{s \in R^c} I^s$ and $I^r = \cup_{s \in R^r} I^s$. Also let $\Theta(R)$ be the set of ordered pairs in R, $\{\langle R^c, R^r \rangle\}$.

The sufficiency of the structure (4.14) for complete separability of U follows immediately from repeated application of the sufficiency part of theorem 3.2a, since (4.14) implies

$$U(X) = \overline{U}(X^c, U^r(X^r)),$$

where $\overline{U}$ is increasing, for all $\langle R^c, R^r \rangle \in \Theta(R)$.

To prove necessity, let $\{R^{c\prime}, R^{c\prime\prime}\}$ and $\{R^{r\prime}, R^{r\prime\prime}\}$ be partitions of R^c and R^r, respectively. As before, let $I^{c\prime} = \cup_{s \in R^{c\prime}} I^s$, and define $I^{c\prime\prime}$, $I^{r\prime}$, and $I^{r\prime\prime}$ analogously. Theorem 4.7, together with the complete strict separability condition, implies that the technology or preference ordering can be represented alternatively by

$$\hat{U}(X) = \hat{U}^{c\prime}(X^{c\prime}) + \hat{U}^{c\prime\prime}(X^{c\prime\prime}) + \hat{U}^r(X^r)$$
$$= \hat{U}^c(X^c) + \hat{U}^r(X^r) \tag{i}$$

or

$$\tilde{U}(X) = \tilde{U}^c(X^c) + \tilde{U}^{r\prime}(X^{r\prime}) + \tilde{U}^{r\prime\prime}(X^{r\prime\prime})$$
$$= \tilde{U}^c(X^c) + \tilde{U}^r(X^r), \tag{ii}$$

[15]This proof of theorem 4.8 is virtually identical to that of Gorman (1968b: pp. 388–389).

where $\hat{U}^c = \hat{U}^{c\prime} + \hat{U}^{c\prime\prime}$ and $\tilde{U}^r = \tilde{U}^{r\prime} + \tilde{U}^{r\prime\prime}$. All of the functions in (i) and (ii) can be made continuous, and $\hat{U}$ and $\tilde{U}$ constitute possibly different renormalizations of the production or utility function; thus

$$\tilde{U}(X) = \phi(\hat{U}(X)) = \psi(U(X)), \tag{iii}$$

where ϕ and ψ are continuous and increasing. Moreover, the aggregator functions mirror the corresponding parent function, and we can normalize so that

$$\hat{U}^c(O^c) = \hat{U}^r(O^r) = 0,$$

where O^c and O^r are the appropriate reference vectors. Thus, we can write

$$\phi(\hat{U}^c(X^c) + \hat{U}^r(X^r)) = \tilde{U}^c(X^c) + \tilde{U}^r(X^r)$$

$$= \phi(\hat{U}^c(X^c)) + \phi(\hat{U}^r(X^r)),$$

where the last equality follows from (iii) and the mirroring property of $\tilde{U}^c$ and $\tilde{U}^r$. As $\hat{U}^c$ and $\hat{U}^r$ vary over a nondegenerate interval containing the origin, this Cauchy equation has the solution

$$\phi(\hat{U}(X)) = \lambda\hat{U}(X), \qquad \lambda \in \Omega^1_+.$$

It is trivial to normalize $\hat{U}$ so that $\lambda = 1$ and the representations (i) and (ii) reflect equivalent renormalizations. Thus,

$$\hat{U}^r(X^r) = \tilde{U}^{r\prime}(X^{r\prime}) + \tilde{U}^{r\prime\prime}(X^{r\prime\prime}) = \hat{U}^{r\prime}(X^{r\prime}) + \hat{U}^{r\prime\prime}(X^{r\prime\prime}),$$

and

$$\hat{U}(X) = \hat{U}^{c\prime}(X^{c\prime}) + \hat{U}^{c\prime\prime}(X^{c\prime\prime}) + \hat{U}^{r\prime}(X^{r\prime}) + \hat{U}^{r\prime\prime}(X^{r\prime\prime}). \tag{iv}$$

The proof is completed by a simple induction. Suppose that

$$U(X) = \sum_{s=1}^{t} \hat{U}^s(X^s) + \check{U}(_{t+1}X), \tag{v}$$

which, by (i), holds for $t = 2$ with $R^{c\prime} = \{1\}$, $R^{c\prime\prime} = \{2\}$, and $R^r = \{3, \ldots, m\}$. But, invoking (iv), with $R^{c\prime} = \{1, \ldots, t-1\}$, $R^{c\prime\prime} = \{t\}$, $R^{r\prime} = \{t+1\}$, and $R^{r\prime\prime} = \{t+2, \ldots, m\}$, we have

$$\hat{U}(X) = \sum_{s=1}^{t+1} \hat{U}^s(X^s) + \bar{U}(_{t+2}X).$$

Thus, (v) holds for all $t \geq 2$ and hence for $t = m$. We can therefore write

$$U(X) = \psi^{-1}\left(\sum_{r=1}^{m} \hat{U}^r(X^r)\right),$$

which is equivalent to (4.14). ‖

The representation (4.14) is a monotone transform of a (groupwise) additive function; consequently, if U is invariant up to monotone functions (i.e., if U represents a preference ordering rather than a production technology), then in some normalization the utility indicator is simply the sum of sectoral utilities, and each U^r mirrors the utility function. As before,

$$U^r(O^r) = 0, \qquad r = 1, \ldots, m,$$

and the macro function satisfies

$$\overline{U}(t) = t$$

for some normalization. Thus

$$U^r(X^r) = U(O^c, X^r)$$

and

$$U(X) = \sum_{r=1}^{m} U^r(X^r).$$

If each sector contains only one element, we have the special case of a Gossen (1854) additive utility function,

$$U(X) = \sum_{i=1}^{n} U^i(x_i).$$

For production technologies, a desirable normalization runs as follows. Given the representation in (4.14), define new aggregator functions, $\tilde{U}^r : \Omega^{(r)} \to \mathbf{R}$, by

$$\tilde{U}^r(X^r) = U^r(X^r) - U^r(O^r), \qquad r = 1, \ldots, m.$$

Also, define a new macro function $\tilde{U} : \sum_{r=1}^{m} \mathcal{R}(U^r) \to \mathbf{R}$ such that

$$\tilde{U}(t) = \overset{*}{U}(t + d),$$

where

$$d = \sum_{r=1}^{m} U^r(O^r).$$

Then

$$U(X) = \overset{*}{U}\left(\sum_{r=1}^{m} U^r(X^r) \right)$$

$$= \tilde{U}\left(\sum_{r=1}^{m} \tilde{U}^r(X^r) \right).$$

Hence

$$\tilde{U}(\tilde{U}^r(X^r)) = U(O^c, X^r).$$

From this we deduce that

$$\overset{*}{U}(U^r(X^r) - U^r(O^r) + d) = U(O^c, X^r).$$

Inverting to solve for $U^r(X^r)$, we have

$$U^r(X^r) = \overset{*}{U}^{-1}(U(O^c, X^r)) + U^r(O^r) - d.$$

Hence for any reference vector O^c, the aggregator function U^r is a monotonic transformation of U with X^c fixed at O^c. Therefore, properties of preference orderings or production technologies that are preserved by monotone transformations—such as (strict) monotonicity, (strict) quasi-concavity, and homotheticity—are inherited from U by each U^r. We formalize the above in the following corollary:

Corollary 4.8.1 *If U is completely strictly separable in $\hat{I}$ ($m>2$) and has any of the following properties, then U^r (and trivially $\overset{*}{U}$) in (4.14) can be chosen to have the same property: (i) positive monotonicity, (ii) strict positive monotonicity, (iii) quasi-concavity, (iv) strict quasi-concavity, and (v) homotheticity.*

On the other hand, it appears that properties which are not necessarily preserved by monotonic transformations—such as differentiability and (strict) concavity—are not necessarily inherited by the aggregator functions. The reason why the aggregators of completely strictly separable representations apparently do not inherit these properties of the parent function, whereas the aggregators of strictly separable representations do, is that we do not have as much freedom to carry out monotonic transformations of additive structures. That is, U^r cannot be transformed monotonically without undermining the additive structure of (4.14). Of course, as complete strict separability is a special case of strict separability, it is always possible to find a strictly separable (i.e., nonadditive) representation in monotonic transformations of the aggregators in (4.14). That is, given the increasing transforms

$$\psi_r : \mathcal{R}(U^r) \rightarrow \mathbf{R}, \qquad r = 1, \ldots, m,$$

there exists an increasing function

$$\psi : \underset{r=1}{\overset{m}{\times}} \mathcal{R}(\psi^r) \rightarrow \mathbf{R}$$

such that

$$\psi\left(\psi^1\left(U^1(X^1)\right), \ldots, \psi^m\left(U^m(X^m)\right)\right) = \overset{*}{U}\left(\sum_{r=1}^{m} \psi^{r^{-1}}\left(\psi^r\left(U^r(X^r)\right)\right)\right)$$

$$= \overset{*}{U}\left(\sum_{r=1}^{m} U^r(X^r)\right).$$

From the discussion of strict separability (more precisely, corollary 4.1.1), we know that these transformations can be chosen to be differentiable, (strictly) concave, or homogeneous [16] if U has the respective property. However, this is not necessarily true of the particular nomalization of the sectoral utility functions in the additively separable representation, $U^r, r = 1, \ldots, m$.

The indirect utility function is completely strictly separable in the partition of $\hat{I}$ if every union of normalized price sectors is separable from all the remaining normalized prices.

Corollary 4.8.2 *Suppose the indirect utility function V is continuous. Then V is completely strictly separable in $\hat{I}$ $(m > 2)$ if and only if there exist functions*

$$V^r : \Omega_+^{(r)} \rightarrow \mathbf{R}, \qquad r = 1, \ldots, m,$$

---

[16]The homogeneity case is discussed more fully below.

and a decreasing function

$$\overset{*}{V}: \sum_{r=1}^{m} \mathscr{R}(V^r) \to \mathbf{R}$$

such that

$$V(P/y) = \overset{*}{V}\left(\sum_{r=1}^{m} V^r(P^r/y) \right). \tag{4.15}$$

Moreover, $\overset{*}{V}$ and each V^r can be chosen to be continuous. Furthermore, if V has any of the following properties, then each V^r can be chosen to have the corresponding property listed in corollary 4.8.1: (i) negative monotonicity, (ii) strict negative monotonicity, (iii) quasi-convexity, (iv) strict quasi-convexity, and (v) homotheticity.

Proof.   Follows from theorem 4.8 and corollary 4.8.1.   ‖

Note that, as in the case of incompletely separable indirect utility functions, we have normalized the V^r, $r = 1, \ldots, m$, to be continuous, nondecreasing, and quasi-concave if V satisfies (R-2). We should also note that complete strict separability of V does not imply, nor is it implied by, complete strict separability of U.

The indirect utility function in nonnormalized prices is completely strictly separable in $\hat{I}$ if every union of nonnormalized price sectors is separable from all remaining nonnormalized prices (but not necessarily income). The representation of this structure is contained in the next corollary to theorem 4.8.

Corollary 4.8.3   *Suppose the indirect utility function W is continuous and satisfies (R-2) in prices. Then W is completely strictly separable in $\hat{I}$ $(m > 2)$ if and only if there exist functions,*

$$W^r: \Omega_+^1 \times \Omega_+^{(r)} \to \mathbf{R}, \qquad r = 1, \ldots, m,$$

and a function

$$\overset{*}{W}: \Omega_+^1 \times \sum_{r=1}^{m} \mathscr{R}(W^r) \to \mathbf{R}$$

such that

$$W(y, P) = \overset{*}{W}\left(y, \sum_{r=1}^{m} W^r(y, P^r) \right), \tag{4.16}$$

where $\overset{*}{W}$ is decreasing in its second argument. Moreover, $\overset{*}{W}$ and each W^r can be chosen to be continuous. Furthermore, if $W(y,\cdot)$ satisfies any of the properties listed in corollary 4.8.2, then each $W^r(y,\cdot)$ can be chosen to have the same property.

Proof. Follows from theorem 4.8 and corollary 4.8.1. ||

If V satisfies (R-2), we adopt the convention of choosing each W^r to be nonincreasing in y and nondecreasing and quasi-concave in P. Also, each W^r must be HDO in its arguments. Moreover, each W^r can be chosen to inherit continuity, monotonicity, curvature, and homotheticity properties from W.

Complete strict separability in $\hat{I}$ of the indirect utility function is a property that does not depend on whether prices are normalized by income. That is, V is completely strictly separable in the partition $\hat{I}$ if and only if W is completely strictly separable in the partition $\hat{I}$. This follows, of course, from the fact that W is HDO in its arguments.

The cost function C is completely (strictly) separable in the partition $\hat{I}$ if every union of price sectors is (strictly) separable from all remaining prices (but not necessarily from output or utility).

Corollary 4.8.4 *Suppose the cost function C is continuous. Then C is completely strictly separable in $\hat{I}$ ($m>2$) if and only if there exist functions*

$$C^r : \mathcal{R}(U) \times \Omega_+^{(r)} \to \Omega_+^1, \qquad r=1,\ldots,m,$$

and an increasing function

$$\overset{*}{C} : \mathcal{R}(U) \times \sum_{r=1}^{m} \mathcal{R}(C^r) \to \Omega_+^1$$

such that

$$C(u,P) = \overset{*}{C}\left(u, \sum_{r=1}^{m} C^r(u,P^r)\right). \tag{4.17}$$

Moreover, each $C^r(u,\cdot)$ can be chosen to inherit from C the properties of continuity, (strict) monotonicity, (strict) quasi-concavity, and homotheticity.

It has not been proved that the aggregator functions C^r, $r=1,\ldots,m$, satisfy all of the regularity conditions (R-3) if C does. In particular, satisfaction of (R-3) by C is insufficient to show that each C^r can be picked concave and PLH in P. If, however, we strengthen the maintained hypotheses, we can prove not only that each C^r inherits concavity and positive linear homogeneity, but that the macro function belongs to the Bergson (1936) class of functions. There are two alternative proofs of this result, requiring substantially different maintained hypotheses. The proof presented for the cost function in Theorem 4.9 below requires not only that the master functions be differentiable, but also that it be possible to choose each aggregator function to be differentiable. On the other hand, no assumptions about the behavior of the function on the boundary of the domain are required. The alternative proof, which is employed in structuring the direct utility function in theorem 4.11, requires only that the master function, or its extension to the boundary, satisfy local nonsatiation on each $\Omega^{(r)}$. In practice, this means that the zero vector can be used as a reference vector in constructing an aggregator function. Because the cost function is defined only on $\mathfrak{R}(U) \times \Omega^n_+$, this latter assumption seems less appropriate for the cost function than for the utility function. Nonetheless, the reader should remember in using theorem 4.9 and its corollaries that if sectoral nonsatiation holds, differentiability can be eschewed.

Theorem 4.9 *Suppose that the cost function C satisfies* (R-3), *is differentiable, satisfies $\partial C(u,P)/\partial p_i > 0$ for all i and for all $P \in \Omega^n_+$, and is completely separable in $\hat{I}$ $(m>2)$. Suppose further that each aggregator function C^r in the representation* (4.17) *can be chosen to be differentiable. Then there exists a function $\Gamma : \mathfrak{R}(U) \to \mathbf{R}$, and m functions,*

$$C^r : \mathfrak{R}(U) \times \Omega^{(r)}_+ \to \Omega^1_+,$$

all satisfying (R-3P), *such that either*

$$C(u,P) = \Gamma(u) \left(\sum_{r=1}^{m} C^r(u,P^r)^{\rho(u)} \right)^{1/\rho(u)}, \qquad 0 \neq \rho(u) \leqslant 1, \quad (4.18a)$$

or

$$C(u,P) = \Gamma(u) \prod_{r=1}^{m} C^r(u,P^r)^{\rho^r(u)}, \qquad \rho^r(u) > 0 \quad \forall r, \quad (4.18b)$$

where $\sum_{r=1}^{m} \rho^r(u) = 1$.

Proof. Note that the first-degree homogeneity of C in P implies that the ratio of any two derivatives of C is HDO in P; that is,

$$\frac{\partial C(u,P)/\partial p_i}{\partial C(u,P)/\partial p_j} = \frac{\partial C^r(u,P^r)/\partial p_i}{\partial C^s(u,P^s)/\partial p_j} = \frac{C^r_i(u,P^r)}{C^s_j(u,P^s)}, \qquad i \in I^r, \ j \in I^s,$$

is HDO in P for all $\langle i,j \rangle \in I \times I$. Pick $r \neq s$ and employ Euler's theorem to arrive at

$$\sum_{k \in I^r} \frac{\partial}{\partial p_k} \left(\frac{C_i^r(u, P^r)}{C_j^s(u, P^s)} \right) p_k + \sum_{k \in I^s} \frac{\partial}{\partial p_k} \left(\frac{C_i^r(u, P^r)}{C_j^s(u, P^s)} \right) p_k = 0,$$

which, after carrying out the indicated differentiation and rearranging, becomes

$$\frac{1}{C_i^r(u, P^r)} \sum_{k \in I^r} C_{ik}^r(u, P^r) p_k = \frac{1}{C_j^s(u, P^s)} \sum_{k \in I^s} C_{jk}^s(u, P^s) p_k. \qquad \text{(i)}$$

The left-hand side of (i) depends only on (u, P^r), whereas the right-hand side depends only on (u, P^s). Hence both sides must be independent of P, so that each side is a function of u only, say $\psi(u)$. Thus

$$\sum_{k \in I^r} C_{ik}^r(u, P^r) p_k = \psi(u) \cdot C_i^r(u, P^r), \quad \text{say}, \qquad \forall i \in I^r, \quad r = 1, \ldots, m. \quad \text{(ii)}$$

This implies that C_i^r is homogeneous of degree $\psi(u)$ in P^r for each $i \in I^r$ for all r.

Next note that

$$\sum_{i \in I^r} \int C_i^r(u, P^r) \, dp_i = C^r(u, P^r) + \theta^r(u), \qquad i \in I^r, \qquad \text{(iii)}$$

where $\theta^r(u)$ is an arbitrary constant of integration, given u. It must also be true that

$$\sum_{i \in I^r} \int C_i^r(u, \lambda P^r) \, d\lambda p_i = C^r(u, \lambda P^r) + \theta^r(u), \qquad i \in I^r, \quad \lambda > 0. \quad \text{(iv)}$$

The homogeneity property of C_i^r deduced from (ii), implies that

$$\sum_{i \in I^r} \int C_i^r(u, \lambda P^r) \, d\lambda p_i = \sum_{i \in I^r} \int \lambda^{\psi(u)} C_i^r(u, P^r) \lambda \, dp_i$$

$$= \lambda^{\psi(u)+1} \sum_{i \in I^r} \int C_i^r(u, P^r) \, dp_i, \qquad i \in I^r. \quad \text{(v)}$$

Together (iii), (iv), and (v) imply that

$$\lambda^{\psi(u)+1} \left[C^r(u, P^r) + \theta^r(u) \right] = C^r(u, \lambda P^r) + \theta^r(u) \qquad \forall \lambda > 0, \quad r = 1, \ldots, m,$$

or, rearranging,

$$C^r(u,\lambda P^r)=\lambda^{\psi(u)+1}C^r(u,P^r)+\theta^r(u)(\lambda^{\psi(u)+1}-1)$$

$$\forall\lambda>0, \quad r=1,\ldots,m. \quad \text{(vi)}$$

Two cases must be considered: $\psi(u)\neq-1$ and $\psi(u)=-1$. Suppose first that $\psi(u)\neq-1$ and define $\tilde{C}^r:\mathfrak{R}(U)\times\Omega_+^{(r)}\to\Omega_+^1$ by

$$\tilde{C}^r(u,P^r)=C^r(u,P^r)+\theta^r(u).$$

We will show that $\tilde{C}^r$ is homogeneous of degree $\psi(u)+1$ in P^r. Note that

$$\tilde{C}^r(u,\lambda P^r)=C^r(u,\lambda P^r)+\theta^r(u), \qquad \forall\lambda>0,$$

and, substituting from (vi),

$$\tilde{C}^r(u,\lambda P^r)=\lambda^{\psi(u)+1}C^r(u,P^r)+\theta^r(u)(\lambda^{\psi(u)+1}-1)+\theta^r(u)$$

$$=\lambda^{\psi(u)+1}(C^r(u,P^r)+\theta^r(u))$$

$$=\lambda^{\psi(u)+1}\tilde{C}^r(u,P^r), \qquad \forall\lambda>0.$$

Now substitute

$$C^r(u,P^r)=\tilde{C}^r(u,P^r)-\theta^r(u), \qquad r=1,\ldots,m,$$

into (4.17) to obtain

$$C(u,P)=\overset{*}{C}\left(u,\sum_{r=1}^m\tilde{C}^r(u,P^r)-\sum_{r=1}^m\theta^r(u)\right)$$

$$=\tilde{C}\left(u,\sum_{r=1}^m\tilde{C}^r(u,P^r)\right)$$

where $\tilde{C}$ is defined by the last equality. Letting $\rho(u)=\psi(u)+1$, the homogeneity properties of C and $\tilde{C}^r,r=1,\ldots,m$, imply that

$$\lambda\tilde{C}\left(u,\sum_{r=1}^m\tilde{C}^r(u,P^r)\right)=\tilde{C}\left(u,\sum_{r=1}^m\tilde{C}^r(u,\lambda P^r)\right)$$

$$=\tilde{C}\left(u,\lambda^{\rho(u)}\sum_{r=1}^m\tilde{C}^r(u,P^r)\right) \qquad \forall\lambda>0,$$

which, in turn, implies that $\tilde{C}$ is homogeneous of degree $1/\rho(u)$ in its second argument. Thus

$$C(u,P) = \left(\sum_{r=1}^{m} \tilde{C}^r(u,P^r) \right)^{1/\rho(u)} \tilde{C}(u,1).$$

Letting

$$\Gamma(u) = \tilde{C}(u,1)$$

and

$$\check{C}^r(u,P^r) = \tilde{C}^r(u,P^r)^{1/\rho(u)}, \qquad r = 1,\ldots,m,$$

we have

$$C(u,P) = \Gamma(u) \left(\sum_{r=1}^{m} \check{C}^r(u,P^r)^{\rho(u)} \right)^{1/\rho(u)}. \tag{vii}$$

where each $\check{C}^r$ is PLH in P^r by construction.

If $\psi(u) = -1$, there are two solutions to (vi). The first implies that each C^r is HDO in P^r and is ruled out by the assumption that C is PLH in P. The second is formed as follows: Since $\theta^r(u)$ is an arbitrary constant (given u), let $\theta^r(u) = \bar{\rho}^r(u)/[\psi(u)+1]$, where $\bar{\rho}^r(u)$ is arbitrary. Then

$$\lim_{\psi(u) \to -1} C^r(u,\lambda P^r) = C^r(u,P^r) + \bar{\rho}^r(u) \lim_{\psi(u) \to -1} \left(\frac{\lambda^{\psi(u)+1} - 1}{\psi(u) + 1} \right)$$

$$= C^r(u,P^r) + \bar{\rho}^r(u) \ln\lambda \qquad \forall \lambda > 0, \quad r = 1,\ldots,m,$$

where the latter equality follows using l'Hôpital's rule. Hence we have

$$C^r(u,\lambda P^r) = C^r(u,P^r) + \bar{\rho}^r(u) \ln\lambda \qquad \forall \lambda > 0, \quad r = 1,\ldots,m.$$

Taking antilogarithms,

$$e^{C^r(u,\lambda P^r)} = e^{C^r(u,P^r)} \lambda^{\bar{\rho}^r(u)}.$$

Let

$$\bar{C}^r(u,P^r) = e^{C^r(u,P^r)}.$$

By construction, $\bar{C}^r$ is homogeneous of degree $\bar{\rho}^r(u)$.

Since

$$C^r(u, P^r) = \ln \overline{C}^r(u, P^r), \qquad r = 1, \ldots, m,$$

the cost function may be written as

$$C(u, P) = \overset{*}{C}\left(u, \sum_{r=1}^{m} \ln \overline{C}^r(u, P^r)\right).$$

$$= \tilde{C}\left(u, \prod_{r=1}^{m} \tilde{C}^r(u, P^r)^{\bar{\rho}^r(u)}\right), \qquad \text{say,}$$

where each

$$\tilde{C}^r(u, P^r) = \left[\overline{C}^r(u, P^r)\right]^{1/\bar{\rho}^r(u)}, \qquad r = 1, \ldots, m,$$

is PLH in prices.

As C is PLH in P, $\tilde{C}$ must be homogeneous of degree $\kappa(u) = (\sum_{r=1}^{m}\bar{\rho}^r(u))^{-1}$ in its second argument. Hence we can write

$$C(u, P) = \tilde{C}(u, 1) \prod_{r=1}^{m} \tilde{C}^r(u, P^r)^{\rho^r(u)},$$

where

$$\rho^r(u) = \bar{\rho}^r(u)\kappa(u), \qquad r = 1, \ldots, m.$$

Finally, letting

$$\Gamma(u) = \tilde{C}(u, 1)$$

we have

$$C(u, P) = \Gamma(u) \prod_{r=1}^{m} \tilde{C}^r(u, P^r)^{\rho^r(u)},$$

where $\sum_{r=1}^{m}\rho^r(u) = 1$.

Finally, note that, as the aggregator functions in (4.18a) and (4.18b) are PLH and quasi-concave in P^r, they satisfy concavity in P^r and hence the regularity conditions (R-3P). ‖

Similar results go through for the transformation function F, which is completely (strictly) separable in $\hat{I}$ if arbitrary unions of quantity variable sectors are (strictly) separable from the set of all other quantity variables (but not necessarily from the output or utility variable).

Corollary 4.8.5 *Suppose the transformation function F is continuous. Then F is completely strictly separable in $\hat{I}$ ($m > 2$) if and only if there exist $m + 1$ functions*

$$F^r : \mathcal{R}(U) \times \Omega_+^{(r)} \to \Omega_+^1, \qquad r = 1, \ldots, m,$$

and

$$\overset{*}{F} : \mathcal{R}(U) \times \sum_{r=1}^{m} \mathcal{R}(F^r) \to \Omega_+^1$$

such that

$$F(u, X) = \overset{*}{F}\left(u, \sum_{r=1}^{m} F^r(u, X^r)\right), \qquad (4.19)$$

where $\overset{*}{F}$ is increasing in its second argument. Moreover, each $F^r(u, \cdot)$ can be chosen to inherit from F the properties of continuity, (strict) monotonicity, (strict) quasi-concavity, and homotheticity.

Corollary 4.9.1 *Suppose that F satisfies (R-4) and is differentiable and completely strictly separable in $\hat{I}$ ($m > 2$). Suppose further that each aggregator F^r in the representation (4.19) can be chosen to be differentiable. Then there exist a function, $\Phi : \mathcal{R}(U) \to \mathbf{R}$, and m functions,*

$$F^r : \mathcal{R}(U) \times \Omega_+^{(r)} \to \Omega^1, \qquad r = 1, \ldots, m,$$

all satisfying (R-4X), such that either

$$F(u, X) = \Phi(u)\left(\sum_{r=1}^{m} F^r(u, X^r)^{\rho(u)}\right)^{1/\rho(u)}, \qquad 0 \neq \rho(u) \leqslant 1 \quad (4.20a)$$

or

$$F(u, X) = \Phi(u) \prod_{r=1}^{m} F^r(u, X^r)^{\rho^r(u)}, \qquad \rho^r(u) > 0 \quad \forall r, \qquad (4.20b)$$

where $\sum_{r=1}^{m} \rho^r(u) = 1$.

Theorems 4.8 and 4.9 and their corollaries elaborate on the nexus between overlapping strict separability and additivity, introduced in theorem 4.7. Complete strict separability induces an additive structure (and, in fact, a CES structure for the cost and transformation functions). Complete (nonstrict) separability, on the other hand, does not induce additivity. The Leontief function, with image

$$U(X) = \min\{x_1, \ldots, x_n\},$$

illustrates this fact. This image can be written

$$U(X) = \min\{x_1, \ldots, x_{n_c}, \min\{x_{n_c+1}, \ldots, x_n\}\}$$

$$= \overline{U}(X^c, U^r(X^r)),$$

given any arbitrary partition,

$$\{I^c, I^r\} = \{\{1, \ldots, n_c\}, \{n_c + 1, \ldots, n\}\},$$

of I; thus it is obvious that the Leontief function is completely separable in arbitrary partitions of $\hat{I}$. Yet this function has no additive representation.

Complete (strict) separability of the direct utility function and that of the indirect utility function are independent of each other, and each is independent of complete (strict) separability of the cost or transformation function. However, complete (strict) separability of the cost function and that of the transformation function are equivalent.

Theorem 4.10 *Suppose U satisfies the regularity conditions* (R-1). *Then the cost function C is completely separable in* $\hat{I}$ *if and only if the transformation function F is completely separable in* $\hat{I}$. *Moreover, if the extensions of C and F to the boundary are locally nonsated on each* $\Omega^{(r)}$, $r = 1, \ldots, m$, *then "separable" may be replaced by "strictly separable" in the above statement.*

Proof. Complete (strict) separability of C in $\hat{I}$ is equivalent to (strict) separability of every proper subset of $\hat{I}$ from its complement in I. By theorem 3.6, this is equivalent to (strict) separability in F of every proper subset of $\hat{I}$ from its complement. This is, in turn, equivalent to complete (strict) separability of F. ‖

By analogy with the noncomplete-separability case, we refer to complete (strict) separability of the cost and transformation function as conjugate complete (strict) separability. Similarly, complete (strict) separability of the direct and indirect utility functions might be called explicit direct and indirect, complete (strict) separability, respectively.

4.5 HOMOTHETICITY. COMPLETE SEPARABILITY, AND DUALITY

4.5.1 Homothetic Separability and Complete Homothetic Separability Contrasted

It will be recalled from section 4.3 that sectoral homotheticity implies that separability in any one of the four representations of the preference ordering or of the technology (U, V, C, or F) is equivalent to separability in each of the other three. Moreover, strengthening sectoral homotheticity to overall homotheticity (of U) induces additional structure on these alternative, equivalent representations. The question that naturally arises is whether or not the same results hold for complete separability. The answer is that the duality results for homothetically separable structures do not go through for complete homothetic separability (complete separability with homothetic aggregators). The three alternative complete separability concepts are equivalent only if the utility or production function is itself homothetic.

These results are presented in this section. We first explain why complete homothetic separability does not in all cases have stronger duality implications than does homothetic separability.[17] We then prove one duality result in which complete homothetic separability has stronger implications than does homothetic separability. We then proceed to examine overall homotheticity, in which case the duality results for complete separability are quite analogous to those for noncomplete separability.

In order to understand the contrast between the dualities of separability on the one hand and complete separability on the other, it is useful to recall that theorem 4.4 (the equivalence of homothetic separability of U and/or V in $\hat{I}$ and separability of C and/or F in $_0\hat{I}$) is proved by straightforward application of Theorem 3.8 (the equivalence of homothetic separability in U and/or in V of I^r from its complement in I and separability in C and/or in F of I^r from its complement in $_0I$). However, theorem 3.8 cannot be used to prove that homothetic complete separability of U implies, say, homothetic complete separability of V, because the condition that orderings on subspaces are homothetic will not in general guarantee that orderings on Cartesian products of these subspaces are homothetic. That is, although homothetic complete separability means that the union of any two separable sectors, say $I^r \cup I^s$, is separable, the

---

[17]Of course, complete homothetic separability of U, say, as a special case of homothetic separability, implies that V is homothetically separable—but not completely—and that C and F are separable—but not completely—in the extended partition (see theorem 4.5).

ordering on $\Omega^{(r)} \times \Omega^{(s)}$ need not be homothetic even though the orderings on $\Omega^{(r)}$ and $\Omega^{(s)}$ are separately homothetic. Thus, although theorem 3.8 can be employed to prove that homothetic complete separability of U in $\hat{I}$ implies that each price sector I^r is homothetically separable, it cannot be used to show that arbitrary unions of price sectors are separable (much less homothetically separable) in V. Thus, using theorem 3.8, we can show that homothetic separability of U implies homothetic separability of V, and no more (about V).

If we restrict our attention to complete strict separability, the additive representations in theorem 4.8 and its corollaries can be exploited to prove duality theorems. However, as it turns out, this fact is of no help in attempting to establish results on homothetic complete separability. To see why this is so, recall that the strategy of the proof of theorem 3.8 exploits a construction in which the homothetic aggregator function is normalized to be PLH. This approach cannot generally be applied to the additive representation of a homothetically completely separable function. To see why, consider a direct utility function with the representation

$$U(X) = \overset{*}{U}\left(\sum_{r=1}^{m} U^r(X^r) \right),$$

where each aggregator function U^r is homothetic, but U itself is not necessarily homothetic. If, by chance, each U^r is PLH, the single argument of $\overset{*}{U}$ is the image of a PLH function. Since $\overset{*}{U}$ is strictly increasing, U, in this case, is a homothetic function. This case is of some interest and is discussed below. On the other hand, if not all the aggregator functions are PLH at the start, it is not possible to renormalize or redefine them to be PLH and, at the same time, preserve the additive representation. This is seen as follows.

Since each U^r is homothetic, each can be written as

$$U^r(X^r) = \tilde{U}^r(\hat{U}^r(X^r)),$$

where $\tilde{U}^r$ is increasing and $\hat{U}^r$ is PLH. Now let $\hat{U}$ be a function whose image is defined by

$$\hat{U}(\hat{U}^1(X^1), \ldots, \hat{U}^m(X^m)) \equiv \overset{*}{U}\left(\sum_{r=1}^{m} \tilde{U}^r(\hat{U}^r(X^r)) \right).$$

Hence, while $\hat{U}$ does represent completely separable preferences and is a function of the images of PLH aggregator functions, the PLH aggregator functions do not themselves constitute the summand in the additive functional form. (If they did, U would be homothetic.)

The foregoing remarks explain why the homothetic complete separability counterpart of theorem 4.4 apparently does not go through. Strengthening homothetic complete separability to overall homotheticity conjoined with complete separability does, however, lead to some useful duality theorems. Before proceeding to the duality results, we first state and prove the appropriate representation theorems for homothetic functions which are also completely separable.

4.5.2   Representation Theorems

The following theorem would be a simple corollary of theorem 4.9 if differentiability of the parent function and the aggregators were assumed. Instead, we assume that U satisfies local nonsatiation on each $\Omega^{(r)}$, which obviates the need for differentiability. Note that neither of these two assumptions is weaker than the other.

Theorem 4.11   *Suppose that U satisfies* (R-1), *homotheticity, complete strict separability with respect to $\hat{I}$ $(m > 2)$, and local nonsatiation on each $\Omega^{(r)}$, $r = 1, \ldots, m$. Then there exist PLH functions*

$$U^r : \Omega^{(r)} \to \Omega^1, \qquad r = 1, \ldots, m,$$

all satisfying (R-1), *and an increasing function $\overset{*}{U}$ such that either*

$$U(X) = \overset{*}{U}\left[\left(\sum_{r=1}^{m} U^r(X^r)^\rho \right)^{1/\rho} \right], \qquad 0 \neq \rho \leqslant 1, \qquad (4.21a)$$

or,

$$U(X) = \overset{*}{U}\left(\prod_{r=1}^{m} U^r(X^r)^{\rho^r} \right), \qquad \rho^r > 0 \quad \forall r. \qquad (4.21b)$$

Proof.   Homotheticity and complete separability of U imply, by theorem 4.8, that we can write

$$\tilde{U}(X) = \phi(U(X)) = \phi\left(\overset{*}{U}\left(\sum_{r=1}^{m} \overset{*}{U}^r(X^r) \right) \right) = \overset{*}{\tilde{U}}\left(\sum_{r=1}^{m} \overset{*}{U}^r(X^r) \right), \qquad (a)$$

where ϕ is increasing, $\tilde{U}$ is PLH, and each $\overset{*}{U}{}^r$ is homothetic. Because U satisfies local nonsatiation on each $\Omega^{(r)}$, $r=1,\ldots,m$, invoking theorem 3.1 and corollary 4.1.2, we can use zero reference vectors to pick each U^r, $r=1,\ldots,m$. That is,

$$U^r(X^r)=\tilde{U}(0^c,X^r),\qquad r=1,\ldots,m,\qquad\text{(b)}$$

and

$$\tilde{U}(X)=\overset{\hat{}}{\tilde{U}}\big(U^1(X^1),\ldots,U^m(X^m)\big).\qquad\text{(c)}$$

Hence, each U^r is PLH. Using (a) we can rewrite (b) as

$$U^r(X^r)=\overset{*}{\tilde{U}}\left[\sum_{\substack{s=1\\ s\neq r}}^{m}\overset{*}{\tilde{U}}{}^s(0^s)+\overset{*}{U}{}^r(X^r)\right],\qquad r=1,\ldots,m.$$

Letting

$$\sum_{\substack{s=1\\ s\neq r}}^{m}\overset{*}{\tilde{U}}{}^s(0^s)=a_r,\qquad r=1,\ldots,m,$$

we get

$$U^r(X^r)=\overset{*}{\tilde{U}}\big(\overset{*}{U}{}^r(X^r)+a_r\big),\qquad r=1,\ldots,m.$$

Exploiting the fact that U^r is PLH yields

$$\tilde{U}\big(\overset{*}{U}{}^r(\lambda X^r)+a_r\big)=\lambda\tilde{U}\big(\overset{*}{U}{}^r(X^r)+a_r\big),\qquad r=1,\ldots,m.\qquad\text{(d)}$$

Homotheticity of each $\overset{*}{U}{}^r$ implies that

$$\phi^r\big(\overset{*}{\tilde{U}}{}^r(X^r)\big)=\overset{*}{U}{}^r(X^r),\qquad r=1,\ldots,m,\qquad\text{(e)}$$

where each ϕ^r is increasing and each $\overset{*}{\tilde{U}}{}^r$ is PLH. Substituting (e) into (d) and letting $\lambda^{-1}=\overset{*}{\tilde{U}}{}^r(X^r)$ yields

$$\overset{*}{\tilde{U}}\big(\phi^r\big(\overset{*}{\tilde{U}}{}^r(X^r)\big)+a_r\big)=\overset{*}{\tilde{U}}{}^r(X^r)\overset{*}{\tilde{U}}\big(\phi^r(1)+a_r\big)$$

$$=\tilde{U}^r(X^r),\quad\text{say},\qquad r=1,\ldots,m.\qquad\text{(f)}$$

Inverting (f) yields

$$\phi^r\big(\overset{*}{\tilde{U}}{}^r(X^r)\big)=\overset{*}{\tilde{U}}{}^{-1}\big(\tilde{U}^r(X^r)\big)-a_r,\qquad r=1,\ldots,m.\qquad\text{(g)}$$

Using (e), substitute (g) into (a) to get

$$\tilde{U}(X) = \overset{*}{\tilde{U}}\left(\sum_{r=1}^{m} \overset{*}{\tilde{U}}^{-1}(\tilde{U}^r(X^r)) + A \right), \tag{h}$$

where $A = -\sum_{r=1}^{m} a_r$. Remembering that $\tilde{U}$ and each $\tilde{U}^r$ are PLH, we have

$$\lambda \overset{*}{\tilde{U}}\left(\sum_{r=1}^{m} \overset{*}{\tilde{U}}^{-1}(\tilde{U}^r(X^r)) + A \right) = \overset{*}{\tilde{U}}\left(\sum_{r=1}^{m} \overset{*}{\tilde{U}}^{-1}(\lambda \tilde{U}^r(X^r)) + A \right).$$

This implies that $\overset{\wedge}{\tilde{U}}$ in identity (c) is a quasi-linear PLH function of the arguments $(\tilde{U}^1(X^1), \ldots, \tilde{U}^m(X^m))$. By a theorem of Eichhorn (1974: p. 24) we get the representation (4.21a) or (4.21b). $\|$

The representation theorem for homothetic and completely separable indirect utility functions is analogous.

Corollary 4.9.2 *Suppose that V satisfies (R-1), differentiability, negative homotheticity, and complete strict separability in $\hat{I}$ ($m>2$). Suppose further that the aggregators in (4.15) are differentiable. Then there exist PLH functions*

$$V^r : \Omega_+^{(r)} \to \Omega^1,$$

all satisfying (R-1), and a decreasing function $\overset{*}{V}$ such that either

$$V(P/y) = \overset{*}{V}\left[\left(\sum_{r=1}^{m} V^r(P^r/y)^\rho \right)^{1/\rho} \right], \qquad 0 \neq \rho \leqslant 1, \tag{4.22a}$$

or

$$V(P/y) = \overset{*}{V}\left(\prod_{r=1}^{m} V^r(P^r/y)^{\rho^r} \right), \qquad \rho^r > 0 \quad \forall r, \; \sum_{r=1}^{m} \rho^r = 1. \tag{4.22b}$$

If the extension of V to the boundary satisfies nonsatiation on each $\Omega^{(r)}$, $r = 1, \ldots, m$, then the differentiability assumption can be deleted.

Proof. The proof uses corollary 4.8.2 and theorem 4.9 (assuming differentiability) and 4.11 (assuming sectoral nonsatiation). $\|$

The dual characterizations of homotheticity and complete separability exploit complete strict separability in $\hat{I}$ and strict separability in the binary partition $_0\tilde{I} = \{\{0\}, I\}$. We formalize the representation theorems for these structures in the next three corollaries.

Corollary 4.9.3 *Suppose that the indirect utility function in nonnormalized prices satisfies (R-2) in prices, and is increasing in y, differentiable in P, and continuous in all of its arguments. Suppose further that W is completely strictly separable in $\hat{I}$ ($m > 2$) and separable in $_0\tilde{I}$, and that the aggregators in (4.16) are differentiable. Then there exist PLH functions*

$$\overline{W}^r : \Omega_+^{(r)} \to \Omega_+^1, \qquad r = 1, \ldots, m,$$

and a decreasing function Υ such that either

$$W(y,P) = \Upsilon\left[\frac{1}{y} \left(\sum_{r=1}^{m} \overline{W}^r (P^r)^\rho \right)^{1/\rho} \right], \qquad 0 \neq \rho \leqslant 1, \qquad (4.23a)$$

or

$$W(y,P) = \Upsilon\left(\frac{1}{y} \prod_{r=1}^{m} \overline{W}^r (P^r)^{\rho^r} \right), \qquad \rho^r > 0 \quad \forall r, \quad \sum_{r=1}^{m} \rho^r = 1. \quad (4.23b)$$

If the extension of $W(y,\cdot)$ to Ω^n by continuity from below satisfies local nonsatiation on each $\Omega^{(r)}$, $r = 1, \ldots, m$, then the differentiability assumption can be eliminated in the above statement.

Proof. Separability of I from $\{0\}$ implies, by lemma 3.4, that V is homothetic, implying that W is homothetic in P. This separability condition also allows us to write

$$W(y,P) = \tilde{W}(y, \hat{W}(P)).$$

Complete strict separability of W in $\hat{I}$ implies that $\hat{W}$ is completely strictly separable in this partition. Thus, we can write

$$\phi(W(y,P)) = \overset{*}{W}\left(y, \sum_{r=1}^{m} W^r (P^r) \right) = \overset{*}{W}\left(1, \sum_{r=1}^{m} W^r (P^r/y) \right)$$

in an appropriate normalization. We can invoke corollary 4.9.2 to obtain

$$W(1,P/y) = \Upsilon\left[\left(\sum_{r=1}^{m} \overline{W}^r (P^r/y)^\rho \right)^{1/\rho} \right], \qquad 0 \neq \rho \leqslant 1,$$

or

$$W(1,P/y) = \Upsilon\left(\prod_{r=1}^{m} \overline{W}^r (P^r/y)^{\rho^r} \right), \qquad \rho^r > 0 \quad \forall r, \quad \sum_{r=1}^{m} \rho^r = 1,$$

where each W^r is PLH. Extracting the scalar y from the sum or the multiple yields the desired representation. ‖

Corollary 4.9.4 *Suppose that the cost function C satisfies (R-3) and is differentiable in P, completely strictly separable in $\hat{I}$ ($m>2$), and strictly separable in the binary partition $_0\tilde{I}$. Suppose further that the aggregators in (4.17) are differentiable. Then there exist PLH functions*

$$\bar{C}^r : \Omega_+^{(r)} \to \Omega_+^1, \qquad r=1,\ldots,m,$$

such that either

$$C(u,P)=\Gamma(u)\left(\sum_{r=1}^m \bar{C}^r(P^r)^\rho\right)^{1/\rho}, \qquad 0\neq\rho\leqslant 1, \qquad (4.24a)$$

or

$$C(u,P)=\Gamma(u)\prod_{r=1}^m \bar{C}^r(P^r)^{\rho'}, \qquad \rho'>0 \quad \forall r, \qquad \sum_{r=1}^m \rho'=1. \quad (4.24b)$$

If the extension of C to $\mathcal{R}(U)\times\Omega^n$ by continuity from above satisfies local nonsatiation on each $\Omega^{(r)}$, $r=1,\ldots,m$, then the differentiability assumption can be eliminated in the above statement.

Proof. As in corollary 4.9.3, we can write

$$C(u,P)=C\left(u, \sum_{r=1}^m C^r(P^r)\right).$$

The technique of proof employed in Theorem 4.9 (given differentiability) or 4.11 (given sectoral nonsatiation) then yields

$$C(u,P)=\tilde{C}\left[u,\left(\sum_{r=1}^m \bar{C}^r(P^r)^\rho\right)^{1/\rho}\right], \qquad 0\neq\rho\leqslant 1,$$

or

$$C(u,P)=\tilde{C}\left(u, \prod_{r=1}^m \bar{C}^r(P^r)^{\rho'}\right), \qquad \rho'>0 \quad \forall r, \qquad \sum_{r=1}^m \rho'=1,$$

where $\tilde{C}$ and each $\bar{C}^r$ are PLH. Extracting the sum or product from $\tilde{C}$ yields the representations (4.24a) and (4.24b) with $\tilde{C}(u,1)=\Gamma(u)$. ‖

Corollary 4.9.5 *Suppose that the transformation function F satisfies (R-4) and is differentiable in X, completely strictly separable in $\hat{I}$ ($m > 2$), and strictly separable in $_0\tilde{I}$. Suppose further that the aggregator functions in (4.19) are differentiable. Then there exist PLH functions*

$$\bar{F}^r : \Omega_+^{(r)} \to \Omega_+^1, \qquad r = 1, \ldots, m,$$

such that either

$$F(u, X) = \Phi(u) \left(\sum_{r=1}^{m} \bar{F}^r (X^r)^\rho \right)^{1/\rho}, \qquad 0 \neq \rho \leqslant 1, \qquad (4.25a)$$

or

$$F(u, X) = \Phi(u) \prod_{r=1}^{m} \bar{F}^r (X^r)^{\rho^r}, \qquad \rho^r > 0 \quad \forall r, \quad \sum_{r=1}^{m} \rho^r = 1. \quad (4.25b)$$

If the extension of F to $\mathcal{R}(U) \times \Omega^n$ by continuity from above satisfies local nonsatiation on each $\Omega^{(r)}$, $r = 1, \ldots, m$, then the differentiability assumption can be deleted in the above statement.

Proof. The proof is identical to the proof of corollary 4.9.4. ‖

4.5.3 Duality Results

We can now state and prove the basic duality conditions for completely separable structures.

Theorem 4.12 *Suppose that U satisfies (R-1). Then the following structures are equivalent:*

(i)   *U is homothetic and completely separable in $\hat{I}$,*
(ii)   *V is homothetic and completely separable in $\hat{I}$,*
(iii)   *W is separable in $_0\tilde{I}$ and completely separable in $\hat{I}$,*
(iv)   *C is separable in $_0\tilde{I}$ and completely separable in $\hat{I}$, and*
(v)   *F is separable in $_0\tilde{I}$ and completely separable in $\hat{I}$.*

Moreover, if the extensions of V, C, and F to the boundary of Ω^n satisfy local nonsatiation on each $\Omega^{(r)}$, $r = 1, \ldots, m$, then "separable" may be replaced by "strictly separable" in the above statement.

Proof. Follows from repeated application of lemma 3.4 and theorem 3.8 after noting that in the presence of overall homotheticity the unions of homothetically separable sets are homothetic. ‖

Theorem 4.12 indicates that overall homotheticity reduces these alternative additive structures [of (i) U, (ii) V, and (iii) C or F] to a single equivalence class. This raises the question of whether overall homotheticity is *necessary* for the conjunction of these three additive structures, or of any two of them. This question has been addressed by Houthakker (1960b), Samuelson (1965, 1969), Hicks (1969), and Lau (1969a). By providing a counterexample to Houthakker's and Samuelson's result, Hicks showed that simultaneous additivity in the partition $\{\{1\},\dots,\{m\}\}$ of the direct and indirect utility functions does not imply homotheticity. This example was extended by Lau to show that simultaneous additivity in a partition $\hat{I}$ does not imply homotheticity (or even homothetic aggregator functions[18]). The question that remains is whether the conjunction of complete strict separability of U and C (or F) or of V and C (or F) (or of all three) implies homotheticity. The following theorem answers this question.

Theorem 4.13 *Suppose that U satisfies* (R-1). *Then homotheticity of U and V is implied by complete strict separability in the partition $\hat{I}$ ($m>2$) of* (i) U *and F,* (ii) U *and C,* (iii) V *and F, or* (iv) V *and C.*

Proof. By theorem 3.9, strict separability of I^r from its complement in I in both U and F implies that I^r is homothetically separable in U. Using theorem 3.8, homothetic separability of I^r in U implies, in turn, that I^r is strictly separable in F from its complement in the extended index set ${}_0I$ (i.e., from the utility or output variable as well as from quantity variables not in I^r).

Since U and F are completely strictly separable the above argument also applies to arbitrary unions of sectors in $\hat{I}$. Consider the two sets $\cup_{r=1}^{m-1}I^r$ and $\cup_{r=2}^{m}I^r$. Complete strict separability of U and F implies that each of these sets is strictly separable from its complement in ${}_0I$ in the function F. Note also that, since $m>2$, the intersection and differences of these two sets are nonempty. Applying Gorman's theorem (theorem 4.7), we find that the union of these two sets, namely I, is strictly separable from its complement in ${}_0I$, namely $\{0\}$. But this in turn implies, using lemma 3.4, that U and V are homothetic.

That complete strict separability of (ii) U and C implies homotheticity of U and V follows immediately from the equivalence of complete strict separability of C and of F (theorem 4.10). The proof that homotheticity of U and V follows from complete strict separability of (iii) V and F or (iv) V and C is dual to the proof that it follows from complete strict separability of (i) U and F or (ii) U and C and need not be written out. ‖

---

[18]Samuelson (1969) and Lau (1969a) do show that the conjunction of direct and indirect additivity implies that at least $m-1$ of the aggregators must be homothetic.

The converse to Theorem 4.13 does not go through, because homotheticity of the conditional orderings on $\Omega^{(r)}$ and $\Omega^{(s)}$, say, does not imply that the conditional preordering on $\Omega^{(r)} \times \Omega^{(s)}$ is homothetic.

4.6 ADDITIVITY IN THE BINARY PARTITION

The representation and duality theorems in sections 4.4 and 4.5 maintain the assumption that the cardinality of the partition $\hat{I}$ is greater than two. If $m = 2$, separability and complete separability are equivalent, and the representation need not be additive. In this section, we examine the conditions for the existence of an additive representation when there are only two groups.

4.6.1 Sono Independence of a Single Variable

Consider the binary partition, $\{I^c, I^r\} = \{\{j\}, I^r\}$. Sono (1945, 1961) found necessary and sufficient conditions for a twice continuously differentiable utility function to be written in the additive form

$$U(X) = \overset{*}{U}\big(U^c(x_j) + U^r(X^r)\big). \tag{4.26}$$

These conditions are that

$$\frac{\partial}{\partial x_j}\left(\ln \frac{\partial U(X)/\partial x_i}{\partial U(X)/\partial x_j}\right) = \psi(x_j) \qquad \forall i \in I^r, \tag{4.27}$$

where ψ is an arbitrary function mapping from Ω^1 into **R**. This condition states that the logarithmic derivative with respect to x_j of the marginal rate of substitution between the jth good and any other good must depend only on x_j (or be constant), and that the nature of this dependence (described by ψ) be the same for all goods in $I - \{j\}$. In this case we say that the variable j is *independent* of its complement $I^r = I - \{j\}$.

Sono's definition of independence presupposed that the set I^r is separable from $\{j\}$. Hence, his result that additivity (4.26) and independence (4.27) are equivalent essentially rested on the maintained hypothesis of the separability of I^r in U. However, in the argument that follows we show that this separability condition need not be a part of the independence definition for the above equivalence to hold. This is because the condition that $\{j\}$ is independent of I^r implies that I^r is separable from $\{j\}$.

Subject to the above proviso, the following result is due to Sono (1961: pp. 265–266).

Lemma 4.1   *Suppose that U is a twice continuously differentiable function. Then the variable j is independent of its complement I^r, (4.27), if and only if U can be written in the additive form (4.26).*

Proof.   The sufficiency of the representation (4.26) is immediate. To simplify the necessity proof, reorder the variable indices so that $j = 1$, letting $c = 1$ and $r = 2$. The independence condition then becomes

$$\frac{\partial}{\partial x_1}\left(\ln \frac{U_i(X)}{U_1(X)}\right) = \psi(x_1) \qquad \forall i \in I^2, \tag{a}$$

where $U_i(X) = \partial U(X)/\partial x_i$. (a) implies that

$$\frac{U_{i1}(X)}{U_i(X)} - \frac{U_{11}(X)}{U_1(X)} = \frac{U_{j1}(X)}{U_j(X)} - \frac{U_{11}(X)}{U_1(X)} = \psi(x_1) \qquad \forall (i,j) \in I^2 \times I^2,$$

where the U_{i1} etc. are second (cross) partial derivatives of U. This implies that

$$U_j(X)U_{i1}(X) - U_i(X)U_{j1}(X) = 0$$

or

$$\frac{\partial}{\partial x_1}\left(\frac{U_i(X)}{U_j(X)}\right) = 0 \qquad \forall (i,j) \in I^2 \times I^2.$$

Thus, I^2 is separable from $\{1\}$. Alternatively, we may express this separability condition as

$$\lambda = \frac{U_{i1}(X)}{U_i(X)}, \qquad i = 2,\ldots,n. \tag{b}$$

The integral of (a) may be written as

$$\ln \frac{U_i(X)}{U_1(X)} = \int \psi(x_1)\,dx_1 + \Theta^i(X^2) \qquad \forall i \in I^2,$$

where $X^2 = (x_2,\ldots,x_n)$. Taking the antilogarithm of each side yields

$$\frac{U_i(X)}{U_1(X)} = \frac{\eta^i(X^2)}{f^1(x_1)}, \tag{c}$$

where $\eta^i(X^2) = \exp[\theta^i(X^2)]$ and $f^1(x_1) = \exp[-\int \psi(x_1)dx_1]$. Partially differentiating each η^i with respect to each x_j, $j \in I^2$, yields

$$\frac{\partial \eta^i(X^2)}{\partial x_j} = \eta^i_j(X^2) = f^1(x_1) \frac{U_1(X)U_{ij}(X) - U_i(X)U_{1j}(X)}{[U_1(X)]^2}.$$

But, because of the separability condition (b), U_{1j} may be replaced by $\lambda U_j(X)$, so that

$$\eta^i_j(X^2) = f^1(x_1) \frac{U_1(X)U_{ij}(X) - \lambda U_i(X)U_j(X)}{[U_1(X)]^2}.$$

This implies that $\eta^i_j(X^2) = \eta^j_i(X^2)$ $\forall (i,j) \in I^2 \times I^2$, which in turn implies that

$$f_1(x_1)dx_1 + \eta^2(X^2)dx_2 + \cdots + \eta^n(X^2)dx_n$$

is an exact total differential. Integration yields

$$\int f_1(x_1)dx_1 + \int \left[\eta^2(X^2)dx_2 + \cdots + \eta^n(X^2)dx_n \right]$$

$$= f(x_1) + \eta(x_2, \ldots, x_n), \qquad \text{say.}$$

At the same time, rearranging (c) and substituting into the total differential of U, we have

$$dU(X) = U_1(X)dx_1 + U_2(X)dx_2 + \cdots + U_n(X)dx_n$$

$$= \frac{U_1(X)}{f^1(x_1)} \left[f_1(x_1)dx_1 + \eta^2(X^2)dx_2 + \cdots + \eta^n(X^2)dx_n \right].$$

Therefore $U(X)$ is a function of $f(x_1) + \eta(X^2)$, say $\overset{*}{U}$:

$$U(X) = \overset{*}{U}\big(f(x_1) + \eta(X^2)\big),$$

which is of the form (4.26).   ‖

4.6.2 Independence of a Set of Variables

In order to generalize Sono's result to the case in which a set of two or more variables is independent of its complement, consider the binary partition $\{I^c, I^r\}$ of I. A set of variables, I^c, is said to be *independent* of its complement I^r if and only if there exist functions $\psi^{ji} : \Omega^{(c)} \to \mathbf{R}$ $\forall (i,j) \in I^c \times I^c$ such that

$$\frac{\partial}{\partial x_i}\left(\ln \frac{\partial U(X)/\partial x_k}{\partial U(X)/\partial x_j}\right) = \frac{\partial}{\partial x_i}\left(\ln \frac{\partial U(X)/\partial x_l}{\partial U(X)/\partial x_j}\right) = \Psi^{ji}(X^c)$$

$$\forall (i,j) \in I^c \times I^c, \quad \forall (k,l) \in I^r \times I^r. \quad (4.28)$$

This independence condition turns out to be necessary but, if the cardinality of I^c exceeds one, not sufficient for the existence of functions $\overset{*}{U}$, U^c, and U^r such that U may be written

$$U(X) = \overset{*}{U}(U^c(X^c) + U^r(X^r)). \quad (4.29)$$

Before proceeding to our formal result, a few comments may be in order. First, the additive form (4.29) clearly implies, but is *not* implied by, strict separability in the partition $\{I^c, I^r\}$. Thus, (4.29) involves more than just a separability condition.

Secondly, as we shall see, the condition that I^c is independent of I^r implies that I^r is separable from I^c. It does *not*, however, imply that I^c is separable from I^r. Thus, when I^c has more than one element, independence of the set I^c does not imply, nor is it implied by, separability of I^c.

To illustrate this point consider the function

$$U(X) = x_1 x_3 x_4 + x_2$$

and the partition $\{I^1, I^2\} = \{\{1,2\}, \{3,4\}\}$. To check for the independence of sector 1, note that, for example,

$$\frac{\partial}{\partial x_1}\left(\ln \frac{U_3(X)}{U_2(X)}\right) = \frac{\partial}{\partial x_1}\left(\ln \frac{U_4(X)}{U_2(X)}\right)$$

$$= \Psi^{21}(x_1, x_2) = \frac{1}{x_1}.$$

The reader may verify that $\Psi^{11}(x_1, x_2) = 1/x_1$, $\Psi^{12}(x_1, x_2) = 0$, and $\Psi^{22}(x_1, x_2) = 0$. Thus I^1 is independent of I^2 but is not separable from I^2, as the reader may also verify. On the other hand I^2 is separable from I^1, with the aggregator $U^2(x_3, x_4) = x_3 x_4$, but is not independent of I^1.

In our generalization of Sono's result, we assume that I^c is both independent of and separable from I^r. This is necessary and sufficient for the additive representation (4.29).[19] The proof exploits the fact that the variables in I^c can be aggregated into a single scalar, say u_c, under the separability assumption. Then, by showing that independence of the variables in I^c is equivalent to independence of the scalar u_c, we can apply Sono's result, lemma 4.1, to complete the proof.

Theorem 4.14 *Suppose that U is a twice continuously differentiable function. The set of variables I^c is independent of its complement I^r (equation (4.28)) and separable from I^r if and only if U can be written in the additive form* (4.29).

Proof. The sufficiency of the representation (4.29) is immediate. The necessity proof is divided into two parts.

First we show that U is separable in the partition $\{I^c, I^r\}$. The independence condition (4.28) implies that

$$\frac{U_{ki}(X)}{U_k(X)} - \frac{U_{ji}(X)}{U_j(X)} = \frac{U_{li}(X)}{U_l(X)} - \frac{U_{ji}(X)}{U_j(X)}$$

$$\forall(i,j)\in I^c\times I^c, \quad \forall(k,l)\in I^r\times I^r.$$

Hence,

$$U_l(X)U_{ki}(X) - U_k(X)U_{li}(X) = 0,$$

or

$$\frac{\partial}{\partial x_i}\left(\frac{U_k(X)}{U_l(X)}\right) = 0 \qquad \forall i\in I^c, \quad \forall(k,l)\in I^r\times I^r,$$

which establishes the separability of I^r from I^c. Since, by assumption, I^c is separable from I^r, U may be written, using theorem 4.1, as

$$U(X) = \hat{U}(U^c(X^c), U^r(X^r)) = \hat{U}(u_c, u_r), \tag{a}$$

where $u_c = U^c(X^c)$ and $u_r = U^r(X^r)$.

Secondly, we show that I^c is independent of I^r in U if and only if u_c is independent of u_r in $\hat{U}$. Using the representation in (a), the independence

---

[19]Geary and Morishima (1973) have similarly extended Sono's result (using a different method of proof), apparently by assuming that both I^r and I^c are separable.

condition (4.28) can be expressed as

$$
\frac{\partial}{\partial x_i} \ln\left(\frac{\hat{U}_r(u_c,u_r)\,U_k^r(X^r)}{\hat{U}_c(u_c,u_r)\,U_j^c(X^c)} \right)
$$

$$
= \frac{\partial}{\partial x_i}\left[\ln \hat{U}_r(u_c,u_r) + \ln U_k^r(X^r) - \ln \hat{U}_c(u_c,u_r) - \ln U_j^c(X^c) \right]
$$

$$
= \frac{\hat{U}_{rc}(u_c,u_r)\,U_i^c(X^c)}{\hat{U}_r(u_c,u_r)} - \frac{\hat{U}_{cc}(u_c,u_r)\,U_i^c(X^c)}{\hat{U}_c(u_c,u_r)} - \frac{U_{ji}^c(X^c)}{U_j^c(X^c)}
$$

$$
= \Psi^{ji}(X^c) \qquad \forall (i,j) \in I^c \times I^c, \quad \forall k \in I^r, \tag{b}
$$

where $\hat{U}_c(u_c,u_r) = \partial\hat{U}(u_c,u_r)/\partial u_c$, $\hat{U}_r(u_c,u_r) = \partial\hat{U}(u_c,u_r)/\partial u_r$, and $\hat{U}_{rc}(u_c,u_r) = \partial^2\hat{U}(u_c,u_r)/\partial u_r\,\partial u_c$. Rearranging yields

$$
\frac{\hat{U}_{rc}(u_c,u_r)}{\hat{U}_r(u_c,u_r)} - \frac{\hat{U}_{cc}(u_c,u_r)}{\hat{U}_c(u_c,u_r)}
$$

$$
= \frac{1}{U_i^c(X^c)}\left(\Psi^{ji}(X^c) + \frac{U_{ji}^c(X^c)}{U_j^c(X^c)} \right) \qquad \forall (i,j) \in I^c \times I^c. \tag{c}
$$

Since the right-hand side of (c) is independent of X^r and the left-hand side is independent of the indices i and j, (c) can be rewritten as

$$
\frac{\partial}{\partial u_c}\left(\ln \frac{\hat{U}_r(u_c,u_r)}{\hat{U}_c(u_c,u_r)} \right) = \rho(X^c). \tag{d}
$$

However, in general the left-hand side of (d) depends only on u_r and u_c, so that

$$
\rho(X^c) = F\big(U^c(X^c), U^r(X^r)\big), \text{ say.}
$$

This implies that

$$
\sum_{i \in I^c} \rho_i(X^c)\,dx_i^c = F_c(u_c,u_r) \sum_{i \in I^c} U_i^c(X^c)\,dx_i^c + F_r(u_c,u_r) \sum_{k \in I^r} U_k^r(X^r)\,dx_k^r.
$$

But the second summation on the right-hand side must be zero, since the left-hand side is independent of dx_k^r $\forall k \in I^r$. This implies that $\rho(X^c)$ and $U^c(X^c)$ are functionally related; i.e., $\rho(X^c) = \overset{*}{F}(U^c(X^c))$, say. Thus, (d) becomes

$$\frac{\partial}{\partial u_c}\left(\ln\frac{\hat{U}_r(u_c,u_r)}{\hat{U}_c(u_c,u_r)}\right)=\overset{*}{F}(u_c),\tag{e}$$

which is the condition for u_c to be independent of u_r in $\hat{U}$. Thus, applying lemma 4.1, $\hat{U}$ (and hence U) can be written with the image

$$U(X)=\hat{U}\left(U^c(X^c),U^r(X^r)\right)$$

$$=\overset{*}{\overline{U}}\left(U^c(X^c)+U^r(X^r)\right),$$

which is desired representation (4.29). ∥

4.7 MULTIPLICATIVE REPRESENTATIONS

4.7.1 Strict Independence

The above characterization of additivity in a binary partition is useful in a wide range of applications where only two groups or two variables are involved. For example, see sections 5.4 and 5.5, where additivity in a binary partition plays an integral role in the theory of price and quantity aggregation. Also, in empirical work two-group additivity is quite commonly employed. Theorem 4.14 indicates that independence, in addition to separability, is needed to rationalize this assumption.

In some applications, particularly in production theory, even independence is not strong enough. Occasionally, a multiplicative decomposition of a function in a binary partition is desired, as in the definition of extended Hicks neutral technical progress (analyzed in chapter 7). It is therefore a matter of some interest to ascertain under what conditions we can write the utility-function image, say, as follows:

$$U(X)=\overset{*}{U}^c(X^c)\cdot\overset{*}{U}^r(X^r).\tag{4.30}$$

Clearly, (4.29) is necessary but not sufficient for (4.30), as (4.29) merely guarantees the existence of a monotone transform of a product. To see this, define $\overset{**}{U}$, $\overset{*}{U}^c$, and $\overset{*}{U}^r$ by

$$\overset{*}{U}^{-1}(t)=\ln\cdot\overset{**}{U}{}^{-1}(t),$$

$$U^c(X^c)=\ln\overset{*}{U}^c(X^c),$$

and

$$U^r(X^r) = \ln \overset{*}{U}{}^r(X^r),$$

which allows us to rewrite (4.29) as

$$U(X) = \overset{*}{U}\big(U^c(X^c) + U^r(X^r)\big) = \overset{**}{U}\left(\overset{*}{U}{}^c(X^c) \cdot \overset{*}{U}{}^r(X^r)\right).$$

In order to eliminate this monotonic transformation (i.e., to make $\overset{**}{U}$ the identity function), conditions even stronger than (4.28) are needed.

The set of variables I^r is said to be *strictly independent* of the set of variables in I^c if there exist functions $\phi^i : \Omega^{(r)} \to \mathbf{R}$ $\forall i \in I^r$ such that

$$\frac{\partial \ln U(X)}{\partial x_i} = \phi^i(X^r) \qquad \forall i \in I^r. \tag{4.31}$$

The next theorem shows that strict independence is necessary and sufficient for a binary multiplicative decomposition of a function.

Theorem 4.15 (Blackorby, Lovell, and Thursby, 1976) *Assume that U is twice continuously differentiable. Then strict independence is necessary and sufficient for (4.30).*

Proof. That (4.30) is sufficient for strict independence is clear. Necessity follows by defining

$$\overset{*}{U}{}^r(X^r) = U(O^c, X^r) \tag{a}$$

for an arbitrary reference vector $O^c \in \Omega^{(c)}$. Equation (4.31) implies that

$$\frac{\partial}{\partial x_i} \ln U(X) = \frac{\partial}{\partial x_i} \ln \overset{*}{U}{}^r(X^r) \qquad \forall i \in I^r, \tag{b}$$

which in turn implies that

$$\frac{U_i(X)}{U(X)} = \frac{\overset{*}{U}{}^r_i(X^r)}{\overset{*}{U}{}^r(X^r)} \qquad \forall i \in I^r,$$

or

$$\frac{U_i(X)}{U(X)} = \phi^i(X^r), \quad \text{say,} \quad \forall i \in I^r. \tag{c}$$

We next show that (c) implies that I^r is both separable from I^c and independent of I^c, allowing us to invoke Theorem 4.14. First note that the condition in (c) implies that the ratio $U_i(X)/U_j(X)$ is independent of X^c for all $(i,j) \in I^r \times I^r$. Hence I^r is separable from I^c.

Next differentiate both sides of the identity (c) with respect to x_k, $k \in I^c$, to obtain

$$U_i(X)U_k(X) - U_{ik}(X)U(X) = 0 \qquad \forall(i,k) \in I^r \times I^c,$$

or

$$\frac{U_{ik}(X)}{U_k(X)} = \frac{U_i(X)}{U(X)} = \phi^i(X^r) \qquad \forall(i,k) \in I^r \times I^c. \qquad (d)$$

To prove independence of I^r from I^c, first note that (d) implies

$$\frac{U_{ik}(X)}{U_k(X)} = \frac{U_{il}(X)}{U_l(X)} = \phi^i(X^r) \qquad \forall(i,k,l) \in I^r \times I^c \times I^c.$$

Subtracting $U_{ij}(X)/U_j(X)$, $j \in I^r$, from these identities yields

$$\frac{\partial}{\partial x_i}\left(\ln \frac{U_k(X)}{U_j(X)}\right) = \frac{\partial}{\partial x_i}\left(\ln \frac{U_l(X)}{U_j(X)}\right) = \phi^i(X^r) - \frac{U_{ij}(X)}{U_j(X)},$$

$$\forall(i,j,k,l) \in I^r \times I^r \times I^c \times I^c.$$

Independence is established by showing that $U_{ij}(X)/U_j(X)$ depends only on X^r. Solving (c) for $U_i(X)$ and differentiating with respect to x_j, $j \in I^r$, yields

$$U_{ij}(X) = U_j(X)\phi^i(X^r) + U(X)\phi_j^i(X^r) \qquad \forall(i,j) \in I^r \times I^r,$$

or

$$\frac{U_{ij}(X)}{U_j(X)} = \phi^i(X^r) + \frac{U(X)}{U_j(X)}\phi_j^i(X^r)$$

$$= \phi^i(X^r) + \frac{\phi_j^i(X^r)}{\phi^j(X^r)}, \qquad \forall(i,j) \in I^r \times I^r.$$

Thus, I^r is independent of I^c.

As I' is both separable and independent of I^c, by theorem 4.14, we can write

$$U(X) = \overset{*}{U}(U^c(X^c) + U^r(X^r)).$$

Taking logarithmic derivatives with respect to x_i, $i \in I'$, yields

$$\phi^i(X^r) = \frac{U_i(X)}{U(X)} = \frac{\overset{*}{U}'(U^c(X^c) + U^r(X^r))U_i^r(X^r)}{\overset{*}{U}(U^c(X^c) + U^r(X^r))}.$$

This identity implies that the ratio,

$$\frac{\overset{*}{U}'(U^c(X^c) + U^r(X^r))}{\overset{*}{U}(U^c(X^c) + U^r(X^r))},$$

does not depend upon X^c and is therefore independent of $U^c(X^c) + U^r(X^r)$. Hence,

$$\frac{\overset{*}{U}'(t)}{\overset{*}{U}(t)} = \alpha \qquad \alpha \neq 0.$$

The solution to this equation is

$$\ln \overset{*}{U}(t) = \alpha t + \beta,$$

where β is an arbitrary constant. Thus

$$\overset{*}{U}(U^c(X^c) + U^r(X^r)) = e^{U^c(X^c) + U^r(X^r) + \beta}$$

$$= e^{U^c(X^c)} e^{U^r(X^r) + \beta}$$

$$= \overset{*}{U}^c(X^c) \overset{*}{U}^r(X^r), \quad \text{say.} \quad \|$$

4.7.2   A Strict-Independence Overlapping Theorem

The essence of the complete separability structure discussed in section 4.4 is distilled in the fundamental theorem of Gorman (1968b)—theorem 4.7. An analogous theorem for structures induced by strict independence has been proved by Primont (1977). As this theorem has useful applications (see, for example, theorem 9.3 on the aggregation property of conditional cost of living subindices), we close this section by proving the following strict-independence overlapping theorem.

Theorem 4.16 *Assume that U is twice continuously differentiable and suppose that I^r and I^s are nonempty subsets of I satisfying $I^r \cap I^s \neq \emptyset$, $I^r - I^s \neq \emptyset$, and $I^s - I^r \neq \emptyset$. Assume also that I^r is strictly separable from its complement in I, that I^s is strictly independent of its complement in I, say I^c, and that $I^s - I^r$ is strictly essential. Then the following sets are all strictly independent of their complements in I: (i) $I^c - I^r$, (ii) $I^r - I^s$, (iii) $I^s - I^r$, (iv) $I^r \cap I^s$, and (v) any union of sets in (i)–(iv).*

Proof. Let $I^1 = I^c - I^r$, $I^2 = I^r - I^s$, $I^3 = I^s - I^r$, and $I^4 = I^r \cap I^s$. Then $I^r = I^2 \cup I^4$, $I^s = I^3 \cup I^4$, and $\hat{I} = \{I^1, I^2, I^3, I^4\}$ is a partition of I.

The symmetry of the structure (4.30) (which by theorem 4.15 is equivalent to strict independence) implies that strict independence is a symmetric concept; hence $I^c = I^1 \cup I^2$ is strictly independent of I^s. As strict independence implies separability, I^c and I^s, as well as I^r, are strictly separable from their respective complements in I. Therefore, using theorem 4.7, every element of the partition $\hat{I}$ is strictly separable from its complement in I. Thus,

$$U(X) = \hat{U}\big(U^1(X^1), U^2(X^2), U^3(X^3), U^4(X^4)\big)$$

$$= h^1\big(U^1(X^1), U^2(X^2)\big)h^2\big(U^3(X^3), U^4(X^4)\big)$$

$$= \bar{g}\big(U^1(X^1), U^3(X^3), g\big(U^2(X^2), U^4(X^4)\big)\big), \qquad \text{(a)}$$

where the second equality follows from strict independence of $I^s = I^3 \cup I^4$ and hence $I^c = I^1 \cup I^2$ and the third equality follows from separability of $I^r = I^2 \cup I^4$. Letting $u_t = U^t(X^t)$, $t = 1, 2, 3, 4$, (a) implies that

$$\frac{\partial \ln U(X)/\partial u_2}{\partial \ln U(X)/\partial u_4} = \frac{\partial \ln h^1(u_1, u_2)/\partial u_2}{\partial \ln h^2(u_3, u_4)/\partial u_4}$$

$$= \frac{\partial g(u_2, u_4)/\partial u_2}{\partial g(u_2, u_4)/\partial u_4}.$$

Rearranging,

$$\frac{\partial \ln h^1(u_1, u_2)}{\partial u_2} = \frac{\partial \ln h^2(u_3, u_4)}{\partial u_4} \frac{\partial g(u_2, u_4)/\partial u_2}{\partial g(u_2, u_4)/\partial u_4}. \qquad \text{(b)}$$

The right-hand side of (b) is independent of u_1; therefore the left-hand side is also. Consequently, variable 2 is strictly independent of variable 1 in h^1 and, using theorem 4.15, we can write

$$h^1(u_1, u_2) = \overset{*}{U}{}^1(u_1)\overset{*}{U}{}^2(u_2).$$

A similar argument allows us to decompose $h^2(u_3, u_4)$ multiplicatively; hence

$$U(X) = \overset{*}{U}{}^1(X^1)\overset{*}{U}{}^2(X^2)\overset{*}{U}{}^3(X^3)\overset{*}{U}{}^4(X^4).$$

Using theorem 4.15, it is apparent that every element of $\hat{I}$ and every union of elements of $\hat{I}$ is strictly independent of its complement in I.   ‖

4.8   CONCLUDING REMARKS

Theorems 4.14 and 4.15 on binary structure underscore the distinction between functional structure and separability. In this chapter we have considered four different restrictions on the technology or preference ordering. Abbreviating these restrictions as (SI) strict independence, (I) independence, (SS) strict separability, and (S) separability, the following logical relationships hold for $m = 2$:

$$\text{(SI)} \quad \Leftrightarrow \quad U(X) = U^c(X^c)U^r(X^r), \tag{4.30}$$

$$\text{(I)}\wedge\text{(SS)} \quad \Leftrightarrow \quad U(X) = \overset{*}{U}(U^c(X^c) + U^r(X^r)) = \overset{**}{U}(U^c(X^c)\cdot U^r(X^r)), \tag{4.29}$$

$$\text{(SS)} \quad \Leftrightarrow \quad U(X) = \hat{U}(U^c(X^c), U^r(X^r)), \tag{4.32}$$

where $\hat{U}$ is increasing, and

$$\text{(S)} \quad \Leftrightarrow \quad U(X) = \hat{U}(U^c(X^c), U^r(X^r)), \tag{4.33}$$

where $\hat{U}$ is nondecreasing. If either sector contains only one variable, (SS) is redundant as a condition for (4.29).

These implications are summarized for convenience below:

$$\text{(SI)} \Rightarrow \text{(I)}\wedge\text{(SS)},$$
$$\text{(SS)} \Rightarrow \text{(S)},$$

and

$$(4.30) \Rightarrow (4.29) \Rightarrow (4.32) \Rightarrow (4.33).$$

[However, (I)$\not\Rightarrow$(SS) and (SS)$\not\Rightarrow$(I).]

Of course, the necessary and sufficient conditions for (4.32) and (4.33) (strict separability and separability) generalize in a straightforward way to arbitrary (m-group) partitions. The conditions (I) and (SS), which are necessary and sufficient for (4.29), clearly generalize in a straightforward way to a *sufficiency* condition for additive structures in the m-group case. The m-group generalization of (I) and (SS) is, however, too strong to provide an equivalent characterization of m-group additivity; it is not implied by complete strict separability. On the other hand, a multiplicative structure (in which monotone transformations are inadmissable) for the m-group case is equivalent to the natural generalization of the necessary and sufficient condition for (4.30):

$$\frac{\partial \ln U(X)}{\partial x_i} = \phi^i(X^r) \quad \forall i \in I^r, \qquad r = 1, \ldots, m-1. \tag{4.34}$$

In fact, (4.34) implies that the same differential restriction holds for all $i \in I^m$.

In some applications (particularly in dynamic-programming problems), it is convenient to work with cardinally additive structures (unique up to a linear transformation):

$$U(X) = \sum_{r=1}^{m} U^r(X^r). \tag{4.35}$$

It is straightforward to show that the necessary and sufficient condition for this structure (for any $m \geq 2$) is

$$\frac{\partial U(X)}{\partial x_i} = \phi^i(X^r) \quad \forall i \in I^r, \qquad r = 1, \ldots, m. \tag{4.36}$$

5

Symmetric Budgeting, Decentralization, and Aggregation

Historically, much of the interest in separability arose from questions associated with the conditions under which economic agents could consistently—in some sense of the word—make certain decisions in a piecemeal fashion. This notion was investigated in the context of consumer theory by Strotz (1957, 1959) and Gorman (1959). Consumer budgeting was defined by Strotz (1957: p. 277) as follows:

> We now wish to deal explicitly with a characterization of what appears to be a familiar budgeting procedure. The individual is thought to deal with his budgeting problem in two stages: first, to decide how much expenditure to allocate to each branch; and then, secondly, to decide how best to spend each allocation on commodities within each branch. The first decision may, moreover, be made on the basis of only a general impression of such magnitudes as "the cost of food," "the cost of transportation," etc.

Strotz and Gorman went on to show that this type of behavior is rationalized by certain separability conditions regarding the consumer's utility function. Moreover, these restrictions on the consumer's preferences imply empirically refutable restrictions on the system of demand functions. There are, however, two distinct concepts embedded in Strotz's (1957, 1959) description of the process of consumer budgeting. It is for this reason that this phenomenon has commonly been referred to as "two-stage optimization". That is, in the first stage the consumer, using price indices as information, allocates total expenditure to budget categories, and in the second stage the category expenditures are allocated among the components of each category. However, the set of necessary and sufficient conditions for this two-stage optimization procedure to yield the correct demands are not necessarily conditions for either one of the two elements of this procedure taken separately. It is therefore instructive to deduce separately the necessary and sufficient conditions for each stage of the consumer budgeting procedure described by Strotz.

We refer to the second stage of the budgeting procedure as decentralization of the optimization problem. In the context of consumer theory, decentralizability refers to the ability of the consumer to make *intrasector* expenditure allocations efficiently (optimally) without knowing all prices and total expenditure. This is, however, just one example of a very broad class of such problems common to many institutional structures. One such example asks under what conditions the detailed decision making in one particular branch of a firm can be left to that branch and still have efficient decisions made. Another example asks under what conditions a planner in an intertemporal environment can leave the details of future plans to later generations, making only current savings and consumption decisions.

Different types of decentralizability arise from imposing separability restrictions on the different representations of a preference ordering or technology. Which set of restrictions is appropriate depends of course on the particular problem which is being modeled.

The first stage of Strotz's budgeting procedure is intimately related to the notion of price aggregation. That is, can the initial expenditure allocation be carried out knowing only price indices—such as the price of "food" —but not necessarily the individual (food) component prices? This is the fundamental issue addressed by Gorman (1959) in his elegant analysis of the Strotz consumer-budgeting problem. There are actually two separate but related price-aggregation issues. The first issue regards the existence of expenditure-allocation functions in which the price arguments are aggregate price indices for each of the budget categories. The second issue regards the existence of price aggregates which, when multiplied by the corresponding composite commodity (e.g., "food"), yield the optimal expenditure on the corresponding budget category.

These price-aggregation results are applicable to the study of decentralized decision making in any organization which allocates expenditure on a set of commodities and/or services subject to parametric prices. This approach is consistent with the traditional Walrasian view that quantities demanded and hence the allocations of expenditure are a function of given prices. However, there is also some justification for specifying a model in which expenditure allocation is a function of quantities rather than prices. Such a model is useful in the study of decision making in an organization which is faced with fixed allotments of inputs and a fixed valuation of total output and which is charged with the responsibility of computing shadow prices to be used by planning authorities in adjusting input allotments. Examples of such organizational structures might be found in planned economies. There is, of course, no need to analyze only those polar extremes. It is easy to imagine hybrid situations in which price aggregation may be appropriate at one level in a hierarchy and quantity aggregation at some other level. This is even more clearly the case if the problem at hand involves aggregation across agents as well as across commodities. Although we are explicitly avoiding the former problem, many of our results are more general than they might at first appear because for each result on price aggregation there is a dual quantity-aggregation result.

There are therefore three concepts embodied in the discussion of consumer budgeting or two-stage optimization—decentralizability, price aggregation, and quantity aggregation—and each has a separate set of necessary and/or sufficient conditions (if known). In fact, it is instructive to dichotomize each of these notions still further. We have already noted in chapters 3 and 4 that indirect structures in normalized prices generally place weaker restrictions on preferences than do structural conditions with respect to nonnormalized prices. Consequently, it turns out that different necessary and sufficient conditions are needed for the rationalization of the concepts discussed above, depending upon whether the allocation of category expenditure is carried out in terms of normalized prices and normalized category income or in terms of their nonnormalized counterparts.

The first section of this chapter lays out the formal definitions of the different forms of decentralization and aggregation. Section 5.2 introduces conditional utility functions which are needed in the proofs of the formal results which follow. Section 5.3 proves some results on the necessary and sufficient conditions for the different decentralizability concepts. Sections 5.4 and 5.5 contain results on price aggregation and quantity aggregation, respectively. It should be noted that all of the notions in this chapter are examined in the context of symmetrically structured preferences. Their nonsymmetric analogues are discussed in chapter 6.

5.1 DEFINITIONS OF DECENTRALIZABILITY AND PRICE AND QUANTITY AGGREGATION

5.1.1 Preliminaries

The fundamental consumer problem is

$$\max_{X} U(X) \quad \text{s.t.} \quad P \cdot X \leqslant y \wedge X \in \Omega^n. \tag{5.1}$$

The solution to (5.1) may be written as

$$X = (X^1, \ldots, X^m) = \left(\bar{\phi}^1(P, y), \ldots, \bar{\phi}^m(P, y) \right),$$

where X^r, $r=1,\dots,m$, is the subvector of quantities in group r. For each sector, the optimal expenditure y_r on goods in that sector can be readily calculated as the inner product of the rth sector's price vector and the rth sector's vector of demands. This defines m sectoral expenditure-allocation functions, $\theta^r : \Omega_+^{n+1} \to \Omega_o^1$, $r=1,\dots,m$, with images

$$y_r = \theta^r(P,y) = P^r \cdot \bar{\phi}^r(P,y), \qquad r=1,\dots,m, \tag{5.2}$$

where $\Omega_o^1 = \Omega_+^1 \cup \{0\}$. The usual properties of demand functions imply (among other things) that each θ^r is homogeneous of degree one in P and y. Thus an alternative to (5.2) is given by the sectoral expenditure-share functions, $\tilde{\theta}^r : \Omega_+^n \to \Omega_o^1$, $r=1,\dots,m$, whose images are defined by

$$\frac{y_r}{y} = \tilde{\theta}^r(P/y) = \theta^r(P/y,1), \qquad r=1,\dots,m. \tag{5.3}$$

A problem which is dual to (5.1) is[1]

$$\min_{P/y} \overset{*}{V}(P/y) \qquad \text{s.t.} \quad \frac{P}{y} \cdot X \leqslant 1 \wedge \frac{P}{y} \in \Omega^n, \tag{5.4}$$

whose solution may be written as

$$\frac{P}{y} = \left(\frac{P^1}{y}, \dots, \frac{P^m}{y} \right) = \left(\xi^1(X),\dots,\xi^m(X) \right),$$

where P^r/y is the subvector of the normalized prices in sector r. In the dual, each sectoral imputation share is calculated as the inner product of the rth-sector quantity vector and the rth-sector vector of normalized shadow prices; this defines m sectoral share functions, $\eta^r : \Omega^n \to \Omega_o^1$, $r=1,\dots,m$, with images

$$\frac{y_r}{y} = \eta^r(X) = \xi^r(X) \cdot X^r, \qquad r=1,\dots,m. \tag{5.5}$$

Just as (5.4) is dual to (5.1), (5.5) is dual to (5.3), since the vector P/y plays the role of X in the dual. The analogue in the dual to (5.2) can be derived from (5.5) by multiplying through by y to get expenditure-alloca-

---

[1] Recall that $\overset{*}{V}$ is the extension to the boundary by continuity from below (see section 2.2).

tion functions $\tilde{\eta}^r : \Omega^n \times \Omega^1_+ \to \Omega^1_o$ with images

$$y_r = \tilde{\eta}^r(X, y) = \eta^r(X) \cdot y, \qquad r = 1, \dots, m, \tag{5.6}$$

where each $\tilde{\eta}^r$ is linear in y.

The first stage of the budgeting process involves the determination of these optimal sector expenditures or imputations. As written above, these allocation functions depend on all prices, as in (5.2) and (5.3), or on all quantities in the dual, as in (5.5) and (5.6). The Strotz-Gorman problem of finding conditions under which these sector expenditures (imputations) depend only on price (quantity) indices is equivalent, as we shall show, to determining the cases under which these functions exhibit certain types of structure (e.g., as induced by separability).

However, we require that the two-stage budgeting process be consistent in the sense that this process yields demand functions which are identical to the solutions of (5.1), or, in the dual, of (5.4). Hence, even if the expenditure (imputation) functions can be structured, the two-stage process is not consistent unless sector expenditures are optimally allocated within each sector (or unless sector imputations are used to calculate correct shadow prices). We first define more precisely this latter problem of decentralizability and then address the problem of price (quantity) aggregation.

5.1.2 Decentralizability

In this section we address the issues associated with the intracategory allocation. For example, can the consumer correctly allocate his food budget without knowing nonfood prices or quantities? Even if total expenditure is correctly allocated to the rth budget category, it does not follow in general that the consumer is able to allocate the category expenditure among the category components optimally without solving the entire optimization problem. It is clear that, in general, the allocation of expenditure among, say, clothing items is not independent of the way in which expenditures are allocated among the other items over which the preference ordering is defined.

(i) *Strong decentralizability.* If it is possible for the consumer to optimally allocate the rth category expenditure, y_r, knowing only intracategory prices, we say that the problem (5.1) is characterized by *strong decentralizability* with respect to sector r. Formally, the problem (5.1) is strongly decentralizable with respect to the partition $\bar{I}$ if there exist

m vector-valued functions $\phi^r : \Omega_+^{(r)} \times \Omega_\circ^1 \to \Omega^{(r)}$ such that

$$X^r = \phi^r(P^r, y_r), \qquad r = 1, \ldots, m, \tag{SD}$$

where ϕ^r is HDO in its arguments and satisfies the Slutsky symmetry conditions; its components are called conditional demand functions.[2] Thus under strong decentralizability, in order to allocate category expenditure correctly, the consumer must know only absolute prices of category components and category expenditure.

(ii) *Weak decentralizability.* We say that the consumer's preferences are characterized by *weak decentralizability* if the consumer need only know *normalized* prices in each category and the sector's *share* of the budget in order to be able to make correct intracategory allocations. Hence, if there exist m vector-valued functions, denoted $\tilde{\phi}^r : \Omega_+^{(r)} \times \Omega_\circ^1 \to \Omega^{(r)}$ such that

$$X^r = \tilde{\phi}^r(P^r/y, y^r/y), \qquad r = 1, \ldots, m, \tag{WD}$$

we say that the (5.1) is *weakly decentralizable* with respect to $\hat{I}$.[3]

In the dual one could similarly define "indirect" versions of strong and weak decentralizability. For example, if (5.4) were weakly decentralizable, the analogous condition in the dual would be that the solution P^r/y depend only on the rth-sector quantities X^r and on the rth-sector share y_r/y. However, under some strong regularity conditions, such a normalized shadow price demand system could be obtained from (WD) by inverting the (WD) system. Thus, this decentralizability condition in the dual would be equivalent to (WD). In the same manner, a system of shadow-price demands in which P^r depended only on X^r and y_r would be equivalent, by inversion, to (SD).

There is an alternative form of decentralizability which is substantively different from (SD) and (WD) and is defined below.

(iii) *Felicitous decentralizability.*[4] In this case, in order to allocate expenditure optimally within group r the consumer needs to know the level of group-r expenditure, y_r; the prices in group r; and the level of "real income", u. Hence, we may think of it as strong decentralizability, given a level surface. Formally, if there exist vector-valued, constant-utility demand functions $\zeta^r : \Re(U) \times \Omega_+^{(r)} \to \Omega^{(r)}$ such that

$$X^r = \zeta^r(u, P^r)y_r, \qquad r = 1, \ldots, m, \tag{DFD}$$

---

[2]This term was coined by Pollak (1969) in an insightful analysis of Hicksian aggregation and Le Châtelier's principle.

[3]This notion was first discussed by Lau (1969b) and Pollak (1970b).

[4]This form of decentralizability was first formulated by Gorman (1970); the name was suggested to us by Philip Neher.

we say that (5.1) is (directly) *felicitously decentralizable* with respect to $\hat{I}$. In addition, we say that a preference ordering is (indirectly) felicitously decentralizable with respect to $\hat{I}$ if there exist vector-valued, constant-utility price-demand functions), $\delta^r : \mathfrak{R}(U) \times \Omega^{(r)} \to \Omega^{(r)}_+$, such that

$$P^r = \delta^r(u, X^r) y_r, \qquad r = 1, \ldots, m. \tag{IFD}$$

We show below that direct and indirect felicitous decentralization are equivalent.

5.1.3 Price Aggregation

In the spirit of Gorman's paper (1959), we define *strong price aggregation* with respect to $\hat{I}$ as the existence of PLH functions

$$\Pi^r : \Omega^{(r)}_+ \to \Omega^1_+, \qquad r = 1, \ldots, m,$$

and PLH expenditure-allocation functions

$$\hat{\theta}^r : \underset{r=1}{\overset{m}{\times}} \mathfrak{R}(\Pi^r) \times \Omega^1_+ \to \Omega^1_\circ, \qquad r = 1, \ldots, m,$$

such that

$$y_r = \hat{\theta}^r \big(\Pi^1(P^1), \ldots, \Pi^m(P^m), y \big), \qquad r = 1, \ldots, m. \tag{SPA}$$

Similarly, we define *weak price aggregation* with respect to $\hat{I}$ as the existence of functions

$$\tilde{\Pi}^r : \Omega^{(r)}_+ \to \Omega^1_+, \qquad r = 1, \ldots, m,$$

and expenditure-share functions

$$\hat{\tilde{\theta}}^r : \underset{r=1}{\overset{m}{\times}} \mathfrak{R}(\tilde{\Pi}^r) \to \Omega^1_\circ, \qquad r = 1, \ldots, m,$$

such that

$$\frac{y_r}{y} = \hat{\tilde{\theta}}^r \big(\tilde{\Pi}^1(P^1/y), \ldots, \tilde{\Pi}^m(P^m/y) \big), \qquad r = 1, \ldots, m. \tag{WPA}$$

Thus, strong price aggregation is defined as the existence of a rule whereby total expenditure can be allocated among the m budget categories, knowing only the values of the category price indices. Weak price aggregation is equivalent to the existence of a rule for determining budget shares, knowing only m price aggregates in normalized prices. It is clear that the homogeneity of degree one of $\hat{\theta}$ in P and y allows us to convert the strong aggregation function into the weak aggregation function. Thus, strong price aggregation implies weak price aggregation. The converse, however, is *not* true, as the aggregators $\tilde{\Pi}^r$ are not necessarily PLH.

If, in addition to the existence of the strong price indices Π^r, $r = 1,\ldots,m$, there exist PLH quantity indices

$$\Gamma^r : \Omega^{(r)} \rightarrow \Omega^1_\circ, \qquad r = 1,\ldots,m,$$

such that

$$\Pi^r(\overset{*}{P}{}^r) \cdot \Gamma^r (\overset{*}{X}{}^r) = \overset{*}{y}_r, \qquad r = 1,\ldots,m, \tag{APA}$$

for optimal triples $(\overset{*}{P}, \overset{*}{X}, \overset{*}{y}_r)$, then we say that the preferences are characterized by *additive price aggregation* with respect to $\hat{I}$. If this condition is satisfied, it is possible to formulate a first-stage optimization problem in which the consumer maximizes utility with respect to the composite commodity quantities $\Gamma^1(X^1),\ldots,\Gamma^m(X^m)$ subject to the summation across r of the above equalities in aggregate prices and commodities.

If, corresponding to the price aggregates in normalized prices, $\tilde{\Pi}^1,\ldots,\tilde{\Pi}^m$, there exist PLH quantity indices $\Gamma^1,\ldots,\Gamma^m$ such that

$$\tilde{\Pi}^r(\overset{*}{P}{}^r/y) \cdot \Gamma^r(\overset{*}{X}{}^r) = \overset{*}{y}_r/y, \qquad r = 1,\ldots,m, \tag{5.7}$$

for optimal triples $(\overset{*}{P}{}^r/y, \overset{*}{X}{}^r, \overset{*}{y}_r/y)$, then we could say that the consumer's preferences are characterized by *weak additive price aggregation* with respect to $\hat{I}$. Clearly, since each Π^r is PLH, additive price aggregation implies weak additive price aggregation. As we have not found weaker sufficient conditions for this concept than for its strong counterpart, we ignore it in what follows.

5.1.4 Quantity Aggregation

Dual to strong price aggregation is *strong quantity aggregation* with respect to $\hat{I}$, which we define as the existence of PLH functions $\Gamma^r : \Omega^{(r)} \rightarrow \Omega^1_\circ$, $r = 1,\ldots,m$, and share imputation functions

$$\hat{\eta}^r : \overset{m}{\underset{r=1}{\times}} \mathcal{R}(\Gamma^r) \rightarrow \Omega^1_\circ, \qquad r = 1,\ldots,m,$$

such that

$$\frac{y_r}{y} = \hat{\eta}^r\big(\Gamma^1(X^1),\ldots,\Gamma^m(X^m)\big), \qquad r=1,\ldots,m. \qquad \text{(SQA)}$$

Similarly, *weak quantity aggregation* with respect to $\hat{I}$ is defined as the existence of functions $\tilde{\Gamma}^r : \Omega^{(r)} \to \Omega_\circ^1$, $r=1,\ldots,m$, and expenditure imputation functions

$$\tilde{\eta}^r : \Omega^1 \times \overset{m}{\underset{r=1}{\times}} \, \mathcal{R}(\tilde{\Gamma}^r) \to \Omega_\circ^1, \qquad r=1,\ldots,m,$$

such that

$$y_r = \tilde{\eta}^r\big(y, \tilde{\Gamma}^1(X^1/y),\ldots,\tilde{\Gamma}^m(X^m/y)\big), \qquad r=1,\ldots,m. \qquad \text{(WQA)}$$

Hence strong quantity aggregation is equivalent to the existence of a rule whereby imputation shares may be calculated for all sectors, knowing only the values of the m quantity indices. Weak quantity aggregation, however, means that sectoral imputations can be calculated for all budget categories when the total expenditure and the values of the m quantity indices are known. Again, it is clear from the homogeneity of $\hat{\eta}^r$ that strong quantity aggregation implies weak quantity aggregation but not conversely.

If, in addition to the existence of the strong quantity indices, there exist price indices Π^r, $r=1,\ldots,m$, such that

$$\overset{*}{y}_r = \Pi^r(\overset{*}{P}{}^r)\Gamma^r(\overset{*}{X}{}^r), \qquad r=1,\ldots,m, \qquad \text{(AQA)}$$

for optimal triples $(\overset{*}{y}_r, \overset{*}{P}{}^r, \overset{*}{X}{}^r)$, then we say that preferences are characterized by *additive quantity aggregation* with respect to $\hat{I}$.

In order to analyze the necessary and/or sufficient conditions for these concepts, we shall want occasionally to exploit the duality between the direct and indirect utility functions in a piecemeal fashion in order to be able to take advantage of the aggregation which has been imposed on one function but not on the other. In order to do this we turn to a discussion of "conditional" utility functions. These functions are representations of the preference ordering in which a partial optimization has been imbedded. The "conditional" direct and indirect utility functions which we derive are closely related to the aggregate utility functions of Hicks's "composite commodity" theorem (1946), rigorously analyzed by Gorman (1953), Pollak (1969), Diewert (1973b), and Epstein (1975).

5.2   CONDITIONAL UTILITY FUNCTIONS

The *conditional indirect utility function*,

$$H : \Omega^m \times \Omega^n_+ \to \mathbf{R},$$

is defined by

$$H(_1 y, P) = \max_X \left\{ U(X) \mid X \in \Omega^n \wedge P^r \cdot X^r \leqslant y_r, r = 1, \ldots, m \right\}, \quad (5.8)$$

where $_1 y = [y_1, \ldots, y_m]$ is a vector of (undetermined) category expenditures. If the utility function satisfies (R-1),[5] then $H(\cdot, P)$ satisfies (R-1) for all $P \in \Omega^n_+$ and $H(_1 y, \cdot)$ satisfies (R-2)[6] for all $_1 y \in \Omega^m$. Furthermore, H is continuous in $(_1 y, P)$ and homogeneous of degree zero in each pair (y_r, P^r) and hence in $(_1 y, P)$. Finally, $H(\cdot, P)$ is strictly quasi-concave for all $P \in \Omega^n_+$ if and only if U is strictly quasi-concave. [See Diewert (1973b) and Epstein (1975) for proofs of these duality results.] If $m = 1$, H becomes, as a special case, the indirect utility function.

Solving the problem

$$\max_{_1 y} H(_1 y, P) \quad \text{s.t.} \quad \sum_{r=1}^m y_r \leqslant y \wedge y_r \in \Omega^1 \; \forall r \quad (5.9)$$

yields the vector-valued expenditure-allocation function $\theta = (\theta^1, \ldots, \theta^m)$, with images[7]

$$y_r = \theta^r(y, P), \qquad r = 1, \ldots, m. \quad (5.2)$$

Substituting these images into H generates the indirect utility function[8]

$$H(\theta^1(y, P), \ldots, \theta^m(y, P), P) = W(y, P)$$

$$= \max_X \left\{ U(X) \mid X \in \Omega^n \wedge P \cdot X \leqslant y \right\}. \quad (5.10)$$

The regularity conditions on $H(\cdot, P)$ together with the maximization in (5.9) underscores an important interpretation of the conditional indirect

[5](R-1): Continuity, positive monotonicity, and quasi-concavity (see section 2.1).

[6](R-2): Continuity, negative monotonicity, and quasi-convexity (section 2.2).

[7]Given the weak regularity conditions (R-1) for U, $\theta^r(y, P)$ is in general set-valued. Paying close attention to this fact would require little modification in the following discussion. We nevertheless find it convenient below to strengthen quasi-concavity to strict quasi-concavity in order to assure that $\theta^r(y, P)$ is a singleton.

[8]If θ is a correspondence, an arbitrary element of the image will do.

utility function: each y_r can be treated as a Hicksian quantity aggregate with a unit price.

Just as H is dual to U, the *conditional direct utility function*

$$G : \Omega^m \times \Omega^n_+ \to \mathbf{R},$$

defined by

$$G(_1y/y, X) = \min_{P/y} \left\{ \overset{*}{V}(P/y) \Big| \frac{P}{y} \in \Omega^n_+ \wedge \frac{P^r}{y} \cdot X^r \leqslant \frac{y_r}{y}, r = 1, \ldots, m \right\},$$

$$(5.11)$$

is dual to $\overset{*}{V}$ (the indirect utility function extended to the boundary by continuity from below). If $\overset{*}{V}$ satisfies (R-2), then $G(_1y/y, \cdot)$ satisfies (R-1) for all $_1y/y \in \Omega^m$ and $G(\cdot, X)$ satisfies (R-2) for all $X \in \Omega^n_+$. In addition, G is jointly continuous in $(_1y/y, X)$ and homogeneous of degree zero in each pair $(y_r/y, X^r)$. The proofs of these assertions parallel the arguments for the properties of H.

By analogy with the above argument regarding the interpretation of y_r in the direct conditional utility function, it is natural to think of y_r/y as a Hicksian price aggregate for one quantity unit.

In order to examine separability properties of the direct and indirect conditional utility functions, it is useful to introduce a partition of $R \cup I$, where, it will be recalled, $R = \{1, \ldots, m\}$ is the set of group (and group-expenditure) indices. Thus, $\overset{\wedge}{RI} = \{\{1\} \cup I^1, \ldots, \{m\} \cup I^m\}$ is a partition of $R \cup I$ that is induced by the partition $\hat{I}$ of I. Separability of $\{r\} \cup I^r$ from its complement in $R \cup I$ is defined analogously to separability in the direct and indirect utility functions. Structures induced by separability—all with respect to the partition $\overset{\wedge}{RI}$—in the direct and indirect conditional utility functions are as follows:

Separability of H:

$$H(_1y, P) = \hat{H}\left(h^1(y_1, P^1), \ldots, h^m(y_m, P^m)\right). \tag{5.12}$$

Complete strict separability of H $(m > 2)$:

$$H(_1y, P) = \overset{*}{H}\left(\sum_{r=1}^{m} h^r(y_r, P^r)\right). \tag{5.13}$$

Separability of G:

$$G(_1y/y, X) = \hat{G}\left(g^1(y_1/y, X^1), \ldots, g^m(y_m/y, X^m)\right). \tag{5.14}$$

Complete strict separability of G ($m > 2$):

$$G(_1 y/y, X) = \overset{*}{G}\left(\sum_{r=1}^{m} g^r(y_r/y, X^r) \right). \tag{5.15}$$

These representations are easily generated by adapting the representation theorems of chapter 4 to the functions H and G. As in those representation theorems, the aggregator functions and macro functions of the above representations can be chosen to inherit the regularity properties of H and G. As these functions are increasing in some arguments and decreasing in others, there is no particularly compelling normalization to be adopted in choosing the monotonicity properties of the macro and aggregator functions. (See the discussion of this issue following corollary 3.2.1.) It is convenient for our purposes to choose h^r and g^r to be increasing in y_r and y_r/y, respectively, and nonincreasing in P^r and X^r, respectively.

The following theorem and corollary relate the structures of H and G to the structures of U and V, respectively.

Theorem 5.1 *Suppose that the direct utility function U satisfies* (R-1). *Then U is separable (completely separable) in the partition $\hat{I}$ if and only if the conditional indirect utility function H is separable (completely separable) in the corresponding partition* $\overset{\wedge}{RI}$. *Moreover, "separable" may be replaced by "strictly separable" in the above statement.*

Proof. If U is separable in $\hat{I}$, its image can be written

$$U(X) = \hat{U}\left(U^1(X^1), \ldots, U^m(X^m) \right),$$

where $\hat{U}$ is nondecreasing. The conditional indirect utility function image is

$$H(_1 y, P) = \max_{X} \left\{ U(X) | X \in \Omega^n \wedge P^r \cdot X^r \leqslant y_r, \forall r \right\}$$

$$= \hat{U}\left(\max_{X^1} \left\{ U^1(X^1) | X^1 \in \Omega^{(1)} \wedge P^1 \cdot X^1 \leqslant y_1 \right\}, \right.$$

$$\left. \ldots, \max_{X^m} \left\{ U^m(X^m) | X^m \in \Omega^{(m)} \wedge P^m \cdot X^m \leqslant y_m \right\} \right)$$

$$= \hat{U}\left(h^1(y_1, P^1), \ldots, h^m(y_m, P^m) \right),$$

proving that H is separable in $\overset{\wedge}{RI}$. Moreover, if $\hat{U}$ is increasing, it follows that H is strictly separable in $\hat{I}$. A similar construction shows that complete (strict) separability of U in $\hat{I}$ implies complete (strict) separability of H in $\overset{\wedge}{\text{RI}}$.

To prove the converse, let

$$\overset{\circ}{\hat{H}}\left(\overset{\circ}{U}^1(X^1),\ldots,\overset{\circ}{U}^m(X^m)\right)$$

$$= \min_{P}\left\{\hat{H}\left(\overset{*}{\hat{h}}{}^1(1,P^1),\ldots,\overset{*}{\hat{h}}{}^m(1,P^m)\right)\middle|P\in\Omega^n\wedge P^r\cdot X^r\leqslant 1, r=1,\ldots,m\right\},$$

where $\overset{*}{\hat{h}}{}^r(1,\cdot)$ is the extension of $h^r(1,\cdot)$ to the boundary by continuity from below, $r=1,\ldots,m$, and $\overset{\circ}{U}^r:\Omega_+^{(r)}\to\mathbf{R}$ is defined by[9]

$$\overset{\circ}{U}^r(X^r)= \min_{P^r}\left\{\overset{*}{\hat{h}}{}^r(1,P^r)\middle|P^r\in\Omega^{(r)}\wedge P^r\cdot X^r\leqslant 1\right\}, \qquad r=1,\ldots,m.$$

But, by theorem A.2 (in the appendix),

$$h^r(1,P^r)= \max_{X^r}\left\{U^r(X^r)\middle|X^r\in\Omega^{(r)}\wedge P^r\cdot X^r\leqslant 1\right\},$$

where U^r is the extension of $\overset{\circ}{U}^r$ to the boundary by continuity from above, so that

$$H(_1 y,P)$$

$$= \max_{X}\left\{\hat{H}\left(U^1(X^1),\ldots,U^m(X^m)\right)\middle|X\in\Omega^n\wedge P^r\cdot X^r\leqslant 1, r=1,\ldots,m\right\},$$

where $\hat{H}$ is the extension of $\overset{\circ}{\hat{H}}$ to the boundary of its domain. Thus,

$$\hat{H}\left(h^1(y_1,P^1),\ldots,h^m(y_m,P^m)\right)$$

$$= \max_{X}\left\{\hat{H}\left(U^1(X^1),\ldots,U^m(X^m)\right)\middle|X\in\Omega^n\wedge P^r\cdot X^r\leqslant y_r, r=1,\ldots,m\right\}.$$

Since, by definition,

$$H(_1 y,P)= \max_{X}\left\{U(X)\middle|X\in\Omega^n\wedge P^r\cdot X^r\leqslant y_r, r=1,\ldots,m\right\},$$

it follows that

$$U(X)=\hat{H}\left(U^1(X^1),\ldots,U^m(X^m)\right).$$

---

[9]This duality argument is carried out at unit category expenditure rather than by normalizing prices by y_r (exploiting the homogeneity property of h^r), since y_r could be zero, in which case P^r/y_r is undefined.

Note that if $\hat{H}$ is increasing, it follows that U is strictly separable in $\hat{I}$. An analogous construction shows that complete (strict) separability of H implies complete (strict) separability of U. ||

Corollary 5.1.1 *Suppose that the extended indirect utility function $\overset{*}{V}$ satisfies (R-2). Then the conditional utility function G is separable (completely separable) in the partition $\hat{\text{RI}}$ if and only if V is separable (completely separable) in the partition $\hat{I}$. Moreover, "separable" can be replaced by "strictly separable" in the above statement.*

Proof. The proof is identical to the proof of Theorem 5.1, apart from a change in notation. ||

We conclude our discussion of conditional utility functions with a lemma that is analogous to Roy's theorem. In the statement and proof of this lemma and in much of what follows it is convenient to strengthen slightly the regularity conditions (R-1). As these stronger regularity conditions will be invoked repeatedly throughout the remainder of this chapter, we list them below for easy reference:

(R-1′) continuity, positive monotonicity, and strict quasi-concavity.[10]

Thus, the difference between (R-1′) and (R-1) is that the former includes *strict* quasi-concavity. We similarly strengthen the regularity conditions for the indirect utility function V to

(R-2′) continuity, negative monotonicity, and strict quasi-convexity.

The stronger curvature assumptions are convenient for the discussion of budgeting, decentralization, and aggregation because they assure uniqueness of the solution to (5.1) and the dual indirect utility minimization problem (5.4). Hence our discussion centers on demand (price and quantity) *functions* rather than correspondences, thus simplifying the exposition.

One should also note that our assumption of strict quasi-concavity is convenient for another reason. Combined with the monotonicity assumption, it implies that U is *increasing*. This in turn has important implications for separability and functional structure, as shown in theorem 3.1; namely, the structure

$$U(X) = \hat{U}\left(U^1(X^1), \ldots, U^m(X^m)\right)$$

is equivalent to strict separability of U in $\hat{I}$, since strict monotonicity of U implies strict monotonicity of $\hat{U}$.

---

[10]Strict quasi-concavity: for all $(X, \hat{X}) \in \Omega^{2n}$ such that $X \neq \hat{X}$, $U(X) \geqslant U(\hat{X}) \Rightarrow U(\theta X + (1 - \theta)\hat{X}) > U(\hat{X})$ for all $\theta \in (0, 1)$. Strict quasi-convexity is defined by reversing the inequalities in the definition of strict quasi-concavity.

Lemma 5.1 *Suppose that the utility function satisfies (R-1′) and that H and the income allocation functions, θ^r, $r = 1,\ldots,m$, are differentiable. If $\theta(y,P)$ is positive, then the vector-valued functions*

$$\tilde{\phi}^r : \Omega^m \times \Omega^a_+ \to \Omega^{(r)}, \qquad r = 1,\ldots,m,$$

defined by

$$\tilde{\phi}^r(_1y,P) = -\frac{\nabla_{P^r}H(_1y,P)}{\nabla_{y_r}H(_1y,P)}, \qquad r = 1,\ldots,m, \tag{5.16}$$

yield as images optimal X^r, $r = 1,\ldots,m$, if $_1y$ is optimal.

Proof. As H is increasing in $_1y$, $\theta(y,P)$ satisfies

$$\sum_{r=1}^{m} \theta^r(y,P) = y. \tag{a}$$

By the hypothesis of the lemma, the solution to the optimization problem (5.9) is interior; hence

$$\frac{\partial H(\theta(y,P),P)}{\partial \theta^r(y,P)} = \lambda(y,P), \qquad r = 1,\ldots,m, \tag{b}$$

where $\lambda(y,P)$ is the saddle-point value of the Lagrangean multiplier corresponding to the optimization problem (5.9). Roy's theorem and the identity (5.10) imply that the optimal value of x_i, where $i \in I^s$, is

$$x_i = -\frac{\partial H(\theta(y,P),P)/\partial p_i}{\partial H(\theta(y,P),P)/\partial y},$$

$$= -\frac{\displaystyle\sum_{r=1}^{m} \frac{\partial H(\theta(y,P),P)}{\partial \theta^r(y,P)} \frac{\partial \theta^r(y,P)}{\partial p_i} + \frac{\partial H(\theta(y,P),P)}{\partial p_i}}{\displaystyle\sum_{r=1}^{m} \frac{\partial H(\theta(y,P),P)}{\partial \theta^r(y,P)} \frac{\partial \theta^r(y,P)}{\partial y}}$$

$$= -\frac{\displaystyle\sum_{r=1}^{m} \frac{\partial \theta^r(y,P)}{\partial p_i} - \frac{\partial H(\theta(y,P),P)}{\partial p_i}}{\displaystyle\sum_{r=1}^{m} \frac{\partial \theta^r(y,P)}{\partial y} - \frac{\partial H(\theta(y,P),P)}{\partial \theta^s(y,P)} \sum_{r=1}^{m} \frac{\partial \theta^r(y,P)}{\partial y}},$$

where the last identity follows from (b). Differentiating the identity (a) with respect to p_i demonstrates that the first term in the above expression vanishes. Differentiating (a) with respect to y yields

$$\sum_{r=1}^{m} \frac{\partial \theta^r (y,P)}{\partial y} = 1,$$

so that the optimal value of x_i is given by

$$x_i = - \frac{\partial H (\theta (y,P),P)/\partial p_i}{\partial H (\theta (y,P),P)/\partial \theta^s (y,P)} . \qquad ||$$

5.3   DECENTRALIZATION

As noted earlier, decentralizability refers to the possibility of making intracategory expenditure allocations optimally and efficiently—that is, without requiring information on all prices and total expenditure. We have introduced in section 5.1 three distinct types of decentralizability—strong, weak, and felicitous. This section examines the known necessity and/or sufficiency conditions for these three concepts.

5.3.1   Strong Decentralizability

Strong decentralizability is the case where only own category prices and own category income are needed. In this case the images of the conditional demand functions are

$$X^r = \phi^r (P^r, y_r), \qquad r = 1, \ldots, m.$$

We first prove sufficient conditions for strong decentralizability.[11]

Theorem 5.2   *If the utility function satisfies* (R-1') *and is separable in the partition* $\hat{I}$, *the optimization problem* (5.1) *is strongly decentralizable with respect to the same partition.*

[11]Proofs of both sufficiency and necessity are in Primont (1970) and Gorman (1971).

Proof. The conditional indirect utility function is generated by

$$\max_{X}\left\{\hat{U}\left(U^{1}(X^{1}),\ldots,U^{m}(X^{m})\right)\middle|X\in\Omega^{n}\wedge P^{r}\cdot X^{r}\leqslant y_{r}\,\forall r\right\}$$

$$=\hat{U}\left(\left\{\max_{X^{1}}U^{1}(X^{1})\middle|X^{1}\in\Omega^{(1)}\wedge P^{1}\cdot X^{1}\leqslant y_{1}\right\},\right.$$

$$\left.\ldots,\left\{\max_{X^{m}}U^{m}(X^{m})\middle|X^{m}\in\Omega^{(m)}\wedge P^{m}\cdot X^{m}\leqslant y_{m}\right\}\right)$$

$$=\hat{U}\left(U^{1}\left(\phi^{1}(P^{1},y_{1})\right),\ldots,U^{m}\left(\phi^{m}(P^{m},y_{m})\right)\right).$$

Moreover, from (5.10),

$$\hat{U}\left(U^{1}\left(\phi^{1}(P^{1},\theta^{1}(y,P))\right),\ldots,U^{m}\left(\phi^{m}(P^{m},\theta^{m}(y,P))\right)\right)$$

$$=\max_{X}\left\{U(X)\middle|X\in\Omega^{n}\wedge P\cdot X\leqslant y\right\},$$

where $\theta(y,P)$ solves

$$\max\hat{U}\left(U^{1}\left(\phi^{1}(P^{1},y_{1})\right),\ldots,U^{m}\left(\phi^{m}(P^{m},y_{m})\right)\right)$$

$$\text{s.t.}\quad {}_{1}y\in\Omega^{m}\wedge\sum_{r=1}^{m}y_{r}\leqslant y.$$

Hence the ϕ^{r}, $r=1,\ldots,m$, are the required decentralization functions. $\parallel$

Stronger maintained assumptions are required in order to show that decentralizability implies separability.

Theorem 5.3 *Suppose that the utility function U satisfies* (R-1') *and that the conditional indirect utility function and the income allocation functions* θ^{r} *are differentiable. If each* $\theta^{r}(P,y)$ *is positive, then separability of U in* $\hat{I}$ *is necessary and sufficient for the decentralizability of* (5.1) *with respect to the same partition.*

Proof. Sufficiency is immediate from theorem 5.2. To prove necessity, note that, as the conditions of Lemma 5.1 are satisfied, we can write

$$\frac{\phi_{i}^{r}({}_{1}y,P)}{\phi_{j}^{s}({}_{1}y,P)}=\frac{\partial H({}_{1}y,P)/\partial p_{i}}{\partial H({}_{1}y,P)/\partial p_{j}}\qquad\forall(i,j)\in I\times I.$$

Decentralizability implies that for $(i,j) \in I' \times I'$, these ratios depend only on y_r and P'. This, however, is the Leontief-Sono separability condition for separability of $\{r\} \cup I'$ from its complement in $R \cup I$. It follows that H is separable in $\overset{\wedge}{RI}$. Hence, by theorem 5.1, U is separable in $\hat{I}$.   ‖

Note that in theorem 5.2 strict separability is not required for decentralization of the utility-maximization problem. For example, the fixed-proportions utility function, defined by

$$U(X) = \min\{x_1, x_2, x_3\},$$

satisfies the sufficient conditions for decentralizability. The solution to

$$\max_{X} \min\{x_1, x_2, x_3\} \qquad \text{s.t.} \quad X \in \Omega^3 \wedge P \cdot X \leqslant y$$

is

$$\phi_i(P,y) = \frac{y}{p_1 + p_2 + p_3}, \qquad i = 1, 2, 3. \tag{a}$$

The solution to

$$\max_{X} \min\{x_1, x_2, x_3\} \qquad \text{s.t.} \quad X \in \Omega^3 \wedge p_1 x_1 \leqslant y_1 \wedge p_2 x_2 + p_3 x_3 \leqslant y_2$$

is

$$\phi^1(P^1, y_1) = \frac{y_1}{p_1}, \tag{b}$$

$$\phi^2(P^2, y_2) = \left(\frac{y_2}{p_2 + p_3}, \frac{y_2}{p_2 + p_3} \right). \tag{c}$$

These functions are the required components of a decentralization algorithm. To make this fact explicit, solve

$$\max_{y_1, y_2} H({}_1 y, P) = \max_{y_1, y_2} \min\left\{ \frac{y_1}{p_1}, \frac{y_2}{p_2 + p_3}, \frac{y_2}{p_2 + p_3} \right\}$$

$$\text{s.t.} \quad {}_1 y \in \Omega^2 \wedge y_1 + y_2 \leqslant y$$

to obtain the allocation functions

$$\theta^1(P,y) = \frac{p_1}{p_1 + p_2 + p_3} y \tag{d}$$

and

$$\theta^2(P,y) = \frac{p_2+p_3}{p_1+p_2+p_3}\, y. \tag{e}$$

Substituting (d) and (e) into (b) and (c) respectively yields the overall solution vector (a).

5.3.2 Weak Decentralizability

It is apparent from the construction in the proof of theorem 5.2 that the decentralized allocation rules are (conditional) demand functions; that is, they are homogeneous of degree zero and, if differentiable, satisfy the Slutsky symmetry conditions. The same cannot be said for the weaker decentralization allocation rule (WD). For correct intracategory allocations to be made under this rule, each division must know its own budget share and its own normalized prices. That is, the intracategory allocation functions have images

$$X^r = \tilde{\phi}^r\left(\frac{P^r}{y}, \frac{y_r}{y}\right), \qquad r=1,\ldots,m. \tag{WD}$$

Since a separable function yields conditional demand functions which are homogeneous of degree zero (as in theorem 5.2), separability of U is sufficient for weak decentralizability. It is not, however, necessary.

The functions $\tilde{\phi}^r$ are allocation devices and not demand functions in the ordinary sense. For example, they are not necessarily homogeneous of degree zero in (P^r, y_r) or in their arguments $(P^r/y, y_r/y)$. These functions also fail to satisfy the symmetry conditions in general. As a result, we do not expect such a clean characterization of weak decentralizability as with strong. The following theorem, however, does provide a sufficient condition.[12]

Theorem 5.4. *Assume that* $\overset{*}{V}$ *satisfies* (R-2′). *Then separability of the indirect utility function in* $\hat{I}$ *implies weak decentralizability with respect to* $\hat{I}$.

Proof. By corollary 5.1.1, G is separable if $\overset{*}{V}$ is. Therefore,

$$G\left({}_1y/y, X\right) = \hat{G}\left(g^1(y_1/y, X^1), \ldots, g^m(y_m/y, X^m)\right).$$

[12]This result was originally proved by Lau (1969b), employing stronger regularity conditions than (R-2′).

The conditional demands for goods in the rth sector make up the vector of solutions to

$$\min_{X^r} \overset{*}{g}{}^r(y_r/y, X^r) \qquad \text{s.t.} \quad \frac{P^r}{y} \cdot X^r \leqslant \frac{y_r}{y}, \qquad r = 1,\ldots,m$$

(where $\overset{*}{g}{}^r$ is the extension of g^r to the boundary by continuity from below); namely,

$$X^r = \tilde{\phi}^r\left(\frac{P^r}{y}, \frac{y_r}{y}\right), \qquad r = 1,\ldots,m. \qquad \|$$

The conditional direct sector utility functions help to explicate the difference between direct and indirect separability and hence between strong and weak decentralizability. Direct strict separability means that the conditional preordering induced on $\Omega^{(r)}$ is independent of quantities of commodities not in the rth sector. Indirect strict separability means that the induced conditional preordering on sector r, represented by the sector utility function g^r, depends on the quantities of commodities outside the rth sector only through the scalar y_r/y, the rth-sector budget share. Using H, one can also characterize direct strict separability as meaning that the induced preordering of prices on $\Omega_+^{(r)}$ depends on prices outside the rth sector only through the scalar y_r. The conditional demand functions derived from a separable conditional *direct* utility function are homogeneous of degree zero in P^r/y and y_r/y and hence could be written as functions of P^r and y_r, as in the case of strong decentralizability. However, as noted before, they do *not* in general satisfy the Slutsky symmetry conditions. This is because the preference ordering induced on goods space by G changes whenever budget shares change.

5.3.3   Felicitous Decentralizability

We turn now to the third type of decentralizability, which occurs quite naturally in the context of cost functions. The relationship between felicitous decentralization and separability of the cost function is captured in the following theorem.

Theorem 5.5   *If the utility function satisfies* (R-1′) *and the cost function is differentiable, then felicitous decentralization relative to* $\hat{I}$ *is equivalent to separability of* C *in* $\hat{I}$.

Proof.   Suppose that C is separable in $\hat{I}$. Using Hotelling's theorem, we obtain the compensated quantity-demand functions as follows:

$$X^r = \frac{\partial C\left(u, C^1(u, P^1),\ldots, C^m(u, P^m)\right)}{\partial C^r(u, P^r)} \cdot \nabla_{P^r} C^r(u, P^r), \qquad r = 1,\ldots,m.$$

Multiplying both sides of the ith component by p_i and summing over $i \in I^r$, we get

$$y_r = \frac{\partial C\left(u, C^1(u, P^1), \ldots, C^m(u, P^m)\right)}{\partial C^r(u, P^r)} \cdot C^r(u, P^r), \qquad r = 1, \ldots, m,$$

by Euler's theorem. Substitution into the demand function yields

$$X^r = \nabla_{P^r} C^r(u, P^r) \cdot \frac{y_r}{C^r(u, P^r)} = \zeta^r(u, P^r) y_r, \qquad r = 1, \ldots, m. \quad \text{(DFD)}$$

Conversely, suppose (DFD) holds; then ratios of quantities in group r depend only upon (u, P^r). Again using Hotelling's theorem, this implies that

$$\frac{\zeta_i(u, P)}{\zeta_j(u, P)} = \frac{\dfrac{\partial C(u, P)}{\partial p_i}}{\dfrac{\partial C(u, P)}{\partial p_j}}$$

depends only upon (u, P^r) for all $(i,j) \in I^r \times I^r$, $r = 1, \ldots, m$, which is the Leontief-Sono separability condition, implying that the cost function is separable in $\hat{I}$. ‖

Corollary 5.5.1 *Preferences exhibit direct felicitous decentralizability if and only if they exhibit indirect felicitous decentralizability.*

Proof. Follows from theorems 4.2 and 5.5. ‖

5.4 PRICE AGGREGATION

Before proceeding to a formal analysis of price aggregation, some additional concepts are needed as well as a preliminary aggregation result. These are taken up in the following two subsections.

5.4.1 The Generalized Gorman Polar Form

By imposing additional restrictions on the conditional utility functions, certain aggregation results become accessible. Suppose the sector functions h^r, $r = 1, \ldots, m$, of a completely strictly separable conditional indirect utility function can be written as

$$h^r(y_r, P^r) = \Psi^r\left(\frac{y_r}{\Pi^r(P^r)}\right) + \Lambda^r(P^r), \qquad \text{(GGPF)}$$

where Ψ^r is increasing in its single argument, Π^r is a PLH function, and Λ^r is homogeneous of degree zero. We call (GGPF) the *generalized Gorman polar form* (Gorman, 1959). The homogeneity properties of Π^r and Λ^r imply that

$$h^r(y_r, P^r) = h^r(y_r/y, P^r/y) = \Psi^r\left(\frac{y_r/y}{\Pi^r(P^r/y)}\right) + \Lambda^r(P^r/y).$$

The function Π^r will turn out to be the price index for the rth sector that is required for price aggregation.

5.4.2 A Preliminary Lemma[13]

A preliminary result, of some interest in its own right, is needed before the main aggregation results can be proved. We are concerned here with solutions to the problem

$$\max_{1^y} H(_1y, P) \qquad \text{s.t.} \quad \sum_{r=1}^{m} y_r = y$$

and the conditions under which they have the form

$$y_r = \hat{\theta}^r\left(\Pi^1(P^1), \ldots, \Pi^m(P^m), y\right), \qquad r = 1, \ldots, m. \qquad \text{(SPA)}$$

We first lighten the notation. Let

$$f(q, z) = H(_1y, P) \qquad \text{for} \quad q \in \Omega^m, \ z \in \Omega^n,$$

and consider the slightly more general problem

$$\max_{q \in \Omega^m} f(q, z) \qquad \text{s.t.} \quad b \cdot q = c, \qquad \text{(a)}$$

where $b = (b_1, \ldots, b_m) \in \Omega_+^m$ and $c \in \Omega_+^1$.

Suppose the solution to (a) has the form

$$q = \phi\left(b, c, \rho^1(z^1), \ldots, \rho^m(z^m)\right) = \phi(b, c, \rho(z)), \qquad \text{(b)}$$

where $\rho(z)$ is the m-tuple of images $(\rho^1(z^1), \ldots, \rho^m(z^m))$. In this case the choice function ϕ, for fixed values of b and c, is separable in some

---

[13]This is taken from Blackorby, Primont, and Russell (1977a).

partition of the set of n variable indices of z. Intuitively, this must mean that the maximand f possesses some structural property that is reflected in the form of the choice function. Our intuition is justified in the following:

Lemma 5.2 *Suppose that $f(\cdot,z)$ satisfies (R-1′), that the (indirect) function $v:\Omega_+^{m+1}\times\Omega^n\to\mathbf{R}$ defined by*

$$v(b,c,z)=f\big(\phi(b,c,\rho(z)),z\big)= \max_q \big\{ f(q,z)|q\in\Omega^m \wedge b\cdot q=c\big\}$$

is continuously differentiable in b and c, and that the solution to (a) is interior. Then the solution to (a) has the form (b) if and only if there exist functions $g:\Omega^m\times\Omega^m\to\mathbf{R}$ and $h:\Omega^n\to\mathbf{R}$ such that

$$f(q,z)=g(q,\rho(z))+h(z). \tag{c}$$

Proof. Maximizing (c) subject to $b\cdot q=c$ clearly gives (b), since the optimal solution for q is independent of the value of $h(z)$. To prove the converse, apply Roy's theorem to the indirect function v for a fixed point $\rho(z)\in\Omega^m$ to get

$$q_i=\phi_i(b,c,\rho(z))=\frac{-\,\partial v(b,c,z)/\partial b_i}{\partial v(b,c,z)/\partial c}, \qquad i=1,\ldots,m.$$

Hence gradients of level sets of v have components

$$\frac{\partial v(b,c,z)/\partial b_i}{\partial v(b,c,z)/\partial b_j}=\frac{\phi_i(b,c,\rho(z))}{\phi_j(b,c,\rho(z))}.$$

Integration over b and c yields

$$v(b,c,z)=w(b,c,\rho(z))+h(z),$$

where $h(z)$ is a constant of integration which, in general, depends on z. Noting that v is homogeneous of degree zero in (b,c), we can write

$$v(b,c,z)=\hat{v}(b/c,z)$$

and

$$w(b,c,\rho(z))=\hat{w}(b/c,\rho(z)).$$

Finally, invoking theorem A.1,

$$f(q,z) = \min_{b/c} \left\{ \overset{*}{\hat{v}}(b/c,z) \,\middle|\, \frac{b}{c} \cdot q \leqslant 1 \right\}$$

$$= \min_{b/c} \left\{ \overset{*}{\hat{w}}(b/c,\rho(z)) + h(z) \,\middle|\, \frac{b}{c} \cdot q \leqslant 1 \right\}$$

$$= g(q,\rho(z)) + h(z),$$

where $\overset{*}{\hat{v}}$ and $\overset{*}{\hat{w}}$ are extensions of $\hat{v}$ and $\hat{w}$ to the boundary by continuity from below.   ‖

5.4.3   Necessary and Sufficient Conditions for Price Aggregation

We are now in a position to characterize, at least to some extent, strong, weak, and additive price aggregation. For easy reference, we repeat below the equalities which define these three concepts:

$$y_r = \hat{\theta}^r\left(\Pi^1(P^1),\ldots,\Pi^m(P^m),y\right), \qquad r=1,\ldots,m, \qquad \text{(SPA)}$$

$$y_r/y = \tilde{\theta}^r\left(\Pi^1(P^1/y),\ldots,\Pi^m(P^m/y)\right), \qquad r=1,\ldots,m, \qquad \text{(WPA)}$$

and

$$y_r = \Pi^r(P^r)\cdot\Gamma(X^r), \qquad r=1,\ldots,m. \qquad \text{(APA)}$$

Theorem 5.6[14]   *Suppose that the utility function U satisfies* (R-1′). *Then price aggregation is possible if the image of U can be written*

$$U(X) = \overset{*}{U}\left(\sum_{r=1}^{d} U^r(X^r) + \hat{U}\left(U^{d+1}(X^{d+1}),\ldots,U^m(X^m)\right)\right), \quad (5.17)$$

where each U^r, $r=1,\ldots,d$, has the generalized Gorman polar form (GGPF) *and each U^r, $r=d+1,\ldots,m$, is homothetic. Moreover, if U is separable, the conditional indirect utility function H is twice continuously differentiable, and each $\theta^r(P,y)$ is positive, then the structure* (5.17) *is necessary for strong price aggregation.*

[14]This theorem and proof are taken from Blackorby, Primont, and Russell (1977b).

Proof. We first prove the sufficiency of the structure (5.17). First note that the homothetic functions U^r, $r = d+1, \ldots, m$, can be normalized to be PLH; thus, assume that they have already been normalized. The conditional indirect utility function has the image

$$H(_1 y, P) = \max_X \left\{ \overset{*}{U} \left(\sum_{r=1}^{d} U^r (X^r) + \hat{U} \left(U^{d+1} (X^{d+1}), \ldots, U^m (X^m) \right) \right) \right|$$

$$\left. X \in \Omega^n \wedge P^r \cdot X^r \leqslant y_r, r = 1, \ldots, m \right\}$$

$$= \overset{*}{U} \left(\sum_{r=1}^{d} h^r (y_r, P^r) + \hat{U} \left(h^{d+1} (y_{d+1}, P^{d+1}), \ldots, h^m (y_m, P^m) \right) \right),$$

where, of course,

$$h^r (y_r, P^r) = \max_{X^r} \left\{ U^r (X^r) \,\middle|\, X^r \in \Omega^{(r)} \wedge P^r \cdot X^r \leqslant y_r \right\}, \qquad r = 1, \ldots, m,$$

and each h^r, $r = d+1, \ldots, m$, is negatively homogeneous (NH) in P^r.[15] Moreover, by hypothesis, using the definition of (GGPF) and lemma 3.4 we can write

$$H(_1 y, P) = \overset{*}{U} \left(\sum_{r=1}^{d} \Psi^r \left(\frac{y_r}{\Pi^r (P^r)} \right) + \Lambda^r (P^r) \right.$$

$$\left. + \hat{U} \left(\frac{y_{d+1}}{\Pi^{d+1} (P^{d+1})}, \ldots, \frac{y_m}{\Pi^m (P^m)} \right) \right) \qquad \text{(a)}$$

where each Π^r, $r = d+1, \ldots, m$, is a PLH function defined by

$$\Pi^r (P^r) = \frac{y_r}{h^r (y_r, P^r)} = \frac{1}{h^r (1, P^r)} \,.$$

As $\overset{*}{U}$ is increasing, maximizing (a) subject to

$$\sum_{r=1}^{m} y_r \leqslant y \qquad \text{(b)}$$

[15]A function f is NH if $f(tX) = t^{-1} f(X)$ for all $t > 0$.

is equivalent to maximizing

$$\sum_{r=1}^{d} \Psi^r\left(\frac{y_r}{\Pi^r(P^r)}\right) + \Lambda^r(P^r) + \hat{U}\left(\frac{y_{d+1}}{\Pi^{d+1}(P^{d+1})},\ldots,\frac{y_m}{\Pi^m(P^m)}\right)$$

subject to (b). But this latter problem gives the same solution as maximizing

$$\sum_{r=1}^{d} \Psi^r\left(\frac{y_r}{\Pi^r(P^r)}\right) + \hat{U}\left(\frac{y_{d+1}}{\Pi^{d+1}(P^{d+1})},\ldots,\frac{y_m}{\Pi^m(P^m)}\right)$$

subject to (b). The solution is clearly of the form

$$y_r = \hat{\theta}^r\left(\Pi^1(P^1),\ldots,\Pi^m(P^m),y\right), \qquad r = 1,\ldots,m. \qquad \text{(SPA)}$$

To prove the necessity condition, suppose that we are given

$$y_r = \hat{\theta}^r(\Pi^1(P^1),\ldots,\Pi^m(P^m),y), \qquad r = 1,\ldots,m, \qquad \text{(SPA)}$$

where each $\hat{\theta}^r$ is PLH in its $m+1$ arguments $\{\Pi^1(P^1),\ldots,\Pi^m(P^m),y\}$ and each Π^r is PLH in P^r. (SPA) is the solution to the problem

$$\max_{1^y} H(_1y,P) \qquad \text{s.t.} \qquad \sum_{r=1}^{m} y_r = y,$$

where H is the conditional indirect utility function. By Lemma 5.2 there exist functions, say $\hat{h}$ and Λ, such that

$$H(_1y,P) = \hat{h}\left(_1y,\Pi^1(P^1),\ldots,\Pi^m(P^m)\right) + \Lambda(P). \qquad \text{(c)}$$

By Theorem 5.1, separability of U in $\hat{I}$ implies that H is separable in the corresponding partition $\hat{R}I$; hence

$$H(_1y,P) = \hat{H}\left(h^1(y_1,P^1),\ldots,h^m(y_m,P^m)\right). \qquad \text{(d)}$$

Moreover, as $\hat{H}$ is increasing, the aggregator functions can be taken as

$$h^r(y_r,P^r) = H\left(O_1,\ldots,y_r,\ldots,O_m,O^1,\ldots,P^r,\ldots,O^m\right), \qquad r = 1,\ldots,m,$$

where O_s and O^s, $s = 1,\ldots,m$, $s \neq r$, are appropriate reference scalars and vectors, respectively (as described in Corollary 4.1.2). Using (c), we can also write

$$h^r(P^r, y_r) = \hat{h}\left(O_1, \ldots, y_r, \ldots, O_m, \Pi^1(O^1), \ldots, \Pi^r(P^r), \ldots, \Pi^m(O^m)\right)$$

$$+ \Lambda(O^1, \ldots, P^r, \ldots, O^m)$$

$$= \hat{h}\left(O_1, \ldots, y_r/\Pi^r(P^r), \ldots, O_m, \Pi^1(O^1), \ldots, 1, \ldots, \Pi^m(O^m)\right)$$

$$+ \Lambda(O^1, \ldots, P^r, \ldots, O^m)$$

$$= \Psi^r\left(\frac{y_r}{\Pi^r(P^r)}\right) + \Lambda^r(P^r), \qquad\qquad\qquad \text{(e)}$$

where the second identity follows from the first-degree homogeneity of Π^r and the zero-degree homogeneity of H in the pair (y_r, P^r) (it is easy to show that zero-degree homogeneity of H implies that Λ is HDO). The functions Ψ^r and Λ^r are defined by the last identity.

Substituting (e) into (d) yields

$$H(_1 y, P) = \hat{H}\left(\Psi^1\left(\frac{y_1}{\Pi^1(P^1)}\right) + \Lambda^1(P^1), \ldots, \Psi^m\left(\frac{y_m}{\Pi^m(P^m)}\right) + \Lambda^m(P^m)\right).$$

$$\text{(f)}$$

It remains to show that H has the structure that is dual to (5.17). In order to show this, we first note that necessary conditions for solving

$$\max_{_1 y} H(_1 y, P) \qquad \text{s.t.} \quad \sum_{r=1}^{m} y_r \leqslant y$$

are

$$\frac{\partial H(_1 y, P)/\partial y_r}{\partial H(_1 y, P)/\partial y_s} = 1 \qquad \forall r, s.$$

Because of (f), these conditions are equivalent to

$$\frac{\hat{H}_r(\psi^1 + \lambda^1, \ldots, \psi^m + \lambda^m)\Psi^{r\prime}\left(\dfrac{y_r}{\Pi^r(P^r)}\right) \cdot \dfrac{1}{\Pi^r(P^r)}}{\hat{H}_s(\psi^1 + \lambda^1, \ldots, \psi^m + \lambda^m)\Psi^{s\prime}\left(\dfrac{y_s}{\Pi^s(P^s)}\right) \cdot \dfrac{1}{\Pi^s(P^s)}} = 1 \qquad \forall r, s,$$

or

$$\frac{\hat{H}_r(\psi^1+\lambda^1,\ldots,\psi^m+\lambda^m)}{\hat{H}_s(\psi^1+\Lambda^1,\ldots,\psi^m+\lambda^m)} = \frac{\Pi^r(P^r)}{\Pi^s(P^s)} \frac{\Psi^{s\prime}\left(\dfrac{y_s}{\Pi^s(P^s)}\right)}{\Psi^{r\prime}\left(\dfrac{y_r}{\Pi^r(P^r)}\right)} \qquad \forall r,s, \qquad \text{(g)}$$

where, of course,

$$\psi^r = \Psi^r\left(\frac{y_r}{\Pi^r(P^r)}\right), \qquad r=1,\ldots,m,$$

$$\lambda^r = \Lambda^r(P^r), \qquad r=1,\ldots,m,$$

$\hat{H}_r$ is the partial derivative of $\hat{H}$ with respect to the rth argument, and $\Psi^{r\prime}$ is the derivative of Ψ^r with respect to its one argument. (The differentiability of $\hat{H}$ and Ψ^r follows from that of H; see corollary 4.1.1.) Substituting in (g) for y_r and y_s using

$$y_r = \hat{\theta}^r\left(\Pi^1(P^1),\ldots,\Pi^m(P^m),y\right), \qquad \text{(SPA)}$$

it is apparent that the ratios in (g) are independent of $\Lambda^r(P^r)$, $r=1,\ldots,m$.

Without loss of generality, suppose that $\Lambda^r(P^r)\neq0$, $r=1,\ldots,d$, and $\Lambda^r(P^r)=0$, $r=d+1,\ldots,m$, where $0\leqslant d\leqslant m$. As the ratios in (g) are independent of $\Lambda^r(P^r)$ for all r, it is apparent that for all r and s such that $r>d$ and $s>d$, the ratio must be independent of the qth argument in $\hat{H}$ for all $q\leqslant d$. Thus, the set of variables $\{d+1,\ldots,m\}$ is separable from the components of $\{1,\ldots,d\}$, and using theorem 3.2 we can aggregate over this separable set:

$$H(_1y,P) = \overline{H}\left(\psi^1+\lambda^1,\ldots,\psi^d+\lambda^d,\overline{U}\left(\psi^{d+1},\ldots,\psi^m\right)\right). \qquad \text{(h)}$$

We now consider successively five cases: (i) $d=0$, (ii) $d=1$, (iii) $d=m=2$, (iv) $d=m>2$, and (v) $m>d\geqslant2$. Establishing the structure (5.17) from (h) requires a somewhat different mode of argument in each case.

Case (i) ($d=0$): In this case, because U is separable,

$$U(X) = \hat{U}\left(U^1(X^1),\ldots,U^m(X^m)\right), \qquad \text{(i)}$$

where

$$U^r(X^r) = \min_{P^r} \left\{ \Psi^r \left[\frac{1}{\overset{*}{\Pi}{}^r(P^r)} \right] \middle| P^r \in \Omega^{(r)} \wedge P^r \cdot X^r \leqslant 1 \right\}$$

and $\overset{*}{\Pi}{}^r$ is the extension of Π^r to the boundary by continuity from above. As Π^r is PLH, U^r is homothetic (using lemma 3.4) and (i) belongs to the class (5.17).

Case (ii) ($d=1$): In this case

$$H(_1 y, P) = \overline{H}\left(\psi^1 + \lambda^1, \overline{U}(\psi^2, \ldots, \psi^m)\right) = \overline{H}(\psi^1 + \lambda^1, \mu),$$

where, of course,

$$\mu = \overline{U}(\psi^2, \ldots, \psi^m).$$

We now show that H satisfies the independence condition for additivity in a binary partition (theorem 4.14). As $\{2, \ldots, m\}$ is separable from $\{1\}$ in H, we need to show that

$$\frac{\partial}{\partial \psi^s} \left[\frac{\hat{H}_1(\psi^1 + \lambda^1, \psi^2, \ldots, \psi^m)}{\hat{H}_r(\psi^1 + \lambda^1, \psi^2, \ldots, \psi^m)} \right] \frac{\hat{H}_r(\psi^1 + \lambda^1, \psi^2, \ldots, \psi^m)}{\hat{H}_1(\psi^1 + \lambda^1, \psi^2, \ldots, \psi^m)}$$

$$= \sigma^{rs}(\psi^2, \ldots, \psi^m), \qquad r, s = 2, \ldots, m. \quad \text{(j)}$$

However, from the above arguments, we know that the ratios

$$\frac{\hat{H}_1(\psi^1 + \lambda^1, \psi^2, \ldots, \psi^m)}{\hat{H}_r(\psi^1 + \lambda^1, \psi^2, \ldots, \psi^m)}, \qquad r = 2, \ldots, m,$$

are themselves independent of $\psi^1 + \lambda^1$. Hence (j) is trivially satisfied, and theorem 4.14 implies that there exist functions $\overset{*}{H}$, ζ, and $\hat{U}$ such that

$$H(_1 y, P) = \overset{*}{H}(\zeta(\psi^1 + \lambda^1) + \hat{U}(\psi^2, \ldots, \psi^m)).$$

Moreover, since

$$\frac{\overset{*}{H}{}'(\zeta(\psi^1 + \lambda^1) + \hat{\mu}) \cdot \zeta'(\psi^1 + \lambda^1)}{\overset{*}{H}{}'(\zeta(\psi^1 + \lambda^1) + \hat{\mu}) \cdot \hat{U}_r(\psi^2, \ldots, \psi^m)}$$

(where $\hat{U}_r$ is the rth partial derivative of $\hat{U}$) is independent of λ^1, ζ must be linear. Thus we can write

$$H\left(_1 y, P\right) = \overset{*}{H}\!\left(\psi^1 + \lambda^1 + \hat{U}\left(\psi^2, \ldots, \psi^m\right)\right).$$

A construction analogous to that in case (i) yields a direct objective function which belongs to the class (5.17).

Case (iii) $(d = m = 2)$: In this case,

$$H\left(_1 y, P\right) = \overline{H}\left(\psi^1 + \lambda^1, \psi^2 + \lambda^2\right),$$

and an argument much the same as that in case (ii) establishes the structure

$$H\left(_1 y, P\right) = \overset{*}{H}\!\left(\psi^1 + \lambda^1 + \psi^2 + \lambda^2\right),$$

which implies the structure (5.17).

Case (iv) $(m = d > 2)$: In this case

$$\frac{\hat{H}_r\left(\psi^1 + \lambda^1, \ldots, \psi^m + \lambda^m\right)}{\hat{H}_s\left(\psi^1 + \lambda^1, \ldots, \psi^m + \lambda^m\right)}$$

is independent of the values of $\psi^t + \lambda^t$ for all $t \in R - \{r, s\}$ for all $(r, s) \in R \times R$. Hence, H is completely separable in the discrete partition $\{\{1\}, \ldots, \{m\}\}$ and therefore additive in its variables (with linear aggregators). Hence we can write

$$\hat{H}\left(\psi^1 + \lambda^1, \ldots, \psi^m + \lambda^m\right) = \overset{*}{H}\!\left(\sum_{r=1}^{m} \psi^r + \lambda^r\right),$$

which implies that U satisfies the structure (5.17).

Case (v) $(m > d \geqslant 2)$: Note that in this case certain ratios of derivatives of $\hat{H}$ and $\overline{H}$ are related by

$$\frac{\hat{H}_r\left(\psi^1 + \lambda^1, \ldots, \psi^d + \lambda^d, \psi^{d+1}, \ldots, \psi^m\right)}{\hat{H}_s\left(\psi^1 + \lambda^1, \ldots, \psi^d + \lambda^d, \psi^{d+1}, \ldots, \psi^m\right)}$$

$$= \frac{\overline{H}_r\left(\psi^1 + \lambda^1, \ldots, \psi^d + \lambda^d, \mu\right)}{\overline{H}_\mu\left(\psi^1 + \lambda^1, \ldots, \psi^d + \lambda^d, \mu\right) \cdot \overline{U}_s\left(\psi^{d+1}, \ldots, \psi^m\right)},$$

$$r = 1, \ldots, d; \ s = d+1, \ldots, m, \qquad \text{(k)}$$

where,

$$\mu = \overline{U}\left(\psi^{d+1}, \ldots, \psi^{m}\right)$$

and $\overline{H}_{\mu}$ and $\overline{U}_{s}$ are derivatives of $\overline{H}$ and $\overline{U}$ with respect to μ and ψ^{s}, respectively. From the above, we know that the left-hand side of (k) is independent of $\psi^{t} + \lambda^{t}$, $t = 1, \ldots, d$; hence the right-hand side is independent of the same arguments. As $\overline{U}_{s}(\psi^{d+1}, \ldots, \psi^{m})$ is trivially independent of these arguments,

$$\frac{\partial}{\partial\left(\psi^{t}+\lambda^{t}\right)}\left[\frac{\overline{H}_{r}\left(\psi^{1}+\lambda^{1}, \ldots, \psi^{d}+\lambda^{d}, \mu\right)}{\overline{H}_{\mu}\left(\psi^{1}+\lambda^{1}, \ldots, \psi^{d}+\lambda^{d}, \mu\right)}\right] = 0, \qquad r = 1, \ldots, d, \quad t = 1, \ldots, d;$$

hence all pairs $\{r, d+1\}$, where $d+1$ indexes μ, are separable from their complements in $\{1, \ldots, d, d+1\}$. Consider, for example, the pairs

$$I^{r} = \{1, d+1\}$$

and

$$I^{s} = \{2, d+1\},$$

whose intersection is

$$I^{q} = \{d+1\}.$$

Applying the Gorman theorem (theorem 4.7) and the argument in case (ii), we can write

$$\overline{H}\left(\psi^{1}+\lambda^{1}, \ldots, \psi^{d}+\lambda^{d}, \mu\right) = \tilde{H}\left(\psi^{1}+\lambda^{1}+\psi^{2}+\lambda^{2}+\mu, \psi^{3}+\lambda^{3}, \ldots, \psi^{d}+\lambda^{d}\right).$$

Note that every argument of $\tilde{H}$ is a term containing some λ^{r}. Hence the ratio of partial derivatives with respect to any two arguments must be independent of all other variables in $\tilde{H}$. This means that $\tilde{H}$ is completely separable in the discrete partition of its variables. Therefore, using theorem 4.8, we can write

$$H\left(_{1}y, P\right) = \overset{*}{H}\left(\sum_{r=1}^{d} g^{r}\left(\psi^{r}+\lambda^{r}\right) + \hat{\mu}\right)$$

$$= \overset{*}{H}\left[\sum_{r=1}^{d}\left(\Psi^{r}\left(\frac{y_{r}}{\Pi^{r}(P^{r})}\right) + \Lambda^{r}(P^{r})\right)\right.$$

$$\left. + \hat{U}\left(\Psi^{d+1}\left(\frac{y_{d+1}}{\Pi^{d+1}(P^{d+1})}\right), \ldots, \Psi^{m}\left(\frac{y_{m}}{\Pi^{m}(P^{m})}\right)\right)\right],$$

where in the first line $\hat{\mu} = g(\mu)$, say, and each $g^r(\psi^r + \lambda^r)$ can be assumed to be linear by the argument given in case (i) for ζ. Finally, a construction analogous to part (i) above yields the structure

$$U(X) = \overset{*}{H}\left(\sum_{r=1}^{d} U^r(X^r) + \hat{U}\left(U^{d+1}(X^{d+1}), \ldots, U^m(X^m) \right) \right), \quad (5.17)$$

where each

$$U^r(X^r) = \min_{P^r}\left\{ \Psi^r\left[\frac{1}{\overset{*}{\Pi}^r(P^r)} \right] + \Lambda^r(P^r) \middle| P^r \in \Omega^{(r)} \wedge P^r \cdot X \leqslant 1 \right\},$$

$$r = 1, \ldots, d,$$

clearly has the generalized Gorman polar form, and each

$$U^r(X^r) = \min_{P^r}\left\{ \Psi^r\left[\frac{1}{\overset{*}{\Pi}^r(P^r)} \right] \middle| P^r \in \Omega^{(r)} \wedge P^r \cdot X^r \leqslant 1 \right\}, \quad r = d+1, \ldots, m,$$

is homothetic by lemma 3.4.   ‖

The salient condition involving (5.17) in theorem 5.6 is essentially a functional structure but not necessarily a separability condition. This is because of the anomalous binary-partition case which arises when $m = d = 2$ or $d = 1$ in equation (5.17). If $m = d = 2$, (5.17) becomes

$$U(X) = \overset{*}{U}\left(U^1(X^1) + U^2(X^2) \right), \quad (5.18)$$

where U^1 and U^2 have the generalized Gorman polar forms. Assuming nonhomothetic separability in the binary partition, this structure is necessary and sufficient for strong price aggregation [maintaining (R-1′), differentiability, and separability] but is *not* implied by complete separability. Similarly, if $d = 1$, (5.17) has the form (5.18) where U^1 has the generalized Gorman polar form and U^2 is homothetic. Again, this structure cannot be characterized by a separability condition. If these two cases are excluded by assumption, the necessary and sufficient conditions for strong price aggregation (the second part of theorem 5.6) can be characterized by separability conditions:

Corollary 5.6.1 (Gorman, 1959) *Suppose that H is differentiable and that U satisfies (R-1') and is separable in the partition $\hat{I}$, where $\hat{I}$ contains more than two elements and where not precisely $m-1$ of the aggregator functions of the separable representation of U are homothetic. Suppose furthermore that the partition $\hat{I}$ is ordered so that all nonhomothetic sectors (if any) precede the homothetic sectors (if any). Then strong price aggregation is possible if and only if*

(i)   U is completely separable in the partition

$$\left\{ I^1,\dots,I^d, \; \bigcup_{r=d+1}^{m} I^r \right\},$$

where d is the number of nonhomothetic sectors, and each aggregator U^r, $r=1,\dots,d$, has the generalized Gorman polar form, and
(ii)   the aggregator over $\cup_{r=d+1}^{m} I^r$ is itself separable in the partition $\{I^{d+1},\dots,I^m\}$.

Two special cases of the sufficiency part of theorem 5.6 which are perhaps most likely to be applied in practice are obtained by letting $d=0$ and $d=m$ respectively.

Corollary 5.6.2 *If U satisfies (R-1'), then homothetic separability implies strong price aggregation.*

Corollary 5.6.3 *If U satisfies (R-1'), then complete separability of U in a partition with more than two groups where each aggregator has the generalized Gorman polar form implies strong price aggregation.*

As strong price aggregation implies weak price aggregation, the above conditions are also sufficient for weak price aggregation. The next theorem provides an alternative sufficient condition for weak price aggregation.

Theorem 5.7 *If the direct utility function U satisfies (R-1'), and the indirect utility function V is differentiable and can be written in the form*

$$V(P/y) = \overset{*}{V}\left(\sum_{r=1}^{m} V^r(P^r/y) \right), \qquad (5.19)$$

then weak price aggregation is possible.

Proof.   Applying Roy's theorem,

$$\phi_i(P/y) = \frac{V_i^r(P^r/y)y}{\displaystyle\sum_{s=1}^{m} \sum_{j\in I^s} V_j^s(P^s/y)\cdot p_j}, \qquad i\in I^r,$$

where $V_j^s(P^s/y)$ is the jth partial derivative of V^s. Multiplying both sides by p_i/y and summing over $i \in I^r$ gives

$$\frac{y_r}{y} = \frac{\tilde{\Pi}^r(P^r/y)}{\sum\limits_{s=1}^{m} \tilde{\Pi}^s(P^s/y)}, \qquad r = 1,\dots,m,$$

where

$$\tilde{\Pi}^s(P^s/y) = \sum_{j \in I^s} V_j^s(P^s/y)\cdot(p_j/y) \qquad s = 1,\dots,m. \qquad \|$$

If $m > 2$ in the structure (5.19), the sufficient condition can be characterized in terms of complete separability of V.

Corollary 5.7.1 (Pollak, 1970) *If U satisfies (R-1′) and V is differentiable and completely separable in a partition with more than two elements, then weak price aggregation is possible.*

Proof. Follows from corollary 4.8.2 and theorem 5.7. $\|$

5.4.4 Necessary and Sufficient Conditions for Additive Price Aggregation

The next theorem proves necessary and sufficient conditions for additive price aggregation.[16]

Theorem 5.8 *If U satisfies (R-1′) and is separable, then homothetic separability is necessary and sufficient for additive price aggregation.*

Proof.
Necessity: We are given price and quantity indices, $\Pi^r(P^r)$ and $\Gamma^r(X^r)$, such that for optimal triples $(\overset{*}{P^r}, \overset{*}{X^r}, \overset{*}{y}_r)$

$$\Pi^r(\overset{*}{P^r})\cdot\Gamma^r(\overset{*}{X^r}) = \overset{*}{y}_r, \qquad r = 1,\dots,m. \qquad \text{(APA)}$$

where each Π^r and each Γ^r is PLH. Since U is separable, the solution

$$\overset{*}{X^r} = \phi^r(\overset{*}{P^r}, \overset{*}{y}_r)$$

to the problem

$$\max_{X^r} U^r(X^r) \qquad \text{s.t.} \quad \overset{*}{P^r}\cdot X^r = \overset{*}{y}_r, \qquad r = 1,\dots,m,$$

---

[16]Using stronger regularity conditions this was proved by Blackorby, Lady, Nissen, and Russell (1970). Sufficiency was proved by Arrow, Barankin, and Shephard (1951), Shephard (1953, 1970), and Gorman (1959). John Weymark referred us to the 1951 article.

picks optimal quantities for the rth sector when the optimal sector allocation is given (see theorem 5.2). Substitution into (APA) yields

$$\overset{*}{y}_r = \Pi^r(\overset{*}{P^r})\Gamma^r(\phi^r(\overset{*}{P^r},\overset{*}{y}_r)),$$

or

$$\frac{\overset{*}{y}_r}{\Pi^r(\overset{*}{P^r})} = \Gamma^r(\phi^r(\overset{*}{P^r},\overset{*}{y}_r)), \qquad r = 1,\ldots,m.$$

Increasing $\overset{*}{y}_r$ by the multiplicative factor λ,

$$\frac{\lambda\overset{*}{y}_r}{\Pi^r(\overset{*}{P^r})} = \Gamma^r(\phi^r(\overset{*}{P^r},\lambda\overset{*}{y}_r)) = \lambda\Gamma^r(\phi^r(\overset{*}{P^r},\overset{*}{y}_r)),$$

shows that the composition $\Gamma^r \circ \phi^r$ is PLH in y_r. Since Γ^r is a PLH function of $\phi^r(\overset{*}{P^r},\overset{*}{y}_r)$, this implies that ϕ^r is PLH in y_r. Hence each U^r is homothetic.

Sufficiency: Homothetic separability implies that $H(_1 y, P)$ may be written as

$$H(_1 y, P) = \hat{H}\left(\frac{y_1}{\Pi^1(P^1)}, \ldots, \frac{y_m}{\Pi^m(P^m)}\right)$$

as in the construction of the sufficiency part of theorem 5.6 (where $d=0$). But, by this construction,

$$\frac{y_r}{\Pi^r(P^r)} = U^r\left(\phi^r(P^r,y_r)\right), r = 1,\ldots,m,$$

so that

$$\overset{*}{y}_r = \Pi^r(\overset{*}{P^r}) \cdot U^r\left(\phi^r(\overset{*}{P^r},\overset{*}{y}_r)\right) = \Pi^r(\overset{*}{P^r}) \cdot \Gamma^r(\overset{*}{X^r}) \qquad \text{(APA)}$$

for optimal triples $(\overset{*}{y}_r, \overset{*}{P^r}, \overset{*}{X^r})$. ‖

It is interesting to note that the quantity aggregator Γ^r is in this case identical to the utility (or output) aggregator U^r. In fact, the constructions in theorems 3.8 and 4.4 make it clear that the PLH aggregator $\bar{F}^r$ in the transformation function is identical to the aggregators U^r and Γ^r. Moreover, the price aggregator Π^r is equivalent to W^r in the indirect objective function and $\bar{C}^r$ in the cost function.

Note also that (APA) implies that

$$\sum_{r=1}^{m} \Pi^r(\overset{*}{P}) \cdot \Gamma^r(\overset{*}{X}^r) = y.$$

Thus, in the homothetic-separability case, the income-allocation functions can be generated by solving

$$\max_{\Gamma^1(X^1),\ldots,\Gamma^m(X^m)} \hat{U}\left(\Gamma^1(X^1),\ldots,\Gamma^m(X^m)\right) \quad \text{s.t.} \quad \sum_{r=1}^{m} \Pi^r(P^r) \cdot \Gamma^r(X^r) \leqslant y,$$

and setting

$$\hat{\theta}^r\left(\Pi^1(P^1),\ldots,\Pi^m(P^m),y\right) = \Pi^r(P^r) \cdot \overset{*}{\Gamma}^r(X^r), \qquad r=1,\ldots,m,$$

where $\left(\overset{*}{\Gamma}^1(X^1),\ldots,\overset{*}{\Gamma}^m(X^m)\right)$ is the solution to this maximization problem.

5.4.5 Examples

The notions of price and quantity aggregation might be explicated by an example. An interesting class of preference orderings (or technologies) is represented in the dual by the *Gorman polar form* (GPF), a special case of the (GGPF) in which Ψ^r is the identity function (see subsection 5.4.1 above). This structure encompasses, as special cases, familiar types of preferences such as those that are affinely homothetic [e.g., the affinely translated CES and its special case, the affinely translated Cobb-Douglas, which generates the linear expenditure system of Stone (1954)] and preferences that are homothetic to minus infinity (see Pollak, 1971b). These special cases are discussed further in sections 8.1.2 and 8.1.3 below. For a more complete characterization of the class of preference orderings represented by the GPF see Blackorby, Boyce, and Russell (1977).

In the notation of subsection 5.4.1, define a function

$$T^r : \Omega^{(r)}_+ \to \Omega^1$$

by

$$T^r(P^r) = \Pi^r(P^r)\Lambda^r(P^r).$$

Then

$$v_r = h^r(y_r, P^r) = \frac{y_r - T^r(P^r)}{\Pi^r(P^r)}.$$

The GPF satisfies (SPA) if U is completely separable. In this case the cost of the rth-sector utility (or intermediate output) is

$$y_r = \Pi^r(P^r)v_r + T^r(P^r),$$

where $T^r(P^r)$ is "committed" cost, independent of v_r, and $\Pi^r(P^r)$ is the marginal cost of rth-sector utility.

Writing the utility function as

$$U(X) = \sum_{r=1}^{m} U^r(X^r) = \sum_{r=1}^{m} u_r$$

in some normalization, the indirect utility function can be derived by

$$V(P/y) = \max_{u_1,\ldots,u_m} \left\{ \sum_{r=1}^{m} u_r \middle| \Pi^r(P^r)u_r \leqslant y - \sum_{r=1}^{m} T^r(P^r) \right\}$$

and has the form

$$V(P/y) = \frac{y - \displaystyle\sum_{r=1}^{m} T^r(P^r)}{\min(\Pi^1(P^1),\ldots,\Pi^m(P^m))}.$$

The associated cost function is

$$C(u,P) = u\min(\Pi^1(P^1),\ldots,\Pi^m(P^m)) + \sum_{r=1}^{m} T^r(P^r).$$

Thus C and the reciprocal of V are Leontief functions of the price indices $\Pi^1(P^1),\ldots,\Pi^m(P^m)$.

On the other hand, if U is separable but not completely separable and each aggregator function has the GPF, then solving

$$\max_{y} \hat{H}\left(\frac{y_1 - T^1(P^1)}{\Pi^1(P^1)}, \ldots, \frac{y_m - T^m(P^m)}{\Pi^m(P^m)} \right) \quad \text{s.t.} \quad \sum_{r=1}^{m} y_r \leqslant y$$

yields income-allocation functions that depend on both $\Pi^r(P^r)$ and $T^r(P^r)$, $r=1,\ldots,m$. Hence (SPA) is *not* satisfied.

A budgeting algorithm analogous to that rationalized by (APA), but using "committed expenditure indices" $T^r(P^r)$, $r=1,\ldots,m$, as well as unit price indices $\Pi^r(P^r)$, $r=1,\ldots,m$, has been employed in the empirical estimation of a model of international trade by Pinard (1975).

For our last example, consider a firm with a production function that is homothetically separable. Thus, we may consider output to be a function of m "intermediate" goods each of which is produced with a homothetic technology. [This is the kind of application of separability that motivated Leontief's (1947a, b) seminal papers.] By redefining the measure of output of each intermediate good, we may take each of the sector production functions to be PLH.

This firm could be organized into m divisions; the manager of each division is responsible for the production of an intermediate good. Manager r computes an input-price index

$$\Pi^r(P^r) = \frac{1}{h^r(P^r)},$$

where

$$h^r(P^r) = \max_{X^r}\left\{U^r(X^r)\,|\,X^r \in \Omega^{(r)} \wedge P^r \cdot X^r \leqslant 1\right\}.$$

For example, if U^r is a Cobb-Douglas function,

$$U^r(X^r) = \prod_{i \in I^r} x_i^{\alpha_i}, \qquad \sum_{i \in I^r} \alpha_i = 1,$$

then

$$\Pi^r(P^r) = \prod_{i \in I^r} (p_i/\alpha_i)^{\alpha_i}.$$

Of course $\Pi^r(\overset{*}{P}{}^r)\cdot U^r(\overset{*}{X}{}^r) = \overset{*}{y}_r$ for the optimal triple $(\overset{*}{P}{}^r, \overset{*}{X}{}^r, \overset{*}{y})$. The profit function is easily calculated as

$$\max_{u,u_1,\ldots,u_m}\left\{pu - \sum_{r=1}^{m}\Pi^r(P^r)u_r\,|\,\hat{U}(u_1,\ldots,u_m) \geqslant u\right\}$$

$$= \pi\big(p, \Pi^1(P^1),\ldots,\Pi^m(P^m)\big).$$

Thus, the firm's supply depends only on the price of output, p, and the m input price indices.

5.5 QUANTITY AGGREGATION

Each of the forms of quantity aggregation is the direct analogue of one of the forms of price aggregation. We begin by showing how known duality results motivate the definitions of quantity aggregation. Recall that the conditional indirect utility function H is dual to the direct utility function. The expenditure allocation functions are derived by the constrained maximization of H with respect to category expenditures. The conditional direct utility function G, which is dual to the indirect utility function V, is a natural counterpart of H. Hence we examine the expenditure-imputation functions derived by the constrained minimization of G.

The solution to

$$\min_{{_1y/y}} G\left({_1y}/y, X\right) \qquad \text{s.t.} \qquad \sum_{s=1}^{m} \frac{y_s}{y} \leqslant 1$$

yields optimal category imputation shares as functions of quantities X. By imposing structural restrictions on G, the imputation functions are endowed with the quantity-aggregation properties that we seek.

Separability of U is part of the sufficiency condition and a maintained hypothesis in the statement of the necessity condition for strong price aggregation in theorem 5.6. In our discussion of the dual notion of quantity aggregation, it therefore makes sense to suppose that V is separable in a partition $\hat{I}$. By corollary 5.1.1, G is therefore separable in the corresponding partition $\overset{\wedge}{RI}$; i.e.,

$$G\left({_1y}/y, X\right) = \hat{G}\left(g^1\left(y_1/y, X^1\right), \ldots, g^m\left(y_m/y, X^m\right)\right).$$

The proof of theorem 5.6 also involves the use of the generalized Gorman polar form, a restriction on h^r, $r = 1, \ldots, m$. Dual to the generalized Gorman polar form is the *generalized Gorman form*, a restriction on g^r:

$$g^r\left(y_r/y, X^r\right) = \Xi^r\left(\frac{y_r/y}{\Gamma^r(X^r)}\right) + \Upsilon^r(X^r), \qquad \text{(GGF)}$$

where Ξ^r is a decreasing function of its single argument, Γ^r is PLH, and Υ^r is homogeneous of degree zero.

In the discussion of quantity aggregation, it is convenient to consider first the special case of theorem 5.6 stated in corollary 5.6.3. Thus, suppose that V is completely separable in $\hat{I}$ (with $m > 2$) and each aggregator function of G has the generalized Gorman form. Then

$$G\left({_1y}/y, X\right) = \overset{*}{G}\left(\sum_{r=1}^{m} \Xi^r\left(\frac{y_r/y}{\Gamma^r(X^r)}\right) + \Upsilon^r(X^r)\right).$$

Minimizing $G({}_1 y/y, X)$ subject to $\sum_{r=1}^{m} y_r/y \leqslant 1$ yields solutions which depend only on $\Gamma^1(X^1), \ldots, \Gamma^m(X^m)$; i.e.,

$$\frac{y_r}{y} = \hat{\eta}^r\left(\Gamma^1(X^1), \ldots, \Gamma^m(X^m)\right), \tag{SQA}$$

which we define as strong quantity aggregation. Multiplying both sides of (SQA) by y and multiplying each argument of $\hat{\eta}^r$ by $y/y = 1$, the positive linear homogeneity of each Γ^r allows us to write

$$y_r = y \cdot \hat{\eta}^r\left(y\Gamma^1(X^1/y), \ldots, y\Gamma^m(X^m/y)\right), \tag{5.20}$$

or alternatively

$$y_r = \tilde{\eta}^r\left(y, \Gamma^1(X^1/y), \ldots, \Gamma^m(X^m/y)\right), \tag{WQA}$$

which is defined as weak quantity aggregation. Hence (SQA) implies (WQA)—but not conversely, because $\tilde{\eta}^r$ does not in general possess any homogeneity properties.

It is interesting to note that X^r is dual to P^r/y, X^r/y is dual to P^r, and y_r/y and y_r are self-dual. Hence, *strong quantity aggregation* is structurally dual to *weak price aggregation*, and *weak quantity aggregation* is structurally dual to *strong price aggregation*. This duality is further explicated by examining the homothetically separable case, remembering that if either the direct or the indirect utility function is homothetically separable, then so is the other. In this case there is a representation of V,

$$V(P/y) = \hat{V}\left(V^1(P^1/y), \ldots, V^m(P^m/y)\right),$$

where each V^r, $r = 1, \ldots, m$, is PLH (corollary 4.1.3). Moreover, the aggregators of G are defined by

$$g^r(y_r/y, X^r) = \frac{y_r/y}{\Gamma^r(X^r)} = \max_{P^r/y}\left\{\overset{*}{V}{}^r(P^r/y)\Big|\frac{P^r}{y} \in \Omega^{(r)} \wedge \frac{P^r}{y} \cdot X^r \leqslant \frac{y_r}{y}\right\},$$

$$r = 1, \ldots, m, \quad (5.21)$$

where $\overset{*}{V}{}^r$ is the extension of $\bar{V}^r$ to the boundary by continuity from above and each $\Gamma^r(X^r)$ is PLH. Therefore G can be written as

$$G({}_1 y/y, X) = \hat{G}\left(\frac{y_1/y}{\Gamma^1(X^1)}, \ldots, \frac{y_m/y}{\Gamma^m(X^m)}\right). \tag{5.22}$$

Minimizing (5.22) subject to $\sum_{r=1}^{m} y_r/y \leqslant 1$ clearly yields (SQA), strong quantity aggregation. If $\overset{*}{P}/y$ is the solution to the maximization problem in (5.21), it follows that

$$\frac{y_r/y}{\Gamma^r(X^r)} = \overset{*}{V}{}^r(\overset{*}{P}/y) = \frac{1}{y}\,\overset{*}{V}{}^r(\overset{*}{P}),$$

where the last equality follows from the positive linear homogeneity of $\overset{*}{V}{}^r$. Thus, letting

$$\Pi^r(\overset{*}{P}) = \overset{*}{V}{}^r(\overset{*}{P}),$$

we have

$$\Pi^r(\overset{*}{P})\cdot\Gamma^r(\overset{*}{X}{}^r) = y_r,$$

which is additive quantity aggregation. It follows that the solution to

$$\max_{\Gamma^1(X^1),\dots,\Gamma^m(X^m)} U\big(\Gamma^1(X^1),\dots,\Gamma^m(X^m)\big) \quad \text{s.t.} \quad \sum_{r=1}^{m} \Pi^r(P^r)\cdot\Gamma^r(X^r) \leqslant y$$

is the optimal solution if and only if the solution to

$$\min_{\Pi^1(P),\dots,\Pi^m(P^m)} V\big(\Pi^1(P^1),\dots,\Pi^m(P^m)\big) \quad \text{s.t.} \quad \sum_{r=1}^{m} \Pi^r(P^r)\cdot\Gamma^r(X^r) \leqslant y$$

is optimal as well. That is, additive price aggregation is possible if and only if additive quantity aggregation is.

The above discussion should make apparent the complete duality between price and quantity aggregation. However, in the interest of completeness, we state the duals to theorems 5.6–5.8 and corollaries 5.6.2, 5.6.3, and 5.7.1. The dual to corollary 5.6.1 is, of course, equally valid, but to avoid repetition of a necessarily awkwardly worded statement, we do not formalize this result for quantity aggregation.

Theorem 5.9 *Suppose that the direct utility function U satisfies (R-1'). Then quantity aggregation is possible if the image of the indirect utility function V can be written*

$$V(P/y) = \overset{*}{V}\bigg(\sum_{r=1}^{d} V^r(P^r/y) + \hat{V}\big(V^{d+1}(P^{d+1}/y),\dots,V^m(P^m/y)\big)\bigg),$$

$$(5.23)$$

where each V^r, $r = 1, \ldots, d$, has the generalized Gorman form and each V^r, $r = d+1, \ldots, m$, is homothetic. Moreover, if V is separable, the direct conditional utility function G is twice continuously differentiable, and each $\eta^r(X)$ is positive, then the structure (5.23) is necessary for strong quantity aggregation.

Proof. The proof is exactly dual to that of theorem 5.6. ‖

Corollary 5.9.1 *If U satisfies (R-1'), homothetic separability implies strong quantity aggregation.*

Corollary 5.9.2 *If U satisfies (R-1'), complete separability of V in a partition with more than two groups where each aggregator has the generalized Gorman form implies strong quantity aggregation.*

Theorem 5.10 *If V satisfies (R-2') and if U is differentiable and can be written in the form*

$$U(X) = \overset{*}{U}\left(\sum_{r=1}^{m} U^r(X^r) \right),$$

then weak quantity aggregation is possible.

Proof. Apply Wold's theorem exactly as Roy's theorem was applied to prove theorem 5.7. ‖

Corollary 5.10.1 *If V satisfies (R-2') and if U is differentiable and completely separable in a partition with more than two groups, then weak quantity aggregation is possible.*

Theorem 5.11 *If U satisfies (R-1') and either U or V is separable, then homothetic separability is necessary and sufficient for additive price aggregation (which is equivalent to additive quantity aggregation).*

5.6 CONCLUSION

At the risk of abandoning rigor, we attempt to summarize below most of the many relationships derived in this chapter. It should be kept in mind that these relationships require an assortment of unlisted conditions. For an exact statement of the implication or equivalence and the maintained assumptions, the reader is referred to the corresponding theorem (T) or corollary (C) listed next to each relationship.

Direct separability $\Leftrightarrow$ Strong decentralizability $\qquad X^r = \phi^r(P^r, y_r)$ $\qquad$ T5.2, 5.3

Indirect separability $\Rightarrow$ Weak decentralizability $\qquad X^r = \tilde{\phi}^r\left(\dfrac{P^r}{y}, \dfrac{y_r}{y}\right)$ $\qquad$ T5.4

Implicit separability $\Leftrightarrow$ Felicitous decentralization
$$\begin{cases} X^r = \zeta^r(u, P^r) y_r & \text{T5.5} \\ P^r = \delta^r(u, X^r) y_r & \text{C5.5.1} \end{cases}$$

Homothetic separability $\Rightarrow$ Strong price aggregation $\qquad y_r = \hat{\theta}^r(y, \Pi(P^1), \dots, \Pi^m(P^m))$ $\qquad$ T5.6.2

Homothetic separability $\Rightarrow$ Strong quantity aggregation $\qquad \dfrac{y_r}{y} = \hat{\eta}^r(\Gamma^1(X^1), \dots, \Gamma^m(X^m))$ $\qquad$ C5.9.1

Homothetic separability $\Rightarrow$ Additive price aggregation $\qquad y_r = \Pi^r(P^r)\Gamma^r(X^r)$ $\qquad$ T5.8

Homothetic separability $\Rightarrow$ Additive quantity aggregation $\qquad y_r = \Pi^r(P^r)\Gamma^r(X^r)$ $\qquad$ T5.8, 5.11

Direct complete separability $\Rightarrow$ Weak quantity aggregation $\qquad y_r = \tilde{\eta}^r\left(\Gamma^1\left(\dfrac{X^1}{y}\right), \dots, \Gamma^m\left(\dfrac{X^m}{y}\right)\right)$ $\qquad$ C5.10.1

Indirect complete separability $\Rightarrow$ Weak price aggregation $\qquad \dfrac{y_r}{y} = \tilde{\theta}^r\left(\tilde{\Pi}\left(\dfrac{P^1}{y}\right), \dots, \tilde{\Pi}^m\left(\dfrac{P^m}{y}\right)\right)$ $\qquad$ C5.7.1

If Indirect separability, then
   Strong quantity aggregation $\Rightarrow$ Homothetic separability or indirect complete separability with
                   generalized Gorman form aggregators $\qquad$ T5.9

If Direct separability, then
   Strong price aggregation $\Rightarrow$ Homothetic separability or direct complete separability with
                   generalized Gorman polar form aggregators $\qquad$ T5.6, C5.6.1

Strong quantity aggregation $\Rightarrow$ Weak quantity aggregation

Strong price aggregation $\Rightarrow$ Weak price aggregation

Direct separability and Additive quantity aggregation $\Rightarrow$ Homothetic separability $\qquad$ T5.8

Indirect separability and Additive price aggregation $\Rightarrow$ Homothetic separability $\qquad$ T5.11

6
Nonsymmetrically Structured Preferences and Technologies

Most research on functional structure and its applications has concentrated on the symmetric structures examined in the previous two chapters. In fact, as was pointed out in the introductory chapter of this book, many practitioners apparently think that separability comes packaged only in these two forms. However, as chapter 3 makes abundantly clear, the notion of separability is an inherently nonsymmetric concept. That is, the separability of I^r from I^s does not imply that I^s is separable from I^r. Indeed, the seminal papers of Leontief (1947a, b) and Sono (1945, 1961) introduced the concept of separability in a nonsymmetric fashion.

Not all applications of separability rely exclusively on the symmetric structures of chapter 4. In one of the first applications of separability, Solow (1955) posited the separability of capital inputs from other inputs (but not the converse) in order to construct an aggregate capital input. A modernized capital-aggregation theorem has been proved more recently by Bliss (1975), who exploited his nonsymmetric separability concept, discussed in chapter 3 above. Pollak (1975a, 1975b) invokes nonsymmetric separability in the construction of subindices and intertemporal indices of the cost of living.

Many problems—particularly those involving time—are inherently conducive to the application of nonsymmetric separability. Habit-formation problems are inherently asymmetric (see, e.g., Pollak, 1970a, 1975a). Large-scale construction projects (e.g., dams) have been studied from the point of view of a nonsymmetrically structured technology set (Marino, 1976), and the notion of intertemporal "impatience" has been studied using nonsymmetric preferences by Koopmans (1960) and by Koopmans, Diamond, and Williamson (1964). Finally, the issue of intertemporal planning consistency (Strotz, 1955; Pollak, 1968; Phelps and Pollak, 1968; and Blackorby, Nissen, Primont, and Russell, 1973) is inherently nonsymmetric. As an application of nonsymmetric structures, we analyze this last problem in chapter 10.

This chapter examines structures that are explicitly nonsymmetric. In particular, we extend the nonsymmetric binary-partitioned structures of chapter 3 to the case where there is an arbitrary (finite) number of sectors. The structures are characterized by nested (finite) sequences of nonsymmetrically separable sets of variables. As in the case of symmetric structures, a natural distinction arises with respect to the completeness of the nonsymmetric separability. This distinction has its origins in a paper by Lady and Nissen (1968). By analogy with chapter 4, we refer to these two basic structures as recursive (strict) separability and completely recursive (strict) separability. The latter structure can also be found in Blackorby and Lady (1967) and Gorman (1968b).

The order of presentation of these two structures does not correspond to the organization of chapter 4; completely recursive structures are examined before noncompletely recursive structures. The reason for this is that completely recursive structures are very similar to structures examined in chapter 3 and sections 4.1 and 4.3. In section 6.1 representation theorems for completely recursive direct and indirect utility functions and cost and transformation functions are stated and proved. Section 6.2 contains representation theorems for homothetically completely recursive functions and ends with two theorems which relate these dual structures to each other. In section 6.3 the above arguments are repeated under the maintained hypothesis of overall homotheticity. Finally, in section 6.4 we analyze (noncompletely) recursive structures. Here we find a plethora of structures, but unfortunately there are few duality results relating these structures to each other. Section 6.5 is the completely recursive analogue of chapter 5 (on decentralization and aggregation), while section 6.6 explores some of the implications for decentralizability of noncompletely recursive structures.

6.1 COMPLETE NONSYMMETRIC SEPARABILITY (COMPLETE RECURSIVITY)

Because nonsymmetric completely separable structures are characterized by properties that are analogous to those of the symmetric structures analyzed in chapters 4 and 5, it is convenient to examine these structures first. Before proceeding, however, additional notation must be introduced, because we need to keep track of the order in which separability is assumed.

6.1.1   Nonsymmetric Notation

Consider the *ordered* partition

$$\langle \hat{I} \rangle = \langle I^1, \ldots, I^m \rangle$$

of the index set I. This notation is contrasted with $\hat{I}$, in which the elements are not ordered. Define the "rth-continuation partition" by

$$\langle {}_r\hat{I} \rangle = \langle I^r, I^{r+1}, \ldots, I^m \rangle.$$

In an analogous fashion, let

$${}_rI = \bigcup_{s=r}^{m} I^s$$

and

$${}_r\hat{I} = \{ I^r, \ldots, I^m \}.$$

Note that this notation is consistent with the notation for the extended-index-set partition of chapter 4. In particular,

$${}_0\hat{I} = \{ I^0, I^1, \ldots, I^m \},$$

which is not ordered, is contrasted with the ordered set

$$\langle {}_0\hat{I} \rangle = \langle I^0, I^1, \ldots, I^m \rangle.$$

Moreover, $\langle {}_1\hat{I} \rangle = \langle \hat{I} \rangle$. Also define the union of preceeding elements by

$${}_1I_r = \bigcup_{s=1}^{r} I^s.$$

Define the rth-continuation subspace orthant by

$${}_r\Omega = \Omega^{(r)} \times \Omega^{(r+1)} \times \cdots \times \Omega^{(m)}.$$

Similarly,

$${}_1\Omega_r = \Omega^{(1)} \times \cdots \times \Omega^{(r)}.$$

Also,

$${}_r\Omega_+ = \Omega_+^{(r)} \times \Omega_+^{(r+1)} \times \cdots \times \Omega_+^{(m)}$$

and

$$_1(\Omega_+)_r = \Omega_+^{(1)} \times \cdots \times \Omega_+^{(r)}.$$

Quantity and price continuation vectors are defined analogously by

$$_rX = [X^r, X^{r+1}, \ldots, X^m] \in {}_r\Omega, \qquad r = 1, \ldots, m,$$

and

$$_rP = [P^r, P^{r+1}, \ldots, P^m] \in {}_r\Omega_+, \qquad r = 1, \ldots, m.$$

Also,

$$_1X_r = [X^1, \ldots, X^r] \in {}_1\Omega_r$$

and

$$_1P_r = [P^1, \ldots, P^r] \in {}_1(\Omega_+)_r.$$

The expenditure continuations, where y_r is the expenditure on group r, are

$$_ry = [y_r, y_{r+1}, \ldots, y_m], \qquad r = 1, \ldots, m.$$

Also,

$$z_r = \sum_{s=r}^{m} y_s$$

is the expenditure on the rth continuation. Note that

$$z_r = {}_rP \cdot {}_rX.$$

For example, in an intertemporal context, z_r represents the funds available from period r to the end of the planning period.

6.1.2   Definitions and Representations

The nonsymmetric analogue of complete (strict) separability is defined as follows. The utility function U is *nonsymmetrically completely (strictly) separable* in the ordered partition $\langle \hat{I} \rangle$ if, for $r = 2, \ldots, m$, the set $_rI$ is (strictly) separable from $_1I_{r-1}$. That is, each continuation of variables is separable from the set of variables that *precede* I^r in the ordered set $\langle \hat{I} \rangle$. Somewhat less descriptively, but also less awkwardly, we refer to this structure as complete (strict) *recursivity*. Noncomplete recursivity is discussed in section 6.4.

Note that Gorman's (1968b) result that unions of intersecting strictly separable sets are strictly separable (see theorem 4.3 above) implies that the above definition of complete strict recursivity is equivalent to the following definition. U is completely strictly recursive in the ordered partition $\langle \hat{I} \rangle$ if each pair $\{I^r, I^{r+1}\}$, $r = 2, \ldots, m-1$, is separable from $_1I_{r-1}$. Note also that complete strict recursivity in every ordered permutation of the set $\hat{I}$ is equivalent to (symmetric) complete strict separability. For example, suppose there are only three sectors and that U is completely strictly recursive in every ordered partition. In particular, it is completely recursive with respect to

$$\langle I^1, I^2, I^3 \rangle$$

and

$$\langle I^3, I^2, I^1 \rangle.$$

This means that $I^2 \cup I^3$ and $I^2 \cup I^1$ are each separable from their respective complements, and in addition have a nonempty intersection, I^2. Applying theorem 4.3, it is clear that every proper subset of $\hat{I}$ is separable from its complement: therefore, U is completely strictly separable. In this sense, complete separability is a special case of complete recursivity.

It is also important to notice that complete recursivity does not imply and is not implied by symmetric separability. Suppose that U is completely recursive with respect to $\langle \hat{I} \rangle$. Only I^m is separable from its complement in I; I^r $(r < m)$ is not separable from $_{r+1}I_m$ unless additional assumptions are made. Thus, complete recursivity does *not* imply symmetric separability. Conversely, suppose that U is separable with respect to $\hat{I}$. Unless additional assumptions are made, no union $I^r \cup I^{r+1}$ can be assumed to be separable from its complement, because unions of disjoint separable sets are not necessarily separable. Obviously the foregoing comments are equally true for strict separability and complete strict recursivity.

Complete recursivity of the indirect utility function V or W, the cost function C, and the transformation function F in the ordered partitions $\langle \hat{I} \rangle$ and $\langle _0\hat{I} \rangle$ are defined analogously to complete recursivity of U.

The fundamental representation theorem for completely recursive structures has been proved by Gorman (1968b) and Primont (1970).

Theorem 6.1 *Suppose that U satisfies the regularity conditions* $(R-1)$.[1] *Then the utility function U is completely recursive in the ordered partition*

---

[1] $(R-1)$: continuity, positive monotonicity, and quasi-concavity (see section 2.2).

$\langle \hat{I} \rangle$ *if and only if there exist m functions*

$$U^{[r]}: \Omega^{(r)} \times \mathcal{R}(U^{[r+1]}) \rightarrow \mathbf{R}, \qquad r = 1, \ldots, m-1,$$

and

$$U^{[m]}: \Omega^{(m)} \rightarrow \mathbf{R},$$

all satisfying (R − 1), *such that*

$$U(X) = U^{[1]}(X^1, u^{[2]}), \tag{6.1a}$$

$$u^{[r]} = U^{[r]}(X^r, u^{[r+1]}), \qquad r = 2, \ldots, m-1, \tag{6.1b}$$

and

$$u^{[m]} = U^{[m]}(X^m). \tag{6.1c}$$

Moreover, if U is completely strictly recursive, each $U^{[r]}$ is increasing in $u^{[r+1]}$, $r = 1, \ldots, m-1$.

Proof. As $_2I$ is separable from I^1, theorems 3.2b and 3.3b imply the existence of functions $U^{[1]}$ and $_2U$, satisfying (R − 1), such that

$$U(X) = U^{[1]}(X^1, {_2U}({_2X})).$$

Moreover, the separability of $_2I$ from I^1 in U and that of $_3I$ from $_1I_2$ in U imply the separability of $_3I$ from I^2 in $_2U$. Hence there exist functions $U^{[2]}$ and $_3U$, satisfying (R − 1), such that

$$_2U({_2X}) = U^{[2]}(X^2, {_3U}({_3X})).$$

Substitution yields

$$U(X) = U^{[1]}(X^1, u^{[2]}),$$

where

$$u^{[2]} = U^{[2]}(X^2, {_3U}({_3X})).$$

Suppose that functions $U^{[1]}, \ldots, U^{[r-1]}, {_rU}$, satisfying (R − 1), such that

$$U(X) = U^{[1]}(X^1, u^{[2]}),$$

$$u^{[s]} = U^{[s]}(X^s, u^{[s+1]}), \qquad s = 2, \ldots, r-1,$$

$$u^{[r]} = {_rU}({_rX})$$

have been constructed in this manner. In this case, since separability of $_{r+1}I$ from $_1I_r$ in U implies separability of $_{r+1}I$ from I^r in $_rU$, there exist functions $U^{[r]}$ and $_{r+1}U$, satisfying $(R-1)$, such that

$$_rU(_rX) = U^{[r]}(X^r, u^{[r+1]})$$

and

$$u^{[r+1]} = _{r+1}U(_{r+1}X).$$

Proceeding sequentially in this manner from $r=1$ to $r=m-1$ and letting

$$_mU(_mX) = U^{[m]}(X^m)$$

completes the construction.

The sufficiency of the representation for complete recursivity follows immediately from repeated application of the sufficiency result in theorem 3.2b if we let

$$U^{[r]}(X^r, U^{[r+1]}(X^{r+1}, \ldots, U^{[m]}(X^m)\ldots)) = _rU(_rX), \qquad r = 2,\ldots,m,$$

and

$$U^{[1]}(X^1, U^{[2]}(X^2, \ldots, _rU(_rX)\ldots)) = \overline{U}(_1X_{r-1}, _rU(_rX)), \qquad r = 2,\ldots,m.$$

For the completely strictly recursive result, repeat the above argument using theorems 3.2a and 3.3a. ‖

An interesting feature of the completely strictly recursive representation is the fact that, unlike the (symmetric) completely strictly separable representation, it is not additive. Basically, the reason that this representation is not additive is that complete strict recursivity is equivalent to (nonsymmetric) strict separability in each of the *binary* partitions $\langle_1I_{r-1}, I\rangle$, $r = 2,\ldots,m$. Thus, each of the representations (6.1b) is essentially equivalent to the simplest structure, which was examined in great detail in chapter 3.

The nested structure of the completely recursive representation can perhaps be explicated by considering the ternary partition

$$U(X) = U^{[1]}(X^1, U^{[2]}(X^2, U^{[3]}(X^3))).$$

More generally, $U^{[1]}$ can be written in nested form as

$$U(X) = U^{[1]}(X^1, U^{[2]}(X^2, U^{[3]}(X^3, \ldots, U^{[m]}(X^m)\ldots))).$$

Note that each $U^{[r]}$, $r = 1, \ldots, m$, is itself a completely recursive function.

The properties of the functions, $U^{[1]}, \ldots, U^{[m]}$, are inherited from the parent utility function U. As in the case of symmetric structures, this inheritance mechanism is patently obvious in the case of strict recursivity because corollary 3.2.0a allows us to choose each $_rU$ so that

$$_rU(_rX) = U(O^1, \ldots, O^{r-1}, _rX), \qquad r = 2, \ldots, m,$$

and hence, by the construction in the proof of theorem 6.1,

$$U^{[r]}(X^r, u^{[r+1]}) = U^{[1]}\big(O^1, U^{[2]}(O^2, \ldots, U^{[r]}(X^r, u^{[r+1]})\ldots)\big)$$

$$= U(O^1, \ldots, O^{r-1}, _rX).$$

where O^r, $r = 1, \ldots, m$, are the arbitrary reference vectors. Of course, if U is endowed with alternative properties, the aggregator functions inherit these alternative properties. The following corollary formalizes this idea somewhat more generally.

Corollary 6.1.1 *Suppose that U satisfies $(R-1)$. If U satisfies any of the following properties, each $U^{[r]}$ can be picked to possess the same property: (i) strict positive monotonicity, (ii) strict quasi-concavity, (iii) positive homotheticity, and (iv) positive linear homogeneity. Moreover, if U is completely strictly recursive, each $U^{[r]}$ inherits partial differentiability whenever U is differentiable.*

Proof. This follows from repeated application of theorems 3.3 and 3.5. ‖

If U is a utility function, each $U^{[r]}$, $r = 2, \ldots, m$, can be thought of as a specific utility function representing the preference ordering on the "consumption continuation space" $_r\Omega$. However, each of these specific utility functions contains only rth-sector quantities X^r; other consumption quantities are reflected in the higher-order aggregator $U^{[r+1]}$. Thus, utility from the consumption of higher-order commodities are successively "marked up" through the sequence of utility aggregators until finally the overall utility is expressed as a function of the first-sector consumption bundle X^1 and the utility of higher-order consumption, $u^{[2]}$. On the other hand, if U is a production function, each $U^{[r]}$ can be thought of as a production function which takes inputs X^r and the "output" of stage $r+1$, $u^{[r+1]}$, and converts them into the "output" of stage r, $u^{[r]}$.

Representations for completely recursive indirect utility functions, cost functions, and transformation functions are contained in the following corollaries to theorem 6.1.

Corollary 6.1.2 *Suppose that the indirect utility function V satisfies $(R-2)$.[2] Then V is completely recursive in the ordered partition $\langle \hat{I} \rangle$ if and only if there exist functions*

$$V^{[r]} : \Omega_+^{(r)} \times \mathcal{R}(V^{[r+1]}) \rightarrow \mathbf{R}, \qquad r = 1, \ldots, m-1,$$

and

$$V^{[m]} : \Omega_+^{(m)} \rightarrow \mathbf{R}$$

such that

$$V(P/y) = V^{[1]}(P^1/y, v^{[2]}), \tag{6.2a}$$

$$v^{[r]} = V^{[r]}(P^r/y, v^{[r+1]}), \qquad r = 2, \ldots, m-1, \tag{6.2b}$$

and

$$v^{[m]} = V^{[m]}(P^m/y), \tag{6.2c}$$

where $V^{[1]}$ satisfies $(R-2)$ and each $V^{[r]}$, $r > 1$, satisfies $(R-1)$. In addition, if V satisfies any of the following properties, $V^{[1]}$ can be picked to possess the same property, while each $V^{[r]}$, $r = 2, \ldots, m$, can be chosen to have the corresponding property listed in corollary 6.1.1: (i) strict negative monotonicity, (ii) strict quasi-convexity, (iii) negative homotheticity, (iv) negative homogeneity. Moreover, if V is completely strictly recursive, each $V^{[r]}$ inherits partial differentiability whenever V is differentiable.

Proof. This follows from an iterative application of corollaries 3.2.1 and 3.5.1. ‖

Notice that we have again normalized in such a fashion that $V^{[1]}$ may be thought of as an indirect utility or production function of its arguments, $(P^1/y, v^{[2]})$, while each $V^{[r]}$ is a reciprocal indirect utility function of its arguments. In general, complete recursivity of U in $\langle \hat{I} \rangle$ does not imply, nor is it implied by, complete recursivity of V in $\langle \hat{I} \rangle$. They represent therefore a different class of technologies or preference orderings. It also follows by analogy with the discussion in chapter 3 that if the indirect utility function in nonnormalized prices, W, is completely recursive with respect to $\langle \hat{I} \rangle$, then this generates the same structure as V in the preceeding corollary. The next two corollaries state the completely recursive representations and inheritance results for the cost and transformation functions, i.e., complete recursivity of C and F in $\langle \hat{I} \rangle$ but not in $\langle_0 \hat{I} \rangle$.

[2]$(R-2)$: Continuity, negative monotonicity, and quasi-convexity (see section 2.2).

Corollary 6.1.3 *Suppose that the cost function C satisfies* $(R-3)$.[3] *Then C is completely recursive in the ordered partition* $\langle \hat{I} \rangle$ *if and only if there exist functions*

$$C^{[r]}: \mathcal{R}(U) \times \Omega_+^{(r)} \times \mathcal{R}(C^{[r+1]}) \rightarrow \Omega_+^1, \qquad r = 1, \ldots, m-1,$$

and

$$C^{[m]}: \mathcal{R}(U) \times \Omega_+^{(r)} \rightarrow \Omega_+^1,$$

all satisfying $(R-3P)$,[4] *such that*

$$C(u, P) = C^{[1]}(u, P^1, c^{[2]}), \tag{6.3a}$$

$$c^{[r]} = C^{[r]}(u, P^r, c^{[r+1]}), \qquad r = 2, \ldots, m-1, \tag{6.3b}$$

and

$$c^{[m]} = C^{[m]}(u, P^m). \tag{6.3c}$$

Moreover, if C is complete strictly recursive in $\langle \hat{I} \rangle$, *the following statements hold:* (a) $C^{[r]}$ *is increasing in* $c^{[r+1]}$, $r = 1, \ldots, m-1$; (b) *each* $C^{[r]}(u, \cdot)$ *inherits differentiability in P;* (c) *each* $C^{[r]}$ *satisfies* $(R-3P)$; *and* (d) *each* $C^{[r]}(\cdot, c^{[r+1]})$ *inherits (strict) convexity and positive linear homogeneity in u.*

Proof. This follows from repeated application of theorem 3.4 and corollary 3.5.2. ‖

Corollary 6.1.4 *Suppose that F satisfies* $(R-4)$.[5] *Then the transformation function F is completely recursive in the ordered partition* $\langle \hat{I} \rangle$ *if and only if there exist functions*

$$F^{[r]}: \mathcal{R}(U) \times \Omega_+^{(r)} \times \mathcal{R}(F^{[r+1]}) \rightarrow \Omega_+^1, \qquad r = 1, \ldots, m-1,$$

and

$$F^{[m]}: \mathcal{R}(U) \times \Omega_+^{(m)} \rightarrow \Omega_+^1,$$

---

[3]$(R-3)$: Continuity in (u, P), strict positive monoticity in u, and positive monotonicity, positive linear homogeneity, and concavity in P (see section 2.4).

[4]$(R-3P)$: Continuity, positive monotonicity, positive linear homogeneity, and concavity in prices and aggregators.

[5]$(R-4)$: Continuity in (u, X), strict negative monotonicity in u, and positive monotonicity, positive linear homogeneity, and concavity in X.

all satisfying $(R-4X)$,[6] *such that*

$$F(u,X) = F^{[1]}(u,X^1,f^{[2]}),$$ (6.4a)

$$f^{[r]} = F^{[r]}(u,X^r,f^{[r+1]}),   r = 2,\ldots,m-1,$$ (6.4b)

and

$$f^{[m]} = F^{[m]}(u,X^m).$$ (6.4c)

Moreover, if F is completely strictly recursive in $\langle \hat{I} \rangle$, *the following statements hold*: (a) $F^{[r]}$ *is increasing in* $f^{[r+1]}$, $r = 1,\ldots,m-1$; (b) *each* $F^{[r]}(u,\cdot)$ *inherits differentiability in* X; (c) *each* $F^{[r]}$ *satisfies* $(R-4X)$; *and* (d) *each* $F^{[r]}(\cdot,f^{[r+1]})$ *inherits (strict) convexity and negative homogeneity in* u.

Proof.   Follows by repeated application of corollaries 3.4.1 and 3.5.3. ||

6.1.3   Conjugate Recursive Duality

As we have noted, complete recursivity of the direct utility function neither implies nor is implied by complete recursivity of the indirect utility function or of the cost or transformation functions. However, by analogy with the structures which are developed in chapter 3, it is not surprising that implicit complete recursivity is a self-dual structure. This is formalized in the next theorem.

Theorem 6.2   *Suppose that U satisfies* $(R-1)$. *Then the cost function is completely recursive in* $\langle \hat{I} \rangle$ *if and only if the transformation function is completely recursive in* $\langle \hat{I} \rangle$. *Moreover, if the extensions of F and C to* $\mathcal{R}(U) \times \Omega^n$ *are locally nonsated on* $\Omega^{(m)}$,[7] *then "recursive" may be replaced by "strictly recursive" in the above statement.*

Proof.   Since local nonsatiation on $\Omega^{(m)}$ implies local nonsatiation on each $,\Omega$, the proof follows from repeated application of theorem 3.6. ||

In order to extend these duality results to a recursive analogue of theorem 3.8, we need to invoke the recursive analogue of homothetic separability.

---

[6]$(R-4X)$: Continuity, positive monotonicity, positive linear homogeneity, and concavity in quantities and aggregators.

[7]See chapter 3 for a discussion of local nonsatiation within a sector.

6.2 HOMOTHETIC COMPLETE RECURSIVITY

As in the case of symmetric structures, homotheticity plays an important role in the analysis of completely recursive structures. Many of the duality equivalences for these structures require a homotheticity condition. Homotheticity is also invoked as a necessary and sufficient condition for nonsymmetric price aggregation in section 6.5 below.

6.2.1 Homothetically Completely Recursive Representations

We first prove a representation theorem which extends the homothetic-separability representation (lemma 3.3).

Theorem 6.3 *Let U satisfy $(R-1)$ and complete recursivity in the ordered partition $\langle \hat{I} \rangle$. If $_rU$ is homothetic,[8] there exists a completely recursive representation in which the $m-r+1$ aggregator functions, $U^{[r]}, \ldots, U^{[m]}$, are PLH in their arguments.*

Proof. Let the completely recursive representation be given by equations (6.1). Recalling lemma 3.3, we note that the homotheticity and complete recursivity of $_rU$ imply that $_sU$ is homothetic for all $s \geqslant r$. In particular, $_mU = U^{[m]}$ is homothetic, and there exist a continuous, strictly increasing function ψ_m and a PLH function $\overset{*}{U}{}^{[m]}$ such that

$$\overset{*}{U}{}^{[m]}(X^m) = \psi_m(U^{[m]}(X^m)). \tag{a}$$

Furthermore, $_{m-1}U$ is homothetic in $_{m-1}X$, and there exist a continuous, strictly increasing function ψ_{m-1} and a PLH function $_{m-1}\overset{*}{U}$ such that

$$_{m-1}\overset{*}{U}(_{m-1}X) = \psi_{m-1}(_{m-1}U(_{m-1}X)). \tag{b}$$

Complete recursivity and (a) imply that

$$_{m-1}U(_{m-1}X) = U^{[m-1]}\left(X^{m-1}, \psi_m^{-1}\left(\overset{*}{U}{}^{[m]}(X^m)\right)\right)$$

$$= \tilde{U}^{[m-1]}\left(X^{m-1}, \overset{*}{U}{}^{[m]}(X^m)\right), \qquad \text{say,}$$

where ψ_m^{-1} is the inverse of ψ_m and the second equality defines $\tilde{U}^{[m-1]}$. But from (b),

$$_{m-1}\overset{*}{U}(_{m-1}X) = \psi_{m-1}\left(\tilde{U}^{[m-1]}\left(X^{m-1}, \overset{*}{U}{}^{[m]}(X^m)\right)\right)$$

$$= \overset{*}{U}{}^{[m-1]}\left(X^{m-1}, \overset{*}{U}{}^{[m]}(X^m)\right), \qquad \text{say,}$$

---

[8]Recall from the proof of theorem 6.1 that $_rU$ maps from $\times_{s=r}^{m}\Omega^{(s)}$ into **R** and therefore has the image $_rU(_rX)$.

where the second equality defines $\overset{*}{U}{}^{[m-1]}$. Finally, as $_{m-1}\overset{*}{U}$ is PLH in $_{m-1}X$ and $\overset{*}{U}{}^{[m]}$ is PLH in X^m, it follows that $\overset{*}{U}{}^{[m-1]}$ is PLH in $[X^{m-1}, \overset{*}{U}{}^{[m]}(X^m)]$, since

$$_{m-1}\overset{*}{U}(\lambda \cdot {}_{m-1}X) = \lambda \cdot {}_{m-1}\overset{*}{U}({}_{m-1}X) \qquad \forall \lambda > 0$$

implies

$$\overset{*}{U}{}^{[m-1]}(\lambda X^{m-1}, \overset{*}{U}{}^{[m]}(\lambda X^m)) = \overset{*}{U}{}^{[m-1]}(\lambda X^{m-1}, \lambda \overset{*}{U}{}^{[m]}(X^m))$$

$$= \lambda \overset{*}{U}{}^{[m-1]}(X^{m-1}, \overset{*}{U}{}^{[m]}(X^m)).$$

Reapplication of the above argument to $_sU$, $s = m-1, \ldots, r$, yields the desired PLH representation:

$$U(X) = U^{[1]}(X^1, u^{[2]}),$$

$$u^{[s]} = U^{[s]}(X^s, u^{[s+1]}), \qquad s = 2, \ldots, r-1,$$

$$u^{[s]} = \overset{*}{U}{}^{[s]}(X^s, u^{[s+1]}), \qquad s = r, \ldots, m-1,$$

$$u^{[m]} = \overset{*}{U}{}^{[m]}(X^m). \qquad \|$$

Note that if $r = 1$ in theorem 6.3, the overall technology or preference ordering is homothetic. The aggregation and duality results for completely recursive structures exploit the weaker structure where $r = 2$ in the statement of the theorem, i.e., where $_2U$ is homothetic. As homotheticity of $_2U$ implies homotheticity of $_sU$, $s = 3, \ldots, m$, we refer to this important structure as *direct homothetic complete recursivity*. Note, however, that homothetic complete recursivity is implied by homotheticity and complete recursivity, but not conversely.

An analogous proof establishes the corresponding result for the indirect utility function.

Corollary 6.3.1 *Let V be completely recursive in the ordered partition $\langle \hat{I} \rangle$. If $_rV$ is negatively homothetic, there exists a completely recursive representation in which the $m - r$ aggregator functions $V^{[r+1]}, \ldots, V^{[m]}$ are PLH in their arguments, and $V^{[r]}$ is NH if $r = 1$ and PLH if $r > 1$.*

If $r = 1$, the indirect utility function is negatively homothetic. By analogy with the direct utility function, a somewhat weaker structure is actually needed for the duality results. We refer to the case where $r = 2$, and hence $_sV$ for $s = 2, \ldots, m$ are homothetic, as *indirect homothetic complete recursivity*.

In the completely separable case, dual structures were found by imposing overall homotheticity on the direct or indirect functions and imposing two different separability conditions simultaneously on the cost and transformation functions. C, for example, was assumed to be separable in $_0\tilde{I}$ and completely separable in $\hat{I}$. It is therefore not surprising that in the completely recursive case more than one partition of the index set is needed. Consequently, we introduce a new ordered binary partition of $_0\tilde{I}$ defined by

$$\langle _0\tilde{I}^1 \rangle = \langle _0I_{1,2}I \rangle = \left(I^0 \cup I^1, \bigcup_{r=2}^{m} I^r \right).$$

Using this new partition in conjunction with the partition $\langle \hat{I} \rangle$, we generate new functional forms for C, F, and W which turn out to be dual to homothetically completely recursive functions. Their representations are generated in the next theorem and the following two corollaries.

Theorem 6.4 *Suppose that C satisfies* (R-3). *Then the cost function C is completely recursive in $\langle _0\tilde{I}^1 \rangle$ and in $\langle \hat{I} \rangle$ if and only if there exist functions*

$$\tilde{C}^{[1]} : \mathcal{R}(U) \times \Omega_+^{(1)} \times \mathcal{R}(\overline{C}^{[2]}) \to \Omega_+^1,$$

$$\overline{C}^{[r]} : \Omega_+^{(r)} \times \mathcal{R}(\overline{C}^{[r+1]}) \to \Omega_+^1, \qquad r=2,\ldots,m-1,$$

and

$$\overline{C}^{[m]} : \Omega_+^{(m)} \to \Omega_+^1$$

such that

$$C(u,P) = \tilde{C}^{[1]}(u, P^1, \bar{c}^{[2]}), \tag{6.7a}$$

$$\bar{c}^{[r]} = \overline{C}^{[r]}(P^r, \bar{c}^{[r+1]}), \qquad r=2,\ldots,m-1, \tag{6.7b}$$

and

$$\bar{c}^{[m]} = \overline{C}^{[m]}(P^m), \tag{6.7c}$$

where $\tilde{C}^{[1]}$ satisfies (R-3) *and each $\overline{C}^{[r]}$ satisfies* (R-3P).

Other properties may also be inherited from C; see corollary 6.1.3.

Proof. Complete recursivity in $\langle \hat{I} \rangle$ implies the representation (6.3), and complete recursivity in $\langle _0\tilde{I}^1 \rangle$ implies that each aggregator $C^{[r]}$, $r=2,\ldots,m$, is independent of the utility index, yielding the representation in the theorem. The inheritance of regularity properties results from sequential application of theorem 3.4 and corollary 3.5.2. ‖

Similar results for the transformation function and the indirect function in nonnormalized prices are stated as corollaries.

Corollary 6.4.1 *Suppose that F satisfies* (R-4). *Then the transformation function is completely recursive in $\langle_0 \tilde{I}^1 \rangle$ and in $\langle \hat{I} \rangle$ if and only if there exist functions*

$$\tilde{F}^{[1]} : \mathcal{R}(U) \times \Omega_+^{(1)} \times \mathcal{R}(\bar{F}^{[2]}) \to \Omega_+^1,$$

$$\bar{F}^{[r]} : \Omega_+^{(r)} \times \mathcal{R}(\bar{F}^{[r+1]}) \to \Omega_+^1, \qquad r = 2, \ldots, m-1,$$

and

$$\bar{F}^{[m]} : \Omega_+^{(m)} \to \Omega_+^1$$

such that

$$F(u, X) = \tilde{F}^{[1]}\big(u, X^1, \bar{f}^{[2]}\big), \tag{6.6a}$$

$$\bar{f}^{[r]} = \bar{F}^{[r]}\big(X^r, \bar{f}^{[r+1]}\big), \qquad r = 2, \ldots, m-1, \tag{6.6b}$$

and

$$\bar{f}^{[m]} = \bar{F}^{[m]}(X^m), \tag{6.6c}$$

where $\tilde{F}^{[1]}$ satisfies (R-4) *and each $\bar{F}^{[r]}$ satisfies* (R-4X).

Proof. This follows from an argument like that for theorem 6.4. ‖

Corollary 6.4.2 *Suppose that V satisfies* (R-2). *Then the indirect utility function W is completely recursive in $\langle_0 \tilde{I}^1 \rangle$ and in $\langle \hat{I} \rangle$ if and only if there exist functions*

$$\tilde{W}^{[1]} : \Omega_+^1 \times \Omega_+^{(1)} \times \mathcal{R}(\overline{W}^{[2]}) \to \mathbf{R},$$

$$\overline{W}^{[r]} : \Omega_+^{(r)} \times \mathcal{R}(\overline{W}^{[r+1]}) \to \mathbf{R}, \qquad r = 2, \ldots, m-1,$$

and

$$\overline{W}^{[m]} : \Omega_+^{(m)} \to \mathbf{R}$$

such that

$$W(y,P) = \tilde{W}^{[1]}(y,P^1,\overline{w}^{[2]}), \tag{6.7a}$$

$$\overline{w}^{[r]} = \overline{W}^{[r]}(P^r,\overline{w}^{[r+1]}), \qquad r = 2,\ldots,m-1, \tag{6.7b}$$

and

$$\overline{w}^{[m]} = \overline{W}^{[m]}(P^m), \tag{6.7c}$$

where $\tilde{W}^{[1]}$ satisfies continuity, (R-2) in $(P^1,\overline{w}^{[2]})$, and positive monotonicity in y, and each $\overline{W}^{[r]}$ satisfies (R-3P).

Proof. As for Theorem 6.4. ||

6.2.2 Homothetic-Complete-Recursivity Equivalences

Although the three basic types of complete recursivity—conjugate implicit, direct, and indirect—generally represent different preference structures, homotheticity of $_2U$ and $_2V$ generates several equivalences. In fact, the following duality result is the completely recursive analogue of theorem 3.8.

Theorem 6.5 *Assume that U satisfies (R-1). Then the following five structures are equivalent:*

(i)   *homothetic complete recursivity of the direct utility function U in $\langle \hat{I} \rangle$,*
(ii) *homothetic complete recursivity of the indirect utility function V in $\langle \hat{I} \rangle$,*
(iii) *complete recursivity of the cost function C in $\langle _0\tilde{I}^1 \rangle$ and in $\langle \hat{I} \rangle$,*
(iv) *complete recursivity of the transformation function F in $\langle _0\tilde{I}^1 \rangle$ and in $\langle \hat{I} \rangle$, and*
(v)   *complete recursivity of the indirect utility function W in $\langle _0\tilde{I}^1 \rangle$ and in $\langle \hat{I} \rangle$.*

Moreover, if the extensions of V, C, and F to the boundary of Ω^n satisfy local nonsatiation on $\Omega^{(m)}$, "recursivity" can be replaced by "strict recursivity" in the above set of equivalences.

Proof. This follows from a simple inductive argument using theorem 3.8. ||

As a result of this set of equivalences, we refer somewhat loosely to each of these structures as homothetic complete (strict) recursivity. Again, by analogy with the equivalence between homothetic strict separability and strict separability of U and F simultaneously, we expect to find a similar equivalence for completely strictly recursive structures. The next theorem states this equivalence explicitly.

Theorem 6.6 *Suppose that U satisfies* (R-1). *Then the utility function U is homothetically completely strictly recursive if and only if U and F are completely strictly recursive in* $\langle \hat{I} \rangle$.

Proof. This follows by repeated application of theorem 3.9.   ‖

Of course, a dual characterization using V and C is also possible.

Corollary 6.6.1 *Suppose that V satisfies* (R-2). *Then the indirect utility function V is homothetically completely strictly recursive if and only if V and C are completely strictly recursive in* $\langle \hat{I} \rangle$.

Proof. Follows by duality from theorem 6.6.   ‖

6.3 OVERALL HOMOTHETICITY AND COMPLETE RECURSIVITY

In Lemma 3.4 it was noted that the assumption of direct or indirect overall homotheticity is also equivalent to certain separability restrictions on the cost and transformation functions. In this section we exploit this equivalence to show that overall homotheticity and complete recursivity is equivalent to a recursivity condition on the cost or transformation function. The condition requires that C, for example, be completely recursive in $\langle_0 \hat{I} \rangle$. Before proceeding to these new equivalences we supply the representation results which are necessary.

Theorem 6.7 *Suppose that C satisfies* (R-3). *Then the cost function C is completely recursive in the ordered partition* $\langle_0 \hat{I} \rangle$ *if and only if there exist functions*

$$\tilde{C}^{[0]} : \mathcal{R}(U) \times \mathcal{R}(\overline{C}^{[1]}) \to \Omega^1_+ ,$$

$$\overline{C}^{[r]} : \Omega^{(r)}_+ \times \mathcal{R}(\overline{C}^{[r+1]}) \to \Omega^1_+ , \qquad r = 1, \ldots, m-1 ,$$

and

$$\overline{C}^{[m]} : \Omega^{(m)}_+ \to \Omega^1_+$$

such that

$$C(u,P) = \tilde{C}^{[0]}(u, \bar{c}^{[1]}) \tag{6.8a}$$

$$\bar{c}^{[r]} = \overline{C}^{[r]}(P^r, \bar{c}^{[r+1]}), \qquad r = 1, \ldots, m-1, \tag{6.8b}$$

and

$$\bar{c}^{[m]} = \overline{C}^{[m]}(P^m),\tag{6.8c}$$

where $\tilde{C}^{[0]}$ satisfies (R-3) and each $\overline{C}^{[r]}$ satisfies (R-3P).

Proof.   As for corollary 6.1.3.   ‖

Corollary 6.7.1   *Suppose that F satisfies (R-4). Then the transformation function F is completely recursive in the ordered partition $\langle_0\hat{I}\rangle$ if and only if there exist functions*

$$\tilde{F}^{[0]}: \mathcal{R}(U) \times \mathcal{R}(\overline{F}^{[1]}) \to \Omega^1_+,$$

$$\overline{F}^{[r]}: \Omega^{(r)}_+ \times \mathcal{R}(\overline{F}^{[r+1]}) \to \Omega^1_+, \qquad r = 1, \ldots, m-1,$$

and

$$\overline{F}^{[m]}: \Omega^{(m)}_+ \to \Omega^1_+$$

such that

$$F(u, X) = \tilde{F}^{[0]}(u, \bar{f}^{[1]}),\tag{6.9a}$$

$$\bar{f}^{[r]} = \overline{F}^{[r]}(X^r, \bar{f}^{[r+1]}), \qquad r = 1, \ldots, m-1,\tag{6.9b}$$

and

$$\bar{f}^{[m]} = \overline{F}^{[m]}(X^m),\tag{6.9c}$$

where $\tilde{F}^{[0]}$ satisfies (R-4) and each $\overline{F}^{[r]}$ satisfies (R-4X).

Proof.   As for corollary 6.1.4.   ‖

Corollary 6.7.2   *Suppose that V satisfies (R-2). Then the indirect utility function W is completely recursive in the ordered partition $\langle_0\hat{I}\rangle$ if and only if there exist functions*

$$\tilde{W}^{[0]}: \Omega^1_+ \times \mathcal{R}(\overline{W}^{[1]}) \to \mathbf{R}$$

$$\overline{W}^{[r]}: \Omega^{(r)}_+ \times \mathcal{R}(\overline{W}^{[r+1]}) \to \mathbf{R}, \qquad r = 1, \ldots, m-1,$$

and

$$\overline{W}^{[m]} : \Omega_+^{(m)} \to \mathbf{R}$$

such that

$$W(y, P) = \tilde{W}^{[0]}(y, \overline{w}^{[1]}) \qquad (6.10a)$$

$$\overline{w}^{[r]} = \overline{W}^{[r]}(P^r, \overline{w}^{[r+1]}), \qquad r = 1, \ldots, m-1, \qquad (6.10b)$$

and

$$\overline{w}^{[m]} = \overline{W}^{[m]}(P^m), \qquad (6.10c)$$

where $\tilde{W}^{[0]}$ satisfies continuity, positive monotonicity in y, and negative monotonicity in $\overline{w}^{[2]}$, and each $\overline{W}^{[r]}$ satisfies (R-3P).

Proof. From corollary 6.4.2. ‖

It is apparent from the representations that complete recursivity in the ordered (extended) partition $\langle_0 \hat{I} \rangle$ of the indirect utility, cost, and transformation functions is related to—in fact, stronger than—homothetic complete recursivity. It is stronger because it implies the existence of a pure price aggregator for all prices $[W^{[1]}(P^1, w^{[2]})$ and $\overline{C}^{[1]}(P^1, \overline{c}^{[2]})]$ or a pure quantity aggregator for all quantities $[\overline{F}^{[1]}(X^1, \overline{f}^{[2]})]$, whereas homothetic complete recursivity implies the existence of such aggregators only for prices and quantities in $_2 I$. As noted previously, this stronger structure is equivalent to complete recursivity and *overall* homotheticity.

Theorem 6.8 *Suppose that U satisfies* (R-1). *Then the following five structures are equivalent:*

(i)   *homotheticity and complete recursivity of the utility function U in $\langle \hat{I} \rangle$,*
(ii) *negative homotheticity and complete recursivity of the indirect utility function V in $\langle \hat{I} \rangle$,*
(iii) *complete recursivity of the indirect utility function W in $\langle_0 \hat{I} \rangle$,*
(iv) *complete recursivity of the cost function C in $\langle_0 \hat{I} \rangle$, and*
(v)   *complete recursivity of the transformation function F in $\langle_0 \hat{I} \rangle$.*

Moreover, if the extensions of V, C, and F to the boundaries of Ω^n are locally nonsated on $\Omega^{(m)}$, "recursivity" can be replaced by "strict recursivity" in the above set of equivalence.

Proof. The proof is a rather trivial extension of lemma 3.4 and theorems 6.3 and 6.4. Assume (i). From lemma 3.4, homotheticity of U implies that the cost, transformation, and indirect utility functions may be written respectively as

$$C(u,P) = \psi_c(u)\hat{C}(P),\tag{a}$$

$$F(u,X) = \frac{\hat{F}(X)}{\psi_f(u)},\tag{b}$$

and

$$W(y,P) = \psi_w(y/\hat{W}(P)),\tag{c}$$

where $\hat{C}$, $\hat{F}$, and $\hat{W}$ are PLH and ψ_c, ψ_f, and ψ_w are increasing. Hence V is negatively homothetic, and both I and I^0 are separable from their complements in C, F, and W.

From theorem 6.3, homotheticity of U implies homotheticity of $_2U$. Since U is homothetically completely recursive, by theorem 6.4, C, W, and F are each completely recursive in $\langle \hat{I} \rangle$ and $\langle _0\hat{I}^1 \rangle$, and V is completely recursive in $\langle \hat{I} \rangle$. Hence C, W, and F are each completely recursive in $\langle _0\hat{I} \rangle$. This proves (i)⇒(ii), (i)⇒(iii), (i)⇒(iv), and (i)⇒(v).

(ii)⇒(iii): By duality, (ii)⇒(i) and hence (ii)⇒(iii).

(iii)⇒(iv): We are given

$$W(y,P) = \tilde{W}^{[0]}(y,\overline{w}^{[1]}).$$

By lemma 3.4,

$$C(u,P) = \psi_c(u)\hat{C}(P),$$

i.e., I and I^0 are each separable from their respective complements. In addition, complete recursivity of W in $\langle _0\hat{I} \rangle$ implies, *a fortiori*, by theorem 6.5 that C is completely recursive in $\langle \hat{I} \rangle$ and $\langle _0\hat{I}^1 \rangle$. Hence C is completely recursive in $\langle _0\hat{I} \rangle$.

(iv)⇒(v): This follows immediately from theorem 6.2 and the equivalence of (iii) and (iv) in theorem 6.5.

(v)⇒(i): We are given

$$\lambda = F(u,X) = \tilde{F}^{[0]}(u,f^{[1]}).$$

By lemma 3.4, U is homothetic. Let $\lambda = 1$ and solve for u to get the completely recursive representation of U.

To obtain the strict-recursivity equivalences, first note that (a)–(c) can be written

$$C(u,P) = \tilde{C}(u, \hat{C}(P)), \tag{a'}$$

$$F(u,X) = \tilde{F}(u, \hat{F}(X)) \tag{b'}$$

and

$$W(y,P) = \tilde{W}(u, \hat{W}(P)), \tag{c'}$$

where $\tilde{C}$, $\tilde{F}$, and $\tilde{W}$ are strictly monotonic in $\hat{C}(P)$, $\hat{F}(X)$, and $\hat{W}(P)$, respectively. Thus, C, F, and W are strictly separable with respect to $\langle_0\tilde{I}^1\rangle$; and V is negatively homothetic if U is homothetic. Next repeat the above argument for nonstrict complete recursivity exploiting the strict-recursivity part of theorem 6.5. ‖

We conclude this section by calling attention again to the fact that the duality results contained in the foregoing theorems and corollaries are very analogous to the symmetric duality theorems of chapter 4. In the next section of this chapter, we see that the same cannot be said about the nonsymmetric analogue of (noncomplete) separability.

6.4   NONSYMMETRIC SEPARABILITY (RECURSIVITY)

The nonsymmetric analogue of separability in $\hat{I}$ is defined as follows. The utility function U is *nonsymmetrically separable* in the ordered partition $\langle\hat{I}\rangle$ if, for $r = 2, \ldots, m$, I^r is separable from $_1I_{r-1}$. That is, each set of variables I^r is separable from the set of variables that *precede* I^r in the ordered set $\langle I\rangle$. We refer to this condition as *recursivity*.

Note that, in the definition of recursivity, I^r is *not* necessarily separable from sectors that *follow* I^r in the ordered set $\langle\hat{I}\rangle$. Indeed, if I^r is separable from variables in succeeding as well as preceding sectors, the utility function is (symmetrically) separable in $\hat{I}$. Thus, separability in $\hat{I}$ is a special case of recursivity in $\langle\hat{I}\rangle$. In fact, separability of U in the partition $\hat{I}$ is equivalent to recursivity of U in *every* ordered permutation of the partition $\hat{I}$.

Recursivity of the indirect utility function W, of the cost function C, and of the transformation function F in the ordered partitions $\langle\hat{I}\rangle$ and $\langle_0\hat{I}\rangle$ are defined analogously.

Representation theorems for recursive structures have been proved by Lady and Nissen (1968) and Primont (1970):

Theorem 6.9   *Suppose U is continuous and nondecreasing. Then the utility function is recursive in the ordered partition $\langle \hat{I} \rangle$ only if there exist functions*

$$U^{(r)}: \Omega^{(r)} \times \overset{m}{\underset{s=r+1}{\times}} \mathscr{R}(U^{(s)}) \to \mathbf{R}, \qquad r = 1, \ldots, m-1,$$

and

$$U^{(m)}: \Omega^{(m)} \to \mathbf{R}$$

such that

$$U(X) = U^{(1)}(X^1, u^{(2)}, \ldots, u^{(m)}), \tag{6.11a}$$

$$u^{(r)} = U^{(r)}(X^r, u^{(r+1)}, \ldots, u^{(m)}), \qquad r = 2, \ldots, m-1, \tag{6.11b}$$

and

$$u^{(m)} = U^{(m)}(X^m), \tag{6.11c}$$

where $U^{(1)}$ is nondecreasing in $u^{(2)}$. If U is strictly recursive in $\langle \hat{I} \rangle$, then each $U^r, r = 1, \ldots, m-1$, is increasing in u^{r+1} and is continuous.

Proof.   By assumption, I^m is separable from its complement in I. Hence, by Theorem 3.2b, there exist functions

$$U^{(m)}: \Omega^{(m)} \to \mathbf{R}$$

and

$$\bar{U}: \Omega^{(1)} \times \cdots \times \Omega^{(m-1)} \times \mathscr{R}(U^{(m)}) \to \mathbf{R}$$

such that

$$U(X) = \bar{U}(X^1, \ldots, X^{m-1}, U^{(m)}(X^m)), \tag{a}$$

where $\bar{U}$ is nondecreasing in $U^{(m)}(X^m)$.

Suppose that there exist functions $\bar{U}^{(r)}$, which are continuous in $_1X_r$ for each $_{r+1}u$, and $U^{(s)}$, $s = r+1, \ldots, m$, satisfying

$$U(X) = \bar{U}^{(r)}(X^1, \ldots, X^r, u^{(r+1)}, \ldots, u^{(m)}), \tag{b}$$

where

$$u^{(s)} = U^{(s)}(X^s, u^{(s+1)}, \ldots, u^{(m)}), \qquad s = r+1, \ldots, m,$$

$$u^{(m)} = U^{(m)}(X^m),$$

and $\overline{U}^{(r)}$ is nondecreasing in $u^{(r+1)}$. Since I^r is separable from $_1I_{r-1}$ given the values of the components of the vector

$$_{r+1}u = [u^{(r+1)}, \ldots, u^{(m)}],$$

we can define the ordering $\succcurlyeq^r_{r+1u}$ (conditional on $_{r+1}u$) by

$$X^r \succcurlyeq^r_{r+1u} \hat{X}^r \Leftrightarrow U^{(r)}(_1X_{r-1}, X^r, _{r+1}u) \geq U^{(r)}(_1X_{r-1}, \hat{X}^r, _{r+1}u) \ \forall_1 X_{r-1} \in {}_1\Omega_{r-1}.$$

As in the proof of theorem 3.2b, it is easily shown that $\succcurlyeq^r_{r+1u}$ is complete, transitive, reflexive, and continuous. Hence the ordering is representable by a function, $U^{(r)}$, which is continuous in X^r for each $_{r+1}u$. Define the function $\overline{U}^{(r-1)}$ by

$$U(X) = \overline{U}^{(r-1)}(_1X_{r-1}, U^{(r)}(X^r, _{r+1}u), _{r+1}u)$$

where $\overline{U}^{(r-1)}$ is nondecreasing in $u^{(r)} = U^{(r)}(X^r, _{r+1}u)$. (Note, however, that no claim has been made for any possible continuity or monotonicity properties of $U^{(r)}$ in $_{r+1}u$.) Repeating the above argument from $r = m-1$ to $r = 2$ yields the representation in (6.11) where $\overline{U}^{(1)} = U^{(1)}$ is nondecreasing in $u^{(2)}$.

If U is strictly recursive, we begin with the representation in (a) where, because of the reference-vector construction,

$$U^{(m)}(X^m) = U(O^1, \ldots, O^{m-1}, X^m),$$

and where, for $r = m-1$ in (b), $\overline{U}^{(m-1)}$ is increasing in $u^{(m)} = U^{(m)}(X^m)$. Next suppose we have the representation in (b) where $\overline{U}^{(r)}$ and $U^{(s)}$, $s = r+1, \ldots, m$, are continuous and $\overline{U}^{(r)}$ is increasing in $u^{(r+1)}$. Since I^r is strictly separable from $_1I_{r-1}$ given $_{r+1}u$, let

$$U^r(X^r, _{r+1}u) = \overline{U}^{(r)}(_1O_{r-1}, X^r, _{r+1}u)$$

where $_1O_{r-1}$ is an arbitrary reference vector. Clearly U^r is continuous in all of its arguments and increasing in $u^{(r+1)}$, inheriting these properties directly from $\overline{U}^{(r)}$. By an argument analogous to the proof of theorem 3.4 there exists a continuous function $\overline{U}^{(r-1)}$ such that

$$U(X) = \overline{U}^{(r-1)}(_1X_{r-1}, U^{(r)}(X^r, _{r+1}u), _{r+1}u)$$

where $\overline{U}^{(r-1)}$ is increasing in $u^{(r)} = U^{(r)}(X^r, _{r+1}u)$. Repeating the above argument recursively from $r = m-1$ to $r = 2$ yields the desired representation in (6.11). $\|$

A consequence of the difference between the recursive and the completely recursive representations is the possible existence of *all* higher-order aggregators in each aggregator function in the recursive structure. Also, in the completely recursive case, many properties of the parent function are inherited by the aggregator functions, whereas apparently very few properties are inherited by the aggregator functions of the noncompletely recursive structure. It is of course true that each $U^{(r+1)}$ inherits from $U^{(r)}$ (and hence from U) properties in X^{r+1} in the strictly recursive case. We have not, however, found general inheritance results with respect to the higher-order aggregators in each term. That is, we do not have general results regarding what properties $U^{(r+1)}$ inherits in $(u^{(r+2)},\ldots,u^{(m)})$ from U^r and its predecessors. This is why theorem 6.9 provides a representation of U which is only necessary for (strict) recursivity.

Relative to the various ordered partitions defined in the previous section, there is a rich assortment of recursive structures which can be imposed upon the utility, cost, and transformation functions. Unfortunately, as noted above, few duality results relating these structures have been proved. We restrict our discussion, therefore, to those structures for which duality results are known and those which have certain interesting decentralization properties to be discussed in section 6.6.

Corollary 6.9.1 *Suppose that V is continuous and nonincreasing. The indirect utility function V is recursive in the ordered partition $\langle \hat{I} \rangle$ only if there exist functions*

$$V^{(r)} : \Omega_+^{(r)} \times \mathop{\times}\limits_{s=r+1}^{m} \mathcal{R}(V^{(s)}) \to \mathbf{R}, \qquad r=1,\ldots,m-1,$$

and

$$V^{(m)} : \Omega_+^{(m)} \to \mathbf{R}$$

such that

$$V(P/y) = V^{(1)}(P^1/y, v^{(2)}, \ldots, v^{(m)}), \tag{6.12a}$$

$$v^{(r)} = V^{(r)}(P^r/y, v^{(r+1)}, \ldots, v^{(m)}), \qquad r=2,\ldots,m, \tag{6.12b}$$

and

$$v^{(m)} = V^{(m)}(P^m/y), \tag{6.12c}$$

where $V^{(1)}$ is nonincreasing in $v^{(2)}$. Moreover, V is strictly recursive only if each $V^{(r)}$, $r = 1, \ldots, m-1$ is strictly monotonic in $v^{(r+1)}$ and continuous.

Proof. This follows as in Theorem 6.9. ‖

Homotheticity of the aggregator functions does not have the same profound implications for recursive structures as for completely recursive structures. Nevertheless, homothetic recursivity is of some interest in the examination of recursive aggregation and budgeting in section 6.6.

Corollary 6.9.2 *Let U be recursive in $\langle \hat{I} \rangle$. Then, if the functions, $U^{(s)}$, $s = r, \ldots, m$, are positively homothetic, there exists a recursive representation in which the $m - r$ aggregators $U^{(r+1)}, \ldots, U^{(m)}$ are PLH in their arguments.*

Proof. The theorem is proved by a construction that is essentially the same as that in the proof of theorem 6.3 above. ‖

Corollary 6.9.3 *Let V be recursive in the ordered partition $\langle \hat{I} \rangle$. Then, if the functions, $V^{(s)}$ $s = r, \ldots, m$, are negatively homothetic, there exists a recursive representation in which the $m - r$ aggregator functions $V^{(r+1)}, \ldots, V^{(m)}$ are PLH in their arguments, and V^r is NH if $r = 1$ and PLH if $r > 1$.*

Of course, $r = 1$ in the statement of the above corollaries implies positive homotheticity or negative homotheticity of U or V. The representations obtained by letting $r = 2$ in the above corollary are referred to as direct and indirect homothetic recursivity, respectively. In order to construct the next three representations, we define a new partition,

$$\langle_0 \tilde{I}^m \rangle = \langle_0 I_1, I^2, \ldots, I^m \rangle.$$

Corollary 6.9.4 *Suppose C is continuous and nondecreasing. Then the cost function is recursive in $\langle_0 \tilde{I}^m \rangle$ only if there exist functions*

$$\overline{C}^{(1)} : \mathcal{R}(U) \times \Omega_+^{(1)} \times \underset{r=2}{\overset{m}{\times}} \mathcal{R}(\overline{C}^{(r)}) \to \Omega_+^1,$$

$$\overline{C}^{(r)} : \Omega_+^{(r)} \times \underset{s=r+1}{\overset{m}{\times}} \mathcal{R}(\overline{C}^{(s)}) \to \Omega_+^1, \qquad r = 2, \ldots, m-1,$$

and

$$\overline{C}^{(m)} : \Omega_+^{(m)} \to \Omega_+^1.$$

such that

$$C(u,P) = \bar{C}^{(1)}(u,P^1,\bar{c}^{(2)},\ldots,\bar{c}^{(m)}), \tag{6.13a}$$

$$\bar{c}^{(r)} = \bar{C}^{(r)}(P^r,\bar{c}^{(r+1)},\ldots,\bar{c}^{(m)}), \qquad r=2,\ldots,m-1, \tag{6.13b}$$

and

$$\bar{c}^m = \bar{C}^{(m)}(P^m), \tag{6.13c}$$

where $\bar{C}^{(1)}$, *is nondecreasing in* $c^{(2)}$. *Moreover,* C *is strictly recursive in* $\langle {}_0\tilde{I}^m \rangle$ *only if each* $\bar{C}^{(r)}$, $r=1,\ldots,m-1$, *is increasing in* $c^{(r+1)}$ *and continuous.*

Corollary 6.9.5 *Suppose that* F *is continuous and nondecreasing in* X. *Then the transformation function* F *is recursive in the ordered partition* $\langle {}_0\tilde{I}^m \rangle$ *only if there exist functions*

$$\bar{F}^{(1)} : \mathcal{R}(U) \times \Omega_+^{(1)} \times \mathop{\mathsf{X}}_{r=2}^{m} \mathcal{R}(\bar{F}^{(r)}) \to \Omega_+^1,$$

$$\bar{F}^{(r)} : \Omega_+^{(r)} \times \mathop{\mathsf{X}}_{s=r+1}^{m} \mathcal{R}(\bar{F}^{(s)}) \to \Omega_+^1, \qquad r=2,\ldots,m-1,$$

and

$$\bar{F}^{(m)} : \Omega_+^{(m)} \to \Omega_+^1$$

such that

$$F(u,X) = \bar{F}^{(1)}(u,X^1,\bar{f}^{(2)},\ldots,\bar{f}^{(m)}), \tag{6.14a}$$

$$\bar{f}^{(r)} = \bar{F}^{(r)}(X^r,\bar{f}^{(r+1)},\ldots,\bar{f}^{(m)}), \qquad r=2,\ldots,m-1, \tag{6.14b}$$

and

$$\bar{f}^{(m)} = \bar{F}^{(m)}(X^m), \tag{6.14c}$$

where $\bar{F}^{(1)}$, *is nondecreasing in* $f^{(2)}$. *Moreover,* F *is strictly recursive in* $\langle {}_0\tilde{I}^m \rangle$ *only if each* $\bar{F}^{(r)}$, $r=1,\ldots,m-1$, *is increasing in* $f^{(r+1)}$ *and continuous.*

Corollary 6.9.6 *Suppose that* W *is continuous and nonincreasing in* P. *Then the indirect utility function* W *is recursive in the ordered partition* $\langle {}_0\tilde{I}^m \rangle$ *only* *if there exist functions*

$$\overline{W}^{(1)}: \Omega^1_+ \times \Omega^{(1)}_+ \times \overset{m}{\underset{r=2}{\times}} \mathcal{R}(\overline{W}^{(r)}) \rightarrow \mathbf{R},$$

$$\overline{W}^{(r)}: \Omega^{(r)}_+ \times \overset{m}{\underset{s=r+1}{\times}} \mathcal{R}(\overline{W}^{(s)}) \rightarrow \mathbf{R}, \qquad r = 2, \dots, m-1,$$

and

$$\overline{W}^{(m)}: \Omega^{(m)}_+ \rightarrow \mathbf{R}$$

such that

$$W(y, P) = \overline{W}^{(1)}(y, P^1, \overline{w}^{(2)}, \dots, \overline{w}^{(m)}), \tag{6.15a}$$

$$\overline{w}^{(r)} = \overline{W}^{(r)}(P^r, \overline{w}^{(r+1)}, \dots, \overline{w}^{(m)}), \qquad r = 2, \dots, m-1, \tag{6.15b}$$

and

$$w^{(m)} = \overline{W}^{(m)}(P^m), \tag{6.15c}$$

where $\overline{W}^{(1)}$ is nonincreasing in $\overline{w}^{(2)}$. Moreover, W is strictly recursive only if each $\overline{W}^{(r)}$, $r = 1, \dots, m-1$, is strictly monotonic in $\overline{w}^{(r+1)}$ and continuous.

These corollaries follow from the construction in theorem 6.9. In addition, it follows from corollaries 6.9.2 and 6.9.3 that in each of the last three results the aggregators can be chosen to be PLH without loss of generality.

The duality theorems 6.2, 6.5, and 6.6 for completely recursive structures do not go through for weakly recursive structures. The recursive analogue of theorem 6.2 (complete recursivity of C $\Leftrightarrow$ complete recursivity of F) cannot be proved, because theorem 3.6 is not applicable. This is because of the existence of the sector $_{r+1}I$, which must be dealt with in forming an aggregator for I^r. Theorems 6.5 and 6.6 rely on the equivalence of separability of the cost and transformation functions and therefore do not have noncomplete recursive analogues.

Known duality results for recursive structures are summarized in the following theorem and corollary:

Theorem 6.10 *Suppose that U satisfies $(R-1)$. Then homothetic recursivity of U in $\langle \hat{I} \rangle$ is equivalent to recursivity of F in $\langle _0\hat{I}^m \rangle$.*

Proof. Homothetic recursivity of U and corollary 6.9.2 allow us to choose U^r, $r = 2, \ldots, m$, in the representation (6.11) to be PLH. Hence,

$$U(X/\lambda) = U^{(1)}(X^1/\lambda, u^{(2)}/\lambda, \ldots, u^{(m)}/\lambda)$$

$$= \tilde{U}^{(1)}(\lambda, X^1, u^{(2)}, \ldots, u^{(m)}), \qquad \lambda > 0.$$

Then max $\{\lambda \epsilon \Omega^1_+ | \tilde{U}^{(1)}(\lambda, \langle X^1, u^{(2)}, \ldots, u^{(m)}) \geq u\}$ equals

$$F(u, X) = \bar{F}^{(1)}(u, X^1, u^{(2)}, \ldots, u^{(m)}),$$

which, given the structure of (6.11b) and (6.11c), implies recursivity of F in $\langle_0 \tilde{I}^m \rangle$. Conversely, letting the expression in (6.14a) equal one and inverting in u yields the structure (6.11). ‖

Corollary 6.10.1 *Suppose that U satisfies $(R-1)$. Then homothetic recursivity of V, recursivity of W in $\langle_0 \tilde{I}^m \rangle$, and recursivity of C in $\langle_0 \tilde{I}^m \rangle$ are equivalent.*

Proof. The proof is analogous to the proof of theorem 6.10 since the derivation of C from V is mathematically equivalent to the derivation of F from U. ‖

6.5 COMPLETELY RECURSIVE AGGREGATION AND DECENTRALIZATION

6.5.1 Introductory Comments

The price and quantity aggregation and decentralization concepts examined in chapter 5 have obvious nonsymmetric analogues. There are, however, important differences. In the symmetric case, direct and indirect separability and homothetic separability play prominent roles in the necessary and sufficient conditions for decentralizability and additive price and quantity aggregation, respectively. In the nonsymmetric case, it is direct and indirect *complete* recursivity and homothetic *complete* recursivity that do the work in the analysis of decentralization and aggregation. Also, (symmetric) complete separability in conjunction with the Gorman (polar) form suffices for quantity (price) aggregation. In the nonsymmetric case, there are in general no additive structures, which means that the Gorman (polar) form cannot be exploited. This also means that the distinction between price aggregation and additive price aggregation vanishes in the nonsymmetric case.

Of course, there may be additive structures if additional assumptions are made. By making such assumptions, many hybrid structures can be generated. For example, suppose that U can be written with the image.

$$U(X) = U^{[1]}(X^1, u^{[2]}),$$

where

$$u^{[2]} = U^{[2]}\left(X^2, \sum_{r=3}^{m} U^r(X^r)\right).$$

Clearly U is completely recursive in $\langle \hat{I} \rangle$, and $_3U$ is completely separable in $_3\hat{I}$, so that stronger results can be obtained by conjoining the nonsymmetric and symmetric theorems.

The chapter closes with a discussion of the relationship between recursive structures and decentralizability. The absence of strong decentralizability properties of these structures is itself interesting because the source of the problem appears to be the "public" nature of higher-order aggregators. Thus, the optimum cannot be decentralized because of the existence of "public goods". Direct and indirect recursivity do, however, rationalize weaker forms of decentralization. Homothetic direct and indirect recursivity strengthen these decentralizability properties; moreover, interesting "public-good accountability" properties can be extracted from these structures.

6.5.2 Recursive Decentralization

Analogously to the symmetric case, *recursive strong decentralizability* is defined as the existence of $m-1$ vector-valued functions

$$\phi^{[r]}: {}_r\Omega_+ \times \Omega^1_+ \to \Omega^{(r)}, \qquad r = 2, \ldots, m,$$

with images

$$X^r = \phi^{[r]}({}_rP, z_r), \qquad r = 2, \ldots, m, \qquad (6.16)$$

which are HDO in their arguments and satisfy the Slutsky symmetry conditions. *Recursive weak decentralizability* is defined by the existence of $m-1$ vector-valued functions

$$\tilde{\phi}^{[r]}: {}_r\Omega_+ \times \Omega^1_+ \to \Omega^{(r)}, \qquad r = 2, \ldots, m,$$

with images

$$X^r = \tilde{\phi}^{[r]}(_rP/y, z_r/y), \qquad r = 2, \dots, m. \tag{6.17}$$

Finally, *recursive felicitous decentralizability* is defined by the existence of $m - 1$ vector-valued functions

$$\zeta^{[r]} : \mathscr{R}(U) \times _r\Omega_+ \to \Omega^{(r)}, \qquad r = 2, \dots, m,$$

with images

$$X^r = \zeta^{[r]}(u, _rP) \cdot z_r, \qquad r = 2, \dots, m. \tag{6.18}$$

Thus, if the utility function is recursively strongly decentralizable, the optimal consumption bundle in the rth sector can be chosen knowing only the optimal expenditure on, and prices of, commodities in the rth and higher-order sectors, $_r\hat{I}$. If the utility function is recursively weakly decentralizable, the informational requirements are the normalized expenditure on, and prices of, the continuation $_rI$. Recursive felicitous decentralization requires the overall utility (or more appropriately output) as well as the continuation expenditure and prices. Note that these decentralization concepts are weaker than their symmetric counterparts, which require only intrasector expenditure and prices. The informational requirements of recursive decentralization are much stronger.

The next three theorems provide conditions for recursive strong and weak decentralizability. As was the case with symmetric decentralization, somewhat stronger maintained hypotheses are needed to generate necessary as well as sufficient conditions for strong decentralization. In order to exploit the symmetric decentralization theorems of chapter 5 in the following proofs, it is useful to consider the following set of optimization problems [assuming that U satisfies $(R-1')$]:[9]

$$H^{[r]}(y_1, \dots, y_{k(r)}, z_r, P)$$

$$= \max_X \left\{ U(X) \,\middle|\, X \in \Omega^n \wedge p_i x_i \leqslant y_i \; \forall i \in {}_1I_{r-1} \wedge {}_rP \cdot {}_rX \leqslant z_r \right\}, r = 2, \dots, m \tag{6.19}$$

where, of course, $k(r) = \sum_{s=1}^{r-1} n_s$. The close relationship of the functions

---

[9]The regularity conditions $(R-1')$, stated in chapter 5, strengthen the quasi-concavity condition of $(R-1)$ (defined in chapter 2) to strict quasi-concavity. The stronger curvature assumption is not essential to what follows, but is convenient because it guarantees unique solutions to the following optimization problems.

$H^{[r]}$, $r=2,\ldots,m$, to the conditional indirect utility functions analyzed in section 5.3 will not escape the reader's attention. Indeed, $H^{[r]}$ is the conditional indirect utility function corresponding to the partition $\{\{1\},\ldots,\{k(r)\},_r I\}$ of I. Thus, solving

$$\max_{y_1,\ldots,y_{k(r)},z_r} H^{[r]}(y_1,\ldots,y_{k(r)},z_r,P) \quad \text{s.t.} \quad \sum_{i=1}^{k(r)} y_i + z_r \leqslant y, \quad r=2,\ldots,m,$$

yields, in part, the recursive system of allocation functions

$$\theta^{[r]} : \Omega_+^1 \times \Omega_+^n \to \Omega_0^1, \quad r=2,\ldots,m,$$

with images

$$z_r = \theta^{[r]}(y,P), \quad r=2,\ldots,m. \tag{6.20}$$

Theorem 6.11 *Suppose that the utility function satisfies* $(R-1')$. *Then complete recursivity of U in the partition $\hat{I}$ is sufficient for recursive strong decentralizability with respect to the same partition. Moreover, if the functions $H^{[r]}$ and $\theta^{[r]}$, $r=2,\ldots,m$, are differentiable, and each $\theta^{[r]}$ is positive-valued, then complete recursivity is necessary for recursive strong decentralizability.*

Proof. Complete recursivity of U in $\hat{I}$ is equivalent to separability in each of the partitions

$$\{\{1\},\ldots,\{k(r)\},_r I\}, \quad r=2,\ldots,m.$$

Therefore, repeated application of theorems 5.2, 5.3 generates a proof. ||

As noted earlier, we are for convenience maintaining strict quasi-concavity in the discussion of recursive decentralization. In conjunction with monotonicity, strict quasi-concavity implies that U is increasing, in which case the distinction between strict and nonstrict recursivity vanishes. Thus, the necessary and sufficient condition (given the differentiability assumptions) of theorem 6.11 is equivalent to complete strict recursivity. If, however, we relax the assumption of strict quasi-concavity, then a weaker condition—complete nonstrict recursivity— is necessary and sufficient for strong recursive decentralizability. For further discussion of this point and an example, see the discussion following theorem 5.3.

Theorem 6.12 *If U satisfies $(R-1)$, complete recursivity of the indirect utility function V is sufficient for recursive weak decentralizability.*

Proof. Noting that complete recursivity of V is equivalent to separability in each of the partitions

$$\{\{1\},\ldots,\{k(r)\},_rI\}, \qquad r=2,\ldots,m,$$

repeated application of theorem 5.4 generates the proof. ∥

Theorem 6.13 *Assume that U satisfies $(R-1')$ and that C is differentiable. Then implicit complete recursivity is necessary and sufficient for recursive felicitous decentralizability.*

Proof. Apply theorem 5.5 recursively as in the above proofs. ∥

As the conditional demand functions $\phi^{[r]}$, $r=2,\ldots,m$, are HDO in their arguments, it is apparent that recursive strong decentralizability implies recursive weak decentralizability. Recursive felicitous decentralizability is neither stronger nor weaker than the other two decentralization concepts.

6.5.3 Recursive Algorithms

Recursive decentralizability rationalizes certain classes of m-stage budgeting procedures, or algorithms—analogues to the two-stage budgeting procedures introduced by Strotz (1957) and discussed in chapter 5. If the utility function is recursively completely decentralizable, the following m-stage algorithm can be used to execute an optimal allocation of total expenditure:

Step 1:

$$\max_{X^m} U^{[m]}(X^m) \qquad \text{s.t.} \quad P^m \cdot X^m \leqslant z_m,$$

where z_m is a dummy variable, yielding

$$X^m = \phi^{[m]}(P^m, z_m).$$

Step 2:

$$\max_{X^{m-1}, z_m} U^{[m-1]}\big(X^{m-1}, \nu^m(P^m, z_m)\big) \qquad \text{s.t.} \quad P^{m-1} \cdot Z^{m-1} + z_m \leqslant z_{m-1}$$

where z_{m-1} is a dummy variable and

$$\nu^m(P^m, z_m) = U^{[m]}\big(\phi^{[m]}(P^m, z_m)\big),$$

yielding

$$X^{m-1} = \phi^{[m-1]}(_{m-1}P, z_{m-1})$$

and

$$z_m = \theta_m(_{m-1}P, z_{m-1}).$$

$$\vdots$$

Step $m - r + 1$:

$$\max_{X^r, z_{r+1}} U^{[r]}\big(X^r, \nu^{r+1}(_{r+1}P, z_{r+1})\big) \qquad \text{s.t.} \quad P^r \cdot X^r + z_{r+1} \leqslant z_r,$$

where z_r is a dummy variable and

$$\nu^{r+1}(_{r+1}P, z_{r+1}) = U^{[r+1]}\big(\phi^{[r+1]}(_{r+1}P, z_{r+1}), \nu^{r+2}(_{r+2}P, \theta_{r+2}(_{r+1}P, z_{r+1}))\big),$$

yielding

$$X^r = \phi^{[r]}(_r P, z_r)$$

and

$$z_{r+1} = \theta_{r+1}(_r P, z_r).$$

$$\vdots$$

Step m:

$$\max_{X^1, z_2} U^{[1]}\big(X^1, \nu^2(_2 P, z_2)\big) \qquad \text{s.t.} \quad P^1 \cdot X^1 + z_2 \leqslant y,$$

where $\nu^2(_2 P, z_2) = U^{[2]}\big(\phi^{[2]}(_2 P, z_2), \nu^3(_3 P, \theta_3(_2 P, z_2))\big)$, yielding

$$X^1 = \phi^{[1]}(_1 P, y)$$

and

$$z_2 = \theta_2(_1 P, y).$$

As y is the (known) total expenditure, these last two equations yield the optimal X^2 and z_2. The remaining consumption quantities are obtained by substituting successively for the z_r using

$$z_r = \theta_r(_{r-1}P, z_{r-1}), \qquad r = 3, \ldots, m.$$

Similar m-stage recursive algorithms can be formulated for recursive weakly decentralizable and recursive felicitously decentralizable functions. The recursive weak-decentralization algorithm is less appealing, since the intrasector allocation functions (6.17) are not derived from an explicit optimization problem.

6.5.4 Recursive Price and Quantity Aggregation

It was mentioned above that nonsymmetric, nonadditive price aggregation turns out to be a vacuous concept. Perhaps a brief discussion of the issue at this point would be instructive.

Recall that (symmetric) price aggregation in chapter 5 was defined as separablity of the expenditure-allocation functions in $\hat{I}$. The nonsymmetric analogue of this concept is not unambiguous. We have thus far employed two alternative sets of recursive allocation functions, one in the proof of recursive strong decentralizability and one in the recursive algorithm discussed above. The two sets of images are repeated here for easy reference:

$$z_r = \theta^{[r]}(y, P), \qquad r = 2, \ldots, m,$$

and

$$z_r = \theta_r(z_{r-1}, {}_{r-1}P), \qquad r = 2, \ldots, m.$$

Price aggregation could be defined by structuring either of these sets of allocation functions with respect to prices, e.g.,

$$\theta^{[r]}(y, P) = \hat{\theta}^{[r]}(y, \pi^{[r]}), \qquad r = 2, \ldots, m,$$

or

$$\theta_r(y, P) = \hat{\theta}_r(z_{r-1}, \pi^{[r]}), \qquad r = 2, \ldots, m,$$

where

$$\pi^{[r]} = \Pi^{[r]}(P^r, \pi^{[r+1]}), \qquad r = 2, \ldots, m-1,$$

and

$$\pi^{[m]} = \Pi^{[m]}(P^m).$$

As it turns out, however, either of these structures, conjoined with complete recursivity (which is necessary for efficient expenditure of the sectoral allocations, as described in theorem 6.11), implies either homothetic complete recursivity of U (which, not surprisingly, turns out to be sufficient for additive recursive price aggregation) or complete (symmetric) separability of U (or some hybrid combination). The reason that the nonhomothetic condition for recursive price aggregation imposes symmetric structure is that, as was pointed out above, complete asymmetric separability does not induce additivity of U; consequently, the generalized Gorman polar form cannot be employed to generate recursive price aggregation.

The foregoing discussion could be formalized by a theorem and a lengthy proof—not unlike the proof of Theorem 5.6—but we spare the reader this exercise and proceed instead to a discussion of additive recursive price aggregation.

Additive recursive price (quantity) aggregation is defined as the existence of price aggregates

$$_r\Pi : {_r\Omega_+} \to \Omega^1, \qquad r = 2, \ldots, m,$$

and quantity aggregates

$$_r\Gamma : {_r\Omega} \to \Omega^1, \qquad r = 2, \ldots, m,$$

such that

$$_r\Pi(_r\overset{*}{P}) \cdot {_r\Gamma}(_r\overset{*}{X}) = \overset{*}{z}_r, \qquad r = 2, \ldots, m,$$

for all optimal triples $(_r\overset{*}{P}, {_r\overset{*}{X}}, \overset{*}{z}_r)$.

Theorem 6.14 *Assume that U satisfies* (R-1′). *Then direct homothetic complete recursivity implies additive recursive price (quantity) aggregation. Moreover, if U is completely recursive, then homothetic complete recursivity is necessary for additive price (quantity) aggregation.*

Proof. As homothetic complete recursivity of U is equivalent to homothetic separability of U in the partitions $\{1, \ldots, \{k(r)\}, {_rI}\}$, $r = 2, \ldots, m$, the theorem follows from recursive application of theorem 5.8. ‖

Homothetic recursivity embellishes the recursive algorithm described above. Employing the recursive price aggregators, the nonsymmetric analogue of homothetic budgeting is described as follows:

Step 1:

$$\max_{X^m} U^{[m]}(X^m) \qquad \text{s.t.} \quad P^m \cdot X^m \leqslant z_m,$$

yielding

$$X^m = \phi^{[m]}(P^m, z_m).$$

Let

$$\pi^{[m]} = V^{[m]}(P^m) = \left[U^{[m]}(\phi^{[m]}(P^m, 1)) \right]^{-1}.$$

Step 2:

$$\max_{X^{m-1}, u^{[m]}} U^{[m-1]}(X^{m-1}, u^{[m]}) \qquad \text{s.t.} \quad P^{m-1} \cdot X^{m-1} + \pi^{[m]} u^{[m]} \leqslant z_{m-1},$$

yielding

$$X^{m-1} = \phi^{[m-1]}(P^{m-1}, \pi^{[m]}, z_{m-1})$$

and

$$u^{[m]} = \hat{\theta}^{[m]}(P^{m-1}, \pi^{[m]}, z_{m-1}).$$

Let

$$\pi^{[m-1]} = V^{[m-1]}(P^{m-1}, \pi^{[m]})$$

$$= \left[U^{[m-1]}(\phi^{[m-1]}(P^{m-1}, \pi^{[m]}, 1), \hat{\theta}^{[m]}(P^{m-1}, \pi^{[m]}, 1)) \right]^{-1}.$$

$$\vdots$$

Step m:

$$\max_{X^1, u^{[2]}} U^{[1]}(X^1, u^{[2]}) \qquad \text{s.t.} \quad P^1 \cdot X^1 + \pi^{[2]} \cdot u^{[2]} \leqslant y,$$

yielding

$$X^1 = \phi^{[1]}(P^1, \pi^{[2]}, y),$$

$$u^{[2]} = \hat{\theta}^{[2]}(P^1, \pi^{[2]}, y).$$

As $y = z_1$ is known expenditure, the optimal consumption bundles are yielded by substituting sequentially for z_r in the conditional demand functions $\phi^{[r]}$, $r = 2, \ldots, m$, using

$$z_r = \pi^{[r]} \hat{\theta}^{[r]} \left(P^{r-1}, \pi^{[r]}, z_{r-1} \right), \qquad r = 2, \ldots, m.$$

This construction elucidates the fact that the price aggregators are themselves completely recursive. Note also that the price indices are, as in the symmetric case, the (normalized) PLH aggregators of the dual homothetically recursive aggregator functions (see theorem 6.5).

Finally, because there is no distinction between price aggregation and additive price aggregation, and because homothetic strong recursivity suffices for both, it is not fruitful to distinguish between recursive price aggregation and quantity aggregation. The symmetric equation (6.21) evinces both price and quantity aggregation.

We repeat the fact that it is complete recursivity that does all of the work in recursive decentralization and aggregation. Noncomplete recursivity plays no role in the above results. Nevertheless, as noted above, recursive structures have some interesting interpretations in the context of decentralization and aggregation. We discuss three recursive structures in the concluding section of this chapter.

6.6   RECURSIVITY, DECENTRALIZATION, AND AGGREGATION

6.6.1   Direct Recursivity

In the case of separable, completely separable, and completely recursive direct utility functions, the specific aggregator functions have two rather natural (mutually consistent) interpretations. On the one hand, they can be thought of as category utility functions; on the other hand, they can be interpreted as amounts of surrogate commodities, each of which is the appropriate argument in the utility function. If, however, the only structure which is imposed upon the direct utility function is recursivity, the first of these two interpretations is inappropriate. It does not make sense to interpret the specific aggregator functions as category utility functions, because the variables in $_{r+1}I$ are contained in other (higher-numbered) aggregator functions as well as $U^{(r)}$. Hence, $U^{(r)}$ cannot be interpreted as "the" (specific) utility function for $_rI$. The interpretation of the recursive aggregators as surrogate commodities, however, becomes somewhat more interesting; in fact, it is suggestive of Lancaster's (1966) idea that satisfaction is derived from the characteristics of commodities, and hence only indirectly from the commodities themselves.

The following example might illuminate these interpretations. Let U be recursive. Then

$$U(X) = U^{(1)}(X^1, {}_2u),$$

where

$$_ru = [u^{(r)}, \ldots, u^{(m)}],$$

$$u^{(r)} = U^{(r)}(X^r, {}_{r+1}u), \qquad r = 1, \ldots, m-1,$$

$$u^m = U^m(X^m).$$

(Note that $m \geqslant 3$, for if $m = 2$ there is no distinction between recursivity and complete recursivity.) Suppose we think of $u^{(q)}$ as being the quantity of the surrogate commodity "warmth". Let X^q be the vector of quantities of different types of clothing, which clearly provide warmth. Let $u^{(r)}$ be the quantity of the surrogate commodity "shelter", where X^r is the vector of quantities of housing services. If $r > q$, then $u^{(r)}$ may be an argument of $U(q)$ and "shelter" helps provide "warmth". Let $u^{(s)}$ and $u^{(t)}$ be the quantities of "recreation" and "food" respectively. Dining out might be considered to add to the amount of "recreation"; hence $u^{(t)}$ is an argument of $U^{(s)}$. Furthermore, vacations are "recreation", and the amount of vacation time which is taken may affect the amount of "shelter". If so, $u^{(s)}$ will be an argument of $U^{(r)}$. As a result, "food" consumption affects the amount of "warmth" by affecting the quantity of "recreation", which in turn affects the quantity of "shelter", which is an argument of $U^{(q)}$. However, it may well be true that "food" consumption affects the amount of "warmth" directly, and may itself be an argument of $U^{(q)}$. If nothing else contributed to the quantity of "warmth", we could write the image of $U^{(q)}$ as

$$u^{(q)} = U^{(q)}\left(X^q, U^{(r)}\left(X^r, U^{(s)}\left(X^s, U^{(t)}(X^t, {}_{t+1}u), {}_{t+1}u\right), U^{(t)}(X^t, {}_{t+1}u)\right)\right),$$

where, for notational convenience, we have assumed that $r = q+1$, $s = q+2$, and $t = q+3$. The reader should refer to figure 6.1 for an illustration of the above example of a recursive structure.

This chart is arranged vertically by levels and horizontally by sectors. At the qth level, if one reads across the chart, there appear all of the arguments of the function $U^{(q)}$. In our example, the clothing sector (X^q), shelter quantity ($u^{(r)}$), food quantity ($u^{(t)}$) and (possibly) $u^{(t+1)}, \ldots, u^{(m)}$ are the arguments of $U^{(q)}$ (warmth). At the sth level, the vacation sector (X^s), food quantity ($u^{(t)}$), and (possibly) $u^{(t+1)}, \ldots, u^m$ are the arguments of $U^{(s)}$ (recreation).

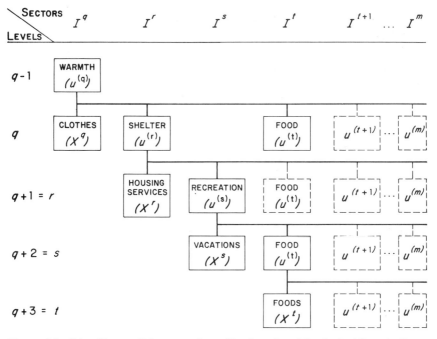

Figure 6.1 "A utility tree" for recursive utility function. The dashed lines indicate agruments that may or may not appear in their indicated positions.

At the tth sector I^t, by reading down the chart, one can find the set of functions (with indices less than t) of which $u^{(t)}$ (food quantity) is an argument. For example, $u^{(t)}$ is an argument of $U^{(q)}$ (warmth), since it is directly connected to $U^{(q)}$ by a solid line. It is also an argument of $U^{(s)}$ (recreation) and (possibly) an argument of $U^{(r)}$ (shelter), for the same reason. On the other hand, $u^{(s)}$ (the amount of recreation), while an argument of $U^{(r)}$ (shelter), is *not* an argument of $U^{(q)}$ (warmth), since it is not connected to $U^{(q)}$ directly, but only indirectly through $U^{(r)}$.

Finally, and perhaps most importantly, the chart is arranged so that each sector is separable from all sectors to its left but is not (necessarily) spearable from sectors to its right. Thus, for example, I^s is separable from I^q and I^r and from I^l, $l = 1, \ldots, q-1$. It is the nonsymmetric separability that accounts for the nonsymmetric appearance of the chart.

The preceding example illustrates the richness of the recursive structure. This very richness, however, presents difficulties for aggregation and decentralization. Surprisingly, even if the function is homothetically recursive, it is not possible to compute a price of say, "warmth" that could be used for the purpose of expenditure allocation. Heuristically, the nonexistence of price aggregates is attributable to the fact that, from the point of view of the rth sector, all higher-order commodities are public goods with respect to the production of the surrogate commodity $U^{(q)}$. They are "public" because the surrogate $U^{(r)}$ not only provides satisfaction directly, but is also used in the production of lower-order surrogate commodities without being diminished.

Although recursive direct utility functions do not possess sufficient structure for aggregation to be possible, a restricted class of decentralization is consistent with this structure. If the optimal expenditure continuation $_r y$ is known, the optimal consumption vector X^r can be found. That is, the conditional demand function images are

$$X^r = \phi^{(r)}(_r P, _r y), \qquad r = 1, \ldots, m. \tag{6.22}$$

If $U^{(r)}, r = 1, \ldots, m$, satisfies $(R-1)$, these conditional demand functions are generated as follows:

Step 1:

$$\max_{X^m} U^{(m)} \qquad \text{s.t.} \quad P^m \cdot X^m \leqslant y_m,$$

yielding

$$X^m = \phi^{(m)}(P^m, y_m).$$

Step 2:

$$\max_{X^{m-1}} U^{(m-1)}(X^{m-1}, u^{(m)}) \qquad \text{s.t.} \quad P^{m-1} \cdot X^{m-1} \leqslant y_{m-1},$$

yielding

$$X^{m-1} = \phi^{(m-1)}\left(P^{m-1}, y_{m-1}, u^{(m)}\right).$$

$$\vdots$$

Step $m - r + 1$:

$$\max_{X^r} U^{(r)}(X^r, _{r+1}u) \qquad \text{s.t.} \quad P^r \cdot X^r \leqslant y_r,$$

yielding

$$X^r = \phi^{(r)}(P^r, y_r, _{r+1}u).$$

$$\vdots$$

Step m:

$$\max_{X^1} U^{(1)}(X^1, _2 u) \qquad \text{s.t.} \quad P^1 \cdot X^1 \leqslant y_1,$$

yielding

$$X^1 = \phi^{(1)}(P^1, y_1, _2u).$$

Then define new functions with images

$$g^{(m)} = G^{(m)}(P^m, y_m) = U^{(m)}\big(\phi^{(m)}(P^m, y_m)\big)$$

and, for $r = m-1, m-2, \ldots, 1$,

$$g^{(r)} = G^{(r)}(P^r, y_r, _{r+1}g) = U^{(r)}\big(\phi^{(r)}(P^r, y_r, _{r+1}g), _{r+1}g\big)$$

where $_{r+1}g = (g^{(r+1)}, \ldots, g^{(m)})$.

Next define new functions with images

$$H^{(m)}(P^m, y_m) = G^{(m)}(P^m, y_m)$$

and, for $r = m-1, m-2, \ldots, 1$,

$$H^{(r)}(_rP, _ry) = G^{(r)}\big(P^r, y_r, H^{(r+1)}(_{r+1}P, _{r+1}y), \ldots, H^{(m)}(P^m, y_m)\big).$$

Finally, solve the problem

$$\max H^{(1)}(_1P, _1y) \qquad \text{s.t.} \quad \sum_{r=1}^{m} y_r \leqslant y,$$

which yields income-allocation functions:

$$\overset{*}{y}_r = \theta^r(P, y), \qquad r = 1, \ldots, m.$$

Substituting optimal sector incomes into each $H^{(r)}$, which in turn are substituted into each $\phi^{(r)}$, yields the optimal values of X, i.e.,

$$\overset{*}{X}^r = \overset{*}{\phi}{}^{(r)}(_rP, _r\overset{*}{y})$$

$$= \phi^{(r)}\big(P^r, \overset{*}{y}_r, H^{(r+1)}(_{r+1}P, _{r+1}\overset{*}{y}), \ldots, H^{(m)}(P^m, \overset{*}{y}_m)\big), \qquad r = 1, \ldots, m.$$

In the above algorithm, the informational requirements of each "division" include expenditure allocations to higher-numbered divisions. This contrasts with the completely recursive decentralization algorithm, in which each division requires as information only the total continuation expenditure, $z_r = \sum_{s=r}^{m} y_s$. In the completely recursive algorithm, each division divides the total continuation expenditure between its own "production", $y_r = P^r \cdot X^r$, and all higher-order production, z_{r+1}. There is no central planning in this structure; the "first" division simply divides the total expenditure y between y_1 and z_2. This type of planning is not optimal in the recursive case, because the public-goods problem must be resolved by the central planner.

A somewhat stronger class of decentralizability is rationalized if we posit *indirect* homothetic recursivity. We turn to a discussion of this structure next.

6.6.2 Indirect Homothetic Recursivity

Previously Corollary 6.10.1 stated that recursivity of W in $\langle_0\tilde{I}^m\rangle$ is equivalent to recursivity of the cost function C in the partition $\langle_0\tilde{I}^m\rangle$. The representation is

$$C(u,P)=\overline{C}^{(1)}(u,P^1,{}_2\bar{c}), \qquad (6.23a)$$

where

$$\bar{c}^{(r)}=\overline{C}^{(r)}(P^r,{}_{r+1}\bar{c}), \qquad r=2,\ldots,m-1, \qquad (6.23b)$$

and

$$\bar{c}^{(m)}=\overline{C}^{(m)}(P^m). \qquad (6.23c)$$

As a PLH function of prices, each $\overline{C}^{(r)}$ in this representation has one property needed for a price index. Although they cannot properly be used in the intercategory allocations, they do have interesting accountability properties. Interpreting $\bar{c}^r$, $r>1$, as the unit price of the rth surrogate commodity implies that

$$\left(\frac{d\overline{C}^{(1)}(u,P^1,{}_2\bar{c})}{d\bar{c}^{(r)}}\right)_u = \sum_{s=2}^r \left(\frac{\partial\overline{C}^{(1)}(u,P^1,{}_2\bar{c})}{\partial\bar{c}^{(s)}}\right)$$

$$\times \left[\sum_{t=s+1}^m \frac{d\overline{C}^{(s)}(P^s,{}_{s+1}\bar{c})}{d\bar{c}^{(t)}} \frac{d\overline{C}^{(t)}(P^t,{}_{t+1}\bar{c})}{d\bar{c}^{t+1}} \cdots \frac{d\overline{C}^{(r-1)}(P^r,{}_r\bar{c})}{d\bar{c}^r}\right]$$

is the compensated demand for the rth surrogate commodity. In a straightforward but messy construction, exploiting Euler's theorem and the positive linear homogeneity of each C^r, it is possible to show that the optimal expenditure on commodities in the rth sector is

$$y_r = \sum_{i\in I^r} p_i\bar{\phi}_i^{(r)}(P^r,{}_{r+1}\bar{c}) = \left(\frac{d\overline{C}^{(1)}(u,P^1,{}_2\bar{c})}{d\bar{c}^r}\right)_u$$

$$\times \left[\overline{C}^{(r)}(P^r,{}_{r+1}\bar{c}) - \sum_{s=r+1}^m \frac{d\overline{C}^{(r)}(P^r,{}_{r+1}\bar{c})}{d\bar{c}^{(s)}}\overline{C}^{(s)}(u,P^s,{}_{s+1}\bar{c})\right].$$

Hence, the income expenditure on the rth sector is equal to the compensated demand for the rth surrogate commodity,

$$\left(\frac{d\bar{C}^{(1)}(u, P^1, {}_2\bar{c})}{d\bar{c}^{(r)}} \right)_u,$$

times the unit price of the rth surrogate, $C^{(r)}(P^r, {}_{r+1}\bar{c})$, minus the optimal amount of higher order surrogates per unit of surrogate r,

$$\frac{d\bar{C}^{(r)}(P^r, {}_{r+1}\bar{c})}{d\bar{c}^s},$$

times the unit price of the higher-order surrogates, $\bar{C}^{(s)}(P^s, {}_{s+1}\bar{c})$. In other words, the expenditure on the rth sector is equal to the expenditure on the rth surrogate minus the indirect expenditure on this surrogate through higher-order (public) surrogate commodities. This means that the amount of "publicness" can at least be costed out in a meaningful manner.

In addition to this nice accountability property, rather stronger decentralization results are available. The application of Roy's theorem generates the following image of the (vector-valued) conditional demand function for the rth category:

$$X^r = \bar{\phi}^{(r)}(P^r, {}_{r+1}\bar{c}, y_r).$$

This is much less information than is needed for decision making in the direct recursive structure. In order to make intracategory allocations, only *own* category expenditure, y_r, needs to be known. In addition, the required information about higher-order prices can be aggregated into price indices.

6.6.3 Recursive Indirect Utility Functions

If the indirect utility function is recursive in normalized but not in nonnormalized prices, the accountability characterized by the preceding structure disappears. Suppose

$$V\left(\frac{P}{y} \right) = V^{(1)}\left(\frac{P^1}{y}, {}_2v \right), \tag{6.24a}$$

$$v^{(r)} = V^{(r)}\left(\frac{P^r}{y}, {}_{r+1}v \right), \qquad r = 1, \ldots, m-1, \tag{6.24b}$$

and

$$v^{(m)} = V^{(m)}\left(\frac{P^m}{y}\right).$$

Only if $V^{(2)}$ were homothetic would there exist price indices as in the previous case. However, by applying Roy's theorem,

$$\frac{x_i}{x_j} = \frac{V_i^{(r)}\left(\frac{P^r}{y}, _{r+1}v\right)}{V_j^{(r)}\left(\frac{P^r}{y}, _{r+1}v\right)} = \psi_{ij}^r\left(\frac{P^r}{y}, _{r+1}v,\right), \quad \text{say,} \quad \forall(i,j)\in I^r\times I^r,$$

$$r = 1,\ldots,m. \tag{6.25}$$

Multiplying by $x_j p_i/y$ and summing over $i\in I^r$, we obtain

$$\frac{y_r}{y} = \sum_{i\in I^r}\frac{p_i}{y}x_i = x_j\sum_{i\in I^r}\frac{p_i}{y}\psi_{ij}^r\left(\frac{p^r}{y}, _{r+1}v\right), \quad \forall j\in I^r,$$

$$r = 1,\ldots,m. \tag{6.26}$$

Solving (6.25) and (6.26) for X^r, $r = 1,\ldots,m$, we have

$$X^r = \phi^{(r)}\left(\frac{P^r}{y}, _{r+1}v, \frac{y_r}{y}\right), \quad r = 2,\ldots,m.$$

Hence, a limited form of decentralization is possible. The intracategory allocations can be made knowing own normalized prices, higher-order aggregators, and only the budget share of that category. This is clearly a weaker form of decentralization than that characterized by a cost function that is recursive in the extended partition.

III

APPLICATIONS
OF SEPARABILITY
AND FUNCTIONAL STRUCTURE

7

Elasticities of Substitution and Neutral Technological Change

This chapter provides two straightforward applications of the theoretical results presented in parts I and II. Both applications are concerned with concepts—the elasticity of substitution and neutral technological change—that are ubiquitous in the literature on production theory, particularly as it relates to the marginal-productivity theory of income distribution. This literature dates back at least to the classic treatise on functional income shares by Hicks (1932). Hicks's analysis is perhaps best remembered for his skillful use of two concepts: the elasticity of substitution between two inputs, and the neutrality of technological progress.

Section 7.1 provides an alternative characterization of separability in terms of restrictions on the Allen (1938) partial elasticities of substitution (first formulated by Allen and Hicks, 1934). This characterization is of more than purely theoretical interest; it may also be of considerable use in empirical work. For example, testing for separability is equivalent in some circumstances to examining the relationship between certain components of the Allen elasticities. More specifically, we show that the Allen elasticity between inputs i and k is equal to that between j and k if and only if $\{i,j\}$ is implicitly separable from $\{k\}$.

In section 7.2, we analyze three different types of neutral technological progress, all of which have at one time or another been referred to as Hicks neutrality. We show that each type of neutrality is related to a particular notion of separability or independence. We conclude the chapter with a discussion of the conditions under which these concepts are the same. This again is of considerable empirical importance; each of these specifications of neutrality has different economic implications. Which specification is appropriate depends of course upon the particular problem being studied.

7.1 THE ALLEN PARTIAL ELASTICITIES OF SUBSTITUTION: EQUALITY RESTRICTIONS AND SEPARABILITY

7.1.1 Definition of the Allen Elasticity

In order to define the Allen elasticity of substitution (henceforth referred to as the AES) and to prove the theorems relating equality conditions on the AES to separability conditions, it is convenient to assume that the cost function satisfies the regularity conditions (R-3'): continuity and strict positive monotonicity in (u, P), and concavity and twice differentiability in P.[1]

Allen's original definition of the elasticity of substitution between two commodities (usually inputs), i and j, is

$$
\sigma_{ij}(X) = \frac{\sum_{k=1}^{n} U_{ik}(X) \cdot x_k}{x_i x_j} \frac{H^{ij}(X)}{H(X)},
$$

where $H(X)$ is the determinant of the (Hessian) matrix of cross partial derivatives of U, evaluated at X, and $H^{ij}(X)$ is the (i,j)th cofactor of this matrix, evaluated at X. Uzawa (1962) has proved that, given the theory of duality (i.e., of output-constrained cost minimization with parametric prices), this definition is equivalent to

$$
\sigma_{ij}(u, P) = \frac{C(u, P)}{\zeta_i(u, P) \zeta_j(u, P)} \frac{\partial \zeta_i(u, P)}{\partial p_j} = \frac{C(u, P) C_{ij}(u, P)}{C_i(u, P) C_j(u, P)}, \quad \text{(AES)}
$$

where, it will be recalled, $\zeta_i(u, P) = C_i(u, P)$ is the demand for input i at given output u and prices P [equivalently, using Hotelling's lemma, the derivative of the cost function C with respect to the ith price, evaluated at (u, P)]. Thus $\partial \zeta_i(u, P) / \partial p_j = C_{ij}(u, P)$ is an expenditure-compensated (constant-output) price derivative (equivalently, a second cross partial derivative of C). The principal attraction of the AES is that the computation allows all other factors of production to adjust optimally to the price change. Because of this property, the AES has been the elasticity definition most frequently employed.

[1]See chapter 2 for precise definitions of these concepts. In addition, note that, given (R-3'), separability and strict separability are equivalent.

7.1.2 Separability and Equality Restrictions

The equality restrictions always involve three different variables; hence we introduce the following notation in the interest of conciseness. For the partition

$$\hat{I} = \{ I^1, \ldots, I^m \},$$

define the set of ordered triples

$$T = \{ \langle i,j,k \rangle \in I \times I \times I \mid i \in I^r \wedge j \in I^r \wedge k \notin I^r \text{ for some } r \}.$$

The equality condition for the AES in the partition $\hat{I}$ is

$$\sigma_{ik}(u, P) = \sigma_{jk}(u, P) \qquad \forall \langle i,j,k \rangle \in T. \tag{E}$$

That is, for every pair of inputs i and j in each sector I^r, and for every input k in some sector other than I^r, the AES between i and k equals the AES between j and k. The following result is due to Blackorby and Russell (1976).

Theorem 7.1 *Assume that the cost function satisfies* (R-3′). *Then the technology is implicitly separable in $\hat{I}$ if and only if the equality condition* (E) *holds. That is,*

$$C(u, P) = \hat{C}\left(u, C^1(u, P^1), \ldots, C^m(u, P^m)\right) = \hat{C}(u, c^1, \ldots, c^m), \qquad \text{say,}$$
$$\tag{7.1}$$

if and only if

$$\sigma_{ik}(u, P) = \sigma_{jk}(u, P) \qquad \forall \langle i,j,k \rangle \in T. \tag{E}$$

Proof. Given (7.1), the elasticities are

$$\sigma_{ik}(u, P) = \frac{\hat{C}(u, c^1, \ldots, c^m)\hat{C}_{rs}(u, c^1, \ldots, c^m)}{\hat{C}_r(u, c^1, \ldots, c^m)\hat{C}_s(u, c^1, \ldots, c^m)} = \sigma_{jk}(u, P) \qquad \forall \langle i,j,k \rangle \in T,$$

which is equivalent to (E). On the other hand, given (E), we have

$$\frac{C_{ik}(u, P)}{C_i(u, P)} = \frac{C_{jk}(u, P)}{C_j(u, P)} \qquad \forall \langle i,j,k \rangle \in T,$$

which is equivalent to

$$\frac{\partial}{\partial p_k}\left(\frac{C_i(u,P)}{C_j(u,P)}\right) = \frac{C_{ik}(u,P)\cdot C_j(u,P) - C_{jk}(u,P)\cdot C_i(u,P)}{C_j(u,P)^2} = 0$$

$$\forall \langle i,j,k \rangle \in T,$$

which implies (7.1) by corollary 4.1.4. ‖

Remembering from theorem 4.5 that the conjunction of implicit and explicit strict separability is equivalent to homothetic separability, it is clear from theorem 7.1 that the conjunction of the equality condition and direct or indirect separability is also equivalent to homothetic separability. The following relationship is due to Russell (1975).

Theorem 7.2 *Suppose that the production function U satisfies (R-1′) and C satisfies (R-3′).[2] Then U is separable in $\hat{I}$ and the equality condition (E) holds if and only if U is homothetically separable in $\hat{I}$.*

Proof. (E) implies, by theorem 7.1, that the cost function is separable in $\hat{I}$. Since U is separable in $\hat{I}$ as well, it is also homothetically separable, by theorem 4.5.

Conversely, if U is homothetically separable in $\hat{I}$, then by theorem 4.5 the cost function is separable in $\hat{I}$. Then (E) is implied by theorem 7.1. ‖

The equality condition (E) does not imply homothetic separability, since it generates the separability of C in $\hat{I}$ but not in $_0\hat{I} = \{I^0, I^1, \ldots, I^m\}$.[3] Intuitively, this is because the equality condition yields information about the curvature property of each level contour of the production function but not about relationships, such as homotheticity, between level surfaces. However, under the maintained hypothesis of overall homotheticity, separability and the equality condition are equivalent. This result is from Berndt and Christensen (1973a).

Theorem 7.3 *Assume that U satisfies (R-1′) and is homothetic, and that C satisfies (R-3′). Then the equality condition (E) holds if and only if U is separable in $\hat{I}$.*

Proof. If the production function is separable and homothetic, it is homothetically separable by corollary 4.1.1, and the equality condition follows from theorem 7.2. To prove the converse, note that the equality condition implies that C is separable in $\hat{I}$, and homotheticity implies that C

[2](R-1′): Continuity, positive monotonicity, and strict quasi-concavity.
[3]See chapter 4 for further discussion.

is separable in the binary partition $_0\tilde{I} = \{I^0, I\}$ by lemma 3.4. Hence each price sector is separable from all prices (separability in $\hat{I}$) and is separable from utility (separability in $_0\tilde{I}$). As a singleton, I^0 is separable from all prices. Hence C is separable in $_0\hat{I}$. By theorem 4.4, this implies that the production function is homothetically separable in $\hat{I}$; it follows, *a fortiori*, that U is separable in $\hat{I}$. $\|$

7.1.3 Complete Separability and the Strong Equality Restrictions

The equality restriction and hence implicit separability do not, in general, imply anything about pairs of elasticities if each variable in the triple comes from a different group. In order to analyze this case, we introduce a strong equality condition which implies but is not implied by (E). For conciseness, we denote the ordered triples

$$T_S = \{\langle i,j,k \rangle \in I \times I \times I | i \in I^r \wedge j \in I^s \wedge k \notin I^r \wedge k \notin I^s \text{ for some } r,s\}.$$

The strong equality condition for the AES in the partition $\hat{I}$ is

$$\sigma_{ik} = \sigma_{jk} \qquad \forall \langle i,j,k \rangle \in T_S. \qquad \text{(SE)}$$

It is readily apparent that (SE) implies (E) but not conversely. The next theorem, due to Blackorby and Russell (1976), characterizes (SE).

Theorem 7.4 *Assume that C satisfies (R-3′). The technology is implicitly completely separable in $\hat{I}$ if and only if the strong equality condition (SE) holds. That is,*

$$C(u,P) = \overset{*}{C}\left(u, \sum_{r=1}^{m} C^r(u,P^r)\right) \qquad (7.2)$$

if and only if

$$\sigma_{ik}(u,P) = \sigma_{jk}(u,P) \qquad \forall \langle i,j,k \rangle \in T_S. \qquad \text{(SE)}$$

Note that, by theorem 4.9, (7.2) is equivalent to

$$C(u,P) = \Gamma(u)\left(\sum_{r=1}^{m} [C^r(u,P^r)]^{\rho(u)}\right)^{1/\rho(u)}, \qquad 0 \neq \rho(u) \leqslant 1,$$

an implicit CES function (or, as $\rho(u) \to 0$, an implicit Cobb-Douglas function.)

Proof. Let $\overset{*}{C}_2$ be the first-order partial derivative of $\overset{*}{C}$ with respect to its second argument, and let $\overset{*}{C}_{22}$ be the corresponding second-order partial derivative. Deriving the AES from (7.2), one gets

$$
\sigma_{ik}(u,P) = \frac{\overset{*}{C}\left(u, \sum_{r=1}^{m} c^r\right) \overset{*}{C}_{22}\left(u, \sum_{r=1}^{m} c^r\right)}{\left[\overset{*}{C}_2\left(u, \sum_{r=1}^{m} c^r\right)\right]^2} = \sigma_{jk}(u,P) \qquad \forall \langle i,j,k \rangle \in T_S,
$$

which is equivalent to (SE).

To show the converse, note that (SE) implies that

$$
\frac{C_{ik}(u,P)}{C_i(u,P)} = \frac{C_{jk}(u,P)}{C_j(u,P)} \qquad \forall \langle i,j,k \rangle \in T_S,
$$

which is equivalent to

$$
\frac{\partial}{\partial p_k}\left(\frac{C_i(u,P)}{C_j(u,P)}\right) = \frac{C_{ik}(u,P)C_j(u,P) - C_{jk}(u,P)C_i(u,P)}{C_j(u,P)^2} = 0
$$

$$
\forall \langle i,j,k \rangle \in T_S,
$$

which implies (7.2) by corollary 4.8.4. ‖

Combining theorems 4.12 and 4.13 one can readily deduce that U and C are simultaneously completely separable in $\hat{I}$ if and only if U is homothetic and completely separable in $\hat{I}$.[4] This result gives us the following complete-separability version of theorem 7.2.

Theorem 7.5 *Assume that U satisfies (R-1′) and C satisfies (R-3′). The production function U is completely separable in $\hat{I}$ and the strong equality condition (SE) holds if and only if U is homothetic and completely separable in $\hat{I}$.*

Proof. The strong equality condition (SE) implies, by theorem 7.4, that the cost function is completely separable in $\hat{I}$. Since U is completely separable as well, it is also homothetic by theorem 4.13.

[4]Thus in lemma S1 and theorem S2 of Blackorby and Russell (1976), the sufficiency condition should be strengthened to read "homothetic and strongly (sic) separable".

To prove the converse, note that the homotheticity and complete separability of U in $\hat{I}$ imply that C is completely separable in $\hat{I}$ by theorem 4.12. Thus (SE) follows from theorem 7.4.   ‖

One implication of theorem 7.5 is that if homotheticity of U is assumed, then complete separability of U implies the strong equality condition. In fact, given the assumption of homotheticity of U, the converse is also true. Since this result is the complete-separability version of theorem 7.3, we state it formally below.

Theorem 7.6 *Suppose the production function U satisfies* (R-1') *and is homothetic, and C satisfies* (R-3'). *Then the strong equality condition* (SE) *holds if and only if the production function is completely separable.*

Proof.   Given the homotheticity of U, if U is also completely separable, then (SE) follows immediately from theorem 7.5.

To prove the converse, first note that the homotheticity of U implies that C is separable in $_o\tilde{I} = \{\{0\}, I\}$ by lemma 3.4. The strong equality condition (SE) implies that C is also completely separable in $\hat{I}$ by theorem 7.4. Thus, by theorem 4.12, U is completely separable in $\hat{I}$.   ‖

Of course, these symmetric restrictions on the AES may be overly restrictive. The nonsymmetric analogues of these equality restrictions are in fact equivalent to certain recursive structures.

7.1.4   Recursivity and Nonsymmetric Equality Restrictions

Again we need some new notation. With respect to the partition $\hat{I}$ define the set of ordered triples

$$T_{SR} = \{\langle i,j,k\rangle \in I \times I \times I | \langle i,j\rangle \in {}_rI \times {}_rI \wedge k \notin {}_rI \text{ for some } r\},$$

where $_rI = \bigcup_{s=r}^{m} I^s$ (see chapter 6). The strong recursive-equality condition is

$$\sigma_{ik}(u,P) = \sigma_{jk}(u,P) \qquad \forall \langle i,j,k\rangle \in T_{SR}. \tag{SRE}$$

Given the ordered partition $\langle \hat{I}\rangle$, this condition says that any two elasticities must be equal if they are computed with respect to a third input which is from a group with a lower number than either of the first two. The next theorem is the implicit strong recursive analogue of theorems 7.1 and 7.4.

Theorem 7.7   *Assume that C satisfies* (R-3'). *Then the technology is implicitly completely recursive if and only if the strong recursive-equality* *condition holds. That is,*

$$C(u,P) = C^{[1]}(u, P^1, c^{[2]}),\tag{7.3}$$

$$c^{[r]} = C^{[r]}(u, P^r, c^{[r+1]}), \qquad r = 2, \ldots, m-1,$$

and

$$c^{[m]} = C^{[m]}(u, P^m)$$

if and only if (SRE) *holds.*

Proof. Recalling that implicit complete recursivity is equivalent to

$$\frac{\partial}{\partial p_k}\left(\frac{C_i(u,P)}{C_j(u,P)}\right) = 0 \qquad \forall \langle i, j, k \rangle \in T_{\mathrm{SR}},$$

the strategy of proof is identical to that of theorem 7.1 (though the differential calculations are much more cumbersome). ‖

The next theorem is the completely recursive version of theorems 7.2 and 7.5.

Theorem 7.8 *Suppose that U satisfies* (R-1′) *and C satisfies* (R-3′). *Then U is completely recursive in* $\langle \hat{I} \rangle$ *and* (SRE) *holds if and only if U is homothetically completely recursive.*

Proof. The proof uses theorems 7.7, 6.2, and 6.6 exactly as the proof of theorem 7.2 uses theorems 7.1 and 4.5. ‖

The final theorem regarding the strong recursive-equality condition is the analogue of theorems 7.3 and 7.6.

Theorem 7.9 *Assume that U satisfies* (R-1′) *and is homothetic, and C satisfies* (R-3′). *Then* (SRE) *holds if and only if U is completely recursive in* $\langle \hat{I} \rangle$.

Proof. Use theorems 7.8 and 6.5, corollary 6.1.1, and lemma 3.4 exactly as the proof of theorem 7.3 uses theorems 7.2 and 4.4, corollary 4.1.1, and lemma 3.4, respectively. ‖

Just as the duality results break down when one is studying recursive rather than completely recursive structures, so there is only one interesting relationship between the AES and recursive functions which we have identified.

Theorem 7.10 *Assume that C satisfies (R-3'). Then C is recursive with respect to $\langle \hat{I} \rangle$, i.e.,*

$$C(u,P) = C^{(1)}(u,P^1,c^{(2)},\ldots,c^{(m)}),\tag{7.4}$$

$$c^{(r)} = C^{(r)}(u,P^r,c^{(r+1)},\ldots,c^{(m)}), \qquad r=2,\ldots,m-1,$$

and

$$c^{(m)} = C^{(m)}(u,P^m),$$

if and only if the recursive equality condition

$$\sigma_{ik}(u,P) = \sigma_{jk}(u,P) \qquad \forall \langle i,j,k \rangle \in T_R \tag{RE}$$

holds, where

$$T_R = \{ \langle i,j,k \rangle \in I \times I \times I | \langle i,j \rangle \in I^r \times I^r \wedge k \notin {}_rI \text{ for some } r \}.$$

Proof. Recalling that C is recursive in $\langle \hat{I} \rangle$ if and only if

$$\frac{\partial}{\partial p_k} \left(\frac{C_i(u,P)}{C_j(u,P)} \right) = 0 \qquad \forall \langle i,j,k \rangle \in T_R,$$

the strategy of proof is identical to that of theorem 7.7, and we again spare the reader the messy differential calculations. $\parallel$

7.1.5 Concluding Remarks

The most important of the above results is the equivalence of (certain) elasticity of substitution equalities and certain *implicit* separability conditions. These equality conditions therefore constitute an alternative characterization of the restrictions imposed upon the underlying technology of structural hypotheses about the cost (or transformation) function. A practical implication of this equivalence is that it might facilitate certain hypothesis tests; testing the appropriate elasticity equality condition is equivalent to testing for separability of the cost and transformation functions in the corresponding partition. Moreover, because of theorems 7.3, 7.6, and 7.9, if overall homotheticity of the production function is maintained, testing the appropriate elasticity equality condition is equivalent to testing for separability of the production function in the appropriate partition, and hence for the existence of aggregate inputs.[5] It should be remembered, however, that if homotheticity is not maintained, these equality conditions are neither necessary nor sufficient for *explicit* separability; hence they are neither necessary nor sufficient for the existence of an aggregate input in a production function.

7.2   HICKS NEUTRAL TECHNOLOGICAL CHANGE[6]

In this section we examine in some detail a type of neutrality first suggested by Hicks (1932), and two variants of Hicks neutrality with which the former has often been confused. Subsection 7.2.1 defines and characterizes functionally these three concepts, and subsection 7.2.2 examines the relationships between them.

7.2.1   Three Concepts of Hicks Neutrality

In *The Theory of Wages* (1932, p. 121), Hicks classified inventions "according as their initial effects are to increase, leave unchanged, or diminish the ratio of the marginal product of capital to that of labor," and referred to them as labor-saving, neutral, or capital-saving, respectively. When considering the effect of technological change, Hicks required that the firm remain in a position of "internal equilibrium". This requirement may be interpreted to mean that the effect of technological change must be examined along the firm's expansion path, where the firm must remain if it is to minimize the cost of producing any given rate of output. Given this interpretation, technological change is Hicks neutral if it is "expansion-path-preserving". Therefore, technological progress is Hicks neutral if the marginal rates of substitution between all pairs of inputs are independent of technological progress. In order to formalize this notion, define a production function, $\mathcal{U} : \Omega^{n+1} \rightarrow \Omega^1$, with the image $u = \mathcal{U}(X, t)$ where X represents the vector of input quantities and t is a scalar representing the state of technology. For the balance of this chapter, we adopt some regularity conditions regarding $\mathcal{U}$ which are frequently stronger than needed but simplify the exposition. The regularity conditions are

(**R-1″**):   Continuity, strict positive monotonicity, and differentiability in (X, t), and quasi-concavity in X.

Hicks neutrality is characterized by the following results.

[5]See Berndt and Christensen (1974a) for an employment of this last procedure.
[6]This section follows Blackorby, Lovell, and Thursby (1976).

Theorem 7.11 *Suppose that $\mathcal{U}$ satisfies regularity conditions* (R-1″). *Then technological progress is Hicks neutral if and only if $\mathcal{U}$ can be written as*

$$\mathcal{U}(X,t) = \overline{\mathcal{U}}(U(X),t), \qquad (7.5)$$

where $\overline{\mathcal{U}}$ and U satisfy (R-1″).

Proof. Follows from theorems 3.2, 3.3, and 3.5. ‖

Several post-Hicksian writers have proposed an alternative definition of neutrality which involves examining the effect of technological change along a ray where factor proportions remain fixed at their initial pre-technological-change values. Technological change is *implicitly Hicks neutral* if it is ray-preserving. The extent to which this notion has gained widespread acceptance can be illustrated by a quotation from Kennedy and Thirwall's recent survey of technical progress; they assert that "Hicks defined a 'neutral' invention as one which *with given factor proportions* raised the marginal product of labor in the same proportion as the marginal product of capital" (1972: p. 20; italics added). Hicks did not impose this restriction, and since it is not generally the same as Hicks's requirement that the firm remain on its expansion path, it leads to a quite different notion of neutrality. In order to characterize functionally this notion of neutrality, we first construct the implicit representation of the technology —the transformation function[7] associated with $\mathcal{U}$—by

$$\mathcal{F}(u,t,X) = \max\left\{\lambda \in \Omega_{+}^{1} \mid \mathcal{U}(X/\lambda,t) \geqslant u\right\}. \qquad (7.6)$$

$\mathcal{F}$ is decreasing in u, PLH in X, and increasing in t. As such it provides a convenient way to represent implicit Hicks neutrality.

Theorem 7.12 *Suppose $\mathcal{U}$ satisfies* (R-1″). *Then technological change is implicitly Hicks neutral if and only if $\mathcal{F}$ can be written as*

$$\mathcal{F}(u,t,X) = \overline{\mathcal{F}}(u,t,F(u,X)), \qquad (7.7)$$

where $\overline{\mathcal{F}}$ is increasing in $F(u,X)$.

Proof. The definition is equivalent to separability in $\mathcal{F}$ of input quantity variables from the technological state variable, but not necessarily from the output variable. By corollary 3.4.1, this separability condition is equivalent to the representation (7.7). ‖

[7]See section 2.4 above.

It is clear that in general Hicks neutrality and implicit Hicks neutrality are not equivalent. Before pursuing the conditions under which they are equivalent, we introduce a third type of technological change which is frequently confused with the former two types. Technological change is said to exhibit *extended Hicks neutrality* if it permits a multiplicative decomposition of the production function into one term involving input variables only and another involving the state-of-technology variable only. That is, technological change is extended Hicks neutral if and only if

$$\mathcal{U}(X,t) = A(t)U(X). \tag{7.8}$$

The next theorem characterizes this case.

Theorem 7.13 *Technological change is extended Hicks neutral (7.8) if and only if the set of input-quantity variables is strictly independent of the state-of-technology variable.*

Proof. Follows immediately from theorem 4.15. ‖

7.2.2 Equivalence Theorems

A casual inspection of equations (7.5) and (7.8) reveals that extended Hicks neutrality implies Hicks neutrality. With this sole exception, none of the three types of Hicks neutrality implies either of the other two unless additional assumptions are made. The first theorem in this section states that input homotheticity is necessary and sufficient for simultaneous Hicks and implicit Hicks neutrality. Thus, homotheticity is a necessary condition for the equivalence of all three types of Hicks neutrality. The second theorem states that input homogeneity is a sufficient condition for the above equivalence.

Theorem 7.14 *Assume that U satisfies (R-1″). Then Hicks neutrality and implicit Hicks neutrality are equivalent if and only if the technology is input-homothetic.*

Proof. First note that technological change is both Hicks neutral and implicitly Hicks neutral if and only if the set of inputs is separable from the state-of-technology variable in both the production function $\mathcal{U}$ and the transformation function $\mathcal{F}$. A minor modification of the argument in the proof of theorem 3.9 establishes that inputs are separable from the technological-change variable in both $\mathcal{U}$ and $\mathcal{F}$ if and only if the input aggregator function U in (7.5) is homothetic. ‖

Corollary 7.14.1 *If technological change is both extended Hicks neutral and implicitly Hicks neutral, the technology is input-homothetic.*

Proof. The representation (7.8) of extended Hicks neutrality clearly implies Hicks neutrality (7.5). This, together with implicit Hicks neutrality, implies, by theorem 7.14, input homotheticity. ‖

Thus the combination of implicit Hicks neutrality and either Hicks neutrality or extended Hicks neutrality implies input homotheticity. However, the remaining possible combination, viz., Hicks neutrality and extended Hicks neutrality, does *not* imply input homotheticity, as the following example shows. Consider the two-factor CRES[8] production function with constant exponential factor augmenting technological change:

$$\mathfrak{U}(x_1, x_2, t) = \left[\delta \left(e^{\alpha t} x_1 \right)^{-\rho_1} + (1 - \delta)\left(e^{\beta t} x_2 \right)^{-\rho_2} \right]^{-1/\rho}. \tag{7.9}$$

Technological change is both Hicks neutral and extended Hicks neutral if and only if $\alpha \rho_1 = \beta \rho_2$, in which case (7.9) can be written as

$$A(t)U(x_1, x_2) = e^{(\alpha \rho_1/\rho)t} \left[\delta x_1^{-\rho_1} + (1 - \delta) x_2^{-\rho_2} \right]^{-1/\rho}.$$

However, this technology is clearly not input homothetic unless $\rho_1 = \rho_2$.

The next example illustrates that the converse to corollary 7.14.1 is not true. Consider the production function with image

$$\mathfrak{U}(x_1, x_2, t) = \ln(x_1 x_2 t),$$

$$= \ln(x_1 x_2) + \ln t,$$

$$= U(x_1, x_2) + A(t).$$

The corresponding transformation-function image is

$$\mathfrak{F}(u, t, x_1, x_2) = e^{-u/2} t^{1/2} (x_1 x_2)^{1/2}$$

$$= e^{-u/2} B(t) F(x_1, x_2), \quad \text{say.}$$

Technological change is both Hicks neutral and implicitly Hicks neutral, since inputs are separable in both $\mathfrak{U}$ and $\mathfrak{F}$. Moreover, this technology is input-homothetic, since U is a homothetic function. However, technological progress is not extended Hicks neutral, since $\mathfrak{U}$ cannot be written in the form (7.8).

A conclusion of the above discussion is that, in the presence of input homotheticity, *only* Hicks neutrality and implicit Hicks neutrality are equivalent. The last example given shows that extended Hicks neutrality is

---

[8]See Mukerji (1963), Gorman (1965), Hanoch (1971) and Färe and Jansson (1975).

not implied by Hicks neutrality and/or implicit Hicks neutrality *even if* input homotheticity is also assumed. This serves to point out the restrictiveness of the extended Hicks neutrality hypothesis.

We end this section with a theorem that gives a sufficient condition for the equivalence of all three types of Hicks neutrality. For an alternative characterization see, Färe (1974). This condition is input homogeneity and is defined as follows. A technology is *input-homogeneous* if $\mathcal{U}$ is homogeneous of degree k in X for all t, where k is a positive constant; i.e.,

$$\mathcal{U}(\lambda X, t) = \lambda^k \mathcal{U}(X, t), \qquad k > 0, \qquad \forall \lambda \geqslant 0, \qquad \forall (X, t) \in \Omega^n \times \Omega^1.$$

Theorem 7.15 *Assume that $\mathcal{U}$ satisfies (R-1″) and is input homogeneous. Then* (i) *Hicks neutrality*, (ii) *implicit Hicks neutrality*, *and* (iii) *extended Hicks neutrality are equivalent.*

Proof. (i)⟺(ii): This follows, *a fortiori*, from Theorem 7.14.

(ii)⟹(iii): As (i) and (ii) are equivalent, (7.5) holds. Moreover, by the hypothesis of the theorem, $\mathcal{U}$ is homogeneous of degree k in X. Take the kth root of each side of (7.5), and define a new function $\widetilde{\mathcal{U}}$ by

$$\mu = u^{1/k} = \widetilde{\mathcal{U}}(U(X), t)$$

$$= \left[\overline{\mathcal{U}}(U(X), t) \right]^{1/k}.$$

Since the value of the "normalized output", μ, is PLH in X, the set of inputs is homothetically separable from t in $\widetilde{\mathcal{U}}$; thus the function U can be chosen to be PLH by lemma 3.3. Assume this has already been done. Then $\widetilde{\mathcal{U}}$ is linear in $U(X)$, and

$$\mu = U(X)\widetilde{\mathcal{U}}(1, t)$$

$$= U(X)A(t), \qquad \text{say.}$$

Raising each side to the kth power yields

$$\mu^k = u = U(X)^k A(t)^k,$$

which implies extended Hicks neutrality.

(iii)⟹(i): This is immediate, even in the absence of input homogeneity. ‖

8

Separability and the Econometric Estimation of Demand Systems

This chapter provides a cursory description of the role of separability in the estimation of systems of demand functions generated by utility or output maximization subject to an expenditure constraint. We distinguish between two approaches. One approach maintains separability in order to facilitate estimation, especially in systems composed of many commodities. The other approach attempts to test for separability restrictions using flexible functional forms. Section 8.1 discusses the first of these approaches, and section 8.2 describes the second. Section 8.3 proves a theorem which generates some skepticism regarding the use of flexible functional forms to test for separability.

8.1 SEPARABILITY AS A MAINTAINED HYPOTHESIS

8.1.1 Estimation of Conditional Demand Systems

Interest in the econometric estimation of theoretically plausible systems of demand functions (i.e., systems generated by expenditure-constrained utility or output maximization), first carried out by Stone (1954), has been revived in recent years. This revival is primarily attributable to the influential work of Houthakker (1960a, 1960b, 1965a). Fairly comprehensive surveys of the literature on estimating theoretically plausible demand systems are given by Goldberger (1967), Brown and Deaton (1972), Phlips (1974), Powell (1974), Lau (1975b), and Barten (1977). These surveys, however, do not cover the more recent literature on the estimation of demand systems generated by flexible functional forms. This very interesting research is discussed below (section 8.2).

As the number of commodities in a typical economy is myriad, the estimation of a truly complete demand system is econometrically intractable. As a result, certain restrictions must be invoked—implicitly if not explicitly—in order to carry out the estimation. One possibility is to estimate demand subsystems—that is, demand systems for subsets of the commodities. The explanatory variables of these demand subsystems are *sectoral* prices and *sectoral* expenditure. This ploy can reduce the number of variables (and presumably the number of parameters) to manageable proportions. Of course, the decentralization theorems of chapter 5 (theorems 5.2 and 5.3) indicate that this estimation procedure is consistent with the underlying theoretical model of utility maximization if and only if the direct objective function is separable in the appropriate partition of the commodities. Similarly, the estimation of subsystems of constant-output demand systems is consistent with the underlying theory if and only if the cost (and transformation) functions are separable in the appropriate partitions (theorem 5.5 and corollary 5.5.1).

Implementation of the above approach to estimating demand systems for large numbers of commodities can exploit theorem 5.1 on the equivalence of separability of U and of the conditional indirect utility function H. Decentralizability implies that this function has the structure

$$H(_1y, P) = \hat{H}\left(h^1(y_1, P^1), \ldots, h^m(y_m, P^m)\right). \tag{8.1}$$

Conditional demand functions are generated by

$$X^r = \phi^r(P^r, y_r) = -\frac{\nabla_{P^r} h^r(y_r, P^r)}{\nabla_{y_r} h^r(y_r, P^r)}, \qquad r = 1, \ldots, m. \tag{8.2}$$

The expenditure-allocation functions are generated by

$$\max_{_1y} \hat{H}\left(h^1(y_1, P^1), \ldots, h^m(y_m, P^m)\right) \qquad \text{s.t.} \quad _1y \in \Omega^m \wedge \sum_{r=1}^{m} y_r \leqslant y,$$

yielding the images

$$y_r = \theta^r(P, y), \qquad r = 1, \ldots, m. \tag{8.3}$$

Substituting (8.3) into (8.2) yields the complete demand system:

$$X = \phi(P, y) = \left(\phi^1(P^1, \theta^1(P, y)), \ldots, \phi^m(P^m, \theta^m(P, y))\right). \tag{8.4}$$

Thus, the simplest way to proceed with a two-stage estimation problem is to specify the forms of the conditional utility aggregator functions $h^r, r = 1, \ldots, m$, and the form of the macro function $\hat{H}$. If the specification satisfies the regularity conditions for H (see section 5.2), this is equivalent to specifying a direct utility function (Epstein, 1975). Of course, it might not be possible to derive the closed-form representation of U from the specified form of H; this, in fact, underscores the advantage of specifying the form of the conditional indirect utility function H rather than the form of the direct utility function U, since the conditional demand systems (8.2) are easily derived from H using lemma 5.1.

With h^r specified, the m systems of demand functions generated by (8.2) can then be estimated using, in each case, data on sectoral expenditure y_r, sectoral prices P^r, and sectoral consumption X^r. The expenditure allocation can then be estimated using the values of the parameters of the systems of conditional demand functions (8.2). This two-stage estimation procedure generates estimates of the values of all parameters of the complete demand system (8.4) and therefore of the conditional utility function (up to monotonic transforms, of course) and the direct utility function as well, if it can be derived from H.

Of course, the estimators of the parameters of systems of conditional demand functions retain their optimal properties only if very restrictive assumptions are made about the error structure. In particular, covariances between error terms in different sectors must vanish. Given the sectoral budget constraints, this means that random disturbances within a sector generate compensating disturbances in other conditional demand equations in the *same* sector. Put differently, the consumer must allocate total expenditure among categories without error. The fact that our discussion emphasizes the theoretical requirements for the nonstochastic structure of the econometric model should not be interpreted as a cavalier disregard of problems associated with the stochastic specification of a demand model. The emphasis merely reflects our assessment of the appropriate division of labor. See Anderson (1976: chapter 3) for an excellent analysis of the stochastic specification of a "two-level" demand system.

The advantage of this two-stage estimation procedure is that each sectoral demand system (8.2) [as well as the system of expenditure allocation functions, (8.3)] has far fewer parameters to be estimated than does the complete system of demand functions, (8.4). (Of course, the two-stage estimation procedure does not economize on degrees of freedom; it only makes the calculations less demanding of computer time and core—a nontrivial saving in nonlinear estimation problems.)

The next two subsections provide some examples of the estimation procedure.

8.1.2   The S-Branch Utility Function

The study of Heien (1974), extending the work of Brown and Heien (1972) to include additional commodities, provides a good example of the above approach to the problem involved in the estimation of large-scale consumer demand systems.[1] The Brown-Heien specification (of the direct utility function) is a CES function of affinely translated CES functions (i.e., CES functions of translated variables, $x_i - \gamma_i$, where γ_i is parametric). That is, the specification—called the "S-branch utility function"—can be written

$$U(X^1,\ldots,X^m) = \left(\sum_{r=1}^{m} \alpha_r U^r (X^r)^\rho \right)^{1/\rho}, \qquad (8.5)$$

where

$$U^r(X^r) = \left(\sum_{i \in I^r}^{m} \alpha_i (x_i - \gamma_i)^{\rho_r} \right)^{1/\rho_r}, \qquad r=1,\ldots,m. \qquad (8.6)$$

Thus, U is a completely strictly separable utility function where each aggregator is affinely homothetic (i.e., homothetic to the point $\gamma^r \in \mathbf{R}^{(r)}$, where $\mathbf{R}^{(r)}$ is a Euclidean space whose dimension equals the cardinality of I^r). Thus, the conditional income-consumption curves in $\Omega^{(r)}$ are linear, and, if extended to $\mathbf{R}^{(r)}$, they would emanate from the point γ^r; similarly, the (linear) income-consumption curves in Ω^n emanate from $\gamma = (\gamma^1,\ldots,\gamma^m)$. The utility function and the induced preference ordering are defined only on the set $\{X \in \Omega^n | X \geqslant \gamma\}$; note that γ is not restricted to be nonnegative. This specification of the aggregator functions is a generalization of the translated Cobb-Douglas utility function that generates the linear expenditure system [first estimated by Stone (1954) and extensively applied over the past twenty years[2]], obtained by letting $\rho_r \to 0$.[3]

---

[1]Other good examples are provided by Braithwait (1975) and Deaton (1975). For applications of this approach to the estimation of models of international trade with many traded commodities, see McMenamin (1975), Pinard (1975) and McMenamin, Pinard, Russell, and Boyce (1977).

[2]See Phlips (1974, pp. 127–128) for citations. The linear expenditure system was first formulated by Klein and Rubin (1947) in their study of cost-of-living indices. The demand system was integrated back to the appropriate utility function by Samuelson (1947) and Geary (1950).

[3]The CES generalization of the linear expenditure system was first estimated by Wales (1972). We focus on the Brown-Heien formulation because of the structure that they impose on this utility function.

It is customary to refer to the vector γ as a "committed" consumption bundle or even as a "minimum survival" bundle. If, however, γ has negative components, this interpretation is nonsensical.

Heien estimated the (nonlinear) conditional demand system

$$
\phi_i(P^r, y_r) = \gamma_i + \frac{\alpha_i^{\sigma_r} p_i^{-\sigma_r}\left(y_r - \sum_{i \in I^r} \gamma_i p_i\right)}{\sum_{i \in I^r} \alpha_i^{\sigma_r} p_i^{1-\sigma_r}} \qquad \forall i \in I^r, \qquad \forall r, \qquad (8.7)
$$

where $\sigma_r = 1/(1 - \rho_r)$, for three categories of (per capita) food expenditure: meats, vegetables, and fruits.[4] He then estimated the remaining parameters ($\rho, \alpha_1, \alpha_2,$ and α_3) by estimating expenditure-allocation functions, defined by

$$
y_r = \frac{\alpha_r^{\sigma}\left(\sum_{i \in I^r} \hat{\alpha}_i^{\hat{\sigma}_r} p_i^{1-\hat{\sigma}_r}\right)^{(1-\sigma)/(1-\hat{\sigma}_r)}}{\sum_{s=1}^{m} \alpha_s^{\sigma}\left(\sum_{i \in I^s} \hat{\alpha}_i^{\hat{\sigma}_s} p_i^{1-\hat{\sigma}_s}\right)^{(1-\sigma)/(1-\hat{\sigma}_s)}}\left(y - \sum_{s=1}^{m} \sum_{i \in I^s} p_i \hat{\gamma}_i\right) + \sum_{i \in I^r} p_i \hat{\gamma}_i,
$$

$$(8.8)$$

where the carets over parameters indicate that they have been estimated in the first stage.

The conditional demand system generated by the rth branch of the S-branch utility tree has $2n_r$ independent parameters, and the income allocation function has m independent parameters. The total number of independent parameters (which must be estimated simultaneously if the complete system of equations is estimated simultaneously) is therefore $2\sum_{r=1}^{m} n_r + m$. In Heien's case there are seven groups, all but one containing three commodities. Hence, all but one sectoral demand system have six independent parameters. The entire system of demand equations has 29 parameters.

The Brown-Heien class of utility functions is particularly interesting because it is a nontrivial example of an aggregator function with a Gorman polar form (GPF) (see section 5.4). The dual to (8.6) in the conditional

---

[4]As these three groups of commodities constitute only a small subset of the complete set of commodities consumed, the estimation of this system requires the maintained hypothesis that the union of these three groups is separable in U from its complement. See the discussion below.

indirect utility function can be written as

$$h^r(y_r, P^r) = \frac{y_r}{\Pi^r(P^r)} - \frac{\Lambda^r(P^r)}{\Pi^r(P^r)}, \tag{8.9}$$

where

$$\Pi^r(P^r) = \left(\sum_{i \in I^r} \alpha_i^{\sigma} p_i^{1-\sigma_r} \right)^{1/(1-\sigma_r)}$$

and

$$\Lambda^r(P^r) = \sum_{i \in I^r} \gamma_i p_i$$

This specification belongs to the special class of generalized Gorman polar forms (GGPF) in which Ψ^r (see subsection 5.4.4) is the identity function. Moreover, the overall indirect utility function corresponding to (8.5) can itself be written as a Gorman polar form. This can be seen by rewriting the expenditure functions (8.8) as

$$y_r = \frac{\alpha_r^{\sigma} \Pi^r(P^r)^{1-\sigma}}{\sum_{s=1}^{m} \alpha_s^{\sigma} \Pi^s(P^s)^{1-\sigma}} \left(y - \sum_{s=1}^{m} \Lambda^s(P^s) \right) + \Lambda^r(P^r).$$

Substituting into the image of the conditional indirect utility function,

$$H(_1 y, P) = \left[\sum_{r=1}^{m} \left(\frac{y_r}{\Pi^r(P^r)} - \frac{\Lambda^r(P^r)}{\Pi^r(P^r)} \right)^{\rho} \right]^{1/\rho},$$

we obtain (after some manipulation)

$$W(y, P) = \frac{y}{\Pi(P)} - \frac{\Lambda(P)}{\Pi(P)},$$

where

$$\Pi(P) = \left(\sum_{r=1}^{m} \alpha_r^{\sigma} \Pi^r(P^r)^{1-\sigma} \right)^{1/(1-\sigma)}$$

and

$$\Lambda(P) = \sum_{r=1}^{m} \Lambda^r(P^r) = \sum_{r=1}^{m} \sum_{i \in I^r} p_i \gamma_i = P \cdot \gamma.$$

Note that although each sectoral utility function U^r in the specification (8.1) has the Gorman polar form, strong price aggregation is not possible. This is because the functions U^r are monotone transformations of the aggregators in the completely separable representation

$$U(X) = \left(\sum_{r=1}^{m} \hat{U}^r(X^r) \right)^{1/\rho},$$

where, of course,

$$\hat{U}^r(X^r) = \alpha_r U^r(X^r)^\rho, \qquad r = 1, \ldots, m.$$

The dual to $\hat{U}^r$ in the conditional indirect utility function is given by

$$\hat{h}^r(y_r, P^r) = \alpha_r \left(\frac{y_r}{\Pi^r(P^r)} - \frac{\Lambda^r(P^r)}{\Pi^r(P^r)} \right)^\rho,$$

where Π^r and Λ^r are defined above. Clearly $\hat{h}^r$ does not belong to the GGPF class.

The demand functions generated by the S-branch specification are linear in income. This can be seen by substituting the allocation-function images (8.8) into the conditional demand systems (8.7). It is in fact characteristic of all members of the GPF class, as is demonstrated by applying Roy's theorem to

$$W(y, P) = \frac{y}{\Pi(P)} - \frac{\Lambda(P)}{\Pi(P)}, \tag{8.10}$$

thus generating the demand system

$$X = \phi(P, y) = \frac{\nabla \Pi(P)}{\Pi(P)} (y - \Lambda(P)) + \nabla \Lambda(P). \tag{8.11}$$

In fact, Gorman (1953, 1961) has shown that the GPF completely characterizes the general class of preferences which are locally linear in income.

The linearity of demand functions in income is a very important property for the purposes of aggregation. In those regions of the price space where all members of the community are consuming positive amounts of the same commodities,[5] a necessary and sufficient condition for the aggregation of preferences across individuals is that each preference ordering is representable by a GPF, where only the marginal expenditure function (Π in our notation) need be common to all individuals.

8.1.3 A More General Specification of the Gorman Polar Form

The Brown-Heien specification is a very special case of the GPF in that it is affinely homothetic (a CES utility function relative to the "translated origin" γ). In general, however, the linear income-consumption curves corresponding to a GPF indirect utility function (or their extensions out of consumption space) radiate from the graph of a function which may, but does not necessarily, lie in the consumption space. When it does, the points on this graph might be interpreted as "subsistence bundles". In this case, and in sharp contrast to the Brown-Heien specification, the "subsistence bundles" are functions of prices. When this function degenerates to a point, the GPF collapses to a dual of an affinely homothetic direct utility function. [For a more extended discussion of this structure, see Blackorby, Boyce, and Russell (1977).]

A generalization of the Brown-Heien S-branch specification, which makes the "subsistence bundle" price-dependent, has been estimated by Boyce (1975) and Blackorby, Boyce, and Russell (1977).[6] This specification retains the Brown and Heien's assumptions that Π in (8.10) is a CES function of sectoral CES price indices. The generalization is in the form of the Λ^r (which are linear in the S-branch specification):

$$\Lambda^r(P^r) = \sum_{i \in I^r} \sum_{j \in I^r} \gamma_{ij} p_i^{1/2} p_j^{1/2}, \quad \gamma_{ij} = \gamma_{ji} \ \forall (i,j) \in I^r \times I^r, \qquad \forall r. \quad (8.12)$$

This Λ^r is a "generalized Leontief" specification (Diewert, 1971), discussed more extensively in section 8.2. Clearly, the S-branch specification is generated by setting $\gamma_{ij} = 0$ for all $(i,j) \in I^r \times I^r$ such that $i \neq j$ for all r, in which case Λ^r is linear. Moreover, the vector from which the linear income-consumption curve emanates, given the specification (8.12), is price-dependent:

$$x_i = \frac{\partial \Lambda(P)}{\partial p_i} = \sum_{j \in I^r} \gamma_{ij} (p_i p_j)^{1/2}, \qquad i \in I^r.$$

---

[5]This restriction to regions of the commodity space is due to Houthakker (1953).

[6]Another specification which makes the "subsistence bundle" price-dependent has been specified and estimated by Deaton (1975). Deaton employs CES Π^r functions and

$$\Lambda^r(P^r) = \sum_{i \in I^r} \left(\alpha_i p_i + \beta_i p_i \ln \frac{\beta \cdot P^r}{p_i} \right),$$

where $\beta \cdot P^r = \sum_{i \in I^r} \beta_i p_i$.

Blackorby, Boyce, and Russell (1977) estimate the demand system generated by this specification and conclude (using a likelihood-ratio test) that the hypothesis that off-diagonal γ_{ij}'s in (8.12) vanish must be rejected. Thus, affine homotheticity of the underlying preference ordering is rejected.

Using the translog specification (Lau and Mitchell, 1971), discussed below in section 8.2, Boyce and Primont (1976a) have gone on to reject the hypothesis, maintained in Blackorby, Boyce, and Russell (1977), that preferences belong to the GPF class (i.e., that expansion paths are linear).

8.1.4 Estimation and Aggregation

The above discussion focused on the estimation of conditional demand systems in order to avoid the problem associated with simultaneous estimation of large-scale, nonlinear systems of equations.

Alternatively, the number of parameters can be reduced by maintaining other structural hypotheses such as *generalized additive separability* (see Pollak (1972) or the *quadratic expenditure* system (see Howe and Pollak (1976)). A more common method of reducing the number of parameters to be estimated simultaneously is to work directly with a small system of commodity aggregates (e.g., food, clothing, housing, and a residual). Similarly, many econometric studies of production functions and derived demand work with highly aggregated inputs such as "capital", "labor", and "energy", abstracting from the obvious fact that there are typically many types of capital, labor, and energy inputs.

Of course, "food", "capital", etc. are not primitive (or homogeneous) commodities; they are composites. Separability of U rationalizes the construction of such composite commodities. However, the econometric modeling of the decision processes employing such composites also requires the existence of price aggregates which can be used as explanatory variables in expenditure-allocation equations:

$$y_r = \hat{\theta}^r \left(\Pi^1(P^1), \ldots, \Pi^m(P^m), y \right), \qquad r = 1, \ldots, m. \tag{8.13}$$

Typically, the econometrician employs Paasche indices (e.g., implicit price deflators available from national-income-accounts data), Laspeyres indices (e.g., fixed-weight indices of consumer price indices), discrete approximations to Divisia indices (see, for example, Christensen and Jorgenson, 1973; Christensen, Jorgenson, and Lau, 1975; Jorgenson and Lau 1975), or discrete approximations to the "marginal-expenditure-effect indices" (see, for example, Barten and Turnovsky, 1966). The Divisia index is defined by

$$\frac{d \ln \Pi^r(P^r(t))}{dt} = \sum_{i \in I^r} w_i(t) \frac{d \ln p_i(t)}{dt}, \tag{a}$$

where $w_i(t) = p_i(t) \cdot x_i(t)/y_r(t)$. The marginal-expenditure-effect index is defined by (a) where $w_i(t) = \partial p_i(t) \cdot x_i(t)/\partial y_r(t)$. Gorman (1959) showed that homothetic separability implies that the sectoral price indices satisfy the differential formula defining Divisia indices. Diewert (1976) showed that the discrete approximation to the Divisia index can be generated only by a homogeneous translog utility or production function (see section 8.2).

In an interesting Monte Carlo study, Anderson (1976) has shed some light on the relative advantages and disadvantages of employing the "true" price index, as opposed to one of these four ad hoc indices, in the estimation of allocation functions (8.13). Anderson specifies a completely separable conditional indirect utility function by

$$H(\iota y, P) = \sum_{r=1}^{m} a_r \left(\frac{y_r}{\Pi^r(P^r)} - b_r \right)^c + \frac{\Lambda^r(P^r)}{\Pi^r(P^r)} \qquad (8.14)$$

where

$$\Pi^r(P^r) = \sum_{i \in I^r} \alpha_i p_i, \qquad r = 1, \ldots, m, \qquad (8.14a)$$

and

$$\Lambda^r(P^r) = \sum_{i \in I^r} \mu_i p_i, \qquad r = 1, \ldots, m.$$

This specification clearly satisfies one of the Gorman conditions for price aggregation (see theorem 5.6)—viz., complete separability with the generalized Gorman polar form.

Anderson generates data sets consistent with the (stochasticized) expenditure-allocation system (8.13) generated by (8.14) and estimates the resultant system five ways, corresponding to five different conditions on the price indices Π^r (viz., the "true forms" (8.14a) and the four commonly employed indices identified above). He concludes that the use of the indices (8.14a) "led to a tighter estimation fit...than did the use of any alternative indices considered" (1976: p. 169) and "produced forecasts of actual expenditures which outperformed those of any other method" (1976: p. 170), but "in estimating the structure generating behavior, the use of perfect price indices did not give results superior to other methods" (1976: p. 170). (Efficiency in "estimating the structure" means that the parameter estimates are "close" to the "true state of the world"). Anderson's study thus indicates that, if one maintains the hypothesis that the complete separability conditions for Gorman price aggregation are satisfied, then using the theoretically consistent price indices, rather than any of the four commonly employed indices, in estimating (8.13) results in a better fit and more accurate forecasting capability, but is not demonstrably superior for the purpose of hypothesis tests regarding the structure of the underlying preference ordering or technology.

Of course, much more research is required before any of the above conclusions can be considered to be definitive. It would, in particular, be interesting to ascertain whether the inconclusiveness of the issue of relative efficiency in determining the true underlying structure would be modified if the true index were assumed to be nonlinear. But certainly it is not unreasonable to contend that if price aggregates are to be used at all, there is some gain to be expected from searching for the "correct" index.

Many econometric studies require that the price indices satisfy the adding-up condition (multiplying the quantity index by the price index yields the optimal expenditure on the respective sector). As was shown in chapter 5 (theorem 5.8), homothetic separability in the appropriate partition is necessary and sufficient (given separability) for the existence of such (additive) price and quantity indices. Unfortunately, homothetic separability is perhaps less plausible than complete separability with the generalized Gorman polar form, because the former assumption implies that sectoral expenditure elasticities are all unitary, in which case overall expenditure elasticities are equal within each group I'. Although this assumption may be plausible in the theory of production, it is unpalatable to most consumer-demand analysts. Nevertheless, practitioners who use additive price indices implicitly assume homothetic separability.

8.1.5 Demand-System Estimation and the Work-Leisure Choice

Viewed from a broader perspective, even "complete" demand systems which allocate total expenditure must be rationalized by maintained separability assumptions. Total expenditure is itself a choice variable. Consumers are endowed with a vector of "primary" commodities, such as leisure, which can be exchanged directly or indirectly for other marketed commodities. Suppose for the sake of illustration that leisure time, l, is the only endowment. The consumer optimization problem is

$$\max_{X,L} U(X,L) \quad \text{s.t.} \quad P \cdot X + wL \leqslant w\bar{L},$$

where $\bar{L}$ is the endowment of leisure time l; L is the amount of leisure time consumed, the remainder $(\bar{L}-L)$ being sold as labor services; and w is the wage rate (the price, or opportunity cost, of l). The solution can be written

$$X = \phi(P, w, \bar{L})$$

and

$$L = \zeta(P,w,\bar{L}).$$

The consumer's gross monetary expenditure is

$$y = w\left[\bar{L} - \zeta(P,w,\bar{L})\right].$$

The econometric models of consumer expenditure can be rationalized by assuming (probably, it must be admitted, without much empirical justification) that I (the set of indices of X) is separable from l in U. In this case, we can write

$$U(X,L) = \bar{U}\left(\hat{U}(X),L\right)$$

and decentralize the consumer expenditure problem as follows:

$$\max_{X} \hat{U}(X) \quad \text{s.t.} \quad P \cdot X \leqslant y,$$

yielding the "conditional" expenditure system

$$X = \hat{\phi}(P,y). \tag{8.15}$$

Of course, optimal total expenditure, or income, is generated by solving

$$\max_{y} \bar{U}\left(\hat{U}(\hat{\phi}(P,y)), \bar{L} - (y/w)\right).$$

The point, however, is that, if data on the allocation of time are not available, the separability (or decentralizability) assumption rationalizes the econometric estimation of (8.15) using consumer expenditure and price data only. (The caveat regarding the stochastic structure of the model, noted above, should be reemphasized here.)

The procedure discussed above can be extended in a fairly straightforward manner to incorporate multiple endowments of commodities, though some minor problems arise if the consumer consumes more than his endowment of some commodity. The procedure can also incorporate nonmarketed commodities and activities into the consumer's feasible consumption set.

8.1.6   Value-Added Production Functions and Input Demand

It is also common in econometric models of production and input demand to abstract from the existence of some inputs. For example, production functions typically include labor and capital inputs but abstract from, say, materials. Often this approach is implemented by working with a "real-value-added" production function (see Arrow, 1974). This can be rationalized by assuming that the set {labor, capital} is (strictly) separable from materials in the gross output production function and that the ordering in the capital-labor subspace is homothetic. That is, assume that the production function image can be written

$$U(K,L,M) = \tilde{U}(\hat{U}(K,L),M),$$

where K, L, and M are the quantities of capital, labor, and material inputs, respectively; $\tilde{U}$ is nondecreasing (increasing) in $\hat{U}(K,L)$; and $\hat{U}$ is homothetic. Then $\hat{U}$ can be normalized to be PLH (lemma 3.3) and there exists a PLH price aggregator Π (theorem 5.8) such that the optimal expenditure on captial and labor (value-added) is

$$v = p_l \overset{*}{L} + p_k \overset{*}{K} = \Pi(p_l, p_k) \cdot \hat{U}\left(\overset{*}{L}, \overset{*}{K}\right),$$

where, of course, $\overset{*}{L}$ and $\overset{*}{K}$ are optimal quantities. (In fact, Π is the dual aggregator in the cost function; see chapter 5). Thus $\Pi(p_l, p_k)$ is the appropriate value-added deflator and $\hat{U}(L,K)$ is real value added.[7] It is now legitimate to examine the technological relationships between labor and capital independently of the materials input by working with the real-value-added production function $\hat{U}$. Unfortunately, the typical value-added deflator is linear and hence is rationalized only by a Leontief (fixed-proportions) value-added production function $\hat{U}$.

8.1.7 Intertemporal Optimization and Current Demand Systems

Maintained separability assumptions can also rationalize the estimation of one-period consumer expenditure systems within the broader intertemporal perspective of multiple-period optimization. It is quite obvious that the assumption of intertemporal separability rationalizes intertemporal decentralization. For the purpose of simple illustration, suppose that U is an intertemporal utility function with image

$$U(X) = U(X^1, \ldots, X^T)$$

[7]The converse of the above argument is also true. That is, suppose that the set {labor, capital} is separable from its complement in the gross output production function, and there exist a PLH real-valued-added function and a PLH value-added deflator whose product is optimal expenditure on labor and capital. Using theorem 5.8 , this implies that the ordering in the capital-labor subspace is homothetic.

where $X^t \in \Omega^{(t)}$ is the tth-period consumption bundle and T is the time horizon. The estimation of current-period expenditure systems independently of future consumption patterns is rationalized by assuming that I^1 is separable in U from its complement in $\cup_{t=1}^t I^t$, in which case we can write, in the notation of chapter 6,

$$U(X) = \overline{U}\left(U^1(X^1), X^2, \ldots, X^T\right) = \overline{U}\left(U^1(X^1), {}_2X\right).$$

Solving

$$\max_{X^1} U^1(X^1) \qquad \text{s.t.} \quad P^1 \cdot X^1 \leqslant y_1$$

yields the (conditional) current demand system,

$$X^1 = \phi^1(P^1, y_1),$$

which can be estimated with current data. (Of course, the optimal current expenditure can be generated by solving

$$\max_{y_1, {}_2X} \overline{U}\left(U^1\big(\phi(P^1, y_1), {}_2X\big)\right) \qquad \text{s.t.} \quad y_1 + {}_2P \cdot {}_2X \leqslant \omega,$$

where ω is the present value of the consumer's wealth and ${}_2P$ is the vector of forward prices.)

8.2   TESTING FOR FUNCTIONAL STRUCTURE

8.2.1   Flexible Functional Forms

As noted in the previous section, in the estimation of demand systems it is frequently convenient (if not necessary) to work with a subset of the complete list of commodities or with aggregate (or composite) commodities (and prices). Such tactics, however, usually require—implicitly if not explicitly—very strong maintained assumptions. Ideally, such assumptions should be tested. However, until recently it was very difficult, if not impossible, to test structural restrictions. Primarily because of the absence of operational nonlinear estimation algorithms, most estimated demand systems were highly structured—i.e., maintained strong homotheticity and/or separability restrictions. Even the quite rigidly sructured systems discussed in the previous section were not estimated until recently; their principal appeal is in fact that they generalize even more highly structured systems (such as the linear expenditure system, the CES, and the Cobb-Douglas specifications) which have typically been employed in empirical analyses of demand and supply.

Recent developments in the implementation of nonlinear estimation programs has made feasible the estimation of less structured functional forms—that is, functional forms that do not maintain, *a priori*, homotheticity or separability restrictions. Econometric estimation of specifications that include, as proper subsets, classes of specifications that incorporate homotheticity and/or separability restrictions makes it possible to test statistically for these structural restrictions.

There is, of course, an uncountable infinity of functional specifications with no homotheticity or separability restrictions. It is therefore obvious that a set of reasonable criteria must be formulated in order to facilitate the choice of functional specification. The art of functional-form specification has been dramatically advanced in recent years, primarily because of the pioneering work of Diewert (1971, 1973a, 1973d, 1974d).

One obvious criterion to be employed in the adoption of functional forms for testing structural hypotheses is that specifications satisfying the structural property be properly nested in the specified class of functions. Another obvious criterion is that the specified functional form be capable of satisfying the appropriate regularity conditions (at least over a region if not globally). A third criterion is that of computational simplicity with respect to the derivation of demand and/or supply functions and with respect to statistical estimation of parameters.

Perhaps the most ingenious criterion proposed by Diewert is that "the functional form contains precisely the number of parameters needed to provide a *second order approximation* to an arbitrary twice differentiable...function satisfying the appropriate regularity conditions..."(1973d: p. 285). A function which satisfies this property is referred to by Diewert as a *flexible* functional form. More precisely, according to Diewert, a functional form is flexible if the parameters of the functional form can be chosen to make the values of its first- and second-order derivatives (and, trivially, the function image itself) equal to the first- and second-order derivatives (and the level) of the function being approximated at any point (of approximation) in the domain. That is, a function $\tilde{U}$ is a second-order approximation to the "true" function U at the point $\overline{X}$ if

$$\tilde{U}(\overline{X}) = U(\overline{X}),$$

$$\nabla \tilde{U}(\overline{X}) = \nabla U(\overline{X}),$$

and

$$\nabla^2 \tilde{U}(\overline{X}) = \nabla^2 U(\overline{X}).$$

Diewert's concept is a fairly weak notion of approximation. A somewhat stronger approximation property is for the functional form to have an interpretation as a Taylor's-series approximation. It is somewhat instructive for our purposes to clarify this notion precisely. Write the true function image as

$$U(x_1,\ldots,x_n) = \overline{U}\left(f_1(x_1),\ldots,f_n(x_n)\right), \tag{8.16}$$

where $f_1,\ldots,f_n$ are arbitrary twice differentiable transformations of the original variables and $\overline{U}$ is defined by (8.16). Taking a twice differentiable monotonic transformation, say ψ, of both sides, we have

$$\psi \circ U(X) = \psi \circ \overline{U}\left(f_1(x_1),\ldots,f_n(x_n)\right).$$

The composition $\psi \circ \overline{U}$ can be represented by a Taylor's-series expansion about $(f_1(\overline{x}_1),\ldots,f_n(\overline{x}_n)) \in \Omega^n_+$:

$$\psi \circ U(X) = \psi \circ \overline{U}\left(f_1(\overline{x}_1),\ldots,f_n(\overline{x}_n)\right)$$

$$+ \sum_{i \in I}\left(\frac{\partial}{\partial x_i}\left[\psi \circ \overline{U}\left(f_1(\overline{x}_1),\ldots,f_n(\overline{x}_n)\right)\right]\right)\left[f_i(x_i) - f_i(\overline{x}_i)\right]$$

$$+ \frac{1}{2}\sum_{i \in I}\sum_{j \in I}\left(\frac{\partial^2}{\partial x_i \partial x_j}\left[\psi \circ \overline{U}\left(f_1(\overline{x}_1),\ldots,f_n(\overline{x}_n)\right)\right]\right)$$

$$\times \left[f_i(x_i) - f_i(\overline{x}_i)\right]\left[f_j(x_j) - f_j(\overline{x}_j)\right]$$

$$+ \ldots$$

$$= \overline{\alpha}_0 + \sum_{i \in I}\overline{\alpha}_i\left[f_i(x_i) - f_i(\overline{x}_i)\right]$$

$$+ \frac{1}{2}\sum_{i \in I}\sum_{j \in I}\overline{\beta}_{ij}\left[f_i(x_i) - f_i(\overline{x}_i)\right]\left[f_j(x_j) - f_j(\overline{x}_j)\right]$$

$$+ \ldots, \qquad \overline{\beta}_{ij} = \overline{\beta}_{ji} \quad \forall (ij) \in I \times I,$$

where, of course, $\bar{\alpha}_0$, $\bar{\alpha}_i$ $(i = 1, \ldots, n)$, and $\bar{\beta}_{ij}$ $(i, j = 1, \ldots, n)$ are the values of the image, the first partial derivatives, and the second partial derivatives of $\psi \circ \bar{U}$ at the point $\bar{X}$. Rearranging terms and eliminating third- and higher-order terms yields the second-order Taylor's-series approximation to $\psi \circ \bar{U}$ at $\bar{X} = 1$

$$\overline{\psi \circ U(X)} = \left(\bar{\alpha}_0 - \sum_{i \in I} \bar{\alpha}_i f_i(\bar{x}_i) + \frac{1}{2} \sum_{i \in I} \sum_{i \in I} \bar{\beta}_{ij} f_i(\bar{x}_i) f_j(\bar{x}_j) \right)$$

$$+ \sum_{i \in I} \left(\bar{\alpha}_i - \sum_{j \in I} \bar{\beta}_{ij} f_j(\bar{x}_j) \right) f_i(x_i)$$

$$+ \frac{1}{2} \sum_{i \in I} \sum_{j \in I} \bar{\beta}_{ij} f_i(x_i) f_j(x_j)$$

or

$$\overline{\psi \circ U(X)} = \alpha_0 + \sum_{i \in I} \alpha_i f_i(x_i) + \frac{1}{2} \sum_{i \in I} \sum_{j \in I} \beta_{ij} f_i(x_i) f_j(x_j),$$

$$\beta_{ij} = \beta_{ji} \quad \forall (i, j) \in I \times I, \tag{8.17}$$

where

$$\alpha_0 = \bar{\alpha}_0 - \sum_{i \in I} \bar{\alpha}_i f_i(\bar{x}_i) + \frac{1}{2} \sum_{i \in I} \sum_{j \in I} \bar{\beta}_{ij} f_i(\bar{x}_i) f_j(\bar{x}_j), \tag{8.17a}$$

$$\alpha_i = \bar{\alpha}_i - \sum_{j \in I} \bar{\beta}_{ij} f_j(\bar{x}_j) \quad \forall i \in I, \tag{8.17b}$$

and

$$\beta_{ij} = \bar{\beta}_{ij} \quad \forall (i, j) \in I \times I. \tag{8.17c}$$

Thus any functional form that can be written as in the right-hand side of (8.17) has a Taylor's-series interpretation; that is, it can be interpreted as a second-order Taylor's-series approximation, in transformed variables, to a monotonic transformation of the "true" underlying function.

In some applications, the distinction between the Diewert concept of approximation and the Taylor's-series-approximation concept might be a matter of some importance. This is because a second-order Taylor's-series approximation has the property of being a numerical approximation —i.e., in any prescribed neighborhood of the point of approximation, the error of the approximation is bounded by the size of the higher-order terms (see Lau, 1974a).

Most flexible-form specifications have interpretations as Taylor's-series approximations. Some commonly employed flexible functional forms are as follows:

Quadratic: $f_i(x_i) = x_i$ $\forall i$ and $\psi(z) = z$.
Generalized Leontief (Diewert, 1971): $f_i(x_i) = x_i^{1/2}$ $\forall i$ and $\psi(z) = z$.
Generalized quadratic mean of order ρ (Kadiyala, 1971–2; Denny, 1972, 1974; Hasenkamp, 1973): $f_i(x_i) = x_i^{\rho/2}$ $\forall i$ and $\psi(z) = z^{1/\rho}$.[8]
Translog (Lau and Mitchell, 1971): $f_i(x_i) = \ln x_i$ $\forall i$ and $\psi(z) = \ln z$.

Examples of commonly used flexible forms which do not have interpretations as Taylor's-series approximations are the generalized Cobb-Douglas form (Diewert, 1973a),

$$U(X) = \prod_{i \in I} \prod_{j \in I} \left(\tfrac{1}{2} x_i + \tfrac{1}{2} x_j \right)^{\beta_{ij}}, \qquad \beta_{ij} = \beta_{ji} \quad \forall (i,j) \in I \times I,$$

and the mean of order two (Diewert, 1974d),

$$U(X) = \sum_{i \in I} \sum_{j \in I} \beta_{ij} \left(\tfrac{1}{2} x_i^2 + \tfrac{1}{2} x_j^2 \right)^{1/2}, \qquad \beta_{ij} = \beta_{ji} \quad \forall (i,j) \in I \times I.$$

The suitability of the above specifications for use in testing functional-structure hypotheses is manifested in their "flexibility". In particular, none of these specifications imposes, *a priori*, separability restrictions on the underlying preferences or technology.[9] Nevertheless, as will be seen below, all of these specifications can generate separable structures as special cases and can therefore be used to test for separability. Moreover, each of these specifications can be constrained to satisfy the regularity conditions (R-1) (continuity, monotonicity, and quasi-concavity) at least over a region of the domain of U.[10]

---

[8]The generalized quadratic mean of order ρ clearly generates the generalized Leontief form as the special case where $\rho = 1$. The quadratic mean of order ρ—the actual specification of Kadiyala, Denny, and Hasenkamp—is obtained by letting $\alpha_i = 0$ $\forall i \in I$.

[9]The four specifications with Taylor's-series-approximation interpretations are also, in general, nonhomothetic, but can generate homothetic functions as special cases. First-order terms can be added to the generalized Cobb-Douglas and the mean-of-order-two specifications to make them nonhomothetic (see, e.g., Diewert, 1974d: p. 128).

[10]The quadratic and translog specifications cannot satisfy monotonicity and quasi-concavity globally. For discussions of the regularity properties of these functional forms, see Diewert (1974d) (quadratic and mean of order two), Diewert (1971) (generalized Leontief), Denny (1972, 1974) and Diewert (1976) (quadratic mean of order ρ), and Lau (1974a) (translog). It is possible either to maintain the regularity properties or to test them using these flexible forms [see Lau (1975a) on this matter].

Although the foregoing exposition of the interpretation and specification of flexible functional forms is couched in terms of the utility or production function, it is quite obvious that the same points are valid for the indirect utility or production function, the cost function, and the transformation function. Of course, in the cases of the cost and transformation functions, one of the variables is utility or output, and the regularity conditions (continuity, monotonicity, concavity, and positive linear homogeneity in P or X and strict monotonicity in u) are much stronger. Consider, for example, the homogeneity condition. This is satisfied automatically by the generalized Cobb-Douglas form and the mean of order two. The quadratic form, generalized Leontief form, and quadratic mean of order ρ in the variables (u, P) are not, in general, PLH in P and increasing in u. In order to employ these specifications in the statistical analysis of cost functions that are consistent with cost-minimizing behavior, it is necessary to impose some structure.

A common approach is to maintain homotheticity of the production function, in which case the cost function has the structure (see lemma 3.4)

$$C(u, P) = \phi(u)\hat{C}(P),$$

where ϕ is increasing and $\hat{C}$ is nondecreasing, concave, and PLH. If $\phi(u) = u$, the production function is PLH and $\hat{C}$ is the unit cost function. One can then specify a flexible functional form for $\hat{C}$ that satisfies the regularity conditions.

An alternative approach, which does not require a homothetic production technology, is to assume that C has the Gorman polar form structure (see subsection 8.1.2)

$$C(u, P) = \phi(u) \cdot \hat{C}(P) + T(P),$$

and specify flexible function forms for the marginal cost function [relative to the transformed output variable $\phi(u)$] $\hat{C}$ and the "committed cost function" T that satisfy the regularity conditions. [This specification of flexible forms for both C and T would involve more parameters than are needed to approximate an arbitrary twice differentiable Gorman-polar-form cost function (see Lau, 1975b).]

In the first approach, any of the above second-order approximations to $\hat{C}$ can be constrained to satisfy the appropriate regularity properties, although the quadratic and translog specifications cannot satisfy monotonicity and concavity globally (see Diewert, 1974d; Lau, 1974a). It is easy to see that the quadratic unit cost function, with image

$$\hat{C}(P) = \alpha_0 + \sum_{i \in I} \alpha_i p_i + \frac{1}{2} \sum_{i \in I} \sum_{j \in I} \beta_{ij} p_i p_j,$$

is **PLH** if and only if $\alpha_0 = \beta_{ij} = 0$ for all $(i,j) \in I \times I$. Thus, if homogeneity is imposed upon the quadratic, it degenerates to a linear function, which cannot provide a second-order approximation to an arbitrary, PLH, twice differentiable unit cost function. That is, the quadratic is "homogeneity-inflexible". The quadratic-mean-of-order-ρ, unit cost function

$$\hat{C}(P) = \left(\alpha_0 + \sum_{i \in I} \alpha_i p_i^{\rho/2} + \frac{1}{2} \sum_{i \in I} \sum_{j \in I} \beta_{ij} p_i^{\rho/2} p_j^{\rho/2} \right)^{1/\rho},$$

$$\beta_{ij} = \beta_{ji} \quad \forall (i,j) \in I \times I,$$

and its special case, the generalized Leontief form ($\rho = 1$), are PLH if and only if $\alpha_0 = \alpha_i = 0$ for all $i \in I$. The resultant expression, containing only second-order terms, can provide a second-order approximation to an arbitrary, PLH, twice differentiable unit cost function and is therefore not homogeneity-inflexible.

If one insists upon an interpretation of this specification as a Taylor's-series approximation, the right-hand side is in fact an approximation of $[\hat{C}(P)]^\rho$ in transformed variables. In this case, positive linear homogeneity requires that $\alpha_0 = 0$ and that $\rho = 1$ and $\alpha_i = 0 \; \forall i \in I$ or $\rho = 2$ and $\beta_{ij} = 0$ $\forall (i,j) \in I \times I$.

The translog specification can be used to approximate the cost function corresponding to a nonhomothetic technology:

$$\ln C(u, P) = a + \alpha_0 \ln u + \sum_{i \in I} \alpha_i \ln p_i + \beta_{00} \ln u \ln u$$

$$+ \sum_{i \in I} \beta_{0i} \ln u \ln p_i + \frac{1}{2} \sum_{i \in I} \sum_{j \in I} \beta_{ij} \ln p_i \ln p_j,$$

$$\beta_{ij} = \beta_{ji} \quad \forall (i,j) \in I \times I.$$

This specification satisfies the homogeneity restriction if and only if

$$\sum_{i \in I} \alpha_i = 1$$

and

$$\sum_{j \in I} \beta_{ij} = 0, \qquad i = 0, 1, \ldots, n,$$

and therefore is not homogeneity-inflexible.

8.2.2 Testing for Separability

The foregoing discussion indicates that any of the flexible functional forms defined above can be used to test the hypothesis of first-degree homogeneity or can be constrained to satisfy this property (though the quadratic has the unattractive property of being homogeneity-inflexible).[11] Of more importance to the subject matter of this book is the use of the flexible functional forms to test separability restrictions. We first briefly describe this procedure in the context of the general class of flexible functional forms (8.17) that have an interpretation as Taylor's-series approximations. Complete fidelity to the approximation interpretation would require that we carry out the entire analysis of separability and flexible funtional forms using the functional notation $\overline{\psi \circ U}$ lest we forget that the right-hand side of (8.17) is only an approximation in transformed variables to a monotonic transformation of the true function. However, consistently with most of the literature on testing separability with flexible functional forms (and consistently with our effort to simplify notation), throughout most of the discussion that follows, we assume that that the form (8.17) is a specification of the true function.

[Assuming that the flexible form holds exactly rather than "approximately" is a matter of some importance, because the approximation to a separable function need not itself be separable (though it will satisfy the differential implications of separability at the point of approximation). See Christensen, Jorgenson, and Lau (1975) and Jorgenson and Lau (1975), who, because of this distinction, test separability restrictions only at the point of approximation.]

Hence we examine the specification

$$U(X) = \alpha_0 + \sum_{i \in I} \alpha_i f_i(x_i) + \frac{1}{2} \sum_{i \in I} \sum_{j \in I} \beta_{ij} f_i(x_i) f_j(x_j),$$

$$\beta_{ij} = \beta_{ij} \quad \forall (i,j) \in I \times I, \tag{8.18}$$

which we refer to as the "generalized quadratic". (Neglecting the monotonic transformation ψ is inconsequential, since separability properties are invariant under monotonic transformations.)

---

[11]Christensen, Jorgenson, and Lau (1973, 1975), Christensen and Manser (1975), and Jorgenson and Lau (1975) have used the translog specification to test for homogeneity. Christensen, Jorgenson, and Lau (1975) and Jorgenson and Lau (1975) have also employed the translog to test for the weaker property of homotheticity at a point (in particular, at the "point of approximation", $\ln X = 0$"). (If the translog is globally homothetic, it is globally homogeneous.) Testing for affine homotheticity (at a point) requires that a third-order translog be employed (see Lau, 1975b; Boyce and Primont, 1976a).

In order to employ the Leontief-Sono differential definition of separability, we assume that the first-order partial derivatives of U do not vanish. The marginal rates of substitution in the generalized quadratic are [12]

$$\frac{\partial U(X)/\partial x_i}{\partial U(X)/\partial x_j} = \frac{U_i(X)}{U_j(X)} = \frac{R_i(X)f_i'(x_i)}{R_j(X)f_j'(x_j)}, \tag{8.19}$$

where

$$R_i(X) = \alpha_i + \sum_{l \in I} \beta_{il} f_l(x_l), \qquad i = 1,\ldots,n, \quad j = 1,\ldots,n \tag{8.20}$$

and f_i' is the derivative of f_i, $i = 1,\ldots,n$. Recall that the pair of variables $\{i,j\}$ is separable from k if and only if the Leontief-Sono condition holds:

$$\frac{\partial}{\partial x_k}\left(\frac{U_i(X)}{U_j(X)}\right) = 0.$$

Using (8.19), this is equivalent to

$$R_i(X)\frac{\partial R_j(X)}{\partial x_k} - R_j(X)\frac{\partial R_i(X)}{\partial x_k} = 0.$$

Evaluating the derivatives in this expression yields

$$\beta_{ik}R_j(X) - \beta_{jk}R_i(X) = 0. \tag{8.21}$$

Substituting from (8.20), we have

$$\alpha_j\beta_{ik} - \alpha_i\beta_{jk} + \sum_{l \in I}(\beta_{jl}\beta_{ik} - \beta_{il}\beta_{jk})f_l(x_l) = 0. \tag{8.22}$$

This equality holds for all points $X \in \Omega^n_+$ if and only if

$$\alpha_j\beta_{ik} - \alpha_i\beta_{jk} = 0. \tag{a}$$

and

$$\beta_{jl}\beta_{ik} - \beta_{il}\beta_{jk} = 0, \qquad l = 1,\ldots,n. \tag{b}$$

[12]The separability restrictions for the generalized Cobb-Douglas form and the mean of order two are derived in section 8.3.

Thus, (a) and (b) are necessary and sufficient for separability of $\{i,j\}$ from k in the generalized quadratic. Given specifications of $f_i(x_i)$, $i=1,\ldots,n$, these parametric restrictions can be tested by executing a likelihood-ratio test where the ratio is calculated by estimating the parameters of the implied demand system with and without the restrictions (a) and (b). [13]

An alternative test procedure, which purports to exploit the approximation property of the generalized quadratic, is to test for separability at the point of approximation (rather than for global separability of the generalized quadratic). Separability of the "true" function implies separability of the approximating function only at the point of approximation. Separability at the point of approximation is equivalent to the parametric restriction [using (8.21)]

$$\alpha_j \beta_{ik} - \alpha_i \beta_{jk} + \sum_{l \in I} (\beta_{jl} \beta_{ik} - \beta_{il} \beta_{jk}) f_l (\bar{x}_l) = 0.$$

It is perhaps natural to interpret the "point of approximation" as the point at which α_i and β_{ij} $(i,j=1,\ldots,n)$ are estimates of the first and second derivatives of the true function. Using (8.17b) and (8.17c), it is apparent that this choice makes $f_i(\bar{x}_i)=0$ $\forall i \in I$,[14] in which case the separability restriction degenerates to a simple parametric restriction,

$$\alpha_j \beta_{ik} - \alpha_i \beta_{jk} = 0. \tag{c}$$

Thus, a test for separability at the "point of approximation" is executed by forming the likelihood ratio obtained by estimating the parameters of the implied demand system both with and without the restriction (c). [15]

[13]See Berndt and Christensen (1973b) for an extended discussion of this test procedure. They also employ a translog unit-cost function (maintaining a PLH production function) to test for the existence of a capital aggregate (i.e., separability of capital inputs from labor) in U. S. manufacturing. In another paper, Berndt and Christensen (1974a) employ a translog unit-cost function to test for the existence of an aggregate labor input (separability of blue-collar and white-collar labor from capital). These hypotheses have been retested by Woodland (1976b), who employs a translog variable profit function. Humphrey (1976), Burgess (1974), and Berndt and Wood (1975) have all employed translog specifications to test for the existence of a real-value-added production function (see subsection 8.1.6 above).

[14]If the point $\bar{X}$ satisfying $f_i(\bar{x}_i)=0$ $\forall i \in I$ is not in the domain of U, the function must be affinely transformed in order to employ this test procedure. [Recall that separability properties are unaffected by monotonic (a fortiori, affine) transformation of U.] As it turns out, only the translog function has been used to test for separability at the "point of approximation" (see the next footnote for references), and $1^n \in \Omega_+^n$ satisfies $f_i(1)=\ln 1=0$.

[15]Jorgenson and Lau (1975) employ translog direct and indirect utility functions to test for separability at $\ln X=0^n$. Earlier, Christensen, Jorgenson, and Lau (1973, 1975) employed the translog specification to test for additivity in the discrete partition $\{\{1\},\ldots,\{n\}\}$ at $\ln X=0^n$.

One possible advantage of testing for a property at a point is that a global test for the property might be computationally infeasible.[16] Of course, if a property is rejected at a point, it is rejected globally; on the other hand, acceptance of a property at a point does not have much statistical power (acceptance at a point does not imply acceptance of the property in any neighborhood—no matter how small—of the test point).

Another possible advantage of testing for separability at a point is attributable to the fact that the flexible functional forms introduced above turn out to be "separability-inflexible" (much as the quadratic is "homogeneity-inflexible"). That is, a separable generalized quadratic cannot provide a second-order approximation to an arbitrary, twice differentiable, separable function. In more practical terms, it turns out that the flexibility of flexible functional forms is seriously impaired by the imposition of separability restrictions; in particular, these flexible functional forms are incapable of modeling many types of functional structures. This is a matter of some importance, because it means that tests for functional structure using these flexible forms in fact test only for special cases of these structures; hence there is a danger of seriously misinterpreting the test outcomes. We turn to a formalization of this problem in the next section.

8.3 THE SEPARABILITY-INFLEXIBILITY
OF FLEXIBLE FUNCTIONAL FORMS

In order to show that the flexible functional forms that have been employed in empirical analyses are unable to model many types of functional structures, we first show that the generalized quadratic is separability-inflexible, providing in the process a complete characterization of those structures which it can model. [17] The specific results for the translog, the mean of order ρ, and the generalized Leontief form are then generated as straightforward examples of our main theorem. We conclude by showing that the generalized Cobb-Douglas form and the mean of order two are even less flexible vis-a-vis separability than is the generalized quadratic.

8.3.1 The Generalized Quadratic

We first characterize the necessary and sufficient conditions for separability of the generalized quadratic, (a) and (b) above, in terms which themselves betray the separability-inflexibility of this form.

---

[16]See, for example, the test of the representative consumer hypothesis using a third-order translog by Boyce and Primont (1976a).

[17]Most of these results are taken from Blackorby, Primont, and Russell (1977c).

For easy reference in the following theorems and proofs we repeat here the expression for the generalized quadratic,

$$U(X) = \alpha_0 + \sum_{i \in I} \alpha_i f_i(x_i) + \frac{1}{2} \sum_{i \in I} \sum_{j \in I} \beta_{ij} f_i(x_i) f_j(x_j),$$

$$\beta_{ij} = \beta_{ji} \quad \forall (i,j) \in I \times I, \tag{8.18}$$

and the necessary and sufficient condition for separability of $\{i,j\}$ from $\{k\}$,

$$\beta_{ik} R_j(X) = \beta_{jk} R_i(X) \tag{8.21}$$

or, equivalently,

$$\alpha_j \beta_{ik} - \alpha_i \beta_{jk} = 0 \tag{a}$$

and

$$\beta_{jl} \beta_{ik} - \beta_{il} \beta_{jk} = 0, \qquad l = 1, \ldots, n. \tag{b}$$

Theorem 8.1. *Assume that $R_i(X) \neq 0$ and $R_j(X) \neq 0$. Then the ith and jth variables are separable from the kth variable in the generalized quadratic function (8.18) if and only if one of the following conditions is met:*

(i) $\beta_{ik} = \beta_{jk} = 0$, or
(ii) the ith and jth variables are separable from all variables $l \in I$ such that $i \neq l \neq j$.

Proof. Sufficiency [(i)⇒(a)&(b) and (ii)⇒(a)&(b)] is immediate. The strategy of the proof of necessity is to show that, given separability, (ii) must hold whenever (i) does not hold.

If (i) does not hold, both β_{ik} and β_{jk} are nonzero. This follows from (8.21) and the assumption that neither $R_i(X)$ nor $R_j(X)$ is zero. If, on the other hand, either β_{jl} or β_{il} is zero, then both are zero. This follows from (b) and the just-established fact that both β_{ik} and β_{jj} are nonzero. Partition I into L_0 and L_1 such that

$$l \in L_0 \quad \Leftrightarrow \quad \beta_{jl} = \beta_{il} = 0$$

and

$$l \in L_1 \quad \Leftrightarrow \quad \beta_{jl} \neq 0 \text{ and } \beta_{il} \neq 0.$$

Then condition (b) is satisfied if and only if

$$\beta_{jl}\beta_{ik} - \beta_{il}\beta_{jk} = 0 \qquad \forall l \in L_1. \tag{b'}$$

Clearly, the ith and jth variables are separable from all variables $l \in L_0 - \{i,j\}$. (A pair of variables cannot be separable from themselves by our definition.) For $l \in L_1$, (b') is equivalent to

$$\frac{\beta_{ik}}{\beta_{jk}} = \frac{\beta_{il}}{\beta_{jl}} \qquad \forall l \in L_1, \tag{c}$$

which implies

$$\frac{\beta_{il}}{\beta_{jl}} = \frac{\beta_{il'}}{\beta_{jl'}}$$

or

$$\beta_{il}\beta_{jl'} = \beta_{il'}\beta_{jl} \qquad \forall (l,l') \in L_1 \times L_1 \tag{d}$$

Moreover, using (a), we deduce from (c) that

$$\frac{\alpha_i}{\alpha_j} = \frac{\beta_{il}}{\beta_{jl}},$$

or

$$\alpha_i \beta_{jl} = \alpha_j \beta_{il} \qquad \forall l \in L_1. \tag{e}$$

Comparing (d) and (e) with (a) and (b') [and hence (a) and (b)] reveals that $\{i,j\}$ is also separable from all $l \in L_1 - \{i,j\}$, completing the proof. ‖

Suppose there is a group of variables—i.e., a sector denoted by I'—for which condition (i) of Theorem 8.1 holds with respect to all variables outside the group. Specifically,

$$\beta_{ik} = \beta_{jk} = 0 \qquad \forall (i,j) \in I' \times I', \quad \forall k \notin I'.$$

In this case, I' is additively separable. On the other hand, if all variables in I' satisfy (b), the rth group can be represented by a linear function of the $f_i(x_i)$, $i \in I'$. As will be seen, it is the degeneracy characterized by the above theorem which restricts the form of the aggregators when condition (b) is satisfied.

In addition, imposing separability on the generalized quadratic allows the macro function to be structured as a quadratic function of the sector specific aggregates. This assertion is justified in the following theorem, which exhaustively characterizes the types of symmetric functional structures that can be modeled by the generalized quadratic.

Theorem 8.2 *Suppose that* $R_i(X) \neq 0$ $\forall i \in I$. *If the sets* I^r, $r = 1, \ldots, d$ $(0 < d < m)$, *are additively separable from their complements in* I, *and the sets* I^r, $r = d+1, \ldots, m$, *are nonadditively separable from their complements in* I, *then the generalized quadratic image can be written as*

$$U(X) = \sum_{r=1}^{m} \kappa_r U^r(X^r) + \sum_{s=d+1}^{m} \sum_{t=d+1}^{m} \delta_{st} U^s(X^s) U^t(X^t), \quad (8.23)$$

where

$$U^r(X^r) = \sum_{i \in I^r} \alpha_i f_i(x_i) + \sum_{j \in I^r} \sum_{k \in I^r} \beta_{jk} f_j(x_j) f_k(x_k), \qquad r = 1, \ldots, d; \quad (8.23a)$$

$$U^s(X^s) = \sum_{i \in I^s} \gamma_i f_i(x_i), \qquad s = d+1, \ldots, m; \quad (8.23b)$$

$\kappa_r = 1$, $r = 1, \ldots, d$; *and* κ_r, γ_i $(i \in I^r)$, *and* δ_{st}, $r, s, t = d+1, \ldots, m$, *are parameters.*

Proof. The strategy of the proof is to show first that additive separability of the first d groups allows us to structure U as the sum of $d+1$ smaller functions of the form (8.23a), where the last group is the union $\cup_{s=d+1}^{m} I^s$. We then show that this last group can itself be structured as a quadratic in the images of functions of the form (8.23b).

Additive separability of the rth group implies that

$$\beta_{ik} = \beta_{jk} = 0 \qquad \forall (i,j) \in I^r \times I^r, \quad \forall k \notin I^r. \tag{a}$$

Symmetry of the second-order coeffients implies, however, that

$$\beta_{ki} = \beta_{kj} = 0 \qquad \forall (i,j) \in I^r \times I^r, \quad \forall k \notin I^r. \tag{b}$$

Hence the complement of I^r is additively separable from I^r. Thus, additive separability implies symmetric separability (I^r separable from I^s implies I^s separable from I^r). In particular, $\tilde{I} = \cup_{s=d+1}^{m} I^s$ is additively separable from its complement. In this case, the matrix of β_{ij}'s is block diagonal in the partition $\{I^1,\ldots,I^d,\tilde{I}\}$, and hence the generalized quadratic can be written

$$U(X)=\sum_{r=1}^{d}U^r(X^r)+\tilde{U}(_{d+1}X),\qquad\qquad(c)$$

where

$$U^r(X^r)=\sum_{i\in I^r}\alpha_i f_i(x_i)+\sum_{j\in I^r}\sum_{k\in I^r}\beta_{jk}f_j(x_j)f_k(x_k),\qquad r=1,\ldots,d,$$

and

$$\tilde{U}(X^{d+1},\ldots,X^m)=\sum_{i\in\tilde{I}}\alpha_i f_i(x_i)+\sum_{j\in\tilde{I}}\sum_{k\in\tilde{I}}\beta_{jk}f_j(x_j)f_k(x_k).$$

It remains to show that $\tilde{U}$ is a quadratic in aggregators of the form (8.23b). To see this, consider the partition of the matrix of β_{ij}'s, $(i,j)\in\tilde{I}\times\tilde{I}$, corresponding to $\{I^{d+1},\ldots,I^m\}$, a partition of $\tilde{I}$:

$$\tilde{B}=[\tilde{B}^{rs}],\qquad r,s=d+1,\ldots,m,$$

where

$$\tilde{B}^{rs}=[\beta_{ij}],\qquad(i,j)\in I^r\times I^s.$$

In order to simplify the notation in the remainder of the proof, we map the set of indices of I into a new set (corresponding to the partition $\hat{I}$ and the corresponding partition of the matrix $\tilde{B}$), defined by

$$\tilde{I}^r=\{1,\ldots,n_r\},\qquad r=1,\ldots,m,$$

and correspondingly introduce new notation for the elements of the matrix as follows:

$$\tilde{B}^{rs}=[\tilde{b}_{ij}^{rs}],\qquad(i,j)\in\tilde{I}^r\times\tilde{I}^s.$$

In terms of this new notation, $\tilde{B}_{i:}^{rs}$ is the ith row of $\tilde{B}^{rs}$ and $\tilde{B}_{\cdot j}^{rs}$ is the jth column. In addition the separability of I^r from its complement I^c can be written as

$$\tilde{b}_{ik}^{rt}\tilde{b}_{jl}^{rs}=\tilde{b}_{jk}^{rt}\tilde{b}_{il}^{rs},\qquad\forall(i,j)\in\tilde{I}^r\times\tilde{I}^r,\quad\forall(k,l)\in\tilde{I}^c\times\tilde{I}.\qquad(d)$$

This condition implies that each row of $[\tilde{B}^{r,d+1},\ldots,\tilde{B}^{rm}]$ is a multiple of every other row in this matrix for all $r = d+1,\ldots,m$, and each column of

$$\begin{bmatrix} \tilde{B}^{d+1,r} \\ \vdots \\ \tilde{B}^{mr} \end{bmatrix}$$

is proportional to every other column in this matrix. Also, using the separability condition, it is possible to show that all diagonal elements of each diagonal submatrix have the same sign. In addition, if one element is zero, all diagonal elements in the submatrix vanish. To see this, recall that $\forall (i,j) \in \tilde{I}^r \times \tilde{I}^r$ and $\forall k \in \tilde{I}^s$, $\tilde{b}_{ik}^{rs} = 0$ if and only if $\tilde{b}_{jk}^{rs} = 0$. Next note that for all r there exists a $k \neq i,j$ such that $\tilde{b}_{ik}^{rs} \neq 0 \neq \tilde{b}_{jk}^{rs}$; otherwise the pair $\{i,j\}$ would constitute an additively separable set and could be excluded from $\tilde{I}$. Successively letting $l = i$ and $l = j$ while $s = r$ in equation (d) yields

$$\tilde{b}_{ii}^{rr} = \frac{\tilde{b}_{ik}^{rt}}{\tilde{b}_{jk}^{rt}} \tilde{b}_{ij}^{rr}$$

and

$$\tilde{b}_{jj}^{rr} = \frac{\tilde{b}_{jk}^{rt}}{\tilde{b}_{ik}^{rt}} \tilde{b}_{ij}^{rr} \qquad \forall (i,j) \in \tilde{I}^r \times \tilde{I}^r, \quad r = d+1,\ldots,m,$$

which shows that all diagonal elements in $\tilde{B}^{rr}$ have the same sign. On the other hand, if one element of the diagonal is zero, not only is the diagonal zero, but also the entire submatrix, because of the proportionality of rows and columns. Such cases can be ignored, since by hypothesis an entire row cannot vanish.

Since the diagonal elements are nonzero, they can be normalized as follows:

$$B^{rs} = [b_{ij}^{rs}] = \frac{1}{\tilde{b}_{11}^{rs}} \tilde{B}^{rs}. \tag{e}$$

Our problem is now reduced to showing that each normalized submatrix can be decomposed as follows:

$$(B_{1.}^{rr})' B_{1.}^{ss} = B^{rs}, \qquad r = d+1,\ldots,m, \quad s = d+1,\ldots,m. \tag{f}$$

To show (f), it is sufficient to show that

$$b_{1i}^{rr} b_{j1}^{ss} = b_{ij}^{rs}, \qquad \forall (i,j) \in \tilde{I}^r \times \tilde{I}^s. \tag{g}$$

The separability of I^r from I^s implies that

$$b_{i1}^{rr}b_{1j}^{rs} = b_{11}^{rr}b_{ij}^{rs} = b_{ij}^{rs}, \qquad \forall (i,j) \in \tilde{I}^r \times \tilde{I}^s, \tag{h}$$

where the last equality follows from the normalization making $b_{11}^{rr} = 1$. The separability of I^s from I^r implies that

$$b_{1j}^{ss}b_{11}^{rs} = b_{11}^{ss}b_{1j}^{rs} \qquad \forall j \in \tilde{I}^s,$$

or

$$b_{1j}^{ss} = b_{1j}^{rs} \qquad \forall j \in \tilde{I}^s, \tag{i}$$

since $b_{11}^{ss} = 1$ and $b_{11}^{rs} = 1$. Substituting the last equation into (h) and invoking symmetry yields (g). This decomposition allows us to write the second-order terms of $\tilde{U}$ in matrix notation as follows, where $f^r(X^r) = (f_i(x_i))_{i \in I^r}'$ is a vector of function images:

$$\sum_{r=d+1}^{m} \sum_{s=d+1}^{m} (f^r(X^r))' \tilde{B}^{rs} (f^s(X^s))$$

$$= \sum_{r=d+1}^{m} \sum_{s=d+1}^{m} \tilde{b}_{11}^{rs} (f^r(X^r))' B^{rs} (f^s(X^s))$$

$$= \sum_{r=d+1}^{m} \sum_{s=d+1}^{m} \tilde{b}_{11}^{rs} (f^r(X^r))' (B_{1.}^{rr})' (B_{1.}^{ss}) (f^s(X^s))$$

$$= \sum_{r=d+1}^{m} \sum_{s=d+1}^{m} \delta_{rs} U^r(X^r) U^s(X^s), \tag{j}$$

where

$$U^r(X^r) = (B_{1.}^{rr})(f^r(X^r)) = \sum_{i \in I^r} \gamma_i f_i(x_i),$$

$$\gamma^r = (\gamma_i)_{i \in I^r} = B_{1.}^{rr}, \qquad r = d+1, \dots, m,$$

and

$$\delta_{rs} = \tilde{b}_{11}^{rs}, \qquad r = d+1, \dots, m, \quad s = d+1, \dots, m.$$

Separability places restrictions on the linear terms as well. In fact the separability condition

$$\alpha_j \beta_{ik} - \alpha_i \beta_{jk} = 0, \tag{a}$$

along with (d), and (g) imply that $\alpha^r = (\alpha_i)_{i \in I^r}$, $r = d+1, \ldots, m$, can be written as

$$\alpha^r = \kappa_r B_1^{rr} = \kappa_r \gamma^r.$$

Therefore, the linear terms of $\tilde{U}$ can be written as

$$\sum_{r=d+1}^{m} \kappa_r U^r (X^r). \tag{k}$$

Substituting (j) and (k) into (c) yields the desired representation.   ‖

Theorem 8.2 indicates that the class of symmetric structures which can be generated by the generalized quadratic is characterized by a quadratic macro function in which all aggregators are themselves generalized quadratic functions and those aggregators which enter the second-order (as well as the first-order) term are generalized linear functions, that is, functions of the form $U^r(X^r) = \sum_{i \in I^r} \gamma_i f_i(x_i)$. This structure can be further explicated by considering the two extreme cases where $d = 0$ and $d = m$. The resultant structures are described in the following corollaries.

Corollary 8.2.1 *If every element of the partition $\hat{I}$ is additively separable from its complement in I, the generalized quadratic function is additive in this partition*:

$$U(X) = \sum_{r=1}^{m} U^r (X^r).$$

Thus, if $m > 2$, only complete separability can be modeled. If $m = 2$, as is common in applications, then testing for additive separability is testing for a structure which is more restrictive than complete separability. (See the discussion in section 4.6.)

Corollary 8.2.2 *If every element of the partition $\hat{I}$ is nonadditively separable from its complement in I, the generalized quadratic specification can be written as a quadratic in generalized linear aggregators.*[18]

[18]A more elegant (but less constructive) proof of the property that separable sets are represented by generalized linear functions employs theorem 8.1 and the Gorman intersection theorem (theorem 4.3). By theorem 8.1, all pairs $(i,j) \in I^r \times I^r$ are separable from all other variables. By theorem 4.3, it follows that the aggregator U^r is separable in the discrete partition of its variables. This implies that in some normalization it is additively separable.

This aspect of the quadratic specification detracts from its usefulness in testing for separability. In fact, separability implies either complete separability or separability with generalized linear aggregators.

Combining symmetric and nonsymmetric separability expands the class of structures that can be modeled by the generalized quadratic. However, completely asymmetric structures for more than two groups cannot be generated. Some symmetry is always implied by nonsymmetric separability. This fact is formalized in the following theorem.

Theorem 8.3 *Suppose that $R_i(X) \neq 0$ $\forall i \in I$. If the generalized quadratic function is recursive or completely recursive in the ordered partition $\langle \hat{I} \rangle$ with more than two elements, then given any triple $\{I^r, I^s, I^t\} \subseteq \hat{I}$, two elements of this triple constitute a symmetrically separable pair.*

Proof. Without loss of generality assume that $t > s > r$ in the order of $\langle \hat{I} \rangle$. By the definition of recursivity and *a fortiori* complete recursivity (chapter 6), I^t is separable from $I^s \cup I^r$ and I^s is separable from I^r. If either I^t or I^s is additively separable, the symmetry of this concept (see the proof of theorem 8.2) implies our result. On the other hand, if I^s is nonadditively separable from I^r, then by theorem 8.1 it is separable from I^t as well. $\|$

Although theorem 8.3 precludes the existence of nontrivial $(m \geqslant 3)$ asymmetric structures, a fairly rich class of (hybrid) structures remains to be modeled. To illustrate the class of functions that can be modeled, consider a ternary partition of I. Suppose I^1 is nonadditively separable from I^2, I^2 is additively separable from I^3, and I^3 is additively separable from I^1. In this case U can be written as

$$U(X) = U^2\big(\overline{U}^1(X^1), X^2\big) + U^3(X^3),$$

where U^2 and U^3 are generalized quadratics and $\overline{U}^1$ is a generalized linear function.

8.3.2 The Translog

As noted in section 8.2, the translog is a special case of the generalized quadratic, obtained by letting $f_i(x_i) = \ln x_i$ and $\psi(z) = \ln z$ in (8.17). Theorem 8.2 indicates that the class of symmetric structures which can be generated by the translog is characterized by a quadratic macro function in which all aggregators are themselves translog functions and those aggregators which enter the second-order (as well as the first-order) term are linear logarithmic (that is, the logarithm of a Cobb-Douglas function).

Corollary 8.2.3 *Assume that $R_i(X) \neq 0$ $\forall i \in I$. If the sets I^r, $r = 1, \ldots, d$ $(0 \leqslant d \leqslant m)$, are additively separable from their complements in I, and the* sets I^r, $r = d+1,\ldots,m$, are *nonadditively separable from their complements in I*, then the translog image can be written as

$$\ln U(X) = \sum_{r=1}^{m} \kappa_r U^r(X^r) + \sum_{s=d+1}^{m} \sum_{t=d+1}^{m} \delta_{st} U^s(X^s) U^t(X^t), \quad (8.24)$$

where

$$U^r(X^r) = \sum_{i \in I^r} \alpha_i \ln x_i + \sum_{j \in I^r} \sum_{k \in I^r} \beta_{jk} \ln x_j \ln x_k, \qquad r = 1,\ldots,d; \quad (8.24a)$$

$$U^r(X^r) = \sum_{i \in I^s} \gamma_i \ln x_i, \qquad s = d+1,\ldots,m; \qquad\qquad (8.24b)$$

$\kappa_r = 1, r = 1,\ldots,d$; *and* κ_r, δ_{rt}, *and* γ_i $(\forall i \in I^r)$, $r,t = d+1,\ldots,m$, *are parameters.*[19]

Proof. Follows the Theorem 8.2. ‖

This structure can be further explicated by considering the two extreme cases where $d=0$ and $d=m$. The resultant structures are described in the following corollaries:

Corollary 8.2.4 *If every element of the partition $\hat{I}$ is additively separable from its complement in I, the translog function is additive in this partition:* [20]

$$\ln U(X) = \sum_{r=1}^{m} U^r(X^r).$$

Thus, if $m>2$, additive separability can only model complete separability. If $m=2$, as is common in translog applications, testing for additive separability is testing for a structure which is separable and independent (see section 4.6).

Corollary 8.2.5 *If every element of the partition $\tilde{I}$ is nonadditively separable from its complement in I, the translog specification can be written as a quadratic in linear-logarithmic aggregators.*

This aspect of the translog specification detracts from its usefulness in testing for separability. In fact, separability of the translog implies either complete separability or homothetic separability (separability with homothetic aggregator functions). That is, the translog cannot model nonhomothetic, nonadditive separability. Combining symmetric and nonsymmetric

---

[19]A special case of this result is stated in Jorgenson and Lau (1975a).
[20]This result can be found in Manser (1974).

separability expands the class of structures that can be modeled by the translog. However, as implied by theorem 8.3, completely asymmetric structures for more than two groups cannot be generated by the translog. Some symmetry is always implied by nonsymmetric separability.

8.3.3 The Generalized Quadratic Mean of Order ρ

The generalized quadratic mean of order ρ is obtained as the special case of (8.17) where $f_i(x_i) = x_i^{\rho/2}$ $\forall i \in I$ and $\psi(z) = z^{1/\rho}$. Thus,

$$\psi(U(X)) = \hat{U}(X) = \left(\sum_{i \in I} \alpha_i x_i^{\rho/2} + \sum_{i \in I} \sum_{j \in I} \beta_{ij} x_i^{\rho/2} x_j^{\rho/2} \right)^{1/\rho}.$$

The structures that can be modeled by the quadratic mean of order ρ are restricted to a class that is analogous to that modeled by the translog.

Corollary 8.2.6 *Assume that $R_i(X) \neq 0$ $\forall i \in I$. If the sets I^r, $r = 1, \ldots, d$ $(0 < d < m)$, are additively separable from their complements in I, and the sets I^r, $r = d+1, \ldots, m$, are nonadditively separable from their complements in I, then the generalized quadratic mean of order ρ can be written as*

$$\hat{U}(X) = \left(\sum_{r=1}^{m} \kappa_r U^r(X^r) + \sum_{s=d+1}^{m} \sum_{t=d+1}^{m} \delta_{st} U^s(X^s) \cdot U^t(X^t) \right)^{1/\rho}, \quad (8.25)$$

where

$$U^r(X^r) = \sum_{i \in I^r} \alpha_i x_i^{\rho/2} + \sum_{i \in I^r} \sum_{j \in I^r} \beta_{ij} x_i^{\rho/2} x_j^{\rho/2}, \qquad r = 1, \ldots, d; \quad (8.25a)$$

$$U^s(X^s) = \sum_{i \in I^s} \gamma_i x_i^{\rho/2}, \qquad s = d+1, \ldots, m; \quad (8.25b)$$

$\kappa_r = 1$, $r = 1, \ldots, d$; *and* $\kappa_r, \gamma_i (i \in I^r)$, *and* δ_{rt} $(r, t = d+1, \ldots, m)$ *are parameters.*

Proof. Follows from Theorem 8.2. ‖

In fact, the generalized quadratic mean of order ρ can be written as a generalized quadratic mean of order ρ in the images of aggregator function; i.e.,

$$\hat{U}(X) = \left(\sum_{r=1}^{m} \kappa_r \hat{U}^r(X^r)^{\rho/2} + \sum_{r=1}^{m} \sum_{s=1}^{m} \hat{\beta}_{rs} \hat{U}^r(X^r)^{\rho/2} \hat{U}^s(X^s)^{\rho/2} \right)^{1/\rho},$$

$$(8.26)$$

where $\kappa_r = 1$, $r = 1, \ldots, d$; $\hat{\beta}_{rs} = 0$ if $r \leqslant d$ or $s \leqslant d$; $\hat{\beta}_{rs} = \delta_{rs}$ if $r > d$ and $s > d$;

$$\hat{U}^r(X^r) = \left(\sum_{i \in I^r} \alpha_i x_i^{\rho/2} + \sum_{i \in I^r} \sum_{j \in I^r} \beta_{ij} x_i^{\rho/2} x_j^{\rho/2} \right)^{1/\rho}, \qquad r = 1, \ldots, d; \quad (8.26a)$$

and

$$\hat{U}^r(X^r) = \left(\sum_{i \in I^r} \gamma_i x_i^{\rho/2} \right)^{2/\rho}, \qquad r = d+1, \ldots, m. \qquad (8.26b)$$

Thus, the aggregator functions for the additively separable sectors are themselves quadratic means of order ρ, and the aggregator functions for the nonadditively separable sectors are CES functions with elasticities of substitution equal to $2/(2 - \rho)$.

The counterparts to corollaries 8.2.1 and 8.2.2 are as follows:

Corollary 8.2.7 *If the generalized mean of order ρ has nonzero partial derivatives and is additively separable in the partition $\hat{I}$, it is a CES function of the images of aggregator functions of the generalized quadratic mean of order ρ [with macro elasticity of substituiton equal to $1/(1 - \rho)$]:*[21]

$$\hat{U}(X) = \left(\sum_{r=1}^{m} \hat{U}^r(X^r)^{\rho} \right)^{1/\rho},$$

where

$$\hat{U}^r(X^r) = \left(\sum_{i \in I^r} \alpha_i x_i^{\rho/2} + \sum_{i \in I^r} \sum_{j \in I^r} \beta_{ij} x_i^{\rho/2} x_j^{\rho/2} \right)^{1/\rho}, \qquad r = 1, \ldots, m.$$

Corollary 8.2.8 *If the generalized quadratic mean of order ρ has nonzero partial derivatives and is nonadditively separable in the partition $\hat{I}$, it is a generalized quadratic mean of order ρ whose arguments are CES aggregator functions (with elasticities of substitution equal to $2/(2 - \rho)$):*

$$\hat{U}(X) = \left(\sum_{r=1}^{m} \kappa_r \hat{U}^r(X^r) + \sum_{r=1}^{m} \sum_{s=1}^{m} \delta_{rs} \hat{U}^r(X^r)^{\rho/2} \hat{U}^s(X^s)^{\rho/2} \right)^{1/\rho},$$

where

$$\hat{U}^r(X^r) = \left(\sum_{i \in I^r} \gamma_i x_i^{\rho/2} \right)^{2/\rho}.$$

[21]Notice that as $\rho \to 0$ this yields $\log \hat{U}(X)$ as a sum of homogeneous translogs.

Of course, analogous results for the generalized Leontief specification are obtained as special cases of corollaries 8.2.6, 8.2.7, and 8.2.8 by letting $\rho=1$ in the representation. In particular, if the first d groups of $\hat{I}$ are additively separable and the last $m-d$ are nonadditively separable from their complements in I, then the utility function has the structure

$$\hat{U}(X)= \sum_{r=1}^{m} \kappa_r \hat{U}^r(X^r)^{1/2}+ \sum_{r=1}^{m} \sum_{s=1}^{m} \hat{\beta}_{rs}\hat{U}^r(X^r)^{1/2}\hat{U}^s(X^s)^{1/2},$$

where $\kappa_r=1$, $r=1,\dots,d$; $\hat{\beta}_{rs}=0$ if $r\leqslant d$ or $s\leqslant d$; $\hat{\beta}_{rs}=\delta_{rs}$ if $r>d$ and $s>d$;

$$\hat{U}^r(X^r)= \sum_{i\in I^r} \alpha_i x_i^{1/2}+ \sum_{i\in I^r} \sum_{j\in I^r} \beta_{ij}x_i^{1/2}x_j^{1/2}, \qquad r=1,\dots,d;$$

and

$$\hat{U}^r(X^r)=\left(\sum_{i\in I^r} \gamma_i x_i^{1/2}\right)^2, \qquad r=d+1,\dots,m.$$

Thus, the macro function is itself a generalized Leontief function, the aggregator functions for additively separable sectors are generalized Leontief functions, and the aggregator functions for nonadditively separable sectors are CES functions (with elasticities of substitution equal to 2). The extreme case where $d=m$ generates a linear function of generalized Leontief aggregates, and if $d=0$ we have a generalized Leontief function of CES aggregators with $\sigma=2$.

Finally, we note that, as is the case with the translog, the generalized quadratic mean of order ρ (and of course, the generalized Leontief form) cannot model many types of nonsymmetric structures with more than two groups; that is, some symmetric separability (I^r separable from I^s implies I^s separable from I^r) is always present in any structured function with more than two groups. The reader can generate the types of structures that can be modeled by the quadratic mean of order ρ by employing the constructive algorithm in the proof of theorem 8.4—in particular, the facts that additive separability is symmetric and implies block additivity and that nonadditive separability implies that $\beta_{ik}=\delta_{rs}\gamma_i\gamma_k$ for all $(i,k)\in I^r\times I^s$.

8.3.4 The Generalized Cobb-Douglas Form

The generalized Cobb-Douglas specification is given by

$$U(X)= \prod_{i\in I} \prod_{j\in I} \left(\tfrac{1}{2}x_i+\tfrac{1}{2}x_j\right)^{\beta_{ij}}, \qquad \beta_{ij}=\beta_{ji} \quad \forall\langle i,j\rangle\in I\times I.$$

Assuming that $\partial U(X)/\partial x_i \neq 0 \; \forall i \in I$, the pair $\{i,j\}$ is separable from k if and only if

$$\frac{\partial}{\partial x_k}\left(\frac{\partial U(X)/\partial x_i}{\partial U(X)/\partial x_j}\right) = \frac{\partial}{\partial x_k}\left(\frac{\partial \ln U(X)/\partial x_i}{\partial \ln U(X)/\partial x_j}\right)$$

$$= \frac{-\dfrac{1}{2}\dfrac{\beta_{ik}}{\left(\frac{1}{2}x_i+\frac{1}{2}x_k\right)^2}\displaystyle\sum_{l\in I}\dfrac{\beta_{jl}}{\left(\frac{1}{2}x_j+\frac{1}{2}x_l\right)}+\dfrac{1}{2}\dfrac{\beta_{jk}}{\left(\frac{1}{2}x_j+\frac{1}{2}x_k\right)^2}\displaystyle\sum_{l\in I}\dfrac{\beta_{il}}{\left(\frac{1}{2}x_i+\frac{1}{2}x_l\right)}}{\left[\displaystyle\sum_{l\in I}\dfrac{\beta_{jl}}{\left(\frac{1}{2}x_j+\frac{1}{2}x_l\right)}\right]^2} = 0.$$

$$(8.27)$$

In contrast to the results obtained for the generalized quadratic, there is only one way that (8.27) can be satisfied.

Theorem 8.4 *Assume that $\partial U(X)/\partial x_i \neq 0 \neq \partial U(X)/\partial x_j$. In the generalized Cobb-Douglas form, the pair $\{i,j\}$ is separable from k if and only if $\beta_{ik} = \beta_{jk} = 0$.*

Proof. Sufficiency is immediate. To prove necessity, first rearrange (8.27) so that

$$\beta_{jk}(x_i+x_k)^2 \sum_{l\in I}\frac{\beta_{il}}{x_i+x_l} = \beta_{ik}(x_j+x_k)^2\sum_{l\in I}\frac{\beta_{jl}}{x_j+x_l}. \qquad (a)$$

Note that (a) implies that β_{ik} and β_{jk} are either both zero or both nonzero. Partially differentiating (a) with respect to x_l, $l \in \bar{I} = I - \{i,j,k\}$, yields

$$\beta_{jk}\beta_{il}\left(\frac{x_i+x_k}{x_i+x_l}\right)^2 = \beta_{ik}\beta_{jl}\left(\frac{x_j+x_k}{x_j+x_l}\right)^2. \qquad (b)$$

For this to hold in any neighborhood of some arbitrary point, we must have

$$\beta_{jk}\beta_{il} = \beta_{ik}\beta_{jl} = 0 \qquad \forall l \in \bar{I}. \qquad (c)$$

To show that $\beta_{ik} = \beta_{jk} = 0$, assume the contrary. Then both β_{ik} and β_{jk} must be nonzero. We will show that this leads to a contradiction. If $\beta_{ik} \neq 0 \neq \beta_{jk}$, (c) implies that $\beta_{il} = \beta_{jl} = 0 \; \forall l \in \bar{I}$. In this case, the logarithm of the generalized Cobb-Douglas can be written as

$$\ln U(X) = \beta_{ii} \ln x_i + 2\beta_{ij} \ln\left(\tfrac{1}{2}x_i + \tfrac{1}{2}x_j\right)$$

$$+ 2\beta_{ik} \ln\left(\tfrac{1}{2}x_i + \tfrac{1}{2}x_k\right) + \beta_{jj} \ln x_j$$

$$+ 2\beta_{jk} \ln\left(\tfrac{1}{2}x_j + \tfrac{1}{2}x_k\right) + \beta_{kk} \ln x_k + \sum_{l \in \bar{I}} \beta_{kl} \ln\left(\tfrac{1}{2}x_k + \tfrac{1}{2}x_l\right)$$

$$+ \sum_{l \in \bar{I}} \sum_{l' \in \bar{I}} \beta_{ll'} \ln\left(\tfrac{1}{2}x + \tfrac{1}{2}x_{l'}\right).$$

Let

$$\bar{U}_i(X) = \frac{\partial \ln U(X)}{\partial x_i} = \frac{\beta_{ii}}{x_i} + \frac{2\beta_{ij}}{x_i + x_j} + \frac{2\beta_{ik}}{x_i + x_k},$$

and similarly for $\bar{U}_j(X)$. Then

$$\frac{\partial}{\partial x_k}\left[\frac{\bar{U}_i(X)}{\bar{U}_j(X)}\right] = \left[\frac{-2\beta_{ik}\bar{U}_j(X)}{(x_i + x_k)^2} + \frac{2\beta_{jk}\bar{U}_i(X)}{(x_j + x_k)^2}\right] \div (\bar{U}_{j'}(X))^2 = 0, \quad \text{(d)}$$

since $\{i,j\}$ is separable from k. Rearranging (d) gives

$$\frac{\bar{U}_i(X)}{\bar{U}_j(X)} = \frac{\beta_{ik}(x_j + x_k)^2}{\beta_{jk}(x_i + x_k)^2}. \qquad \text{(e)}$$

Partially differentiating (e) with respect to x_k and invoking separability yields

$$\frac{\partial}{\partial x_k}\left(\frac{U_i(X)}{U_j(X)}\right)$$

$$= \frac{2\beta_{jk}(x_i + x_k)^2\beta_{ik}(x_j + x_k)}{\beta_{jk}^2(x_i + x_k)^4} - \frac{2\beta_{ik}(x_j + x_k)^2\beta_{jk}(x_i + x_k)}{\beta_{jk}^2(x_i + x_k)^4} = 0. \qquad \text{(f)}$$

This is easily reduced to

$$x_i - x_j = 0,$$

which is an absurdity. ∥

Theorem 8.5 *Assume that $\partial U(X)/\partial x_i \neq 0 \ \forall i \in I$. In the generalized Cobb-Douglas form, if each component of the partition $\hat{I}$ is separable from its complement in I, the image can be written as a Cobb-Douglas function of generalized Cobb-Douglas aggregators:*

$$U(X) = \prod_{r=1}^{m} \left(\prod_{i \in I^r} \prod_{j \in I^r} \left(\tfrac{1}{2}x_i + \tfrac{1}{2}x_j \right)^{\beta_{ij}} \right). \tag{8.28}$$

Proof. Follows immediately from theorem 8.4. ∥

Thus, the generalized Cobb-Douglas form can only model complete separability. Separable structures and nonsymmetric structures cannot be generated by this specification (I^r separable from I^s implies I^s separable from I^r).

8.3.5 The Mean of Order ρ

The mean of order ρ, defined by

$$U(X) = \sum_{i \in I} \sum_{j \in I} \beta_{ij} \left(\tfrac{1}{2}x_i^{\rho} + \tfrac{1}{2}x_j^{\rho} \right)^{1/\rho}, \qquad \beta_{ij} = \beta_{ji} \ \ \forall (i,j) \in I \times I,$$

like the generalized Cobb-Douglas form, can model only additive structures.

Corollary 8.5.1 *Assume that $\partial U(X)/\partial x_i \neq 0 \ \forall i \in I$. If I^r, $r = 1,\ldots,m$, is separable from its complement in the mean of order ρ, then its image can be written as a sum of mean-of-order-ρ aggregators:*

$$U(X) = \sum_{r=1}^{m} \left(\sum_{i \in I^r} \sum_{j \in I^r} \beta_{ij} \left(\tfrac{1}{2}x_i^{\rho} + \tfrac{1}{2}x_j^{\rho} \right)^{1/\rho} \right). \tag{8.29}$$

Proof. Repeating the argument in the proof of theorem 8.4 shows that $\beta_{ik} = 0$ for all (i,k) such that $i \in I^r$ and $k \notin I^r$, $r = 1,\ldots,m$. ∥

8.3.6   Concluding Remarks

The salient conclusion that should be drawn from the separability-inflexibility of the commonly employed flexible functional forms—demonstrated in the preceding theorems and corollaries—is that testing for separability using these forms is really testing for complete separability (or, if $m=2$, the stronger independence condition) or homothetic separability. Neither of these conditions is necessary for the existence of an aggregate commodity or input. Hence, using these flexible forms as exact functions, an apparent rejection of the hypothesis that an aggregate input exists might in fact be a rejection of homotheticity of the aggregator function and of additivity of the macro function. Accordingly, negative tests results should be skeptically received. In support of this skepticism, the reader is referred to the paper by Woodland (1976b), in which many of the negative test results of Berndt and Christensen (1973b, 1974b) are reversed by an ingenious test procedure in which, to a certain extent, the problems raised in this section are circumvented.

9

Indices and Subindices of the Cost of Living and the Standard of Living

This chapter uses the notions of duality and functional structure to discuss the construction of theoretically plausible cost- and standard-of-living indices and their corresponding subindices. In the tradition of early works by Konyus (1924), Frisch (1936), and Wold (1943), we only study those cost-of-living indices which can be derived from an underlying preference ordering. As normative connotations are usually ascribed to cost-of-living indices, the existence of an underlying preference ordering which can rationalize a particular index is a matter of some importance.

There has also been a recent resurgence of interest in "mechanistic" economic indices—indices which do not have the characteristic that prices and quantities are related and which do not necessarily have normative connotations. These studies concentrate instead on the consistency of certain sets of properties of economic indices (see Fisher, 1922; Frisch, 1930, 1936; Swamy, 1965; Eichhorn, 1976; Vartia, 1976; and Eichhorn and Voeller, 1976).

In addition to overall cost-of-living indices, various statistical agencies regularly compute subindices of the cost of living, e.g., the "cost of food" and the "cost of travel". A theoretical rationale for these cost-of-living subindices must be provided if they are to be interpreted in a meaningful manner. We proceed by first defining cost- and standard-of-living indices, using the transformation-function notions of chapter 2. We then use the separability notions of chapters 3 and 4 to construct various types of subindices and discuss their respective interpretations.[1]

---

[1] In addition to the many published works on which we have drawn in writing this chapter (for example, Afriat, 1972; Fisher and Shell, 1972; Samuelson and Swamy, 1974; Diewert 1974b, 1976; Pollak, 1975a), we have also drawn heavily upon unpublished surveys by Pollak (1971a) and Diewert (1973c) to which we had access.

9.1 THE THEORY OF THE COST-OF-LIVING INDEX

In general, a cost-of-living index is the ratio of the costs of realizing a particular level of "real income" (or utility or output) in different situations (e.g., different places or dates). The exposition of this concept is facilitated by exploiting the fact that the cost function can be interpreted as a transformation function in price space. Recall from chapter 2 that the cost function can be expressed as a transformation function derived from the indirect utility function V:

$$C(u,P) = \min\{\lambda \in \Omega_+^1 \mid V(P/\lambda) \geqslant u\}, \qquad (9.1)$$

where $u \in \mathcal{R}(U)$. Let the solution to the problem in (9.1) be represented by the image[2]

$$\overset{*}{\lambda}(u,P).$$

It follows that

$$V(P/\overset{*}{\lambda}(u,P)) = u$$

and

$$C(u, P/\overset{*}{\lambda}(u,P)) = 1 \qquad \forall (u,P) \in \mathcal{R}(U) \times \Omega_+^n.$$

Let t and t' stand for different situations, and let $P(t)$ and $P(t')$ represent the respective price vectors. In figure 9.1 it can be seen that $\overset{*}{\lambda}(u,P(t))$ is the multiplicative factor by which $P(t)$ must be reduced to get to $\bar{P}$ where $V(\bar{P}) = u$; similarly, $1/\overset{*}{\lambda}(u,P(t'))$ is the multiplicative factor by which $P(t')$ must be expanded to get to $\bar{P}$ where $V(\bar{P}) = u$ as well. It seems natural that, given the level of utility u, an index of the cost of living at prices $P(t)$ relative to $\bar{P}$ should be constructed as

$$\frac{C(u,P(t))}{C(u,\bar{P})} = \frac{C(u,P(t))}{C(u,P(t))/\overset{*}{\lambda}(u,P(t))} = \overset{*}{\lambda}(u,P(t)),$$

where the first identity exploits positive linear homogeneity of $C(u,\cdot)$. That is, if a consumer first faced prices $\bar{P}$ and prices rose to $P(t)$, we would have

---

[2]Of course, $C(u,P) = \overset{*}{\lambda}(u,P) \ \forall (u,P) \in \mathcal{R}(U) \times \Omega_+^n$. We use two different symbols to emphasize the fact that C can be interpreted as either a cost function (C) or a distance function ($\overset{*}{\lambda}$).

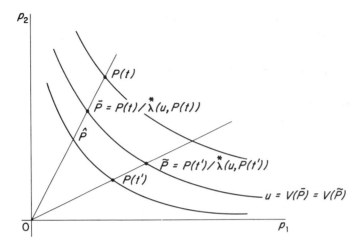

Fig. 9.1

to increase his income by a factor of $\overset{*}{\lambda}(u, P(t))$ in order to make him as well off as before the price change. Similarly, had the consumer faced prices $\tilde{P}$ which then fell to $P(t')$, the consumer's income could be reduced by the factor $\overset{*}{\lambda}(u, P(t'))$ without changing his level of utility. Therefore, the appropriate cost-of-living index in this case is

$$\frac{C(u, P(t'))}{C(u, \tilde{P})} = \frac{C(u, P(t'))}{C(u, P(t'))/\overset{*}{\lambda}(u, P(t'))} = \overset{*}{\lambda}(u, P(t')).$$

This says nothing more than that if all prices rise (fall) by $x\%$, the cost-of-living index should also rise (fall) by $x\%$.

In a somewhat different but equally plausible vein, it makes sense to compare different prices which generate the same level of utility. For example, we would write the index of the cost of living at $\bar{P}$ relative to $\tilde{P}$ as

$$\frac{C(u, \bar{P})}{C(u, \tilde{P})}.$$

But because this cost function is a distance function, and $V(\bar{P}) = V(\tilde{P}) = u$ by construction, both the numerator and the denominator are equal to one. Therefore,

$$\frac{C(u, \bar{P})}{C(u, \tilde{P})} = 1.$$

It is, however, intuitively less clear how to compare different price situations which involve neither proportionality nor the same level of utility. This is accomplished by appealing to one of Irving Fisher's "reasonable" conditions which index numbers should satisfy[3]—the *circularity* condition. In order to describe the circularity property, let the cost-of-living index between t and t' be represented by the function $\Pi: \mathcal{R}(U) \times \Omega_+^{2n} \to \Omega_+^1$, with image $\Pi(u, P(t), P(t'))$. Given three situations t, t', and t'', Π satisfies the *circularity test* if

$$\Pi(u, P(t), P(t'')) = \Pi(u, P(t), P(t')) \cdot \Pi(u, P(t'), P(t'')).$$

For proportional changes, the cost-of-living index clearly satisfies the circularity test. For example, compare $P(t)$, $\bar{P}$, and $\hat{P}$, which all lie on the same ray in figure 9.1:

$$\Pi(u, P(t), \hat{P}) = \frac{C(u, P(t))}{C(u, \hat{P})} = \frac{\overset{*}{\lambda}(u, P(t))}{\overset{*}{\lambda}(u, \hat{P})},$$

$$\Pi(u, P(t), \bar{P}) = \frac{C(u, P(t))}{C(u, \bar{P})} = \overset{*}{\lambda}(u, P(t)),$$

and

$$\Pi(u, \bar{P}, \hat{P}) = \frac{C(u, \bar{P})}{C(u, \hat{P})} = \frac{1}{\overset{*}{\lambda}(u, \hat{P})}.$$

Therefore,

$$\Pi(u, P(t), \hat{P}) = \Pi(u, P(t), \bar{P}) \cdot \Pi(u, \bar{P}, \hat{P}).$$

The indices comparing prices which generate the same level of utility are all equal to one and therefore trivially satisfy the circularity test.

We now construct a general cost-of-living index that satisfies the circularity test for all price combinations. Referring back to figure 9.1, define the cost-of-living index between t and t' by

$$\Pi(u, P(t), P(t')) = \Pi(u, P(t), \bar{P}) \cdot \Pi(u, \bar{P}, \tilde{P}) \cdot \Pi(u, \tilde{P}, P(t'))$$

$$= \overset{*}{\lambda}(u, P(t))(1) \frac{1}{\overset{*}{\lambda}(u, P(t'))}.$$

<hr>

[3]In fact, Fisher proposed five tests which index numbers should satisfy, but this turns out to be unduly demanding (see Swamy, 1965; Eichhorn, 1976).

However, from (9.1) we know that

$$C(u, P(t)) = \overset{*}{\lambda}(u, P(t))$$

and

$$C(u, P(t')) = \overset{*}{\lambda}(u, P(t')).$$

By substitution, this yields

$$\Pi(u, P(t), P(t')) = \frac{C(u, P(t))}{C(u, P(t'))}. \tag{9.2}$$

It is important to remember that this cost-of-living index depends upon the surface which is picked to measure the level of "real income" or utility. In fact, it is clear from the construction that this index is independent of the level of utility if and only if the underlying preference ordering is homothetic. This follows because Π is independent of u if and only if u is multiplicatively separable from P in the cost function. However, by lemma 3.4, this is equivalent to overall homotheticity. One interpretation of this dependence, which is due to Pollak (1971a), is as follows. From an indifference map we pick a particular indifference surface as our basis for comparison. From this base surface we construct a new indifference map by radial expansions and contractions of the base indifference manifold. This new "pseudo" indifference map is of course homothetic. The cost-of-living index Π is independent of the level of "real income" with respect to this pseudo indifference map. Of course, the original map and the pseudo map coincide if preferences are homothetic.

We turn now to the construction of a standard-of-living index.

9.2 A THEORY OF THE STANDARD-OF-LIVING INDEX

Superficially, it might appear natural to let the utility-function image $U(X)$ represent the standard of living. A standard-of-living index, showing the standard of living in situation t relative to situation t', might then be represented by $U(X(t))/U(X(t'))$, where $X(t)$ and $X(t')$ are the consumption bundles in the two situations. However, this index is unappealing because it is not invariant under monotonic transformations of the utility indicator. This cardinality property contrasts with the ordinal measurement of utility underlying the cost-of-living index. There is, however, no reason why a standard-of-living index should require cardinalization of the utility representation. In fact, exploiting the duality theory exposited in chapter 2, we argue in this section that the appropriate standard-of-living index is exactly dual to the cost-of-living index.[4]

Recall that the transformation function F can be expressed as a distance function,

$$F(u,X) = \max_{\lambda} \left\{ \lambda \in \Omega^1_+ \mid U(X/\lambda) \geq u \right\}, \qquad (9.3)$$

or a cost-imputation function,

$$F(u,X) = \min_{P} \left\{ P \cdot X \mid \overset{*}{V}(P) \leq u \wedge P \in \Omega^n \right\}. \qquad (9.4)$$

(Recall from section 2.2 that $\overset{*}{V}$ is the extension of V to the boundary by continuity from below.)

Consider figure 9.2, which is the quantity analogue of figure 9.1. Letting the solution to the problem in (9.3) be given by $\overset{*}{\lambda}(u,X)$, it follows that

$$U\left(X/\overset{*}{\lambda}(u,X)\right) = u$$

and that

$$F\left(u,X/\overset{*}{\lambda}(u,X)\right) = 1 \qquad \forall(u,X) \in \mathcal{R}(U) \times \Omega^n_+.$$

Consider the two bundles $X(t)$ and $X(t')$ in figure 9.1. Clearly $U(X(t)) > U(X(t'))$; hence a standard-of-living index should have a value greater than one when comparing situation t to situation t'. The problem of constructing such an index might be viewed as that of evaluating the pairs of consumption bundles. This problem can in turn be viewed as that of assigning shadow prices to the n goods. But recall that $F(u,X)$ can be interpreted as the evaluation of X at the shadow prices corresponding to the consumption bundle with direction $X/|X|$ that yields utility level u. This construction therefore suggests a method of evaluating consumption bundles in the computation of a standard-of-living index.

We proceed with this construction in a way that is dual to the construction of the cost-of-living index in section 2. First, we compare bundles $X(t)$ and $\overline{X}$ by comparing their shadow values. Let the standard-of-living index be

$$\Gamma : \mathcal{R}(U) \times \Omega^{2n}_+ \rightarrow \Omega^1_+$$

[4]This construction was first proposed by Malmquist (1953).

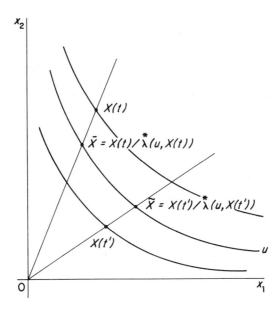

Fig. 9.2

with the image

$$\Gamma\big(u,X(t),\overline{X}\big)=\frac{F\big(u,X(t)\big)}{F\big(u,\overline{X}\big)}=\frac{F\big(u,X(t)\big)}{F\big(u,X(t)\big)/\overset{*}{\lambda}(u,X(t))}=\overset{*}{\lambda}(u,X(t)),$$

where the second identity exploits the positive linear homogeneity of $F(u,\cdot)$. That is, if the consumption of all commodities increases (decreases) by $x\%$, the imputed value must increase (decrease) by $x\%$ as well. Similarly, set the standard-of-living index between $\overline{X}$ and $\tilde{X}$ $[U(\overline{X})=U(\tilde{X})]$ equal to

$$\Gamma(u,\overline{X},\tilde{X})=\frac{F(u,\overline{X})}{F(u,\tilde{X})}=1,$$

as the numerator and denominator are equal to one. Using the circularity test again, we find that the index relating any two consumption bundles is

$$\Gamma\big(u,X(t),X(t')\big)=\frac{F\big(u,X(t)\big)}{F\big(u,X(t')\big)}.\qquad(9.5)$$

Several observations should be made regarding this index. First, the choice of the utility level and hence the shadow prices to use in the evaluation of the consumption bundles are arbitrary. There is, however, no escaping this arbitrariness in the construction of the standard-of-living index, any more than in the construction of a cost-of-living index. It is also interesting to note that, unless the consumption pair lies on a ray, the bundles are evaluated using different shadow-price vectors. A dual phenomenon is embodied in the construction of the cost-of-living index. Evaluating $\Pi(u, P(t), P(t'))$ at utility level u is equivalent to weighting the prices $P(t)$ and $P(t')$ with the optimal consumption bundles on the u-level surface at prices with directions $P(t)/|P(t)|$ and $P(t')/|P(t')|$, respectively.

Note also that the construction of the standard-of-living index does not imply a cardinalization of the utility indicator. The index itself is explicitly cardinal, as is the cost-of-living index. However, neither of the constructions implies any more than a monotone numbering of the indifference surfaces.

However, this statement must be carefully construed. Suppose the standard-of-living index is

$$\Gamma(u, X(t), X(t')) = \frac{F(u, X(t))}{F(u, X(t'))}$$

for some monotone numbering of indifference surfaces. For some other numbering, $v = \Psi(u)$, where Ψ is increasing, the index becomes

$$\hat{\Gamma}(v, X(t), X(t')) = \frac{\hat{F}(v, X(t))}{\hat{F}(v, X(t'))} = \Gamma(u, X(t), X(t')),$$

where $\hat{\Gamma}$ is, of course, the transformation (or indirect cost) function corresponding to the new utility indicator. In other words, the standard-of-living index is constructed by picking a base indifference surface and *not* by picking a base level of utility. Hence, the index is independent of the numbering of indifference surfaces—i.e., invariant with respect to monotone transforms of U.

Finally, note that $\Gamma(u, X(t), X(t'))$, like the cost-of-living index, is independent of the level of utility if and only if the underlying preference ordering is homothetic.

9.3   COST-OF-LIVING SUBINDICES

Practically all indices which are computed are really subindices. That is, important variables are being left out of the computation. For example, intertemporal alternatives, leisure, and environmental effects are seldom accounted for in the construction of cost-of-living indices. This omission can only be rationalized by some theory about the construction of subindices. Moreover, even abstracting from such variables, it is common to compute cost-of-living subindices for categories such as food, etc.

From the analysis of sections 2 and 3, it is clear that the construction of cost-of-living indices must depend crucially upon the construction of sector-specific cost functions (of some kind) which can in turn be used to build the relevant indices. We begin by examining two alternatives put forward by Pollak (1975a), which involve the construction of sector-specific "conditional" and "partial" cost functions. Then, using the notion of implicit separability, we construct sector-specific cost-of-living indices as ratios of sector-specific cost functions which can be aggregated meaningfully into an overall cost function. Then, by imposing direct separability on the preference ordering as well, we get homothetic separability and hence subindices which are independent of the level of "real income" even though the overall cost-of-living index does depend upon the base indifference manifold. Finally, we show that if there exists a cost of living subindex which can be aggregated into an overall cost of living index, then the cost function is an implicit Cobb-Douglas function of the sector-specific cost functions.

9.3.1 Conditional Cost Functions

A sector-specific, conditional cost function for sector r gives the minimum cost of generating a given level of utility, given the amount consumed in all sectors other than r. Hence, in the notation of section 3.1.1, we define the "conditional" cost function for sector r,

$$\check{C}^r : \mathcal{R}(U) \times \Omega_+^{(r)} \times \mathop{\mathsf{X}}_{\substack{s=1 \\ s \neq r}}^{m} \Omega^{(s)} \to \Omega_+^1,$$

by

$$\check{C}^r (u, P^r, X^c) = \min_{X^r} \left\{ P^r \cdot X^r \mid U(X^c, X^r) \geqslant u \wedge X^r \in \Omega^{(r)} \right\}.$$

This conditional cost function has the appropriate properties in u and P^r (increasing in u and PLH, concave, and nondecreasing in P^r), but is difficult to use in the construction of sector-specific cost-of-living indices because of the dependence on X^c. Put differently, there is a different sector-specific cost function, mapping from utility and sector-specific prices, for every vector of consumption quantities outside of the relevant sector. Because of this dependence, the sector-specific cost-of-living subindex,

$$\check{\Pi}^r(u, P^r(t), P^r(t'), X^c) = \frac{\check{C}^r (u, P^r(t), X^c)}{\check{C}^r (u, P^r(t'), X^c)}, \qquad \text{say,}$$

cannot in general be used to construct an overall cost-of-living index. Moreover, these conditional cost functions cannot in general be used to construct an overall cost function. If the nature of this dependence were known, however, it might be easier to interpret this conditional cost-of-living subindex.

Substituting $u = U(X^c, X^r)$ into the above sector-specific cost-of-living subindex reveals that X^c affects the subindex in two different ways. Thus, there are at least two different ways of examining the dependence of $\check{\Pi}^r$ on X^c. One is to examine the conditions under which $\check{\Pi}^r$ is independent of its last argument X^c for a fixed level of utility u; the other is to examine the conditions under which $\check{\Pi}^r$ is independent of X^c taking both of its effects into account. Deferring the former approach until a later subsection, we pursue the latter notion of independence in the following theorem, which is due to Pollak (1975a):

Theorem 9.1   *Suppose that U satisfies $(R-1')^5$ and that C is differentiable. Then the conditional cost-of-living index is independent of X^c,*

$$\check{\Pi}^r(U(X^c, X^r), P^r(t), P^r(t'), X^c) = \tilde{\check{\Pi}}^r(X^r, P^r(t), P^r(t')),$$

if and only if I^r is separable from I^c in the direct utility function U.

Proof.   First note that as strict quasi-concavity and monotonicity of U imply strict monotonicity of U and hence sectoral nonsatiation on $\Omega^{(r)}$, separability and strict separability are equivalent by theorem 3.1.

That direct separability is sufficient is immediate from the definition of $\check{C}^r$; for if I^r is separable from I^c then

$$\{\hat{X}^r \in \Omega^{(r)} U(X^c, \hat{X}^r) \geqslant U(X^c, X^r)\} = \{\hat{X}^r y^r \in \Omega^{(r)} \wedge U^r(\hat{X}^r) \geqslant U^r(X^r)\}.$$

Hence $\check{C}^r$ is independent of X^c and so is $\check{\Pi}^r$.

Next suppose I^r is not separable from I^c but that the conditional cost-of-living index depends only on variables in I^r. That is,

$$\tilde{\check{\Pi}}^r(X^r, P^r(t), P^r(t')) = \frac{\check{C}^r(U(X), P^r(t), X^c)}{\check{C}^r(U(X), P^r(t'), X^c)}. \qquad (a)$$

The left-hand side of (a) does not depend on variables in I^c, hence the right-hand side does not either. By theorem 2 in section 7.1.1 of Aczel (1966) we can write $\check{C}^r$ as

$$\check{C}^r(U(X), P^r(t), X^c) = \alpha(X)\tilde{\check{C}}^r(X^r, P^r(t)), \text{ say.}$$

---

[5] (R_i-1'): Continuity, positive monotonicity, and strict quasi-concavity (see subsection 2.1.1 and footnote 10 in section 5.2).

But, by Hotelling's lemma, this implies that the direction of the (unique) optimal demand vector in $\Omega^{(r)}$ depends only on $(X^r, P^r(t))$. That is

$$\overset{*}{X}{}^r / \|\overset{*}{X}{}^r\| = \tilde{\phi}^r(X^r, P^r(t)), \qquad \text{say.} \tag{b}$$

By the strict quasi-concavity of U, there exists a price vector $\bar{P}^r \in \Omega^{(r)}$ such that

$$X^r / \|X^r\| = \tilde{\phi}^r(X^r, \bar{P}^r). \tag{c}$$

Therefore the normal of the supporting hyperplane at each $X^r \in \Omega^{(r)}$ is independent of X^c, implying that I^r is separable from I^c in U. ‖

9.3.2 Partial Cost Functions

Theorem 9.1 suggests that a natural technique to avoid the dependence of $\check{\Pi}^r$ on commodities in other groups is to assume that the direct utility function is separable in the partition $\hat{I}$; in this case, it will be recalled from chapter 4 (theorem 4.1) that the utility-function image can be written as

$$U(X) = \hat{U}\big(U^1(X^1), \ldots, U^m(X^m)\big).$$

The "partial cost function" for sector r, $\hat{C}^r : \mathcal{R}(U^r) \times \Omega_+^{(r)} \to \Omega_+^1$, is then defined by

$$\hat{C}^r(u^r, P^r) = \min_{X^r} \big\{ P^r \cdot X^r \mid U^r(X^r) \geqslant u^r \wedge X^r \in \Omega^{(r)} \big\}, \qquad r = 1, \ldots, m.$$

This partial cost function is PLH, concave, and nondecreasing in P^r and increasing in u^r. Furthermore, it does not depend upon values of variables in different sectors. Notice also that this partial cost function depends not upon the overall utility level but rather upon the level of "utility" in sector r, u^r.

A cost-of-living subindex for sector r,

$$\frac{\hat{C}^r(u^r, P^r(t))}{\hat{C}^r(u^r, P^r(t'))},$$

can be constructed by knowing P^r at t and t' and by specifying the level of "real income" u^r to be generated by sector r. The chief difficulty with these partial cost functions is that in general they cannot be used to construct an overall cost function. Hence, the sector subindices cannot be used, in general, to construct an aggregate cost-of-living index. In fact, if U satisfies (R-1), each sector is strictly essential (see subsection 3.3.3), and U

and C satisfy sectoral nonsatiation in X and P, respectively,[6] these partial cost functions can be used to construct an overall cost function if and only if the utility function is homothetically separable, in which case the cost-of-living subindex is independent of u^r. This is most easily seen as follows. Constrain u^r by $u^r = u$, $r = 1,\ldots,m$, so that the partial cost functions have the images

$$\hat{C}^r(u, P^r), \qquad r = 1,\ldots,m.$$

These can be aggregated into an overall cost function only if the overall cost function $\hat{C}$ is separable with respect to the partition $\hat{I}$. Sectoral nonsatiation of C implies that C is strictly separable in $\hat{I}$ (theorem 3.1). Finally, the conjunction of strict separability of U (implied by sectoral nonsatiation and separability of U and theorem 3.1) and of C implies, by theorem 4.5, that U is homothetically separable. Thus, in spite of the fact that these cost-of-living subindices have a meaningful interpretation, in general they cannot be used to generate overall cost-of-living indices.

9.3.3 Implicitly Separable Cost Functions

This subsection presents an alternative to the preceding construction of cost-of-living subindices. The approach (which follows Blackorby and Russell, 1977) is grounded in the contention that it is more natural to structure the cost function than to structure the utility function in rationalizing such subindices. This approach is perhaps most easily related to the preceding discussion by reexamining the nature of the dependence of the conditional cost-of-living subindex upon X^c. To do this, we follow up the earlier question which asked under what conditions $\check{\Pi}^r$ is independent of X^c for a fixed level of "real income" u.

This notion is captured in the following theorem.

Theorem 9.2 *Suppose that U satisfies (R-1') and that C is differentiable. Then the conditional cost-of-living index $\check{\Pi}^r$ is independent of X^c for a given level of "real income" u if and only if I^r is separable from I^c in the cost function (or its conjugate, the transformation function).*

Proof. To prove necessity, write

$$\hat{\Pi}^r(u, P^r(t), P^r(t')) = \check{\Pi}^r(u, P^r(t), P^r(t'), X^c) = \frac{\check{C}^r(u, P^r(t), X^c)}{\check{C}^r(u, P^r(t'), X^c)}. \qquad \text{(a)}$$

---

[6]See the paragraph before theorem 3.1 for the definition of sectoral nonsatiation. If either U or C does not satisfy sectoral nonsatiation, it is not known whether the conjunction of separability of C and U implies homothetic separability.

As the left-hand side of (a) does not depend upon X^c given u, neither does the right-hand side. Hence we can rewrite $\check{C}^r$ as

$$\check{C}^r\left(u,P\left(t\right),X^c\right)=C^r\left(u,P^r\right)D\left(u,X^c\right),\qquad\text{say.}\qquad\text{(b)}$$

Applying Hotelling's lemma, we obtain the conditional-demand-function images,

$$x_i=C_i^r\left(u,P^r\right)D\left(u,X^c\right),\qquad\forall i\in I^r.$$

Substituting the optimal vector of demands for X^c, we obtain the constant-output demand functions:

$$\zeta_i\left(u,P\right)=C_i^r\left(u,P^r\right)D\left(u,\zeta^c\left(u,P\right)\right)=C_i^r\left(u,P^r\right)\psi(u,P),\qquad\text{say,}\quad\forall i\in I^r.$$

Thus, ratios of constant-output demands in I^r depend only on (u,P^r); that is,

$$\frac{\zeta_i\left(u,P\right)}{\zeta_j\left(u,P\right)}=\frac{C_i\left(u,P\right)}{C_j\left(u,P\right)}=\frac{C_i^r\left(u,P^r\right)}{C_j^r\left(u,P^r\right)},\qquad\forall(i,j)\in I^r\times I^r,$$

implying that I^r is separable from I^c in C. By theorem 3.6, I^r is separable from I^c in the transformation function F as well.

To prove sufficiency, let I^r be separable from I^c in C and F so that

$$F\left(u,X\right)=\bar{F}\left(u,X^c,F^r\left(u,X^r\right)\right).$$

The conditional cost function is defined by

$$\check{C}^r\left(u,P^r,X^c\right)=\min_{X^r}\left\{P^r{\cdot}X^r|X^r\in\Omega^{(r)}\wedge\bar{F}\left(u,X^c,F^r\left(u,X^r\right)\right)\geqslant1\right\}$$

$$=C^r\left(u,P^r\right)\min\left\{\lambda\in\Omega^1|\bar{F}\left(u,X^c,\lambda\right)\geqslant1\right\}$$

$$=C^r\left(u,P^r\right)D\left(u,X^c\right),\qquad\text{say,}$$

where

$$C^r\left(u,P^r\right)=\frac{1}{\lambda}\min_{X^r}\left\{P^r{\cdot}X^r|X^r\in\Omega^{(r)}\wedge F^r\left(u,X^r\right)\geqslant\lambda\right\}$$

$$=\min_{X^r/\lambda}\left\{P^r{\cdot}\left(X^r/\lambda\right)|\left(X^r/\lambda\right)\in\Omega^{(r)}\wedge F^r\left(u,X^r/\lambda\right)\geqslant1\right\}.$$

Thus,

$$\frac{\check{C}^r\left(u,P^r\left(t\right),X^c\right)}{\check{C}^r\left(u,P^r\left(t'\right),X^c\right)} = \frac{C^r\left(u,P^r\left(t\right)\right)}{C^r\left(u,P^{\mathord{\mskip0mu}r}\left(t'\right)\right)},$$

and the conditional cost-of-living index is independent of X^c.   ‖

In this subsection we pursue the implications of conjugate implicit separability for the construction of subindices, not only because of the independence demonstrated above, but, as importantly, because aggregation is possible with conjugate implicit separability as a maintained hypothesis.

If the transformation function is separable in $\hat{I}$, the cost function has the image (see corollary 4.14)

$$C(u,P)=\hat{C}\left(u,C^1\left(u,P^1\right),\dots,C^m\left(u,P^m\right)\right). \tag{9.6}$$

Hence, the rth-sector cost-of-living subindex can be written as

$$\hat{\Pi}^r(u,P^r\left(t'\right),P^r\left(t\right))=\frac{C^r\left(u,P^r\left(t'\right)\right)}{C^r\left(u,P^r\left(t\right)\right)},\qquad r=1,\dots,m. \tag{9.7}$$

That these indices conform to our common-sense notions of cost-of-living indices follows from the following relationship between the sectoral cost function C^r and the sectoral transformation function F^r (see section 3.5).

$$C^r\left(u,P^r\right)=\min_{X^r}\left\{P^r{\cdot}X^r|X^r\in\Omega^{(r)}\overset{*}{F}{}^r(u,X^r)\geqslant 1\right\},\qquad r=1,\dots,m, \tag{9.8}$$

where $\overset{*}{F}{}^r$ is the extension of F^r to the boundary of $\Omega^{(r)}$ by continuity from above.

Two distinctions between these subindices and those of the preceding two subsections should be noted. First, it is only necessary to specify the overall level of utility in order to construct all of the above subindices, whereas the subindices constructed from partial cost functions require an entire vector of utility levels, one for each sector subindex. This reduced informational requirement might be viewed intuitively as a relaxation of the arbitrariness of the normalization procedure. [Of course, if the subindices are to be calculated at "base period" (or terminal period) utility level(s), then all three of the above constructions (using $\check{C}^r$, $\hat{C}^r$, or C^r) require as data *all* prices and the total expenditure for the construction of *each* subindex.]

More importantly, the sector cost functions in (9.7) can be used to construct the aggregate cost function using (9.6). Consequently, the cost-of-living subindices can be used to construct (indirectly) the overall cost-of-living index.

It is apparent that, in general, the sector-specific cost-of-living indices cannot be used directly to compute the aggregate index. In practice, however, if we know how to construct the subindices of the cost of living, we also know the sector-specific implicit cost functions which can be aggregated to the overall cost function. This in turn is used to construct the aggregate cost-of-living index. This provides an indirect procedure which is theoretically consistent for aggregating cost-of-living subindices into an overall index.

If the stronger assumption of implicit complete separability is posited, a much more direct and perhaps more appealing aggregation procedure is rationalized. If C is completely separable in $\hat{I}$, the image can be written as

$$C(u,P) = \overset{*}{C}\left(u, \sum_{r=1}^{m} C^r(u,P^r)\right). \tag{9.9}$$

In fact, from theorem 4.9, we know that (9.9) can be written as

$$C(u,P) = \left[\sum_{r=1}^{m} C^r(u,P^r)^{\rho(u)}\right]^{1/\rho(u)}, \qquad 0 \neq \rho(u) \leqslant 1, \tag{9.10a}$$

or

$$C(u,P) = \Gamma(u) \prod_{r=1}^{m} C^r(u,P^r)^{\rho^r(u)}, \qquad \rho^r(u) > 0 \quad \forall r, \qquad \sum_{r=1}^{m} \rho^r(u) = 1. \tag{9.10b}$$

If the cost function is an implicit CES cost function as in (9.10a), then the rth subindex can now be written as

$$\hat{\Pi}^r(u, P^r(t'), P^r(t)) = \left[\frac{C^r(u, P^r(t'))}{C^r(u, P^r(t))}\right], \qquad r = 1, \dots, m.$$

The aggregate cost-of-living index, Π, can therefore be bounded from above directly by summing the subindices:

$$\Pi(u, P(t'), P(t)) \leqslant \left[\sum_{r=1}^{m} \hat{\Pi}^r(u, P^r(t'), P^r(t))^{\rho}\right]^{1/\rho}.$$

Of course, the exact aggregate index can be found by reconstructing the overall cost function first, and then forming the aggregate index.

On the other hand, if the cost function is an implicit Cobb-Douglas function, as in (9.10b), the rth subindex can be written as

$$\hat{\Pi}^r(u, P^r(t'), P^r(t)) = \frac{C^r(u, P^r(t'))}{C^r(u, P^r(t))}.$$

In this case, the aggregate cost-of-living index can be calculated, directly from the subindices:

$$\Pi(u, P(t'), P(t)) = \prod_{r=1}^{m} \hat{\Pi}^r(u, P^r(t'), P^r(t))^{\rho^r(u)}.$$

The chief difference between the subindices constructed from partial cost functions and those constructed from implicit cost functions can be summarized as follows. In the former case, one structures the direct utility function and calculates "partial (sector-specific) cost functions" using the specific utility aggregators

$$\hat{C}^r(u^r, P^r) = \min_{X^r} \{ P^r \cdot X^r \,|\, U^r(X^r) \geq u^r \wedge X^r \in \Omega^{(r)} \}, \qquad r = 1, \ldots, m.$$

These partial cost functions, which are used to construct cost-of-living subindices, are difficult to interpret; after all, the cost function itself has no structure. The ethereal nature of the $\hat{C}^r$, $r = 1, \ldots, m$, is simply the other side of the aggregation coin.

The implicit-cost-function approach, on the other hand, entails structuring the cost function directly and using the cost aggregators to construct the cost-of-living subindices. It is possible to define associated "sector utility functions" by inverting

$$F^r(u, X^r) = 1, \qquad r = 1, \ldots, m,$$

to obtain

$$u = \hat{U}^r(X^r), \qquad r = 1, \ldots, m,$$

but this sector utility function is as ethereal as the partial cost function. Separability of the cost (and hence the transformation) function does not imply that the utility function is structured. Thus, the sector utility functions $\hat{U}^r$, $r = 1, \ldots, m$, cannot be aggregated into an overall utility function. It may be, however, that the lack of structure on the utility function is of little consequence for the construction of cost-of-living subindices. It is the cost function that should be structured, because it is cost aggregators—not utility aggregators—that are used in the construction of cost-of-living subindices and their (indirect) aggregation into an aggregate index.

9.3.4   Homothetic Separability and Cost-of-Living Subindices

If strict separability prevails, conjoining the maintained hypotheses of the last two subsections gives homothetic separability by theorem 4.5. In this case, the cost function has the image (see corollary 4.1.7)

$$C(u,P) = \tilde{C}\left(u, \overline{C}^1(P^1), \ldots, \overline{C}^m(P^m)\right). \qquad (9.11)$$

If only (nonstrict) separability holds, separability in $_0\hat{I}$ needs to be assumed directly. The rth-sector cost-of-living subindex can be written as

$$\overline{\Pi}^r\left(P^r(t), P^r(t')\right) = \frac{\overline{C}^r\left(P^r(t)\right)}{\overline{C}^r\left(P^r(t')\right)}, \qquad r = 1, \ldots, m. \qquad (9.12)$$

These cost-of-living subindices are not only independent of the level of real income but are also equal to ratios of price indices. Recall from chapter 5 that the sectoral unit cost function is in fact a price index; i.e.,

$$\overline{C}^r(P^r) = \Pi^r(P^r),$$

and hence

$$\overline{\Pi}^r\left(P^r(t), P^r(t')\right) = \frac{\Pi^r\left(P^r(t)\right)}{\Pi^r\left(P^r(t')\right)}, \qquad r = 1, \ldots, m.$$

For a detailed discussion of these homothetically separable indices and their implementation, see Diewert (1974b, 1976).

9.4   STANDARD-OF-LIVING SUBINDICES

Section 9.2 developed a theory of the standard-of-living index that is dual to the theory of the cost-of-living index. The transformation function, which is dual to the cost function, is central to the construction of the standard-of-of-living index. A theory of standard-of-living subindices (e.g., the "food standard of living") that is dual to the theory of cost-of-living subindices can clearly be developed by structuring the transformation function.

If the transformation function is separable, it has the image (see corollary 4.1.5),

$$F(u,X) = \hat{F}\left(u, F^1(u,X^1),\ldots,F^m(u,X^m)\right). \tag{9.13}$$

Furthermore, by construction, each sector-specific indirect cost function can be defined by the following suboptimization problem:

$$F^r(u,X^r) = \min_{P^r}\left\{ P^r \cdot X^r \mid \overset{*}{C}{}^r(u,P^r) \geqslant 1 \wedge P^r \in \Omega^{(r)} \right\}, \qquad r=1,\ldots,m,$$

where $\overset{*}{C}{}^r$ is the extension of C^r to $\mathcal{R}(U) \times \Omega^{(r)}$ by continuity from below. Hence, given the overall utility level and quantities consumed at t and t' in sector r, the standard-of-living subindex can be constructed as

$$\Gamma^r(u,X^r(t),X^r(t')) = \frac{F^r(u,X^r(t))}{F^r(u,X^r(t'))}, \qquad r=1,\ldots,m. \tag{9.14}$$

Furthermore, these subindices can be used to construct consistent aggregate standard-of-living index using (9.13).

Note that because separability of the transformation function and of the cost function are equivalent, implicit standard-of-living subindices exist if and only if implicit cost-of-living subindices exist. Hence the discussion in subsections 9.3.3–4 is equally applicable here.

Finally note that "conditional" and "partial" standard of living subindices can be constructed by replacing U by V and C by F in subsections 9.3.1–2. In particular the quantity analogues of theorems 9.1 and 9.2 hold.

Corollary 9.1.1 *Suppose that $\overset{*}{V}$, the extension of V to Ω^n by continuity from below, satisfies* (R-2')[7] *and that F is differentiable. Then the conditional standard-of-living subindex, $\check{\Gamma}^r\left(V\left(\dfrac{P^c}{y},\dfrac{P^r}{y}\right), X^r(t), X^r(t'), \dfrac{P^c}{y}\right)$, is independent of $\dfrac{P^c}{y}$ if and only if I^r is separable from I^c in the indirect utility function.*

Proof. Follows by duality from theorem 9.1. ‖

[7](R-2'): continuity, negative monotonicity, and strict quasi-convexity (see subsection 2.2.1 and footnote 10 in section 5.2).

Corollary 9.2.1. *Suppose that* $\overset{*}{V}$ *satisfies* (R-2′) *and that F is differentiable. Then the conditional standard-of-living subindex,* $\hat{\Gamma}^r\!\left(u, X^r(t), X^r(t'), \dfrac{P^c}{y}\right)$, *is independent of* P^c/y *if and only if* I^r *is separable from* I^c *in the cost* (*and transformation*) *function.*

Proof. Follows by duality from theorem 9.2. ‖

9.5 AGGREGABLE SUBINDICES

So far our discussion has centered on the construction and interpretation of plausible subindices. We have also noted that in general these subindices cannot be used to construct the overall index, although in the implicitly separable and homothetically separable cases the sector-specific cost functions can be used to construct the overall cost function. In this section, which follows Primont (1977), we explore the implications of assuming the existence of a subindex which enters into the overall cost (or standard)-of-living index.

Remembering the definition of an overall cost-of-living index in (9.2) we say that a subindex for group r,

$$\Pi^r : \mathcal{R}(U) \times \Omega_+^{(r)} \times \Omega_+^{(r)} \to \Omega_+^1,$$

with image $\Pi^r(u, P^r(t), P^r(t'))$, is *aggregable* if there exists a function,

$$\overline{\Pi} : \mathcal{R}(U) \times \Omega_+^{(c)} \times \Omega_+^{(c)} \times \mathcal{R}(\Pi^r) \to \Omega_+^1,$$

whose image is defined by

$$\Pi(u, P(t), P(t')) = \overline{\Pi}\big(u, P^c(t), P^c(t'), \Pi^r(u, P^r(t), P^r(t'))\big) \quad (9.15)$$

where $\overline{\Pi}$ is increasing in $\Pi^r(u, P^r(t), P^r(t'))$.

Aggregability is certainly another desirable property of a cost-of-living subindex. If a subindex exists, it merely requires the existence of an aggregate index which depends on the subindex. Using (9.2) and (9.15) we know that group r is aggregable if and only if

$$\overline{\Pi}\big(u, P^c(t), P^c(t'), \Pi^r(u, P^r(t), P^r(t'))\big) = \frac{C(u, P(t))}{C(u, P(t'))}. \quad (9.16)$$

The next theorem states that if group r is aggregable then the overall cost function is an implicit Cobb-Douglas function.

Theorem 9.3 *Suppose that C satisfies* $(R\text{-}3P)^8$ *and is twice continuously differentiable and that* I^c *is strictly essential (see subsection 3.3.3) in C. Then a cost-of-living subindex is aggregable as in (9.16) if and only if there exist functions* $\rho^c: \mathcal{R}(U) \to \Omega^1_+$, $\rho^r: \mathcal{R}(U) \to \Omega^1_+$, $\phi: \mathcal{R}(U) \to \Omega^1_+, C^c: \mathcal{R}(U) \times \Omega^{(c)}_+ \to \Omega^1_+$, *and* $C^r: \mathcal{R}(U) \times \Omega^{(r)}_+ \to \Omega^1_+$ *such that the image of the overall cost function can be written as*

$$C(u,P) = \phi(u) C^c (u,P^c)^{\rho^c(u)} C^r (u,P^r)^{\rho^r(u)} \qquad (9.17)$$

where C^c *and* C^r *satisfy* $(R\text{-}3P)$ *and*

$$\rho^c(u) + \rho^r(u) = 1.$$

Proof. Sufficiency is immediate. To prove necessity, let $\overset{*}{I} = \{I^c(t), I^r(t), I^c(t'), I^r(t')\}$ be a quaternate partition of $I \times I$. Using (9.15) we see that $A = I^r(t) \cup I^r(t')$ is strictly separable from its complement in $I \times I$. On the other hand (9.16) implies that $B = I^c(t') \cup I^r(t')$ is strictly independent of its complement in $I \times I$. Since A and B overlap, theorem 4.16 implies that every element of $\overset{*}{I}$ is strictly independent of its complement in $I \times I$. Hence there exist functions $\Pi^c_t, \Pi^r_t, \Pi^c_{t'}$, and $\Pi^r_{t'}$, such that

$$\Pi^c_t(u,P^c(t)) \Pi^r_t(u,P^r(t)) \Pi^c_{t'}(u,P^c(t')) \Pi^r_{t'}(u,P^r(t')) = \frac{C(u,P(t))}{C(u,P(t'))}.$$

$$(9.17)$$

Rearranging (9.17) yields

$$\frac{\Pi^c_t(u,P^c(t)) \Pi^r_t(u,P^r(t))}{C(u,P(t))} = \frac{\Pi^c_{t'}(u,P^c(t'))^{-1} \Pi^r_{t'}(u,P^r(t'))^{-1}}{C(u,P(t'))}. \qquad (9.18)$$

As the left side depends on $P(t)$ and u while the right side depends on $P(t')$ and u, each must be equal to some function of u. Hence

$$C(u,P^c(t),P^r(t)) = \phi(u) \Pi^c_t(u,P^c(t)) \Pi^r_t(u,P^r(t)), \qquad (9.19)$$

and

$$C(u,P^c(t'),P^r(t')) = \phi(u) \Pi^c_{t'}(u,P^c(t'))^{-1} \Pi^r_{t'}(u,P^r(t'))^{-1}. \qquad (9.20)$$

---

^{8}(R-3P): continuity, positive monotonicity, positive linear homogeneity, and concavity in P.

When $t = t'$, (9.19) and (9.20) are identical; hence, without loss of generality, we can write

$$\Pi_t^c(u, P^c) = \Pi_{t'}^c(u, P^c)^{-1}$$

and

$$\Pi_t^r(u, P^r) = \Pi_{t'}^r(u, P^r)^{-1}.$$

Now define functions $\bar{C}^c = \Pi_t^c$ and $\bar{C}^r = \Pi_t^r$ such that (9.19) (or (9.20)) becomes (suppressing t)

$$C(u, P) = \phi(u)\bar{C}^c(u, P^c)\bar{C}^r(u, P^r). \qquad (9.21)$$

Since C is PLH in P, Euler's theorem implies that

$$\bar{C}^c(u, P^c)\nabla_r\bar{C}^r(u, P^r) \cdot P^r + \bar{C}^r(u, P^r)\nabla_c\bar{C}^c(u, P^c) \cdot P^c =$$

$$\bar{C}^c(u, P^c)\bar{C}^r(u, P^r), \qquad (9.22)$$

where $\nabla_r\bar{C}^r$ and $\nabla_c\bar{C}^c$ are the vectors of partial derivatives of $\bar{C}^r$ and $\bar{C}^c$ with respect to P^r and P^c, respectively. Dividing (9.22) by the right-hand side and rearranging yields

$$\frac{\nabla_r\bar{C}^r(u, P^r) \cdot P^r}{\bar{C}^r(u, P^r)} = 1 - \frac{\nabla_c\bar{C}^c(u, P^c) \cdot P^c}{\bar{C}^c(u, P^c)}. \qquad (9.23)$$

Since the right-hand side of (9.23) is independent of P^r, the left-hand side can depend only on u. Let

$$\rho^r(u) = \frac{\nabla_r\bar{C}^r(u, P^r) \cdot P^r}{\bar{C}^r(u, P^r)}$$

or

$$\nabla_r\bar{C}^r(u, P^r) \cdot P^r = \rho^r(u)\bar{C}^r(u, P^r), \qquad (9.24)$$

which by Euler's theorem implies that $\bar{C}^r$ is homogeneous of degree $\rho^r(u)$ in P^r. A similar argument establishes that $\bar{C}^c$ is homogeneous of degree $\rho^c(u)$ in P^c. Moreover, positive linear homogeneity of C in P implies that

$$\rho^c(u) + \rho^r(u) = 1.$$

Define

$$C^r(u, P^r) = \bar{C}^r(u, P^r)^{1/\rho^r(u)} \qquad (9.25)$$

and

$$C^c(u, P^c) = \bar{C}^c(u, P^c)^{1/\rho^c(u)}. \qquad (9.26)$$

Substituting (9.25) and (9.26) into (9.21) yields

$$C(u, P) = \phi(u) C^c(u, P^c)^{\rho^c(u)} C^r(u, P^r)^{\rho^r(u)}. \qquad (9.27)$$

Continuity, concavity, and monotonicity are immediate properties of the aggregators in the representation (9.27). ‖

Nothing in the preceding argument depended on the existence of only one aggregable subindex. We can therefore generalize theorem 9.3 as follows.

Corollary 9.3.1 *Suppose that C satisfies* (R-3P) *and is twice continuously differentiable and that each sector in $\hat{I}$ is strictly essential in C. Then there exist m aggregable cost-of-living subindices if and only if there exist functions, $\rho^r: \mathfrak{R}(U) \to \Omega^1_+, r = 1,\ldots,m, \phi: \mathfrak{R}(U) \to \Omega^1_+$, and $C^r: \mathfrak{R}(U) \times \Omega^{(r)}_+ \to \Omega^1_+, r = 1,\ldots,m$, such that the image of the cost function can be written as*

$$C(u, P) = \phi(u) \prod_{r=1}^{m} C^r(u, P^r)^{\rho^r(u)}, \qquad (9.28)$$

where

$$\sum_{r=1}^{m} \rho^r(u) = 1.$$

and C^r satisfies (R-3P).

Proof. By repeated application of theorem 9.3. ‖

Of course the duality between cost and transformation functions is such that an analogous result holds for standard-of-living subindices.

Corollary 9.3.2 *Suppose that F satisfies* (R-4X)[9] *and is twice continuously differentiable and that each sector in $\hat{I}$ is strictly essential in F. Then there exist m aggregable standard-of-living subindices if and only if there exist functions $\rho^r: \mathfrak{R}(U) \to \Omega^1_+, r = 1,\ldots,m, \psi: \mathfrak{R}(U) \to \Omega^1$, and $F^r: \mathfrak{R}(U) \times \Omega^{(r)}_+ \to \Omega^1_+, r = 1,\ldots,m$ such that the image of the transformation function can be Ω^1_+*

---

[9](R-4X): continuity, positive monotonicity, positive linearity homogeneity in X (see subsection 3.3.3.).

written as

$$F(u,X) = \psi(u) \prod_{r=1}^{m} F^r(u, X^r)^{\rho^r(u)},$$

where

$$\sum_{r=1}^{m} \rho^r(u) = 1$$

and each F^r satisfies $(R\text{-}4X)$.

Proof.   As in corollary 9.3.1.   ‖

Lastly we note that there exist aggregable cost-of-living subindices if and only if there exist aggregable standard-of-living indices.

Theorem 9.4   *Suppose that C and F satisfy $(R\text{-}3P)$ and $(R\text{-}4X)$, respectively, are twice continuously differentiable and that I^c is strictly essential in C and F. Then there exist aggregable cost-of-living subindices if and only if there exist corresponding aggregable standard-of-living subindices.*

Proof.   Suppose there exists an aggregable cost-of-living subindex for group r. Then from theorem 9.3

$$C(u, P) = \phi(u) C^c(u, P^c)^{\rho^c(u)} C^r(u, P^r)^{\rho^r(u)}.$$

The transformation function is derived from C by

$$F(u, X) = \min_{X} \left\{ P \cdot X \mid X \in \Omega^n \wedge \overset{*}{C}(u, P) \geqslant 1 \right\}$$

$$= \min_{X} \left\{ P \cdot X \mid X \in \Omega^n \wedge \phi(u) \overset{*}{C}{}^c(u, P^c) \rho^c(u) \overset{*}{C}{}^r(u, P^r) \rho^r(u) \geqslant 1 \right\}$$

$$= \min_{\lambda_c, \lambda_r} \left\{ \min_{X^c} \left\{ P^c \cdot X^c \mid X^c \in \Omega^{(c)} \wedge \overset{*}{C}{}^c(u, P^c) \geqslant \lambda_c \right\} \right.$$

$$+ \min_{X^r} \left\{ P^r \cdot X^r \mid X^r \in \Omega^{(r)} \wedge \overset{*}{C}{}^r(u, P^r) \geqslant \lambda_r \right\}$$

$$\left. \mid (\lambda_c, \lambda_r) \in \Omega^2_+ \wedge \phi(u) \lambda_c^{\rho^c(u)} \lambda_r^{\rho^r(u)} \geqslant 1 \right\}$$

$$= \min_{\lambda_c, \lambda_r} \left\{ \lambda_c F^c(u, X^c) + \lambda_r F^r(u, X^r) \right.$$

$$\left. \mid (\lambda_c, \lambda_r) \in \Omega^2_+ \wedge \phi(u) \lambda_c^{\rho^c(u)} \lambda_r^{\rho^r(u)} \geqslant 1 \right\},$$

where

$$F^t(u, X^t) = \min_{X^t} \left\{ P^t \cdot X^t \mid X^t \in \Omega^{(t)} \wedge \overset{*}{C}{}^t(u, P^t) \geqslant 1 \right\}, \qquad t = c, r.$$

As $\rho^r(u) > 0$ and C^r is PLH for each r, the constraints in these problems are equalities at the optimum; hence, the method of Lagrange can be used to obtain

$$F(u, X) = \phi(u)^{-1} \rho^c(u)^{-\rho^c(u)} \rho^r(u)^{-\rho^r(u)} F^c(u, X^c)^{\rho^c(u)} F^r(u, X^r)^{\rho^r(u)},$$

$$(9.29)$$

which completes the proof.   ‖

10

Intertemporal Consistency and Intergenerational Conflict

10.1 NAIVE PLANNING AND INTERTEMPORAL CONSISTENCY

This chapter is an application of functional structure to a class of intertemporal optimization problems. More specifically, we consider a society's (or individual's) specification of a plan which dictates its consumption behavior from the present to the end of the planning period. The intertemporal society which we consider is ahistorial; that is, preferences are only defined over the consumption possibilities of present and future generations.[1] The problem—first posed by Samuelson (1937: p. 160)—is one of intergenerational conflict and was summarized by Strotz (1955: p. 165) as follows:

> An individual is imagined to choose a plan of consumption for a future period of time so as to maximize the utility of the plan as evaluated at the present moment. His choice is, of course, subject to a budget constraint. Our problem arises when we ask: If he is free to reconsider his plan at later dates, will he abide by it or disobey it—*even though his original expectations of future desires and means of consumption are verified?*

The answer which was provided by Strotz, and which has since been verified by others under more general conditions, is negative. Among the many unpleasant features of inconsistent planning is that if an individual or a society behaves myopically by continually executing the present portion of the plan, then the behavior, *ex post*, makes no sense from any point of view. Therefore, Strotz proceeded to suggest various strategies which could be adopted to overcome this intertemporal inconsistency. Later, these strategies were correctly characterized by Pollak (1968).

[1]For an elegant analysis without this restriction the reader is referred to Hammond (1973).

341

This chapter will follow the more general characterization of this problem which was presented in Blackorby, Nissen, Primont, and Russell (1973). (Also see Heal, 1973, ch. 10.) We consider various types of intertemporal societies and examine the conditions under which the implied behavior is consistent. For so-called "naive" societies we show that intertemporal optimization is consistent only if intertemporal preferences are so structured that the future is separable from the present—i.e., completely recursive (in the language of chapter 6). We then consider the "sophisticated solution" which has been considered as a planning strategy when the intertemporal preference ordering is not completely recursive.

10.1.1   The Intertemporal Society

The intertemporal society with which we are concerned survives m periods. Each period is associated with precisely one generation which makes and executes the plan for that period. This does not preclude this particular generation from existing before and after the period in question; however, each generation makes and executes but one plan. In addition, each generation is assumed to care about the consumption of future generations. Notice that if any particular generation cares not at all about the future, there is no planning problem, as that generation will simply consume everything, leaving nothing for its heirs. Hence, we rule out malevolence as well as indifference toward future generations. More specifically, we consider an intertemporal society to be a collection of m sequential generations, each having preferences which are defined over its own consumption and the consumption of all of its heirs. The preferences of the rth generation are represented by a utility function, $U^r: {}_r\Omega \to \mathbf{R}$, whose image is written

$$U^r(X^r, \ldots, X^m) = U^r({}_rX).$$

The discussion of intertemporal consistency below requires that each U^r satisfy (R-1').[2]

We now interpret the vector $X^r \in \Omega^{(r)}$ as the consumption of generation r, and a consumption plan or program for society is ${}_1X = (X^1, \ldots, X^m) \in \Omega^n$. The rth generation is only concerned with the rth continuation of a particular plan, ${}_rX = (X^r, \ldots, X^m) \in {}_r\Omega$. The prices associated with a particular plan, ${}_1P = (P^1, \ldots, P^m)$, are "forward" prices, i.e., cross-temporal exchange ratios in terms of the first-period numeraire. The wealth available

---

[2](R-1'): continuity, monotonicity, and strict quasi-concavity. Note also that, given (R-1'), separability and strict separability are equivalent. (See section 5.2.)

for generation r and its successors is denoted z_r, and $z_1 = y$ is the initial wealth. One additional bit of notation is necessary because different generations may make independent choices of the same alternative. We let the tth continuation of a program which was chosen by generation s, $s \leqslant t$, be denoted by $_t \overset{*}{X}_{(s)} = (\overset{*}{X}^t_{(s)}, \ldots, \overset{*}{X}^m_{(s)})$. For example, $\overset{*}{X}^m_{(s)}$ is the consumption bundle which generation s plans for generation m. In general, the subscript in parentheses refers to the generation which made the plan, while the superscript or presubscript refer to the period or periods for which the plan was made.

Each generation is presumed to maximize its utility subject to an inherited wealth constraint. We assume that this wealth constraint is sufficient information about the availability of commodities to be supplied at any point in time. This could be rationalized in more detail by assuming a linear intertemporal production technology and known intertemporal resource constraints. We focus instead upon the planning portion of this problem. We are in particular concerned with the ways in which an intertemporal society can avoid so-called naive behavior. We therefore need a precise notion of naive planning. A *naive plan* is formed by first allowing each generation, $r = 1, \ldots, m$, to solve

$$\max_{_rX} U^r(_rX) \qquad \text{s.t.} \qquad _rP \cdot _rX \leqslant z_r,$$

to obtain

$$_r \overset{*}{X}_{(r)} = {_r\phi_{(r)}}(z_r, {_rP}), \qquad r = 1, \ldots, m.$$

Each generation behaves myopically (naively) by executing that portion of the plan over which it has control—the current planned consumption $\overset{*}{X}^r_{(r)}$, and then bequeaths z_{r+1} to its heirs, where

$$z_{r+1} = z_r - P^r \cdot \overset{*}{X}^r_{(r)}, \qquad r = 1, \ldots, m-1.$$

Hence a naive plan is $^n\overset{*}{X} = (\overset{*}{X}^1_{(1)}, \overset{*}{X}^2_{(2)}, \ldots, \overset{*}{X}^m_{(m)})$, say, which by construction satisfies the wealth constraint. Notice that, in general, no generation (other than the mth) will have planned to follow a path such as $^n_r\overset{*}{X} = (\overset{*}{X}^r_{(r)}, \ldots, \overset{*}{X}^m_{(m)})$. In such a case, the path which the society actually follows does not make sense from the point of view of any generation, except the last one. In this sense, a naive plan does not appear to enjoy any advantage over not planning at all. We are therefore primarily interested in the conditions under which an intertemporal society will behave consistently.

Intertemporal consistency is the requirement that each generation behave in accordance with the plans of its predecessors; that is, in our notation,

$$_r \overset{*}{X}_{(1)} = {}_r \overset{*}{X}_{(r)}, \qquad r = 1, \ldots, m. \tag{10.1}$$

10.1.2 Necessary and Sufficient Conditions for Intertemporal Consistency

In what follows we describe several different intertemporal societies and establish necessary and sufficient conditions for their intertemporal consistency. Before proceeding, we introduce another bit of notation. A pair of utility functions, U and $\hat{U}$, which are defined on the same domain are *equivalent*, $U \sim \hat{U}$, if they induce the same preference ordering on that domain.

Society I (Intertemporal Paternalism)[3]   In this society preferences are either inherited or imposed. Hence the preferences of generation r are determined by generation $r-1$, $r = 2, \ldots, m$.

Theorem 10.1   *Assume that each $U^r, r = 1, \ldots, m$, satisfies (R-1'). Society I is intertemporally consistent if and only if the preference-inheritance mechanism entails that*

$$U^r(\cdot) \sim U^{r-1}\left(\overset{*}{X}{}^{r-1}_{(r-1)}, \cdot \right), \qquad r = 2, \ldots, m. \tag{10.2}$$

Proof.   We first show that (10.2) implies consistency. Noting that (10.2) implies

$$U^r\left(\overset{*}{X}{}^r_{(r)}, \cdot \right) \sim U^{r-1}\left(\overset{*}{X}{}^{r-1}_{(r-1)}, \overset{*}{X}{}^r_{(r)}, \cdot \right), \qquad r = 2, \ldots, m$$

(i.e., the conditional preorderings on $_{r+1}\Omega$ are equivalent), a simple recursive argument yields

$$U^r(\cdot) \sim U^1\left(\overset{*}{X}{}^1_{(1)}, \ldots, \overset{*}{X}{}^{r-1}_{(r-1)}, \cdot \right), \qquad r = 2, \ldots, m. \tag{a}$$

In addition, the condition (10.2) implies that, under an appropriate normal-

---

[3]The names of these societies have been borrowed from Archibald and Donaldson (1976), who use these concepts in considering atemporal general equilibrium. In writing this chapter we have benefited from discussions with them.

ization,

$$\max_{,X} \left\{ U^r(,X) \middle|\, _rX \in {}_r\Omega \land {}_rP \cdot {}_rX \leqslant z_r \right\}$$

$$= \max_{,X} \left\{ U^{r-1} \left(\overset{*}{X}{}^{r-1}_{(r-1)}, {}_rX \right) \middle|\, _rX \in {}_r\Omega \land {}_rP \cdot {}_rX \leqslant z_r \right\};$$

hence

$$_r\overset{*}{X}_{(r)} = {}_r\overset{*}{X}_{(r-1)}, \qquad r = 1, \ldots, m. \tag{b}$$

This, by substitution, implies consistency; i.e.,

$$_r\overset{*}{X}_{(r)} = {}_r\overset{*}{X}_{(1)}, \qquad r = 1, \ldots, m. \tag{c}$$

Given consistency (c), we find that (c) implies (b) by recursion. From the regularity properties (R-1′), we know that every bundle $_rX \in {}_r\Omega$ is optimal at some price-wealth configuration. This implies (10.2). ‖

Note that intertemporal paternalism is really equivalent to allowing the first generation to impose its preferences upon all heirs. Plans which achieve consistency in this fashion are what Strotz (1955) calls a "precommitment path" and Pollak (1968) calls a "commitment optimum" path. Preference imposition is merely one way of following such paths. In practice social customs may succeed in generating paternalistic societies in a variety of ways. Education is, of course, the most obvious way of forcing one's heirs to see the world in the same way as their ancestors. The custom of keeping the capital intact is another preference-inheritance mechanism insofar as the ownership of capital also molds one's preferences.

Society II (Intertemporal Independence) In this society each generation has preferences over present and future consumption without constraining or being constrained by the preferences of its ancestors or its heirs.

The next theorem is a statement of the conditions under which intertemporal independence is compatible with intertemporal consistency. For society II a sufficient condition for consistency is rather immediate. Consider the collection of m utility functions $U^{[r]}$, $r = 1, \ldots, m$, defined by

$$U^1(_1X) = U^{[1]}(X^1, u^{[2]}), \tag{10.3}$$

$$u^{[r]} = U^r(,X) = U^{[r]}(X^r, u^{[r+1]}), \qquad r = 2, \ldots, m-1,$$

and

$$u^{[m]} = U^m(X^m) = U^{[m]}(X^m),$$

where each $U^r, r = 1, \ldots, m-1$, is increasing in $u^{[r+1]}$. Note that each $U^{[r]}$ is completely strictly recursive with aggregator functions that are identical to the utility functions of future generations. Thus for $r < s$ the conditional preference ordering of individual r over the subspace $_s\Omega$ is both independent of sectors $I^r, \ldots, I^{s-1}$ (complete strict recursivity) and identical to the preference ordering of individual s over $_s\Omega$. Hence we call (10.3) a *recursively compatible* system of intertemporal utility functions.

The result of theorem 6.11 immediately implies that maximizing each $U^{[r]}(X^r, u^{[r+1]})$ separately subject to a budget constraint $_rP\cdot_rX \leqslant \overset{*}{z}_r$, where $\overset{*}{z}_r$ is optimal, is equivalent to the straightforward constrained maximization of $U^{[1]}(X^1, u^{[2]})$. Therefore, recursive compatibility is sufficient for intertemporal consistency in society II.

However, proof that recursive compatibility is also necessary for consistency is more complicated. Suppose we have a system of intertemporal demand functions,

$$\phi^{[s]}_{(r)} : {}_r\Omega_+ \times \Omega^1_+ \to \Omega^{(s)}, \qquad r = 1, \ldots, m, \quad s = r, \ldots, m, \qquad (10.4a)$$

which have images

$$\overset{*}{X}{}^s_{(r)} = \phi^{[s]}_{(r)}({}_rP, z_r), \qquad r = 1, \ldots, m, \quad s = r, \ldots, m. \qquad (10.4b)$$

Further, suppose that this system exhibits intertemporal consistency. In this case (10.4) can be collapsed to a much simpler system:

$$\phi^{[r]} : {}_r\Omega_+ \times \Omega^1_+ \to \Omega^{(r)}, \qquad r = 1, \ldots, m, \qquad (10.5a)$$

which have images

$$\overset{*}{X}{}^r = \phi^{[r]}({}_rP, z_r), \qquad r = 1, \ldots, m. \qquad (10.5b)$$

We shall show that intertemporal consistency and hence (10.5) imply the existence of the utility functions in (10.3) which are recursively compatible. But there are two separate issues involved. The first is the existence of a continuous, well-behaved utility function which, when maximized subject to a budget constraint, generates the demand functions in (10.5). The second issue is the structure, if any, of the utility function we find.

The first issue has received considerable attention in the literature.[4] We shall exploit a theorem by Stigum (1973: theorem 1). In that theorem Stigum uses the following Lipschitz condition:

(L)   There exists a positive finite constant K such that, if $\bar{P} > 0$, if $\hat{P} > 0$ and if $P(t) = \bar{P} + t(\hat{P} - \bar{P})$, then for all $t \in [0,1]$ and all $y \geqslant 0$, $y_0 \geqslant 0$,

$$\|\phi(P(t),y) - \phi(P(t),y_0)\| \leqslant K|y - y_0|,$$

where K is independent of t, and ϕ is the demand function.

In addition, the demand function ϕ is assumed to be "well behaved". Call this assumption W:

(W)

(a) ϕ is well defined, single-valued, and continuous on $\Omega_+^n \times \Omega_o^1$. Moreover, for any infinite sequence of price vectors $\{P^{(\nu)} \in \Omega_+^n, \nu = 1,2,\ldots\}$ which has a limit $P^{(0)}$ on the boundary of Ω^n, we have $\limsup_{\nu \to \infty} \|\phi(P^{(\nu)},y)\| = \infty$ for all $y > 0$.

(b) All income is spent; i.e., $P \cdot \phi(P,y) = y$.

(c) For every commodity bundle $X \in \Omega^n$, there exist a price vector and a level of income $(P,y) \in \Omega_+^n \times \Omega_o^1$ such that $X = \phi(P,y)$ is purchased. Moreover, if $X \in \Omega_+^n$, then P/y is unique.

(d) If X and $\hat{X}$ belong to Ω^n, $X \notin \Omega_+^n$, $X = \phi(P,y)$, and $P \cdot X > P \cdot \hat{X}$, then there exists a point $\bar{X} \in \Omega^n$ such that $\bar{X} \leqslant X$, $\bar{X} \neq X$, $\bar{X} = \phi(\bar{P},\bar{y})$, and $\bar{P} \cdot \bar{X} > \bar{P} \cdot \hat{X}$.

(e) The demand function satisfies the strong axiom of revealed preference (Houthakker, 1950).

Stigum proved that if the demand function, $\phi : \Omega_+^n \times \Omega_o^1 \to \Omega^n$, satisfies (L) and (W), then the consumer acts as if he were maximizing a continuous, increasing, strictly quasi-concave function which has differentiable level sets in Ω_+^n.

Theorem 10.2   *Suppose the demand functions*

$$\overset{*}{X}{}_{(r)}^r = \phi_{(r)}^{[r]}(_r P, z_r), \qquad r = 1,\ldots,m, \tag{10.6}$$

of Society II satisfy (L) and (W).

(a) (Stigum, 1973). Then there exists a continuous, increasing, strictly quasi-concave utility function U with differentiable level sets on Ω_+^n such that

---

[4] Rather than give a long list of references, we refer the reader to Chipman, Hurwicz, Richter, and Sonnenschein (1971). A more recent treatment can be found in Newman and Unger (1977).

for all $(P,y) \in \Omega^n_+ \times \Omega^1_0$

$$U(\phi(P,y)) = \max\{ U(X) | X \in \Omega^n P \cdot X \leqslant y \}$$

(b) *Suppose further that the conditional indirect utility functions* $H^{[r]}, r = 2,\ldots,m$, *derived from* U *by* (6.19), *and the income-allocation functions,* $\theta^{[r]}, r = 2,\ldots,m$, *defined by* (6.20), *are differentiable and positive valued. Then the demand functions are intertemporally consistent if and only if the underlying preferences represented by* U *are recursively compatible.*

Proof. (a) See Stigum (1973). (b) The utility function U which generates (10.6) satifies $(R-1')$ by the Stigum theorem. Under the additional maintained hypotheses in (b), theorem 6.11 states that the demand functions have the form (10.6) if and only if U is completely recursive. ‖

Theorem 10.2 says that if society II follows a consistent plan, then in fact it acts as if it were maximizing a single intertemporal social welfare function which has a completely recursive structure.

This leads us to consider a third naive society.

Society III (Intertemporal Noninterference)   In this society each generation adopts the preferences of all succeeding generations as its own. This means that the preferences of generation r can be represented by a utility function whose image is

$$u^{(r)} = U^r(,X) = U^{(r)}(X^r, u^{(r+1)},\ldots,u^{(m)}), \qquad r = 1,\ldots,m-1,$$

$$u^{(m)} = U^m(X^m) = U^{(m)}(X^m).$$

Theorem 10.3   *Suppose that the demand functions of Society* III *satisfy* (L) *and* (W) *and that the regularity conditions of theorem* 10.2(b) *are satisfied. Then the demand functions are intertemporally consistent if and only if the underlying preferences are recursively compatible.*

Proof.   This follows from theorem 10.2. ‖

Consistent intertemporal noninterference has several nice features. First of all, preferences over any continuation of programs must be independent of viewpoint. Hence, the tradeoff between the consumptions of any two generations is independent of their relative time distance; that is, their relative importance does not depend upon whether they are immediate heirs or are in the distant future. A second feature of consistent intertemporal noninterference is that it embodies a nice "responsibility inheritance" mechanism. In constructing the representation $U^{[r]}$, generation r accounts for all subsequent generations by "marking up" the effect of $U^{[r+1]}$ in its evaluation. Having accomplished this, the detailed planning of future consumption, $_{r+1}X$, can be left safely in the care of future generations. A third interesting feature of consistent intertemporal noninterference relates to more general measurement issues in the following way. Generation r is capable of cardinally comparing any two future generations. If generation r picks some numbering scheme for its indifference map, then by virtue of this "responsibility inheritance" mechanism it is also labeling the indifference maps of all future generations. Of course, generation r is free to choose any increasing sequence of numbers for its indifference map, but having done so it can (and must) compare the "utils" of future generations. In one sense at least, it is because of this latter fact that the problem of intergenerational conflict admits of a solution at all.

Intertemporal noninterference may appear to be too strong. It is easy to imagine one generation not wanting to interfere with the preferences of some succeeding generation, say r, over generation r's consumption but still not wanting to accept generation r's evaluation of its heirs. This suggests the formulation of an intertemporal version of the "nonpaternalistic society" of Archibald and Donaldson (1976):

Society IV (Intertemporal Nonpaternalism)   In this society each generation r accepts the ordering of each future generation—say s, $s > r$—over that future generation's consumption X^s, as its own ordering on the subspace $\Omega^{(s)}$.

Of course, the rth generation in this society has a consistent preference ordering over $_r\Omega$ only if I^s is separable from $_{s+1}I$ in the preference ordering of the sth generation, $s > r$. Otherwise, the conditional ordering of the sth generation over $\Omega^{(s)}$ is dependent upon $_{s+1}X$. It may appear to be the case that, in incorporating the sth generation's ordering into its own intertemporal welfare function, the rth generation could simply choose a reference vector $_{s+1}O \in {}_{s+1}\Omega$. For example, if $s = r+1$, the representation of the rth generation's intertemporal preferences is

$$U^r\left(_rX\right) = \hat{U}^r\left(X^r, U^{r+1}\left(X^{r+1}, {}_{r+2}O\right), \ldots, U^m\left(X^m\right)\right).$$

However, unless I^s is separable from $_{s+1}I$ for all $s > r$, the conditional ordering of the rth generation on the sth subspace does not conform to that of the sth generation for values of $_{s+1}X \neq {}_{s+1}O$. This violates the nonpaternalistic condition. Thus, the utility functions of the intertemporal nonpaternalistic society have the following images:

$$U^1\left(_1X\right) = \hat{U}^1\left(X^1, \overline{U}^2\left(X^2\right), \ldots, \overline{U}^m\left(X^m\right)\right),$$

$$U^2\left(_2X\right) = \hat{U}^2\left(\overline{U}^2\left(X^2\right), \ldots, \overline{U}^m\left(X^m\right)\right),$$

$$\vdots$$

$$U^m\left(X^m\right) = \overline{U}^m\left(X^m\right).$$

Finally, applying theorem 10.2, we know that the demand functions of the intertemporal nonpaternalistic society are intertemporally consistent if and only if the underlying preferences are recursively compatible. In this case the preferences are represented by

$$U^1({}_1X) = \tilde{U}^1(X^1, u^2),$$

$$u^r = U^r({}_rX) = \tilde{U}^r\left(\overline{U}^r(X^r), u^{r+1}\right), \qquad r = 2, \ldots, m-1,$$

and

$$u^m = \overline{U}^m(X^m).$$

Thus, the conjunction of intertemporal nonpaternalism and intertemporal consistency is equivalent to an intertemporal preference structure that is stronger than recursive compatibility. The rth generation's preferences ($r \neq 1$) are separable in the binary partition $\{I^r, {}_{r+1}I\}$ as well as completely recursive.

10.2 SOPHISTICATED PLANNING

The theme of the preceding section is that naive intertemporal planning is consistent if and only if the preference orderings of successive generations are completely recursive and compatible. Although there exist plausible (and perhaps morally compelling) arguments for intertemporal compatibility, there is little reason to believe that "the future is separable from the present". We should therefore address the case where the intertemporal society does not have recursively compatible preferences and in addition is either unable or unwilling to impose plans on succeeding generations. In this situation, society may behave in a myopic fashion. Each generation computes a plan from now to the end of the planning period. It then executes the current portion of the plan, leaving the appropriate bequest for the future. The next generation will, however, not be content with this plan, because preferences are not intertemporally compatible. It will therefore revise the plan and then execute the current portion of the revision, and so on. In this context planning appears to make little sense, because the consumption program which is actually followed is not optimal from any point of view; it has been planned by none.

10.2.1 The Sophisticated Society

One solution which has been suggested as a way out of this dilemma places a high value on consistency: the so-called "sophisticated" optimal solution.[5] In a "sophisticated" society each generation is cognizant of the preferences of future generations and takes these preferences into account in constructing a consistent intertemporal plan. Then each generation chooses a plan which, according to its own preferences, is the optimum among that set of plans which will, in fact, be carried out by successive generations.

We illustrate this planning problem in the case of only two generations, where generation 1 has but one commodity and generation 2 has two commodities from which to choose. Let x_1^1 and (x_1^2, x_2^2) represent the consumption bundles of these two generations. Generation 1 has preferences over Ω^3 but can in fact only choose x_1^1 and z_2—the size of the bequest. The triangle abc in figure 10.1 is the budget constraint facing the first generation, while the line Ode is the income-consumption curve of generation 2; given any bequest z_2, the second generation will choose a point on the locus Ode. Because the first generation cannot control the expenditure of generation 2, it chooses a plan which from its point of view is the best of those which will actually be followed; it treats the locus Ode as a constraint. In figure 10.1 this is pictured by projecting the locus Ode onto the budget constraint abc to get the actual "sophisticated" constraint which faces generation 1. It will pick its most preferred point on the constructed locus ad.

This, however, presents several problems. These problems are depicted in figure 10.2, which consists of the budget plane abc and the sophisticated-constraint locus ad. The circles are equal-utility loci, and the point m is generation 1's maximum subject to the constraint abc. The point m is not on a path which will be followed by generation 2. From the point of view of generation 1, the best of all those paths which will actually be followed consists of the locus of points from s^1 to s^2 and the point s^3. Generation 1 is indifferent between all of these "sophisticated" solutions, and by picking one such bundle a consistent plan will be followed. However, in the case of more than two generations, this nonuniqueness presents serious existence problems, to which we return after some formal definitions.

In order to describe the sophisticated solution, define, for all r the budget sets

$$B_r(z_r) = \left\{ {}_rX \in {}_r\Omega \mid_r P \cdot {}_rX \leqslant z_r \wedge z_r \in \Omega_\circ^1 \right\}$$

and the "choice sets"

$$A_r = \left\{ X^r \in \Omega^{(r)} \mid X^r = \phi^r(z_r, {}_rP) \text{ for some } z_r \in \Omega_\circ^1 \right\}, \qquad r = 2, \ldots, m,$$

[5]This planning procedure was suggested by Strotz (1955), and his formulation was corrected by Pollak (1968). An approach that is similar to Pollak's can be found in Blackorby (1967). The sensibleness of this procedure is carefully discussed in Hammond (1976).

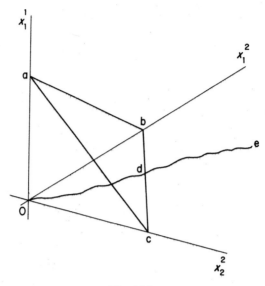

Fig. 10.1

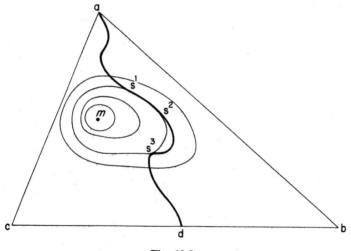

Fig. 10.2

where ϕ^r is the vector-valued choice function of the rth generation. [The sets $B_r(z_r)$ and A_r depend upon $_rP$ and hence, strictly speaking, should be indexed by $_rP$. However, in what follows $_rP$ is fixed, and in the interest of notational simplicity, we suppress the index $_rP$.] The set A_r thus contains all bundles X^r that would be chosen by the rth generation at (nonnegative) values of wealth z_r, given the set of prices $_rP$. Thus, this set is nothing more than the projection of the "income-consumption curve" of the rth generation onto its own consumption space $\Omega^{(r)}$.

The sophisticated path $_1\hat{X}$ is generated by the following sequence of problems:

$$\max_{_rX} U^r(_rX) \quad \text{s.t.} \quad _rX \in B_r(z_r) \text{ and } X^{r+s} \in A_{r+s}, \quad s=1,\ldots,m-r,$$

to obtain

$$\hat{X}^r = \phi^r(z_r, _rP), \quad r=m,\ldots,1.$$

The z_r's are then found by

$$z_1 = y$$

and

$$z_{r+1} = z_r - P^r \cdot \phi^r(z_r, _rP), \quad r=1,\ldots,m-1.$$

Thus the sophisticated path is generated by a recursive programming procedure in which the mth choice function is derived first and the first choice function is derived last. This solution is consistent because the choice functions of future generations are treated as constraints in the optimization problem. Although this solution is not Pareto optimal, it has the attractive property that $_r\hat{X}$ is preferred by the rth generation to all other paths which will be followed by subsequent generations.

10.2.2 The Existence of a Sophisticated Optimum

A serious problem with the sophisticated society is that, even though U^r is assumed to be strictly quasi-concave, the rth optimum may not be unique, in which case planning is indeterminate at the $(r-1)$th stage.[6] To see this, note that the sets $A_{r+s}, s=1,\ldots,m-r$, are not necessarily convex. Consequently, the optimum might not be unique, as demonstrated in the previous example. Although the rth generation is indifferent between the

[6]This fact was first pointed out to us by Robert Pollak. The problem is discussed in Phelps and Pollak (1968) and in Peleg and Yaari (1973).

alternative plans, the $(r-1)$th generation would need to know how the "tie" in the rth period is going to be resolved in order to formulate its own plan.

Three possible escapes from this dilemma are as follows:[7] First, we might permit a type of weak precommitment in which the first generation affected by the prospect of future multiple optima commits the relevant generation to a specific plan among the set of optima. Second, we could adopt a probabalistic approach to deal explicitly with the uncertainty regarding the choices of future generations. Finally, we could posit a strong ordering of consumption programs $_rX$, for $r = 2, \ldots, m - 1$, in which case the optimum is unique despite the possibility of a nonconvex feasible set.

The problem with the last approach is that a strong ordering cannot be represented by a continuous, order-preserving, real-valued function. The other two approaches do not resolve a more fundamental problem generated by nonconvex feasible sets. If, in period r, the feasible set is not convex, the choice function might not be upper hemicontinuous, in which case the feasible set in period $r - 1$ might not be closed. In this case, an optimum might not exist even if the $(r - 1)$th generation can precommit future generations in their choice among multiple optima.[8]

In addition to the assumption of strong orderings of consumption programs, sufficient conditions for a unique sophisticated path to exist are embodied in the following theorem.[9] In the previous example, this condition amounts to forcing the lines Ode and ad to be straight, which, along with strict quasi-concavity, insures uniqueness.

Theorem 10.4 *If the utility functions U^r, $r = 2, \ldots, m$, are homothetic and satisfy* (R-1′), *then a unique sophisticated path $_1\hat{X}$ exists for all $_1P \in \Omega^n_+$ for all $y \in \Omega^1_+$.*

Proof. As the mth maximization is constrained only by the budget constraint, the assumptions regarding U^m imply that the vector-valued demand function ϕ^m exists and is linear in z_m. The proof therefore proceeds by induction.

---

[7]All three of these solutions have been suggested to us by Robert Pollak.

[8]For an example, see Peleg and Yaari (1973: pp. 393–394).

[9]This theorem is analogous to theorem 8.1 of Peleg and Yaari (1973: p. 401). The latter authors deal, however, with the existence of a Nash game equilibrium rather than the sophisticated solution. A set of choice functions is a Nash equilibrium if the choice function of each generation yields maximal utility for that generation, given the choice functions of all other generations. A set of choice functions generates a sophisticated path, on the other hand, if the choice function of each generation yields maximal utility for that generation given the choice functions of all *succeeding* generations for *any* feasible choice functions of *preceeding* generations. A sophisticated solution is a game-equilibrium solution, but the converse does not hold (see Peleg and Yaari, 1973: p. 395).

Suppose that the functions ϕ^s, $s = r+1, \ldots, m$, exist and are linear in z_s. Then each set A_{r+s}, $s = 1, \ldots, m-r$, is a ray in $\Omega^{(r+s)}$. The set of constraints expressed by the condition

$$X^{r+s} \in A_{r+s}, \qquad s = 1, \ldots, m-r,$$

can be expressed equivalently as $_rX \in A_r^\times$, where

$$A_r^\times = \Omega^{(r)} \times \left(\overset{m-r}{\underset{s=1}{\times}} A_{r+s} \right).$$

Clearly, $A_r^\times$ is a closed, convex cone. The feasible set for the rth problem is therefore

$$F_r(z_r) = A_r^\times \cap B_r(z_r),$$

a compact, convex subset of $_r\Omega$. Thus, the nondecreasing, continuous, strictly quasi-concave function U^r reaches a unique maximum on the upper boundary of $F_r(z_r)$. Moreover, at the optimum, $_r\hat{X}$, the (unique) gradient of the upper boundary of the set $F_r(z_r)$ belongs to the set of subgradients of the convex function whose epigraph is the set

$$S_r(_r\hat{X}) = \left\{ _rX \mid U^r(_rX) \geqslant U^r(_r\hat{X}) \wedge _rX \in _r\Omega \right\}$$

It remains to show that the function ϕ^r is linear in z_r for $r = m-1, \ldots, 2$. As the set

$$\lambda B_r(z_r) = \left\{ _rX \mid _rX \in B_r(\lambda z_r)\ \forall \lambda \in \Omega_\circ^1 \right\}$$

is a closed, convex cone,

$$\lambda F_r(z_r) = A_r^\times \cap \lambda B_r(z_r)$$

is also a closed convex cone. Hence $\lambda F_r(z_r)$ contains the ray

$$\left\{ _rX \mid _rX = \lambda \cdot {}_r\hat{X}\ \forall \lambda \in \Omega_\circ^1 \right\}.$$

For given $_rP$, the gradient of the upper boundary of $F_r(\lambda z_r)$, for $\lambda \in \Omega^1$, is independent of λ. But, by homotheticity, the sets of subgradients of the functions defined by the epigraphs $S_r(\lambda \cdot {}_rX)$ are independent of λ, so that $\phi^r(\lambda z_r, {}_rP) = \lambda \hat{X}^r$ for $r = m-1, \ldots, 2$. $\parallel$

The sophisticated solution (if it exists) would appear to be an improvement over naive planning. By explicitly considering future preferences, each generation realizes a level of utility at least as great as that which is possible under inconsistent naive planning (given the plans of previous generations[10]), and at least one generation enjoys a higher utility (if preferences are not intertemporally compatible of course). Despite this improvement, however, it is still not clear in what sense, if any, the sophisticated solution is optimal, since each generation's utility is maximized subject to some rather unconventional constraints.

To answer this question, it seems reasonable to seek the conditions under which the system of sophisticated demand functions can be integrated into a system of intertemporal utility functions of the form $U^r(_rX)$, $r = 1, \ldots, m$. That is, we seek the conditions under which a sophisticated society would act as if it were maximizing a sequence of intertemporal utility functions subject to conventional constraints. This, together with the fact that the demand functions are intertemporally consistent, would then imply integrability into a single utility function U. These conditions are given by the following proposition.

Theorem 10.5 *Suppose that the utility functions of the sophisticated society satisfy* (R-1'), *that the demand functions satisfy* (L) *and* (W), *and that the regularity conditions of theorem 10.2(b) are satisfied. An intertemporal utility function which generates these demand functions exists if and only if the society's preferences are recursively compatible with the representation* (10.3).

Proof.   This follows immediately from theorem 10.2.   ‖

The above result indicates that the sophisticated society acts "rationally" under alternative price and wealth configurations if and only if its preferences are recursively compatible. That is, unless the society's intertemporal preferences are of this form, it may violate the transitivity axiom. This, of course, is not surprising, since the sophisticated optimum path is a "second-best" solution unless the society's preferences are recursively compatible.

---

[10]It is *not* true that a sophisticated planning is partly superior to naive planning for the intertemporal society as a whole.

Appendix: Duality Theorems and Proofs

In the main text of the book, the twelve optimization problems in figure 2.4 are repeatedly employed in the derivation and recovery of the alternative representations of the consumer preference ordering or production technology. We also exploit the regularity properties of derived functional representations. It is therefore important that we document the validity of these derivations and inherited regularity properties. The following twelve theorems and proofs correspond to the twelve relationships depicted in figure 2.4. Where possible, we cite results that are readily accessible in the duality literature.

However, the maintained regularity properties for the utility or production function and the derived properties of the dual representations that are convenient if not essential for the purposes of this book are substantially different from those that are maintained and derived in the existing treatments of duality theory. For example, global nonsatiation is a *regularity* property which greatly facilitates duality proofs but which is inconvenient for our purposes because it is not a property that is inherited by (Bliss or Gorman) aggregator functions. Moreover, the duality theorems that follow are repeatedly applied to the aggregator functions as well as the parent functions. Hence, we must allow for the possibility of a region of global satiation in each of the following proofs. This allowance is not very problematic in the case of the duality between direct and indirect utility functions [where we are able to modify straightforwardly the proofs of Diewert (1974a)]. However, proofs of the many other duality relationships (involving the cost and transformation functions as well as the direct and indirect utility or production functions) are rather substantially complicated by this weakening of the monotonicity conditions that are maintained in other duality studies.

An example of a *derived* property that is essential for our purposes, but which has not (to our knowledge) been proved in the existing duality literature (under our maintained regularity conditions), is provided by the

357

joint continuity in utility (output) and prices of the cost function and joint continuity in utility (output) and quantities of the transformation function. Most of the representation and duality theorems for separable structures in chapters 3–6 require joint continuity. Proof (using the maximum theorem) of joint continuity of the cost or transformation function requires that the upper-level-set mapping (that maps utility levels into upper-level sets in the consumption or price space) be shown to be continuous. Proving the latter turns out to be nontrivial; indeed, the only proof that we have managed to devise relies crucially on two recent theorems of Heller (1977).[1]

Although we have not been able to adopt directly the duality theorems in the literature, the influence of this literature on the proofs that follow is pervasive. Were it not for careful reading of the seminal works of Diewert, Gorman, McFadden, Shephard, and others, we certainly would not have had the temerity to attempt the writing of this appendix.

Theorem A.1 *Suppose that U satisfies (R-1). Then V, defined by (2.1), satisfies (R-2). Moreover, if $\bar{U}$ is derived from $\overset{*}{V}$ (the extension of V to the boundary by continuity from below) by (2.2), and if $\overset{*}{U}$ is the extension of $\bar{U}$ to the boundary by continuity from above, then $\overset{*}{U} = U$.*

Proof. Continuity and monotonicity of V and convexity of lower level sets of V are proved by Diewert (1974a: Theorem 3.2). It remains to show that local nonsatiation of U (except perhaps for a region of global satiation) implies local nonsatiation of V (except perhaps for a region of global satiation). Given $\bar{P}/y \in \Omega^n_+$ and $\varepsilon > 0$, choose $\hat{P}/y = \lambda \bar{P}/y$ such that $0 < \lambda < 1$ and $d(\hat{P}/y, \bar{P}/y) < \varepsilon$. Letting

$$B(P/y) = \left\{ X \in \Omega^n | (P/y) \cdot X \leqslant 1 \right\},$$

clearly $B(\bar{P}/y) \subset B(\hat{P}/y)$. Therefore, for each $\bar{X} \in \phi(\bar{P}/y)$ there exists a $\delta > 0$ such that

$$N_\delta(\bar{X}) = \left\{ X \in \Omega^n | d(X, \bar{X}) < \delta \right\}$$

is a proper subset of $B(\hat{P}/y)$. By local nonsatiation at $\bar{X}$, there exists an $\tilde{X} \in N_\delta(\bar{X}) \subset B(\hat{P}/y)$ such that $U(\tilde{X}) > U(\bar{X})$. Therefore, $V(\hat{P}/y) > V(\bar{P}/y)$.

---

[1]It might be noted that proof of the continuity of the variable profit function (the profit function with fixed input), as in Gorman (1968a) and McFadden (1970), generates, as a special case, proof of the joint continuity of the cost function (interpreting utility as a "fixed inputs"). Unfortunately, both of the above writers *maintain* continuity of the upper-level-set-mapping—precisely what we need to prove.

The second part of the theorem has been proved by Diewert (1974a: Theorem 3.8) under weaker assumptions. ‖

Theorem A.2 *Assume that* $\overset{*}{V}$, *the extension of V to the boundary, satisfies* (R-2). *Then* $\overline{U}$, *defined by* (2.2), *satisfies* (R-1). *Moreover, if* $\overline{V}$ *is derived from* $\overset{*}{U}$ *(the extension of* $\overline{U}$ *to the boundary by continuity from above) by* (2.1), *then* $\overline{V} = V$.

Proof. Follows by duality from Theorem A.1 (see Diewert, 1974a: theorems 3.5 and 3.8). ‖

Theorem A.3 *Assume that* U *satisfies* (R-1). *Then* C, *defined by* (2.9), *satisfies* (R-3). *Moreover, if* $\overset{*}{U}$ *is in turn derived from* C *by* (2.10), *then* $\overset{*}{U} = U$.

Proof. Monotonicity, concavity, and positive linear homogeneity of $C(u, \cdot)$ for each $u \in \mathcal{R}(U)$ have been proved by Diewert (1971: theorem 3).

Next we prove that C is continuous in (u, P). The strategy is to redefine the feasible set of the cost-minimization problem in such a way that it becomes a compact set without affecting the cost-minimization solution. This restatement allows us to appeal to the maximum theorem (Debreu, 1952, 1959b; Berge, 1963; Hildenbrand, 1974).

Let $L: \mathcal{R}(U) \to \mathcal{P}(\Omega^n)$ be the level-set mapping:

$$L(u) = \{X \in \Omega^n | U(X) \geqslant u\}.$$

Conditional on the vector $(u^0, P^0) \in \mathcal{R}(U) \times \Omega^n_+$, choose[2] $\hat{X} \in \text{int}\, L(u^0)$ and define the mapping $M: \Omega^n_+ \to \mathcal{P}(\Omega^n)$ by

$$M(P) = \{X \in \Omega^n | P \cdot X \leqslant P \cdot \hat{X}\}.$$

Finally, let $\hat{L}$ be the restriction of L to $\{u \in \mathcal{R}(U) | u \leqslant U(\hat{X})\}$, let $\mathcal{D}(\hat{L})$ be the effective domain of $\hat{L}$, and let Φ be the intersection of $\hat{L}$ and M:

$$\Phi(u, P) = \{X \in \Omega^n | U(X) \geqslant u \wedge P \cdot X \leqslant P \cdot \hat{X}\}.$$

$\Phi(u, P)$ is clearly compact and nonempty for all (u, P) in the domain of Φ. Moreover, at (u^0, P^0), (2.9) can be rewritten as

$$C(u^0, P^0) = \min_X \{P^0 \cdot X | X \in \Phi(u^0, P^0)\},$$

[2] $\text{int}\, A$ is the interior of the set A.

since the solution to the cost-minimization problem, $\zeta(u^0, P^0)$, must be on the boundary of $L(u^0)$ and must satisfy $P^0 \cdot \zeta(u^0, P^0) \leqslant P^0 \cdot \hat{X}$. If Φ is continuous at (u^0, P^0), then, by the maximum theorem, C is continuous at (u^0, P^0). As (u^0, P^0) was chosen arbitrarily, the above construction can be repeated for any $(u, P) \in \mathcal{R}(U) \times \Omega^n_+$ to prove global joint continuity of C.

The upper hemicontinuity of Φ follows from the continuity of U. That is, let $(u^\nu, P^\nu) \to (u^0, P^0)$, $X^\nu \in \Phi(u^\nu, P^\nu)$, and $X^\nu \to X^0$. Suppose that Φ is not upper hemicontinuous at (u^0, P^0); then $X^0 \notin \Phi(u^0, P^0)$. By the definition of Φ, $U(X^\nu) \geqslant u^\nu$ and $P^\nu \cdot X^\nu \leqslant P^\nu \cdot \hat{X}$ for all ν; moreover, $X^0 \notin \Phi(u^0, P^0)$ implies that $U(X^0) < u^0$ or $P^0 \cdot X^0 > P^0 \cdot \hat{X}$. The first violates the continuity of U and the second the continuity of the inner-product mapping. Thus $X^0 \in \Phi(u^0, P^0)$.

The lower hemicontinuity of Φ is established by invoking some powerful results of Heller (1977). We say that $\hat{L}$ is *locally interior* if, for any $u^0 \in \mathcal{D}(\hat{L})$ and each $X^0 \in \hat{L}(u^0)$, there exist an $\bar{X} \in \text{int}\,\hat{L}(u^0)$ and a continuous function $f: [0, 1] \to \hat{L}(u^0)$ such that $f(0) = \bar{X}$, $f(1) = X^0$, and $f(\theta) \in \text{int}\,\hat{L}(u^0)$ $\forall \theta \in (0, 1)$ (Heller, 1977). $\hat{L}$ is *locally constant* if, for any $u^0 \in \mathcal{D}(\hat{L})$, $X^0 \in \text{int}\,\hat{L}(u^0)$ implies that $X^0 \in \text{int}\,\hat{L}(u)$ for all u in a neighborhood of u^0 (Heller, 1977). Local interiority and local constancy of M are defined similarly. The strategy is to show that $\hat{L}$ and M both satisfy local interiority and local constancy, in which case both are lower hemicontinuous, as is their intersection Φ.

As $M(P)$ and $\hat{L}(u)$ are convex with nonempty interiors for all $P \in \Omega^n_+$ and for all $u \in \mathcal{D}(\hat{L})$, respectively, both M and $\hat{L}$ are locally interior (Heller, 1977). The convex-combination mapping, defined by $f(\theta) = \theta X^0 + (1 - \theta)\bar{X}$, serves as an appropriate f in Heller's definition of local interiority.

Let $X^0 \in \text{int}\,\hat{L}(u^0)$ for an arbitrary $u^0 \in \mathcal{D}(\hat{L})$. If $u^0 = \max\{u | u \in \mathcal{D}(\hat{L})\}$ [i.e., if $u^0 = U(\hat{X})$], then $(\bar{u}, u^0]$ is open relative to $\mathcal{D}(\hat{L})$ for any $\bar{u} \in \mathcal{D}(\hat{L})$ satisfying $\bar{u} < u^0$. Moreover, $X^0 \in \hat{L}(u)$ $\forall u \in (\bar{u}, u^0]$. If $u^0 \neq \max\{u | u \in \mathcal{D}(\hat{L})\}$, the quasi-concavity of U implies that $U(X^0) > u^0$. For $\varepsilon < \min\{U(X^0) - u^0, u^0 - \inf \mathcal{R}(U)\}$, the interval $(u^0 - \varepsilon, u^0 + \varepsilon)$ is an open subset of $\mathcal{D}(\hat{L})$ (by continuity of U). Moreover, $X^0 \in \hat{L}(u)$ $\forall u \in (u^0 - \varepsilon, u^0 + \varepsilon)$. Thus, $\hat{L}$ is locally constant.

Finally, as $\hat{X} \in \text{int}\,L(u^0) \subseteq \Omega^n$ and Ω^n is convex, M is also locally constant (Heller, 1977).

As $\hat{L}$ and M are locally constant and locally interior, both are lower hemicontinuous by corollary 3.1 of Heller (1977).[3] Finally, as $\Phi = \hat{L} \cap M$, and $\Phi(u, P)$ is nonempty for all (u, P) in the domain of Φ, Φ is lower

---

[3]In fact, the lower hemicontinuity of M was proved by Debreu (1959b), since our assumption that $\hat{X} \in \text{int}\,L(U(X^0))$ implies Debreu's assumption of an interior endowment.

hemicontinuous by proposition 3.4 of Heller (1977). This establishes the continuity of Φ at (u^0, P^0), as was required to invoke the maximum theorem.

It remains to show that $\overset{*}{U}$, derived by

$$\overset{*}{U}(\hat{X}) = \max_u \{ u \in \mathcal{R}(U) | C(u, P) \leqslant P \cdot \hat{X} \quad \forall P \in \Omega_+^n \}, \qquad (2.10)$$

is equivalent to U. Clearly, $U(\hat{X})$ satisfies the constraint in (2.10), since

$$C(U(\hat{X}), P) = \min_X \{ P \cdot X | U(X) \geqslant U(\hat{X}) \wedge X \in \Omega^n \}.$$

Thus $U(\hat{X}) \leqslant \overset{*}{U}(\hat{X})$.

To show that $U(\hat{X}) = \overset{*}{U}(\hat{X})$ it suffices to show that $u > U(\hat{X})$ implies that u does not satisfy the constraint in (2.10) for some $P \in \Omega_+^n$. The continuity and quasi-concavity of U imply that $L(u) = \{ X \in \Omega^n | U(X) \geqslant u \}$ is a closed, convex set. Hence there exists a hyperplane $H(P, \alpha)$ that strictly separates $\{\hat{X}\}$ and $L(u)$ (Rockafellar, 1970: corollary 11.4.2). Moreover, by the monotonicity of U, the recession cone of $L(u)$ contains Ω_+^n; hence the normal, P, of the strictly separating hyperplane is nonnegative. Thus there exist a scalar $\varepsilon > 0$ and a vector $P \in \Omega^n$ such that

$$P \cdot X > P \cdot \hat{X} + \varepsilon \qquad \forall X \in L(u).$$

Let $z_i = \sup\{ \hat{x}_i - x_i | x_i \in \rho_i(L(u)) \}$, where $\rho_i(L(u))$ is the projection of $L(u)$ onto the ith coordinate axis. Let $\delta \in \Omega_+^n$ satisfy $\delta \cdot z = \delta \cdot [z_1, \ldots, z_n] \leqslant \varepsilon$. Then

$$P \cdot X > P \cdot \hat{X} + \delta \cdot z \qquad \forall X \in L(u),$$

which implies that

$$P \cdot X > P \cdot \hat{X} + \delta \cdot (\hat{X} - X) \qquad \forall X \in L(u),$$

and thus

$$P \cdot X + \delta \cdot X > P \cdot \hat{X} + \delta \cdot \hat{X} \qquad \forall X \in L(u).$$

Letting $\hat{P} = P + \delta$, we have

$$\hat{P} \cdot X > \hat{P} \cdot \hat{X} \qquad \forall X \in L(u),$$

where, by construction, $\hat{P} \in \Omega_+^n$. Therefore,

$$C(u, \hat{P}) > \hat{P} \cdot \hat{X},$$

implying that u violates the constraint in (2.10).   ‖

Theorem A.4 *Suppose that $\overset{*}{C}$, the extension of C to the boundary of Ω_+^n, satisfies (R-3). Then $\overset{*}{U}$, derived from C by (2.10), satisfies (R-1). Moreover, if $\overline{C}$ is in turn derived from $\overset{*}{U}$ by (2.9), then $\overline{C} = C$.*

Proof. To prove continuity of $\overset{*}{U}$, we first reformulate the optimization problem (2.10). Let $\hat{\mathcal{R}}(U) = \mathcal{R}(U) \cup \inf \mathcal{R}(U)$ and let $\mathcal{P}(\hat{\mathcal{R}}(U))$ denote the power set of $\hat{\mathcal{R}}(U)$. For a given vector $P \in \Omega_+^n$, define the mapping $I_P : \Omega^n \to \mathcal{P}(\hat{\mathcal{R}}(U))$ whose image set is given by

$$I_P(X) = \{ u \in \mathcal{R}(U) | C(u, P) \leqslant P \cdot X \} \cup \inf \mathcal{R}(U).$$

Since $C(\overset{*}{U}(X), P) \leqslant P \cdot X$, $I_P(X)$ is nonempty for all $X \in \Omega^n$. Moreover, since C is continuous and increasing in u, $I_P(X)$ is a compact interval for each $X \in \Omega^n$. [If $\mathcal{R}(U)$ is unbounded from below, we can renormalize to make $I_p(X)$ a bounded interval.]

Next we show that I_p is closed, and therefore, since $I_p(X)$ is compact for all $X \in \Omega^n$, upper hemicontinuous (see Berge, 1963: corollary, p. 112). Consider any sequence $\{X^\nu\}$ in Ω^n such that $X^\nu \to X^0$, and a corresponding sequence $\{u^\nu\}$ in $\hat{\mathcal{R}}(U)$ such that $u^\nu \in I_p(X^\nu) \; \forall \nu$ and $u^\nu \to u^0$. Thus,

$$C(u^\nu, P) \leqslant P \cdot X^\nu \qquad \forall \nu.$$

But, as $C(\cdot, P)$ is continuous,

$$C(u^0, P) \leqslant P \cdot X^0.$$

Thus $u^0 \in I_p(X^0)$, proving that I_p is a closed mapping.

Next define the correspondence $I : \Omega^n \to \hat{\mathcal{R}}(U)$ by

$$I(X) = \bigcap_{P \in \Omega_+^n} I_p(X)$$

$$= \{ u \in \mathcal{R}(U) | C(u, P) \leqslant P \cdot X \; \forall P \in \Omega_+^n \} \cup \inf \mathcal{R}(U).$$

$I(X)$ is clearly nonempty for all $X \in \Omega^n$ and $\overset{*}{U}(X) = \max_u I(X)$. Moreover, as the intersection of a family of upper hemicontinuous mappings, I is upper hemicontinuous (Berge, 1963: theorem 2′, p. 114).

I is lower hemi-continuous if, for all $\varepsilon > 0$, $u^0 \in I(X^0)$ implies that there exists a $\delta > 0$ such that

$$X \in N_\delta(X^0) \quad \Rightarrow \quad I(X) \cap N_\varepsilon(u^0) \neq \emptyset.$$

Suppose not; then there is an $\varepsilon > 0$ such that, for each $\delta > 0$, there exists a point $X(\delta) \in N_\delta(X^0)$ such that $I(X(\delta)) \cap N_\varepsilon(u^0) = \emptyset$. In other words, there exists a sequence $\{X^\nu\}$ in Ω^n such that $X^\nu \to X^0$ and

$$I(X^\nu) \cap N_\varepsilon(u^0) = \emptyset \qquad \forall \nu.$$

Thus $u^0 \notin I(X^\nu)$, and hence for each ν there is a price vector $P^\nu \in \Omega^n_+$ such that

$$C(u^0, P^\nu) > P^\nu \cdot X^\nu.$$

(Note that $u^0 \neq \inf \mathcal{R}(U)$ since $\inf \mathcal{R}(U) \in I(X) \; \forall X \in \Omega^n$.) By continuity of $C(\cdot, P)$, this in turn implies that, for some $\bar{u} \in \mathcal{R}(U)$ satisfying $\bar{u} < u^0$,

$$C(\bar{u}, P^\nu) > P^\nu \cdot X^\nu \qquad \forall \nu.$$

As C is PLH in P, this implies that

$$C(\bar{u}, \tilde{P}^\nu) > \tilde{P}^\nu \cdot X^\nu \qquad \forall \nu,$$

where $\tilde{P}^\nu = P^\nu / \|P^\nu\|$. Thus, $\{\tilde{P}^\nu\}$ is a sequence in the bounded set $B \cap \Omega^n_+$, where B is the closed unit ball. Consequently, $\{\tilde{P}^\nu\}$ contains a subsequence $\{\tilde{P}^{\nu_k}\}$ that converges in the compact set $B \cap \Omega^n$. Let $\{X^{\nu_k}\}$ be the corresponding subsequence of $\{X^\nu\}$; thus $X^{\nu_k} \to X^0$. Let $(\tilde{P}, X^0)$ denote the limit of $(\tilde{P}^{\nu_k}, X^{\nu_k})$. Then

$$C(\bar{u}, \tilde{P}^{\nu_k}) > \tilde{P}^{\nu_k} \cdot X^{\nu_k} \qquad \forall k,$$

and since $\overset{*}{C}$, the extension of C to the boundary, is continuous,

$$\overset{*}{C}(\bar{u}, \tilde{P}) \geqslant \tilde{P} \cdot X^0. \tag{a}$$

On the other hand, since $u^0 \in I(X^0)$,

$$C(u^0, P) \leqslant P \cdot X^0 \qquad \forall P \in \Omega^n_+. \tag{b}$$

Moreover, by continuity of $\overset{*}{C}$, (b) implies, in particular, that

$$\overset{*}{C}(u^0, \tilde{P}) \leqslant \tilde{P} \cdot X^0. \tag{c}$$

Since $\overset{*}{C}$ is increasing in u, and $\bar{u} < u^0$, (c) implies that

$$\overset{*}{C}(\bar{u}, \tilde{P}) < \tilde{P} \cdot X^0,$$

which contradicts (a). Thus, I must be lower hemicontinuous at X^0.
The optimization problem (2.10) can be reformulated as follows:

$$\overset{*}{U}(X) = \max\{u | u \in I(X)\}.$$

Since I is continuous, $\overset{*}{U}$ is continuous by the maximum theorem.

Monotonicity of $\overset{*}{U}$ follows from monotonicity of C in u. Since C is increasing in u, if $\hat{X} \geqslant X$, $I(X) \subseteq I(\hat{X})$ and hence $\overset{*}{U}(\hat{X}) \geqslant \overset{*}{U}(X)$.

To prove convexity of the upper level sets, suppose that $\overset{*}{U}(\bar{X}) \geqslant \overset{*}{U}(\hat{X})$. Then $I(\hat{X}) \subseteq I(\bar{X})$. Suppose further that $u \notin I(\theta \bar{X} + (1-\theta)\hat{X})$, $\theta \in (0,1)$. Then there exists a $\tilde{P} \in \Omega^n_+$ such that

$$C(u, \tilde{P}) > \theta \tilde{P} \cdot \bar{X} + (1-\theta)\tilde{P} \cdot \hat{X},$$

which in turn implies

$$C(u, \tilde{P}) > \min\{\tilde{P} \cdot \bar{X}, \tilde{P} \cdot \hat{X}\}.$$

Hence $u \notin I(\hat{X}) \cap I(\bar{X}) = I(\hat{X})$. The contrapositive statement is that $u \in I(\hat{X})$ implies $u \in I(\theta \bar{X} + (1-\theta)\hat{X})$; therefore, $\overset{*}{U}(\theta \bar{X} + (1-\theta)\hat{X}) \geqslant U(\hat{X})$.

It remains to prove local nonsatiation. Consider a neighborhood $N_\varepsilon(\bar{X})$. Choose $\hat{X} \in N_\varepsilon(\bar{X})$ such that $\hat{X} > \bar{X}$. The strict monotonicity of $C(\cdot, P)$ implies that $\overset{*}{U}(\hat{X}) > \overset{*}{U}(\bar{X})$.

Proof that $\overset{*}{C} = C$ can be found in Diewert (1971: theorem 4). $\parallel$

Proofs of the two theorems regarding the relationships between the utility and transformation functions and their properties require the following two lemmas (which are also invoked repeatedly in the main body of the text):

Lemma A.1 *Suppose that U satisfies (R-1), and define F by (2.11). Then*[4]

$$F(u,X)=\lambda \Rightarrow U(X/\lambda)=u \qquad \forall(u,X)\in\mathcal{R}(U)\times\Omega_+^n \qquad (a)$$

and

$$U(X/\lambda)=u \Rightarrow \left[F(u,X)=\lambda \text{ or } X/\lambda\in\operatorname{int}L(\sup\mathcal{R}(U))\right]$$

$$\forall(\lambda,X)\in\Omega_+^{n+1}. \qquad (b)$$

Proof. If $F(\mathring{u},X)=\lambda^*$, then λ^* must be feasible in (2.11), and hence

$$U(X/\lambda^*)\geqslant\mathring{u}. \qquad (c)$$

Construct a monotonically decreasing sequence $\{\lambda^\nu\}$ which converges to λ^*, i.e.,

$$\lambda^\nu>\lambda^{\nu+1} \qquad \forall\nu$$

and

$$\lambda^\nu\to\lambda^*.$$

Since $\lambda^\nu>\lambda^*$, λ^ν is not feasible in (2.11). Thus,

$$U(X/\lambda^\nu)<\mathring{u} \qquad \forall\nu. \qquad (d)$$

Since U is continuous and $\lambda^\nu\to\lambda^*$, (d) implies that

$$U(X/\lambda^*)\leqslant\mathring{u}. \qquad (e)$$

Together, (c) and (e) imply that $U(X/\lambda^*)=\mathring{u}$.

To prove (b), note that, if $U(X/\lambda)=\mathring{u}$, λ is feasible in (2.11) and hence $\lambda\leqslant F(\mathring{u},X)=\lambda^*$. The latter equality and (a) imply that $U(X/\overset{*}{\lambda})=\mathring{u}$; hence $U(X/\lambda)=U(X/\lambda^*)$. This implies that either $\lambda=\lambda^*$ or X/λ is in the interior of a region of global satiation of U. $\|$

---

[4]Note that commonly employed special cases of (a) and (b) are $F(u,X)=1 \Rightarrow U(X)=u$ $\forall(u,X)\in\mathcal{R}(U)\times\Omega_+^n$ and $U(X)=u \Rightarrow [F(u,X)=1 \text{ or } X\in\operatorname{int}L(\sup\mathcal{R}(U))]$ $\forall(u,X)\in\mathcal{R}(U)\times\Omega_+^n$.

Lemma A.2 *Suppose that F satisfies (R-4) and define $\overset{*}{U}$ by (2.13). Then*[5]

$$F(u,X)=\lambda \Rightarrow \overset{*}{U}(X/\lambda)=u \qquad \forall (u,X)\in \mathcal{R}(U)\times \Omega_+^n \tag{a}$$

and

$$\overset{*}{U}(X/\lambda)=u \Rightarrow \left[F(u,X)=\lambda \text{ or } X/\lambda \in \text{int } \overset{*}{L}\left(\sup \mathcal{R}(U)\right)\right] \tag{b}$$

$$\forall (\lambda,X)\in \Omega_+^{n+1},$$

where

$$\overset{*}{L}(u)=\left\{ X\in \Omega^n |\, \overset{*}{U}(X)\geqslant u\right\}.$$

Proof.   Rewrite (2.13) as

$$\overset{*}{U}(X/\lambda)=\max\{u\in \mathcal{R}(U)|\, F(u,X)\geqslant \lambda\}. \tag{c}$$

If $F(\bar{u},X)=\lambda$ for some $\bar{u}\in \mathcal{R}(U)$ then $\bar{u}$ is feasible in (c). Thus $\overset{*}{U}(X/\lambda)\geqslant \bar{u}$. Since $\overset{*}{U}(X/\lambda)$ must be feasible in (c) it follows that $F(\overset{*}{U}(X/\lambda),X)\geqslant \lambda = F(\bar{u},X)$. Thus, by the negative monotonicity of $F(\cdot,X)$, we also have

$$\overset{*}{U}(X/\lambda)\leqslant \bar{u}.$$

Hence

$$\overset{*}{U}(X/\lambda)=\bar{u}.$$

To prove (b), note that, if $\overset{*}{U}(X/\lambda)=\bar{u}$, then $\bar{u}$ is feasible in (c) and hence $F(\bar{u},X)\geqslant \lambda$. Suppose $F(\bar{u},X)>\lambda$. If $\bar{u}\neq \sup \mathcal{R}(U)$ then, since $\mathcal{R}(U)$ is an interval, there exists an $\varepsilon>0$ and a scalar $\hat{u}\in N_\varepsilon(\bar{u})$ such that $\hat{u}>\bar{u}$ and $F(\hat{u},X)>\lambda$, which violates the optimality property of $\bar{u}$. Hence either $F(\bar{u},X)=\lambda$ or $\bar{u}=\sup \mathcal{R}(U)$. In the latter case, if $F(\bar{u},X)>\lambda$, then $X/\lambda \in \text{int } \overset{*}{L}(\sup \mathcal{R}(U))$.   ‖

---

[5]Note that the special cases of (a) and (b) indicated in footnote 4 also apply here.

Theorem A.5 *Suppose that U satisfies* (R-1). *Then F, defined by* (2.11), *satisfies* (R-4). *Moreover, if $\overset{*}{U}$ is derived from F by* (2.13) *and extension to the boundary, then $\overset{*}{U} = U$.*

Proof. To prove continuity of F, define the mapping $\Lambda: \mathcal{R}(U) \times \Omega^n_+ \to \mathcal{P}(\Omega^1_+ \cup \{0\})$ by

$$\Lambda(u, X) = \{\lambda \in \Omega^1_+ \mid U(X/\lambda) \geqslant u\} \cup \{0\}.$$

The monotonicity of U implies that the feasible set in (2.11) is nonempty. Hence (2.11) is equivalent to

$$F(u, X) = \max_{\lambda} \{\lambda \mid \lambda \in \Lambda(u, X)\}.$$

If Λ is continuous, then, by the maximum theorem, so is F.

The (R-1) properties of U imply that $\Lambda(u, X)$ is a closed and bounded interval and is therefore compact. To prove that Λ is closed, consider a sequence $\{u^\nu, X^\nu\} \subseteq \mathcal{R}(U) \times \Omega^n_+$ satisfying

$$(u^\nu, X^\nu) \to (u^0, X^0) \in \mathcal{R}(U) \times \Omega^n_+,$$

and a corresponding sequence $\{\lambda^\nu\} \subseteq \Omega^1_+ \cup \{0\}$, satisfying

$$\lambda^\nu \in \Lambda(u^\nu, X^\nu) \qquad \forall \nu$$

and

$$\lambda^\nu \to \lambda^0.$$

Then

$$U(X/\lambda^\nu) \geqslant u^\nu \qquad \forall \nu$$

and, as U is continuous,

$$U(X^0/\lambda^0) \geqslant u^0.$$

Hence $\lambda^0 \in \Lambda(u^0, X^0)$, and Λ is upper hemicontinuous.

To prove lower hemicontinuity of Λ, we again invoke the theorem of Heller (1977). As a compact nondegenerate[6] interval, $\Lambda(u, X)$ is a convex set with a nonempty interior; hence, Λ is trivially locally interior.

---

[6]Recall the maintained assumption that U is not the constant function.

To see that Λ is locally constant, consider $\lambda^0 \in \mathrm{int}\,\Lambda(u^0, X^0)$ and define $\bar{\lambda} = \max \Lambda(u^0, X^0)$. [$\bar{\lambda}$ exists, since $\Lambda(u^0, X^0)$ is compact.] If $U(X^0/\lambda^0)$ is not maximal on $\mathcal{R}(U)$, then, by monotonicity of U and local nonsatiation at X^0/λ^0 (implied by quasi-concavity),

$$U(X^0/\lambda^0) > U(X^0/\bar{\lambda}).$$

The continuity of U implies the existence of an $\varepsilon > 0$ such that

$$X \in N_\varepsilon(X^0) \subseteq \Omega_+^n \quad \Rightarrow \quad U(X/\lambda^0) > U(X^0/\bar{\lambda}) \geqslant u^0.$$

As

$$U(X/\lambda^0) > u^0 \qquad \forall X \in N_\varepsilon(X^0),$$

the continuity of U implies the existence of a $\bar{u} > u^0$ such that

$$U(X/\lambda^0) > \bar{u} \qquad \forall X \in N_\varepsilon(X^0).$$

Let $\delta = \bar{u} - u^0$, and define the open neighborhood

$$N(u^0, X^0) = (u^0 - \delta, u^0 + \delta) \times N_\varepsilon(X^0).$$

By construction,

$$U(X/\lambda^0) > u \qquad \forall (u, X) \in N(u^0, X^0).$$

Thus, Λ is locally constant, and by corollary 3.1 of Heller (1977), Λ is lower hemicontinuous. By the maximum theorem, F is therefore continuous.

We now establish that F is decreasing in u. Suppose $\hat{u} < \bar{u}$ and let $\hat{\lambda} = F(\hat{u}, X)$ and $\bar{\lambda} = F(\bar{u}, X)$. Then, invoking Lemma A.1,

$$U(X/\hat{\lambda}) = \hat{u} < U(X/\bar{\lambda}) = \bar{u},$$

and the monotonicity of U implies that $\hat{\lambda} > \bar{\lambda}$.

To prove that F is nondecreasing in X, suppose that $\bar{X} \geqslant \hat{X}$, where $\bar{X} \in \Omega_+^n$ and $\hat{X} \in \Omega_+^n$. Let $\bar{\lambda} = F(u, \bar{X})$ and $\hat{\lambda} = F(u, \hat{X})$, and use Lemma A.1 to write

$$u = U(\bar{X}/\bar{\lambda}) = U(\hat{X}/\hat{\lambda}).$$

Since $\bar{X} > \hat{X}$, the monotonicity of U implies that

$$U(\bar{X}/\bar{\lambda}) > U(\hat{X}/\bar{\lambda}),$$

and hence that

$$U(\hat{X}/\hat{\lambda}) > U(\hat{X}/\bar{\lambda}).$$

Since U is monotonic, it follows that $\bar{\lambda} > \hat{\lambda}$.

To see that F is PLH in X, note that for any $\theta > 0$,

$$F(u, \theta X) = \max_{\lambda} \left\{ \lambda \in \Omega^1_+ \,|\, U(\theta X/\lambda) > u \right\}$$

$$= \theta \max_{\lambda/\theta} \left\{ \frac{\lambda}{\theta} \in \Omega^1_+ \,\left|\, U\left(\frac{X}{\lambda/\theta}\right) > u \right. \right\} = \theta F(u, X).$$

To prove concavity of F in X, consider $(u, \hat{X}, X') \in \Re(U) \times \Omega^{2n}_+$ such that

$$\hat{\lambda} = F(u, \hat{X}) > F(u, X') = \lambda'. \tag{a}$$

Thus, using Lemma A.1,

$$U(\hat{X}/\hat{\lambda}) = U(X'/\lambda') = u,$$

and, using (a) and the monotonicity of U,

$$U(\hat{X}/\lambda') > U(X'/\lambda') = u. \tag{b}$$

Quasi-concavity of U, together with (b), implies that

$$U(\theta \hat{X}/\lambda' + (1-\theta)X'/\lambda') > u \qquad \forall \theta \in [0,1],$$

which, in turn, implies that

$$F\left(u, \frac{\theta \hat{X} + (1-\theta)X'}{\lambda'}\right) > 1 \qquad \forall \theta \in [0,1]. \tag{c}$$

Exploiting the positive linear homogeneity of F in X, (c) implies

$$F(u, \theta \hat{X} + (1-\theta)X') > \lambda' = F(u, X') \qquad \forall \theta \in [0,1],$$

proving that F is quasi-concave in X. But, by a theorem of Newman (1969), quasi-concavity and positive linear homogeneity of $F(u, \cdot)$ imply that $F(u, \cdot)$ is concave for all $u \in \mathcal{R}(U)$.

Letting $\mathring{U}$ be the restriction of U to Ω_+^n it remains to show that $\overset{*}{U} = \mathring{U}$. Suppose $\overset{*}{u} = \overset{*}{U}(\overline{X}) \neq \mathring{U}(\overline{X}) = \mathring{u}$ for some $\overline{X} \in \Omega_+^n$. Then, by Lemma A.1, $F(\overset{*}{u}, \overline{X}) = 1$ and $F(\mathring{u}, \overline{X}) = 1$, or $\overline{X}$ is in the interior of a region of global satiation. But $F(\mathring{u}, \overline{X}) = 1$ and $F(\overset{*}{u}, \overline{X}) = 1$ jointly contradict the strict monotonicity of $F(\cdot, X)$. Moreover, if $\overline{X}$ is in the interior of a region of global satiation, then $F(\mathring{u}, \overline{X}) > 1$, and, by the strict negative monotonicity of $F(\cdot, X)$,

$$\overset{*}{u} > \mathring{u} = \mathring{U}(\overline{X}) = \max \mathcal{R}(U),$$

implying $\overset{*}{u} \notin \mathcal{R}(U)$, a contradiction. $\|$

Theorem A.6 *Suppose that F satisfies* (R-4). *Then $\overset{*}{U}$, defined by* (2.13), *satisfies* (R-1). *Moreover, if $\overset{*}{F}$ is derived from $\overset{*}{U}$ by* (2.11), *then $\overset{*}{F} = F$.*

Proof.   To prove continuity, define the mapping $\Gamma : \Omega_+^n \to \mathbf{R}$ by

$$\Gamma(X) = \left\{ u \in \hat{\mathcal{R}}(U) \,\middle|\, F(u, X) \geqslant 1 \right\}.$$

For each $X \in \Omega_+^n$, $\Gamma(X)$ is a compact, nondegenerate interval [$\inf \mathcal{R}(U)$, $U(X)$]. (If necessary, renormalize U to a bound $\mathcal{R}(U)$ from below.) Moreover,

$$\overset{*}{U}(X) = \max_u \left\{ u \,\middle|\, u \in \Gamma(X) \right\}.$$

As $\Gamma(X)$ is a convex set with a nonempty interior for all $X \in \Omega_+^n$, Γ is locally interior. To see that Γ is locally constant, consider a point $\mathring{u} \in \text{int}\,\Gamma(\overline{X})$. Then $F(\mathring{u}, \overline{X}) > 1$. The continuity of F implies, therefore, that there exists a neighborhood $N(\overline{X}) \subseteq \Omega_+^n$ such that

$$X \in N(\overline{X}) \;\Rightarrow\; F(\mathring{u}, X) > 1 \;\Rightarrow\; \mathring{u} \in \Gamma(X).$$

Hence Γ is locally constant as well as locally interior, and, by corollary 3.1 of Heller (1977), Γ is lower hemicontinuous.

Suppose that Γ is not upper hemicontinuous. Then, as $\Gamma(X)$ is compact for all $X \in \Omega_+^n$, there exist a sequence $\{X^\nu\} \subseteq \Omega_+^n$ such that $X^\nu \to X^0$ and a corresponding sequence $\{u^\nu\} \subseteq \hat{\mathcal{R}}(U)$ such that $u^\nu \to \mathring{u}$ and $\mathring{u} \notin \Gamma(X^0)$. That is, $F(u^\nu, X^\nu) \geqslant 1 \; \forall \nu$, but $F(u^0, X^0) < 1$, violating the continuity of F.

To prove quasi-concavity of $\overset{*}{U}$, consider $(\hat{X}, X') \in \Omega^{2n}$ such that $\overset{*}{U}(\hat{X}) > \overset{*}{U}(X')$, or

$$\max_u \left\{ u \in \mathcal{R}(U) | F(u, \hat{X}) \geqslant 1 \right\} > \max_u \left\{ u \in \mathcal{R}(U) | F(u, X') \geqslant 1 \right\}.$$

Note that $\overset{*}{U}(X') < \sup \mathcal{R}(U)$ since $\overset{*}{U}(X') < \overset{*}{U}(\hat{X})$. As F is decreasing in u,

$$F\left(\overset{*}{U}(X'), \hat{X} \right) > F\left(\overset{*}{U}(\hat{X}), \hat{X} \right) \geqslant F\left(\overset{*}{U}(X'), X' \right) = 1, \tag{a}$$

where the last equality follows from Lemma A.2, since $\overset{*}{U}(X') < \sup \mathcal{R}(U)$.

The quasi-concavity of F in X (implied by the concavity of F in X), together with (a), yields (again invoking Lemma A.2)

$$F\left(\overset{*}{U}(X'), \theta \hat{X} + (1-\theta)X' \right) > F\left(\overset{*}{U}(X'), X' \right) = 1 \qquad \forall \theta \in (0, 1).$$

As $F(\cdot, X)$ is decreasing and Lemma A.2 implies that either

$$F\left(\overset{*}{U}(\theta \hat{X} + (1-\theta)X'), \theta \hat{X} + (1-\theta)X' \right) = 1$$

or $\overset{*}{U}(\theta \hat{X} + (1-\theta)X') = \sup \mathcal{R}(U), \; \forall \theta \in (0, 1)$, it follows that

$$\overset{*}{U}(\theta \hat{X} + (1-\theta)X') > \overset{*}{U}(X') \qquad \forall \theta \in (0, 1),$$

proving the quasi-concavity of $\overset{*}{U}$.

To see that $\overset{*}{U}$ is nondecreasing, consider $\hat{X} \geqslant X'$. For any $u \in \mathcal{R}(U)$, $F(u, \hat{X}) \geqslant F(u, X')$. As F is decreasing in u,

$$\max_u \left\{ u \in \mathcal{R}(U) | F(u, \hat{X}) \geqslant 1 \right\} \geqslant \max_u \left\{ u \in \mathcal{R}(U) | F(u, X') \geqslant 1 \right\},$$

which implies that $\overset{*}{U}(\hat{X}) \geqslant \overset{*}{U}(X')$.

It remains to show that $\overset{*}{F}=F$. Given an arbitrary $(\bar{u},\bar{X})\in\mathcal{R}(U)\times\Omega_+^n$ let

$$\bar{\lambda}=F(\bar{u},\bar{X}).\tag{b}$$

Then from Lemma A.2

$$\bar{u}=\overset{*}{U}(\bar{X}/\bar{\lambda}).\tag{c}$$

Since F is PLH in X

$$F(\bar{u},\bar{X}/\bar{\lambda})=1$$

and

$$F(\bar{u},\bar{X}/\delta)<1\qquad\forall\delta>\bar{\lambda}.$$

Since F is continuous and decreasing in u, there exists a scalar $\hat{u}<\bar{u}$ such that

$$F(\hat{u},\bar{X}/\delta)=1.$$

From Lemma A.2 this implies that

$$\hat{u}=\overset{*}{U}(\bar{X}/\delta)$$

and hence

$$\overset{*}{U}(\bar{X}/\delta)<\overset{*}{U}(\bar{X}/\bar{\lambda})\qquad\forall\delta>\lambda.$$

This establishes that $\bar{X}/\bar{\lambda}$ cannot be in the interior of a region of global satiation for $\overset{*}{U}$ since every neighborhood of $\bar{X}/\bar{\lambda}$ of radius $\epsilon=\delta-\lambda$ contains at least one point $(\bar{X}/\delta)$ for which $\overset{*}{U}(\bar{X}/\delta)$ takes on a lower value. Since $\overset{*}{U}$ satisfies $(R-1)$, (c) implies that

$$\overset{*}{F}(\bar{u},\bar{X})=\bar{\lambda}$$

by Lemma A.1. This together with (b) implies that

$$F(\bar{u},\bar{X})=\overset{*}{F}(\bar{u},\bar{X})\qquad\forall(\bar{u},\bar{X})\in\mathcal{R}(U)\times\Omega_+^n.\quad\|$$

Lemma A.3 *Suppose that U satisfies $(R\text{-}1)$ and define F by (2.11). Then*

$$U(X/\lambda) \geqslant u \Leftrightarrow F(u,X) \geqslant \lambda \qquad \forall (u,\lambda,X) \in \mathcal{R}(U) \times \Omega_+^{n+1}.$$

Proof. By Lemma A.1

$$F(u,X) = \lambda \Rightarrow U(X/\lambda) = u \qquad \forall (u,X) \in \mathcal{R}(U) \times \Omega_+^n \qquad \text{(a)}$$

and

$$U(X/\lambda) = u \Rightarrow F(u,X) = \lambda \qquad \forall (\lambda,X) \in \Omega_+^{n+1} | X/\lambda \notin \text{int } L(\sup \mathcal{R}(U)). \tag{b}$$

The monotonicity of U and (2.11) yield

$$F(u,X) > \lambda \Rightarrow U(X/\lambda) \geqslant u \qquad \forall (u,\lambda,X) \in \mathcal{R}(U) \times \Omega_+^{n+1}. \qquad \text{(c)}$$

If X/λ is a point of global satiation [i.e. $X/\lambda \in L(\sup \mathcal{R}(U))$] then $F(u,X) \geqslant \lambda \ \forall \ u \in \mathcal{R}(U)$, so that, using (b),

$$U(X/\lambda) = u \Rightarrow F(u,X) \geqslant \lambda \qquad \forall (\lambda,X) \in \Omega_+^{n+1}. \qquad \text{(d)}$$

Hence, again using (2.11) and the monotonicity of U,

$$U(X/\lambda) > u \Rightarrow F(u,X) > \lambda \qquad \forall (\lambda,X) \in \Omega_+^{n+1}. \qquad \text{(e)}$$

Implications (a), (c), (d) and (e) jointly yield

$$U(X/\lambda) \geqslant u \Leftrightarrow F(u,X) \geqslant \lambda \qquad \forall (u,\lambda,X) \in \mathcal{R}(U) \times \Omega_+^{n+1}. \quad \|$$

Theorem A.7 *Suppose that F is derived from U satisfying $(R\text{-}1)$ by (2.11). Then $\overline{C}$, derived by (2.31) from the extension $\overset{*}{F}$ of F to the boundary, equals C, derived from U by (2.9).*

Proof. C and $\overline{C}$ are defined by

$$C(u,P) = \min_X \{ P \cdot X | X \in \Omega^n \wedge U(X) \geqslant u \} \tag{2.9}$$

and

$$\overline{C}(u,P) = \min_X \{ P \cdot X | X \in \Omega^n \wedge \overset{*}{F}(u,X) \geqslant 1 \}, \tag{2.31}$$

respectively. F is derived from U by

$$F(u,X) = \max_{\lambda} \left\{ \lambda \in \Omega^1_+ \mid U(X/\lambda) \geqslant u \right\}. \tag{2.11}$$

It suffices to show that

$$U(X) \geqslant u \Leftrightarrow \overset{*}{F}(u,X) \geqslant 1 \qquad \forall (u,X) \in \mathcal{R}(U) \times \Omega^n_+. \tag{a}$$

From Lemma A.3. we have

$$U(X) \geqslant u \Leftrightarrow F(u,X) \geqslant 1 \qquad \forall (u,X) \in \mathcal{R}(U) \times \Omega^n_+. \tag{b}$$

Moreover, as $\overset{*}{F}$, the extension of F to the boundary of Ω^n_+ by continuity from above, is unique (b) yields the desired equivalence. $\parallel$

Theorem A.8 *Suppose that C is derived from U satisfying (R-1) by (2.9). Then $\bar{F}$, derived by (2.32) from the extension, C^*, of C to the boundary, equals F, derived from U by (2.11).*

Proof.[7] F and $\bar{F}$ are defined by

$$F(u,X) = \max_{\lambda} \left\{ \lambda \in \Omega^1_+ \mid U(X/\lambda) \geqslant u \right\} \tag{2.11}$$

and

$$\bar{F}(u,X) = \min_{P} \left\{ P \cdot X \mid \overset{*}{C}(u,P) \geqslant 1 \wedge P \in \Omega^n \right\}, \tag{2.32}$$

respectively. In order to show that F and $\bar{F}$ are equal, it is sufficient to show that L and $\bar{L}$ are the same, where

$$L(u) = \left\{ X \mid X \in \Omega^n \wedge \overset{*}{F}(u,X) \geqslant 1 \right\}$$

and

$$\bar{L}(u) = \left\{ X \mid X \in \Omega^n \wedge \overset{*}{\bar{F}}(u,X) \geqslant 1 \right\},$$

where $*$ indicates closure by continuity from above.

[7] This proof follows Shephard [1970, Proposition 44, p. 157].

First we show that $L(u) \subseteq \bar{L}(u)$. Suppose that $\tilde{X} \in L(u)$. From (2.9), the definition of C, (2.11), and theorem A.7, we know that

$$C(u,P) = \min_X \left\{ P \cdot X \mid X \in \Omega^n \wedge U(X) \geqslant u \right\} \tag{2.9}$$

$$= \min_X \left\{ P \cdot X \mid X \in \Omega^n \wedge \overset{*}{F}(u,X) \geqslant 1 \right\}$$

$$= \min_X \left\{ P \cdot X \mid X \in L(u) \right\}.$$

This implies that

$$C(u,P) \leqslant P \cdot \tilde{X} \qquad \forall P \in \Omega_+^n. \tag{a}$$

Since $\tilde{X} \in L(u)$, $\overset{*}{F}(u,\tilde{X}) = \tilde{\lambda} \geqslant 1$. The continuity and monotonicity of U imply that $\tilde{X}/\tilde{\lambda}$ is on the boundary of $L(u)$. Since $L(u)$ is closed and convex, there exists a supporting hyperplane passing through $\tilde{X}/\tilde{\lambda}$ and hence, by the monotonicity of U, a price vector $\hat{P} \neq 0$ such that

$$\overset{*}{C}(u,\hat{P}) = \hat{P} \cdot (\tilde{X}/\tilde{\lambda}) \leqslant \hat{P} \cdot X \qquad \forall X \in L(u).$$

Let

$$\tilde{P} = \frac{\tilde{\lambda}\hat{P}}{\hat{P} \cdot \tilde{X}}.$$

Then

$$\overset{*}{C}(u,\tilde{P}) = 1 \leqslant \tilde{P} \cdot X \qquad \forall X \in L(u). \tag{b}$$

We now show that $\tilde{P}$ is a solution to the problem that defines $\bar{F}$:

$$\bar{F}(u,\tilde{X}) = \min_P \left\{ P \cdot \tilde{X} \mid P \in \Omega^n \wedge \overset{*}{C}(u,P) \geqslant 1 \right\}. \tag{c}$$

$\tilde{P}$ is feasible by construction; suppose it is not optimal. Then there exists a price vector $\overset{*}{P}$ such that $\overset{*}{C}(u,\overset{*}{P}) \geqslant 1$ and

$$\overset{*}{P} \cdot \tilde{X} < \tilde{P} \cdot \tilde{X}.$$

Dividing by $\tilde{\lambda}$,

$$\overset{*}{P} \cdot (\tilde{X}/\tilde{\lambda}) < \tilde{P} \cdot (\tilde{X}/\tilde{\lambda}) = 1.$$

Thus, since $U(\tilde{X}/\tilde{\lambda}) = u$,

$$\overset{*}{C}\left(u, \overset{*}{P}\right) < 1,$$

which implies that $\overset{*}{P}$ is not feasible in (c), which is a contradiction. Hence $\tilde{P}$ is optimal in (c).

From (c) we have

$$\bar{F}(u, \tilde{X}) = \overset{*}{F}(u, \tilde{X}) = \tilde{P} \cdot \tilde{X}. \tag{d}$$

From (a) and the definition of $\overset{*}{C}$, we know that

$$\overset{*}{C}(u, \tilde{P}) \leqslant \tilde{P} \cdot \tilde{X},$$

which, together with (b) and (d), implies that

$$\overset{*}{F}(u, \tilde{X}) \geqslant 1.$$

Hence $\tilde{X} \in \bar{L}(u)$.

To show that $\bar{L}(u) \subseteq L(u)$, we show that

$$\tilde{X} \in \bar{L}(u) \quad \Rightarrow \quad \tilde{X} \in L(u);$$

this, however, is equivalent to the contrapositive statement,

$$\tilde{X} \notin L(u) \quad \Rightarrow \quad \tilde{X} \notin \bar{L}(u).$$

$L(u)$ is convex and closed, and F is nondecreasing in X; thus, if $\tilde{X} \notin L(u)$, there exists a strictly separating hyperplane, and hence a nonnegative price vector, $\tilde{P} \neq 0$, such that

$$\tilde{P} \cdot \tilde{X} < \tilde{P} \cdot X \qquad \forall X \in L(u).$$

In particular,

$$\tilde{P} \cdot \tilde{X} < \overset{*}{C}(u, \tilde{P}). \tag{e}$$

Dividing both sides by $\overset{*}{C}(u,\tilde{P})$ and letting

$$\hat{P} = \frac{\tilde{P}}{\overset{*}{C}(u,\tilde{P})},$$

(e) becomes

$$\hat{P} \cdot \tilde{X} < 1.$$

Also, since $\overset{*}{C}$ is PLH in P,

$$\overset{*}{C}(u,\hat{P}) = 1.$$

Thus, $\hat{P}$ is feasible in (2.32) and

$$\bar{F}(u,X) \leqslant \hat{P} \cdot \tilde{X} < 1.$$

Hence, $\overset{*}{\bar{F}}(u,\tilde{X}) < 1$, and this implies that $\tilde{X} \notin \bar{L}(u)$.   ‖

Theorem A.9 *Suppose that V is derived from U, satisfying (R-1), by (2.1). Then $\bar{C}$, derived from V by (2.14), equals C, derived from U by (2.9).*

Proof.   This result was proved in section 2.3.3.   ‖

From theorem A.9 we know that the cost function may be derived from the indirect utility function by

$$C(u,P) = \min\{\lambda \in \Omega_+^1 | V(P/\lambda) \geqslant u\}. \tag{2.14}$$

As this problem has the same formal structure as the derivation of F from U by (2.11), the following results are analogous to lemmas A.1–3.

Lemma A.4 *Suppose that V satisfies (R-2) and define C by (2.14). Then*

$$C(u,P) = \lambda \;\Rightarrow\; V(P/\lambda) = u \qquad \forall (u,P) \in \mathcal{R}(U) \times \Omega_+^n \tag{a}$$

and

$$V(P/\lambda) = u \;\Rightarrow\; C(u,P) = \lambda \quad \text{or} \quad P/\lambda \in \text{int} M\big(\sup(\mathcal{R}(U))\big)$$

$$\forall (\lambda, P) \in \Omega_+^{n+1} \tag{b}$$

where

$$M\big(\sup(\mathcal{R}(U))\big) = \{P \in \Omega_+^n | V(P) = \sup(\mathcal{R}(u))\}.$$

Proof.   If $C(\overset{*}{u},P)=\lambda^*$, then λ^* must be feasible in (2.14), and hence

$$V(P/\lambda^*) \geqslant \overset{*}{u}.\tag{c}$$

Construct a monotonically increasing sequence which converges to λ^*, i.e.

$$\lambda^\nu < \lambda^{\nu+1}\qquad \forall\nu$$

and

$$\lambda^\nu \to \lambda^*.$$

Since $\lambda^\nu < \lambda^*, \lambda^\nu$ is not feasible in (2.14). Thus,

$$V(P/\lambda^\nu) < \overset{*}{u}\qquad \forall\nu.\tag{d}$$

Since V is continuous and $\lambda^\nu \to \lambda^*$, (d) implies that

$$V(P/\lambda^*) \leqslant \overset{*}{u}.\tag{e}$$

Together, (c) and (e) imply that $V(P/\lambda^*) = \overset{*}{u}$.

To prove (b), note that, if $V(P/\lambda) = \overset{*}{u}$, λ is feasible in (2.14) and hence $\lambda \geqslant C(\overset{*}{u},P)=\lambda^*$. Then from (a) we have $V(P/\lambda^*) = \overset{*}{u}$ and hence $V(P/\lambda) = V(P/\lambda^*)$. This implies that either $\lambda=\lambda^*$ or P/λ is in the interior of a region of global satiation of V.   ‖

Lemma A.5   *Suppose that V satisfies $(R\text{-}2)$ and define C by (2.14). Then*

$$C(u,P) \leqslant \lambda \Leftrightarrow V(P/\lambda) \geqslant u\qquad \forall(u,\lambda,P)\in \mathcal{R}(U)\times\Omega_+^{n+1}.$$

Proof.   By Lemma A.4,

$$C(u,P)=\lambda \Rightarrow V(P/\lambda)=u\qquad \forall(u,P)\in \mathcal{R}(U)\times\Omega_+^n,\tag{a}$$

and

$$V(P/\lambda)=u \Rightarrow C(u,P)=\lambda\qquad \forall(\lambda,P)\in\Omega_+^{n+1}\tag{b}$$

where $P/\lambda \notin \operatorname{int}M(\sup \mathcal{R}(U))$.
The monotonicity of V and (2.14) yield

$$C(u,P)<\lambda \Rightarrow V(P/\lambda) > u\qquad \forall(u,\lambda,P)\in \mathcal{R}(U)\times\Omega_+^{n+1}.\tag{c}$$

If P/λ is a point of global satiation then $C(u,P) \leqslant \lambda \quad \forall u \in \mathcal{R}(U)$. Thus, using (b),

$$V(P/\lambda) = u \Rightarrow C(u,P) \leqslant \lambda. \qquad \forall(\lambda, P) \in \Omega_+^{n+1}. \qquad \text{(d)}$$

Hence, again using (2.14) and the monotonicity of V,

$$V(P/\lambda) > u \Rightarrow C(u,P) < \lambda \qquad \forall(u, \lambda, P) \in \mathcal{R}(U) \times \Omega_+^{n+1}. \qquad \text{(e)}$$

Implications (a), (c), (d) and (e) jointly yield

$$V(P/\lambda) \geqslant u \Leftrightarrow C(u,P) \leqslant \lambda \quad \forall(u, \lambda, P) \in \mathcal{R}(U) \times \Omega_+^{n+1}. \quad \|$$

Lemma A.6   *Suppose V satisfies $(R\text{-}2)$ and define C by (2.14). Then*

$$C(u,P) \geqslant \lambda \Leftrightarrow V(P/\lambda) \leqslant u \qquad \forall(u, \lambda, P) \in \mathcal{R}(U) \times \Omega_+^{n+1}.$$

where $P/\lambda \notin \mathrm{int}\, M(\sup \mathcal{R}(U))$

Proof.   From Lemma A.4,

$$C(u,P) = \lambda \Leftrightarrow V(P/\lambda) = u \qquad \forall(u, \lambda, P) \in \mathcal{R}(U) \times \Omega_+^{n+1}.$$

where $P/\lambda \notin \mathrm{int}\, M(\sup \mathcal{R}(U))$
Moreover, from Lemma A.5

$$C(u,P) > \lambda \Leftrightarrow V(P/\lambda) < u \qquad \forall(u, \lambda, P) \in \mathcal{R}(U) \times \Omega_+^{n+1}.$$

Combining these results completes the proof. $\|$

Theorem A.10   *Suppose that C is derived from U satisfying $(R\text{-}1)$ by (2.9). Then $\bar{V}$, derived from C by (2.19), is equal to V, derived from U by (2.1).*

Proof.   For $\lambda = 1$, the statement of Lemma A.6 becomes

$$C(u,P) \geqslant 1 \Leftrightarrow V(P) \leqslant u \qquad \forall(u,P) \in \mathcal{R}(U) \times (\Omega_+^n - \mathrm{int}\, M(\sup \mathcal{R}(U))).$$

Hence, for $P \notin M(\sup \mathcal{R}(U))$

$$\bar{V}(P) = \min_u \{ u \in \mathcal{R}(U) | C(u,P) \geqslant 1 \} \qquad \text{(2.19)}$$

can be rewritten as

$$\bar{V}(P) = \min_u \{ u \in \mathcal{R}(U) | V(P) \leqslant u \} = V(P). \qquad \text{(a)}$$

Thus $V(P) = \overline{V}(P)$ $\forall P \in \Omega_+^n - M(\sup \mathcal{R}(U))$. However, if $P \in M(\sup \mathcal{R}(U))$, then the feasible sets for (2.19) and (a) are each the singleton $\{\sup \mathcal{R}(U)\}$. Thus

$$V(P) = \overline{V}(P) \qquad \forall P \in \Omega_+^n. \quad \|$$

Theorem A.11 *Suppose that V is derived from U satisfying (R-1) by (2.1). Then $\overline{F}$, derived from its closure $\overset{*}{V}$ by (2.26), equals F derived from U by (2.11) over the interior of its domain,* int $(\mathcal{R}(U) \times \Omega_+^n)$.[8]

Proof. $\overline{F}$ and F are defined by

$$\overline{F}(u,X) = \min_P \left\{ P \cdot X \mid P \in \Omega^n \wedge \overset{*}{V}(P) \leqslant u \right\} \qquad (2.26)$$

and

$$F(u,X) = \max_\lambda \left\{ \lambda \in \Omega_+^1 \mid U(X/\lambda) \geqslant u \right\}. \qquad (2.11)$$

From Lemma A.6 we know that $C(u,P) \geqslant 1 \Leftrightarrow V(P) \leqslant u$. It follows immediately that $\overset{*}{C}(u,P) \geqslant 1 \Leftrightarrow \overset{*}{V}(P) \leqslant u$ $\forall (u,P) \in \mathcal{R}(U) \times \Omega^n - M(\sup \mathcal{R}(U))$. Hence

$$\overline{F}(u,X) = \min_P \left\{ P \cdot X \mid P \in \Omega^n \wedge \overset{*}{C}(u,P) \geqslant 1 \right\}.$$

By theorem A.8, $\overline{F} = F$. $\quad \|$

Theorem A.12 *Suppose that F is derived from U satisfying (R-1) by (2.11). Then $\overline{V}$, derived from F by (2.30), equals V derived from U by (2.1) over the restricted domain* $\overset{\circ}{\Omega}_+^n = \{ P \in \Omega_+^n \mid V(P) < \sup \mathcal{R}(U) \}$[9]

Proof. $\overline{V}$ and V are defined by

$$\overline{V}(P) = \min_u \left\{ u \in \mathcal{R}(U) \mid F(u,X) \leqslant P \cdot X \quad \forall X \in \Omega_+^n \right\} \qquad (2.30)$$

and

$$V(P) = \max_X \left\{ U(X) \mid X \in \Omega^n \wedge P \cdot X \leqslant 1 \right\}. \qquad (2.1)$$

---

[8]Note that the definition of $\overline{F}$ can easily be modified to make $\overline{F}(u,X) = F(u,X)$ for $u = \sup \mathcal{R}(U)$.

[9]Redefining $\overline{F}$ as in footnote 8 would obviate the need for the restriction of the domain.

By theorem A.11,

$$F(u,X)= \min_{P} \left\{ P{\cdot}X \,|\, P \in \Omega^n \wedge \overset{*}{V}(P) \leqslant u \right\} \qquad \forall(u,X) \in \mathrm{int}(\mathcal{R}(U) \times \Omega^n_+).$$

Hence, using (2.30), by duality with theorem A.3,

$$V(P)= \min_{u} \left\{ u \in \mathcal{R}(U) \,|\, F(u,X) \leqslant P{\cdot}X \ \forall X \in \Omega^n_+ \right\} \qquad \forall P \in \overset{\circ}{\Omega}{}^n_+.$$

Thus, $\overline{V}=V$. ‖

REFERENCES

Aczel, J. 1966. *Lectures on Functional Equations and Their Applications*. New York: Academic.

Afriat, S. N. 1972. The Theory of international comparisons of real incomes and prices, In *International Comparisons of Prices and Outputs* (D. J. Daly, ed.). New York: National Bureau of Economic Research, pp. 13–69.

Allen, R. G. D. 1938. *Mathematical Analysis for Economists*. New York: Macmillan.

———, and J. R. Hicks. 1934. A reconsideration of the theory of value, II. *Economica*, 1: 196–219.

Anderson, R. W. 1976. *Commodity Aggregation in Demand Analysis*. Ph. D. dissertation, University of Michigan.

Archibald, G. C., and D. Donaldson. 1976. Non-paternalism and the basic theorems of welfare economics. *Canadian Journal of Economics*, 9: 492–507.

Arrow, K. J. 1974. The measurement of real value added. In *Nations and Households in Economic Growth* (P. A. David and M. W. Reder, eds.). New York: Academic, pp. 3–19.

———, E. W. Barankin, and R. W. Shephard. 1951. Note on the problem of aggregation. Research Memorandum 674, The Rand Corporation.

Barten A. P. 1977. The systems of consumer demand functions approach: a review. *Econometrica*, 45: 23–52.

———, A., and S. Turnovsky. 1966. Some aspects of the aggregation problem for composite demand equations. *International Economic Review*, 7: 231–259.

Berge, C. 1963. *Topological Spaces*. Edinburgh and London: Oliver and Boyd.

Bergson (Burk), A. 1936. Real income, expenditure proportionality, and Frisch's new method of measuring marginal utility. *Review of Economic Studies*, 4: pp. 33–52.

Bergstrom, T. 1970. A "Scandinavian consensus" solution for efficient income distribution among non-malevolent consumers. *Journal of Economic Theory*, 2: 383–398.

Berndt, E. R., and L. R. Christensen. 1973a. The internal structure of functional relationships: Separability, substitution, and aggregation. *Review of Economic Studies*, 40: 403–410.

_____, and _____. 1973b. The translog function and the substitution of equipment, structures, and labor in U. S. manufacturing, 1929–1968. *Journal of Econometrics*, 1: 81–114.

_____, and _____. 1974a. Testing for the existence of a consistent aggregate index of labor inputs. *American Economic Review*, 64: 391–404.

_____, and _____. 1974b. The specification of technology in U. S. manufacturing. Discussion Paper 73–17, University of British Columbia.

_____, and D. O. Wood. 1975. Technology, prices, and the derived demand for energy. *The Review of Economics and Statistics*, 43: 259–268.

Blackorby, C. 1967. *Rational Rules for Intertemporal Decision Making.* Ph. D. Dissertation, The Johns Hopkins University.

_____, R. Boyce, and R. R. Russell. 1977. Estimation of demand system generated by the Gorman polar form: a generalization of the *S*-branch utility tree. *Econometrica*, forthcoming.

_____, and G. Lady. 1967. Structural characteristics of recursive optimization. Unpublished manuscript.

_____, _____, D. Nissen, and R. R. Russell. 1970. Homothetic separability and consumer budgeting. *Econometrica*, 38: 469–472.

_____, C. A. K. Lovell, and M. Thursby. 1976. Extended Hicks neutral technical change. *Economic Journal*, 86: 845–852.

_____, D. Nissen, D. Primont, and R. R. Russell 1973. Consistent intertemporal decision making. *Review of Economic Studies*, 40: 239–248.

_____, _____, _____, and _____. 1974. Recursively decentralized decision making. *Econometrica*, 42: 487–496.

_____, D. Primont, and R. R. Russell. 1975a. Budgeting, decentralization, and aggregation. *Annals of Economic and Social Measurement*, 4: 23–44.

_____, _____, and _____. 1975b. Some simple remarks on duality and the structure of utility functions. *Journal of Economic Theory*, 11: 155–160.

_____, _____, and _____. 1977a. Dual price and quantity aggregation. *Journal of Economic Theory,* 14: 130–148.

_____, _____, and _____. 1977b. An extension and alternative proof of Gorman's price aggregation theorem. In *Theory and Applications of Economic Indices* (W. Eichhorn, ed.). Würstburg-Wien: Physica, forthcoming.

_____, _____, and _____. 1977c. On testing separability restrictions with flexible functional forms. *Journal of Econometrics*, 5: 195–209.

_____, and R. R. Russell. 1975. Conjugate implicit separability. Discussion Paper 75-12, Department of Economics, University of California, San Diego.

_____, and _____. 1976. Functional structure and the Allen partial elasticities of substitution: an application of duality theory. *Review of Economic Studies*, 43: 285–292.

_____, and _____. 1977. Indices and subindices of the cost of living and the standard of living. *International Economic Review*, 18, forthcoming.

Bliss, C. J. 1975. *Capital Theory and the Distribution of Income*. New York: North Holland/American Elsevier.

Boyce, R. 1975. Estimation of dynamic Gorman polar form utility functions. *Annals of Economic and Social Measurement*, 4: 103–116.

_____, and D. Primont. 1976a, An econometric test of the representative consumer hypothesis. Discussion Paper No. 76-31, Department of Economics, University of British Columbia.

_____, and _____. 1976b. An econometric test for cost of living subindexes. Delivered to the meeting of the Econometric Society, Atlantic City.

Braithwait, S. 1975. Consumer demand and cost of living indexes for the U. S.: an empirical comparison of alternative multi-level demand systems. Working Paper 45, Bureau of Labor Statistics, U. S. Department of Labor.

Brown, J. A. C., and A. Deaton. 1972. Surveys in applied economics: models of consumer behavior. *Economic Journal*, 82: 1145–1236.

Brown, M., and D. Heien. 1972. The *S*-branch utility tree: a generalization of the linear expenditure system, *Econometrica*, 40: 737–747.

Burgess, D. 1974. Production theory and the derived demand for imports. *Journal of International Economics*, 4: 103–117.

Burk (Bergson), A. 1936. Real income, expenditure proportionality, and Frisch's new methods of measuring marginal utility, *Review of Economic Studies*, 4: 33–52.

Chipman, J. S., L. Hurwicz, M. K. Richter, and H. F. Sonnenschein. 1971, eds. *Preferences, Utility, and Demand*. New York: Harcourt Brace Jovanovich.

Christensen, L. R., and D. W. Jorgensen. 1973. U. S. income, savings, and wealth, 1929–1969. *Review of Income and Wealth*, 4: 329–362.

_____, _____, and L. J. Lau. 1973. Transcendental logarithmic production frontiers. *Review of Economics and Statistics*, 65: 28–45.

_____, _____, and _____. 1975. Transcendental logarithmic utility functions. *American Economic Review*, 65: 367–383.

_____, and M. E. Manser 1975. Cost of living indexes and price indexes for U. S. meat and produce, 1947–1971. In *Household Production and Consumption* (N. Terleckyj, ed.). New York: National Bureau of Economic Research.

_____, and _____. 1977. Estimating U. S. consumer preferences for meat with a flexible utility function. *Journal of Econometrics*, 5: 37–54.

Darrough, M. 1975. *Intertemporal Allocations of Consumption, Savings, and Leisure:*

An Application Using Japanese Data. Ph. D. dissertation, University of British Columbia.

Deaton, A. 1975. *Models and Projections of Demand in Post-War Britain.* London: Chapman and Hall.

Debreu, G. 1952. A social equilibrium existence theorem. *Proceedings of the National Academy of Sciences of USA*, 38: 886–893.

_____. 1954. Representation of a preference ordering by a numerical function. In *Decision Processes* (R. Thrall, C. Coombs, and R. Davis, eds.). New York: Wiley, pp. 159–165.

_____. 1959a, Topological methods in cardinal utility theory. In *Mathematical Methods in the Social Sciences* (K. Arrow, S. Karlin, and P. Suppes, eds.). Stanford: Stanford U. P.

_____. 1959b. *Theory of Value.* New York: Wiley.

Denny, M. 1972. *Trade and the Production Sector: An Exploration of Models of Multi-product Technologies.* Ph. D. dissertation, University of California, Berkeley.

_____. 1974. The relationship between functional forms for the production system. *Canadian Journal of Economics*, 7: 21–31.

Diewert, W. E. 1971, An application of the Shephard duality theorem: a generalized Leontief production function. *Journal of Political Economy*, 79: 481–507.

_____. 1973a. Separability and a generalization of the Cobb-Douglas cost, production, and indirect utility function. Technical Report No. 86, Institute for Mathematical Studies in the Social Sciences, Stanford University.

_____.1973b. Hicks' aggregation theorem and the existence of a real value added function. Department of Manpower and Immigration, Ottawa. Also in *An Econometric Approach to Production Theory* (M. Fuss and D. McFadden, eds.), forthcoming.

_____.1973c. *Lecture Notes on Aggregation and Index Number Theory.* Unpublished manuscript.

_____.1973d. Functional forms for profit and transformation functions. *Journal of Economic Theory*, 6: 284–316.

_____.1974a, Applications of duality theory. In *Frontiers of Quantitative Economics, II* (M. Intrilligator and D. Kendrick, eds.). Amsterdam: North Holland.

_____.1974b, Homogeneous weak separability and exact index numbers. Technical Report No. 122, Institute for Mathematical Studies in the Social Sciences, Stanford University.

_____.1974c. Intertemporal consumer theory and the demand for durables. *Econometrica*, 42: 497–516.

_____.1974d. Functional forms for factor and revenue requirement functions. *International Economic Review*, 15: 119–130.

_____.1976. Exact and superlative index numbers. *Journal of Econometrics*, 4: 115–146.

Eichhorn, W. 1974. Characterization of the CES production functions by quasilinearity. In *Production Theory* (W. Eichhorn, R. Henn, O. Opitz, and R. W. Shephard, eds.), Lecture Notes in Economics and Mathematical Systems (M. Beckman and H. P. Künzi, eds.), Vol. 99. Berlin: Springer-Verlag.

_____.1976. Fisher's test revisited. *Econometrica*, 44: 247–256.

_____.1977. *Functional Equations in Economics*. Reading, Mass.: Addison-Wesley.

_____, and J. Voeller. 1976. *Theory of the Price Index*. Lecture Notes in Economics and Mathematical Systems (M. Beckman and H. P. Künzi, eds.), Vol.140 Berlin: Springer-Verlag.

Epstein, L. 1975. A disaggregate analysis of consumer choice under uncertainty. *Econometrica*, 43: 877–892.

Färe, R. 1974. A characterization of Hicks neutral technical progress. In *Production Theory* (W. Eichhorn, R. Henn, O. Opitz, and R. W. Shephard, eds.), Lecture Notes in Economics and Mathematical Systems (M. Beckman and H. P. Künzi, eds.), Vol. 99. Berlin: Springer-Verlag.

_____, and L. Janssen. 1975. On VES and WDI production functions. *International Economic Review*, 16: 745–750.

Fisher, F. M. 1965. Embodied technical change and the existence of an aggregate capital stock. *Review of Economic Studies*, 32: 263–288.

_____. 1968a. Embodied technology and the existence of labor and output aggregates. *Review of Economic Studies*, 35: 391–412.

_____. 1968b. Embodied technology and the aggregation of fixed and moveable capital goods. *Review of Economic Studies*, 35: 417–428.

_____. 1969. The existence of aggregate production functions. *Econometrica*, 37: 553–577.

_____, and K. Shell. 1972. *The Economic Theory of Price Indices*. New York: Academic.

Fisher, I. 1922. *The Making of Index Numbers*. Boston and New York: Houghton Mifflin.

Frisch, R. 1930. Necessary and sufficient conditions regarding the form of an index number which shall meet certain of Fisher's tests. *Journal of the American Statistical Association*, 25: 397–406.

_____. 1936. Annual survey of general economic theory: the problem of index numbers. *Econometrica*, 4: 1–39.

Geary, P. T., and M. Morishima. 1973. Demand and supply under separability. In *Theory of Demand: Real and Monetary*. M. Morishima and others, Oxford: Clarendon Press.

Geary, R. C. 1950. A note on "A constant utility index of the cost of living". *Review of Economic Studies*, 18: 65–66.

Goldberger, A. 1967. Functional forms and utility: a review of consumer demand theory. Report 6703, University of Wisconsin: Social Systems Research Institute.

Goldman, S. M. and H. Uzawa. 1964. A note on separability and demand analysis. *Econometrica*, 32: 387–398.

Gorman, W. M. 1953. Community preference fields. *Econometrica*, 21: 63–80.

———. 1959. Separable utility and aggregation. *Econometrica*, 27: 469–481.

———. 1961. On a class of preference fields. *Metroeconomica*, 13: 53–56.

———. 1965. Production functions in which the elasticities of substitution stand in fixed proportion to each other. *Review of Economic Studies*, 32: 217–224.

———. 1968a. Measuring the quantities of fixed factors. In *Value, Capital, and Growth* (J. N. Wolfe, ed.). Edinburgh: Edinburgh.

———. 1968b. The structure of utility functions. *Review of Economic Studies*, 35: 369–390.

———. 1968c. Conditions for additive separability. *Econometrica*, 36: 605–609.

———. 1970. Quasi-separability. Unpublished paper, London School of Economics and Political Science.

———. 1971. Two stage budgeting. Unpublished paper, London School of Economics and Political Science.

———. 1976. Tricks with utility functions. In *Essays in Economic Analysis* (M. Artis and R. Nobay, Eds.). Cambridge: Cambridge U.P.

Gossen, H. H. 1854. *Entwicklung der Gesetze des menschlichen Verkehrs*. Berlin: Praeger.

Green, H. A. J. 1964. *Aggregation in Economic Analysis: An Introductory Survey*. Princeton, N. J.: Princeton U. P.

Hammond, P. J. 1973. *Consistent Planning and Intertemporal Welfare*, Ph.D. dissertation, Cambridge University.

———. 1976. Changing tastes and coherent dynamic choice. *Review of Economic Studies*, 43: 159–174.

Hanoch, G. 1970. Generation of new production functions through duality. Discussion Paper 118, Harvard Institute of Economic Research.

———. 1971. CRESH production functions. *Econometrica*, 39: 695–712.

———. 1975. Symmetric duality and polar production functions. In *An Econometric Approach to Production Theory* (M. Fuss and D. McFadden, Eds.). North Holland, forthcoming.

Hasenkamp, E. 1973. *Specification and Estimation of Multiple Output Production Functions*. Ph.D. dissertation, University of Wisconsin, Madison.

Heal, G. M. 1973. *The Theory of Economic Planning*. New York: North Holland/American Elsevier.

Heien, D. 1974. Some further results on the estimation of the *S*-branch utility tree. Research Discussion Paper No. 10, Price Research Division, U.S. Bureau of Labor Statistics.

Heller, W. P. 1977. Continuity in general nonconvex economies (with applications to the convex case). In *Equilibrium and Disequilibrium in Economic Theory* (G. Schwödiauer, ed.). Dordrecht: D. Reidel Publishing Co.

Hicks, J. R. 1932. *Theory of Wages*. London: Macmillan.

_____. 1946. *Value and Capital*. Oxford: Clarendon.

_____.1969. Direct and indirect additivity. *Econometrica*, 37: 353–354.

Hotelling, H. 1932. Edgeworth's taxation paradox and the nature of supply and demand functions. *Journal of Political Economy*, 40: 557–616.

Houthakker, H. S. 1950. Revealed preference and the utility function. *Economica*, 17: 159–174.

_____. 1953. La Forme des Courbes d'Engel. *Cahiers du Seminaire d'Econometrie*, 2: 59–66.

_____. 1960a. The influences of prices and income on household expenditure. *Bulletin de l'Institute International de Statistique*, 37: 9–22.

_____. 1960b. Additive preferences. *Econometrica*, 28: 244–257.

_____. 1961. The present state of consumption theory. *Econometrica*, 29: 704–740.

_____. 1965a. New evidence on demand elasticities. *Econometrica*, 33: 277–288.

_____. 1965b. A note on self dual preferences. *Econometrica*, 33: 797–801.

Hildenbrand, W. 1974. *Core and Equilibria of a Large Economy*. Princeton: Princeton University.

Howe, H. and R. Pollak. 1976. Estimation of a quadratic expenditure system. Mimeo: University of Pennsylvania.

Hulten, C. 1973. Divisia index numbers. *Econometrica*, 41: 1017–1025.

Humphrey, D. 1976. Empirical estimates of factor-intermediate substitution and separability: implication for effective protection *Journal of International Economics*, forthcoming.

Jorgensen, D. W., and L. J. Lau. 1975. The structure of consumer preferences. *Annals of Economic and Social Measurement*, 4: 49–102.

Kadiyala, K. 1971–2. Production functions and the elasticity of substitution. *Southern Economic Journal*, 38: 281–284.

Katzner, D. W. 1970. *Static Demand Theory*. New York: Macmillan.

Kennedy, C., and A. Thirwall. 1972. Technical progress: a survey. *Economic Journal*, 82: 11–72.

Klein, L. R. 1946. Macroeconomics and the theory of rational behavior. *Econometrica*, 14: 93–108.

_____, and H. Rubin. 1947. A constant-utility index of the cost of living. *Review of Economic Studies*, 15: 84–87.

Konyus, A. 1924. The problem of the true index of the cost of living. Translation in *Econometrica* (1939), 7: 10–29.

Konyus, A. and S. Byushgens 1926. K probleme pokupatel'noi cili deneg. *Voprosi Konyunkturi*, 2: 151–171. [English title: On the problem of the purchasing power of money. In *The Problems of Economic Conditions* (supplement to the Economic Bulletin of the Conjuncture Institute)].

Koopmans, T. C. 1960. Stationary ordinal utility and impatience. *Econometrica*, 28: 287–309.

_____. 1972. Representation of preference ordering with independent components of consumption. In *Decision and Organization* (C. B. McGuire and R. Radner, eds.). Amsterdam: North Holland.

_____. P. Diamond, and R. Williamson. 1964. Stationary utility and time perspective, *Econometrica* 32: 82–100.

Lady, G. M., and D. H. Nissen, 1968. Functional structure in demand analysis. Econometric Society Winter Meetings, Washington, D. C.

Lancaster, K. 1966. A new approach to consumer theory. *Journal of Political Economy*, 74: 132–157.

Lau, L. J. 1969a. Duality and the structure of utility functions. *Journal of Economic Theory*, 1: 374–396.

_____. 1969b. Budgeting and decentralization of allocation decisions. Memorandum No. 89, Center for Research in Economic Growth, Stanford University.

_____. 1969c. Some applications of profit functions. Memorandum 96, Research Center in Economic Growth, Stanford University.

_____. 1974a. Applications of duality theory: a comment. In *Frontiers of Quantitative Economics II* (M. Intrilligator and D. Kendrick, eds.). Amsterdam: North Holland.

_____. 1974b. Private correspondence.

_____. 1975a. Econometrics of monotonicity, convexity and quasi-convexity. *Econometrica*, forthcoming.

_____. 1975b. Complete systems of consumer demand functions through duality. Paper presented at the Third World Congress of the Econometric Society, Toronto.

_____, and B. N. Mitchell. 1971. A linear logarithmic expenditure system: an application to U.S. data (Abstract). *Econometrica*, 39: 87–88.

_____, and S. Tamura. 1972. Economies of scale, technical progress, and the nonhomothetic Leontief production function: an application to the Japanese petrochemical industry. *Journal of Political Economy*, 80: 1167–1187.

Leontief, W. W. 1947a. A note on the interrelation of subsets of independent variables of a continuous function with continuous first derivatives. *Bulletin of the American Mathematical Society*, 53: 343–350.

_____. 1947b. Introduction to a theory of the internal structure of functional relationships. *Econometrica*, 15: 361–373.

McFadden, D. 1966. Cost, revenue, and profit functions: a cursory review. Working Paper No. 86, IBER, Department of Economics, University of California, Berkeley.

_____. 1970. Cost, revenue and profit functions. In *An Econometric Approach to Production Theory* (M. Fuss and D. McFadden, eds.), North Holland, forthcoming.

McKenzie, L. 1955. Demand theory without a utility index. *Review of Economic Studies*, 24: 185–189.

McMenamin, S. 1975. *A Disaggregated International Linkage Model: The Supply Price Approach*. Ph.D. dissertation, University of California, San Diego.

_____, J. Pinard, R. Russell, and R. Boyce. 1977. Estimation of conditional import demand systems. Discussion Paper 77-18, University of California, San Diego.

Malmquist, S. 1953. Index numbers and indifference surfaces. *Trabajos de Estatistica*, 4: 209–242.

Manser, M. E. 1974. *Estimating Consumer Preferences and Cost of Living Indices for U. S. Meat and Produce, 1947–1971*. Ph.D. dissertation, University of Wisconsin, Madison.

Marino, A. 1976. Optimal capacity expansion with economies of scale and growing demand. Working Paper #63, Economics Department, Kansas University.

Morishima, M. 1952. Consumers' behavior and liquidity preference. *Econometrica*, 20: 223–246.

Mukerji, V. 1963. Generalized SMAC function with constant ratios of elasticities of substitution. *Review of Economic Studies*, 30: 233–236.

Nataf, A. 1948. Sur la Possibilité de Construction de Certains Macromodèles. *Econometrica*, 16: 232–244.

Negishi, T. 1964. Conditions for neutral money. *Review of Economic Studies*, 31: 147–148.

Newman, P. 1969. Some properties of concave functions. *Journal of Economic Theory*, 1: 291–314.

_____, and K. Unger. 1977. Integrability conditions for set-valued demand. *International Economic Review*, forthcoming.

Pearce, I. F. 1961. An exact method of consumer demand analysis. *Econometrica*, 30: 499–516.

_____. 1964. *A Contribution to Demand Analysis*, Oxford: Oxford U. P.

Peleg, B., and M. E. Yaari. 1973. On the existence of a consistent course of action when tastes are changing. *Review of Economic Studiies*, 40: 391–402.

Phelps, E. and R. Pollak. 1968. On second-best national saving and game-equilibrium growth. *Review of Economic Studies*, 35: 185–199.

Phlips, L. 1974. *Applied Consumption Analysis*. Amsterdam: North Holland.

Pinard, J. P. 1975. *A Disaggregated International Linkage Model: The Profit Function Approach*. Ph.D. dissertation, University of California, San Diego.

Pokropp, F. 1972. A note on the problem of aggregation. *Review of Economic Studies*, 39: 221–230.

Pollak, R. A. 1968. Consistent planning. *Review of Economic Studies*, 35: 201–208.

_____. 1969. Conditional demand functions and consumption theory. *Quarterly Journal of Economics*, 83: 60–78.

_____.1970a. Habit formation and dynamic demand functions. *Journal of Political Economy*, 78: 745–763.

_____. 1970b. Budgeting and decentralization, Discussion Paper 157, Department of Economics, University of Pennsylvania.

_____. 1971a. The theory of the cost of living index. Research Paper No. 11, Research Division, Office of Prices and Living Conditions, U. S. Bureau of Labor Statistics.

_____. 1971b. Additive utility functions and linear Engel Curves. *Review of Economic Studies*, 37: 401–413.

_____. 1971c. Conditional demand functions and the implications of separability. *Southern Economic Journal*, 37: 423–433.

_____. 1972. Generalized separability. *Econometrica*, 40: 431–453.

_____. 1975a. Subindexes of the cost of living. *International Economic Review*, 16: 135–150.

_____. 1975b. The intertemporal cost of living index. *Annals of Economic and Social Measurement*, 4: 179–196.

Powell, A.A. 1974. *Empirical Analytics of Demand Systems*. Lexington: Heath.

Primont, D. 1970. *Functional Structure and Economic Decision Making*. Ph.D. dissertation, University of California, Santa Barbara.

_____. 1977. Necessary and sufficient conditions for the consistent aggregation of cost-of-living subindexes. Discussion Paper 77–08, Department of Economics, University of British Columbia.

Rockafellar, R. T. 1970. *Convex Analysis*. Princeton, N. J.: Princeton U. P.

Roy, R. 1942. *De l'Utilitè*. Paris: Hermann.

_____. 1947, La distribution du revenue entre les divers biens. *Econometrica*, 15: 205–225.

Russell, R. R. 1975. Functional separability and partial elasticities of substitution. *Review of Economic Studies*, 42: 79–86.

Samuelson, P. 1937. A note on the measurement of utility. *Review of Economic Studies*, 5: 155–218.

_____. 1947. Some implications of linearity. *Review of Economic Studies*, 15: 88–90.

_____. 1953. Prices of factors and goods in general equilibrium. *Review of Economic Studies*, 21: 1–20.

_____. 1960. Structure of a minimum equilibrium system. In *Essays in Economics and Econometrics* (R. W. Pfouts, ed.). Chapel Hill: University of North Carolina Press, pp. 1 – 33.

_____. 1965. Using full duality to show that simultaneously additive direct and indirect utilities imply unitary price elasticity of demand. *Econometrica*, 33: 781–796.

_____. 1969. Corrected formulation of direct and indirect additivity. *Econometrica*, 37: 355–359.

_____. and S. Swamy, 1974. Invariant economic index numbers and canonical duality: survey and synthesis. *American Economic Review*, 64: 566–593.

Shephard, R. W. 1953. *Cost and Production Functions*. Princeton, N. J.: Princeton U. P.

_____. 1970. *Theory of Cost and Production Functions*. Princeton, N. J.: Princeton U. P.

Solow, R. N. 1955. The production function and the theory of capital. *Review of Economic Studies*, 23: 101–108.

Sono, M. 1945. The effect of price changes on the demand and supply of separable goods (in Japanese). *Kokumin Keisai Zasshi*, 74: 1–51.

_____. 1961. The effect of price changes on the demand and supply of separable goods. *International Economic Review*, 2: 239–271.

Stigum, B. P. 1967. On certain problems of aggregation. *International Economic Review*, 8: 349–367.

_____. 1973. Revealed preference—a proof of Houthakker's theorem. *Econometrica*, 41: 411–424.

Stone, R. 1954. Linear expenditure systems and demand analysis: an application to the pattern of British demand. *The Economic Journal*, 64: 511–527.

Strotz, R. H. 1955. Myopia and inconsistency in dynamic utility maximization. *Review of Economic Studies*, 23: 165–180.

_____. 1957. The empirical implications of a utility tree. *Econometrica*, 25: 269–280.

_____. 1959. The utility tree—a correction and further appraisal. *Econometrica*, 27: 482–488.

Swamy, S. 1965. Consistency of Fisher's tests, *Econometrica*, 33: 619–623.

Unger, K. 1974. *Monotone Operators and Revealed Preferences*, Ph.D. dissertation, Johns Hopkins University.

Uzawa, H. 1962. Production functions with constant elasticities of substitution. *Review of Economic Studies*, 29: 291–299.

_____. 1964. Duality principles in the theory of cost and production. *International Economic Review*, 5: 216–220.

Vartia, Y. 1976. *Relative Changes and Index Numbers*. Helsinki: Research Institute of the Finnish Economy.

Wales, T. W. 1972. A generalized linear expenditure model of demand for nondurable goods in Canada. *Canadian Journal of Economics*, 4: 471–484.

Winter, S. J., Jr. 1969. A simple remark on the second optimality theorem of welfare economics. *Journal of Economic Theory*, 5: 99–103.

Wold, H.O.A. 1943. A synthesis of pure demand analysis, I., II. *Skandinavisk Akguarietidskrift*, 26: 85–118, 220–263.

_____. 1944. A synthesis of pure demand analysis, III. *Skandinavisk Akguarietidskrift*, 27: 60–120.

_____. in association with L. Juréen. 1953. *Demand Analysis.* New York: Wiley.

Woodland, A. D. 1977. Estimation of a variable profit and planning price functions for Canadian manufacturing, 1947–1970. *Canadian Journal of Economics*, 10: 355–377.

_____, 1976a. Joint outputs, intermediate inputs, and international trade theory. *International Economic Review*, forthcoming.

_____, 1976b. On testing for weak separability. Discussion Paper 76–28, University of British Columbia.

Yasui, T. 1944. Relation between homogeneity postulate and separability notion in Slutsky theory (in Japanese). *Keizai oyobi Keizaigaku no Saishuppatsu*, 5: 189–206.

Index